Slavery and Forced Migration in the Antebellum South

American slavery in the antebellum period was characterized by a massive wave of forced migration as millions of slaves were moved across state lines to the expanding southwest, scattered locally, and sold or hired out in towns and cities across the South. This book sheds new light on domestic forced migration by examining the experiences of American-born slave migrants from a comparative perspective. Juxtaposing and contrasting the experiences of long-distance, local, and urban slave migrants, it analyzes how different migrant groups anticipated, reacted to, and experienced forced removal, as well as how they adapted to their new homes.

Damian Alan Pargas is an associate professor of social and economic history at Leiden University. Specializing in North American slavery, he is the author of *The Quarters and the Fields: Slave Families in the Non-Cotton South* (2010) as well as numerous academic articles for journals such as *Slavery & Abolition*, the *Journal of Family History*, the *Journal of Early American History*, and *American Nineteenth Century History*. In 2011, he was granted a prestigious three-year Veni postdoctoral fellowship from the Dutch Council for Scientific Research (NWO) and a visiting research fellowship from the John F. Kennedy Institute for North American Studies at the Freie Universität of Berlin. Pargas is also an editor for the journal *Itinerario: Journal of European Expansion and Globlisation* and the secretary of the Netherlands Association for American Studies.

Cambridge Studies on the American South

Series Editors

Interdisciplinary in its scope and intent, this series builds upon and extends Cambridge University Press's long-standing commitment to studies on the American South. The series will not only offer the best new work on the South's distinctive institutional, social, economic, and cultural history but will also feature works in a national, comparative, and transnational perspective.

Titles in the Series

Robert E. Bonner, *Mastering America: Southern Slaveholders and the Crisis of American Nationhood*
Ras Michael Brown, *African-Atlantic Cultures and the South Carolina Lowcountry*
Christopher Michael Curtis, *Jefferson's Freeholders and the Politics of Ownership in the Old Dominion*
Louis A. Ferleger and John D. Metz, *Cultivating Success in the South: Farm Households in Postbellum Georgia*
Craig Friend and Lorri Glover, *Death and the American South*
Luke E. Harlow, *Religion, Race, and the Making of Confederate Kentucky, 1830–1880*
Ari Helo, *Thomas Jefferson's Ethics and the Politics of Human Progress: The Morality of a Slaveholder*
Susanna Michele Lee, *Claiming the Union: Citizenship in the Post–Civil War South*
Scott P. Marler, *The Merchants' Capital: New Orleans and the Political Economy of the Nineteenth-Century South*
Peter McCandless, *Slavery, Disease, and Suffering in the Southern Lowcountry*
Barton A. Myers, *Rebels against the Confederacy: North Carolina's Unionists*
Johanna Nicol Shields, *Freedom in a Slave Society: Stories from the Antebellum South*
Damian Alan Pargas, *Slavery and Forced Migration in the Antebellum South*
Brian Steele, *Thomas Jefferson and American Nationhood*
Jonathan Daniel Wells, *Women Writers and Journalists in the Nineteenth-Century South*

Slavery and Forced Migration in the Antebellum South

DAMIAN ALAN PARGAS
Leiden University

CAMBRIDGE
UNIVERSITY PRESS

CAMBRIDGE
UNIVERSITY PRESS

32 Avenue of the Americas, New York, NY 10013-2473, USA

Cambridge University Press is part of the University of Cambridge.

It furthers the University's mission by disseminating knowledge in the pursuit of education, learning, and research at the highest international levels of excellence.

www.cambridge.org
Information on this title: www.cambridge.org/9781107658967

First published 2015

Printed in the United States of America

A catalog record for this publication is available from the British Library.

Library of Congress Cataloging in Publication Data
Pargas, Damian Alan.
Slavery and forced migration in the antebellum South / Damian Alan Pargas (Leiden University).
pages cm. – (Cambridge studies on the American South)
Includes bibliographical references and index.
ISBN 978-1-107-03121-0 (hardback) – ISBN 978-1-107-65896-7 (paperback)
1. Slavery – Southern States – History – 19th century. 2. Slave trade – Southern States – History – 19th century. 3. Forced migration – Southern States – History – 19th century. 4. Migration, Internal – Southern States – History – 19th century. 5. Slaves – Southern States – Social conditions – 19th century. 6. Migrant labor – Southern States – History – 19th century. 7. Assimilation (Sociology) – Southern States – History – 19th century. 8. Southern States – Social conditions – 19th century. 9. Southern States – Race relations – History – 19th century.
I. Title.
E449.P235 2014
306.3'62097509034–dc23 2014026588

ISBN 978-1-107-03121-0 Hardback
ISBN 978-1-107-65896-7 Paperback

Contents

List of Illustrations

Acknowledgments

The preparation of this book would not have been possible without the generous support of various institutions, colleagues, friends, and family. The entire manuscript was researched and written between 2011 and 2014 during a Veni postdoctoral fellowship from the Netherlands Organization for Scientific Research (NWO). This fellowship exempted me from most of my teaching and administrative duties, funded all of my research trips, and provided me with the time and space to pursue various avenues of scholarly inquiry. I am extremely grateful to NWO for the opportunity to expand my ideas on slave migration into a book. The John F. Kennedy Institute for North American Studies of the Freie Universität in Berlin also granted me a one-month research fellowship in early 2011, permitting me to commence my research in their fantastic library, to which I returned several times during the writing of this manuscript. The microfilm collections at the JFK Institute are unparalleled in Europe and are something of a godsend to scholars working on this side of the Atlantic. The library staff is also extremely helpful and knowledgeable, making it a pleasure to work there. I am also grateful to the staff of the Library of Congress and National Archives and Records Administration in Washington, as well as Hill Memorial Library in Baton Rouge, for helping me to locate various sources that were relevant to my research.

The content of this book benefited from both discussions arising from papers I presented at various institutions during the past three years and the feedback I received on articles that I published with *Slavery & Abolition* and the *Journal of Early American History*. I extend my thanks to the editorial boards at both journals. I am particularly grateful to Bertrand van Ruymbeke (Université Paris 8) for inviting me to present my research plans at his Atlantic History seminar in Paris in April 2011 and for co-chairing our panel on Jefferson's "Empire of Liberty" at the European Association of American Studies conference in The Hague in April 2014. Joris van Eijnatten at Utrecht University also provided me with an early forum to test my ideas at his Cultural History seminar in February 2011, and Marlou Schrover and Leo Lucassen at Leiden University invited me to present parts of Chapter 6 at their Social History seminar in 2013, which generated useful feedback and tips.

I cannot express enough gratitude to Leiden University for providing me with a quiet and amenable workplace to finish my manuscript. Leiden exempted me from all duties during the last six months of this project, encouraged me to set up a Slavery Study Group with other colleagues working on global slavery as a forum to exchange ideas and methods, and supported me in every other possible way. This book benefited from conversations with several friends and colleagues, especially Jeff Fynn-Paul, Karwan Fatah-Black, Lotte Pelckmans, Cátia Antunes, Gert Oostindie, Henk den Heijer, Chris Quispel, Piet Emmer, Marlou Schrover, Leo Lucassen, and many others too numerous to mention. I would also like to thank the students from my undergraduate seminar on slavery and emancipation, from whom I learned more than they did from me.

I am extremely grateful to Cambridge University Press for guiding this project from its early stages in mid-2011 to its final publication. The series editors, Mark Smith and David Moltke-Hansen, provided encouragement and constructive criticism on my research proposal and all of my chapters. This book would not have been possible without their support and tireless effort. I also extend my thanks to the press editor, Lewis Bateman, and to the rest of the Cambridge University Press staff engaged in this project.

Writing this book has had its ups and downs, but my family has never failed to provide me with encouragement and support when I needed it most. I extend my deepest gratitude to the Pargas-Errico family in the United States, the Pargas-Gesto family in Uruguay, and the Bos family in Holland. Nobody lived with this project more than my wife Tamara, however. For three years this book took up space in our household and dominated our conversations. For her advice, encouragement, and, above all, her patience, I am infinitely grateful.

Introduction

> *The being of slavery, its soul and body, lives and moves in the chattel principle, the property principle, the bill of sale principle... You are a slave, a being in whom another owns property.*
>
> Former slave James W.C. Pennington, 1849[1]

Upon leaving a Louisiana sugar plantation during his travels through the southern states in 1854, Frederick Law Olmsted, landscape architect and newspaper reporter for the *New York Daily Times*, struck up a conversation with the "talkative and communicative" slave named William who was charged with driving his buggy to his next destination. In the course of their journey of some twenty miles together, the two men broadly discussed various issues of local and national interest, including sugar cultivation, slavery, and master–slave relations in the Deep South. Interestingly, however, the very first thing William said to Olmsted as he stepped into the carriage was the seemingly irrelevant reassurance "that he was not a 'Creole nigger'; he was from Virginia," having been sold and shipped to Louisiana via the domestic slave trade as an adolescent.[2]

Not being mistaken for a Louisiana-born slave was obviously of profound importance to the thirty-three-year-old forced migrant even though he had lived in Louisiana for twenty years, learned to speak French fluently, and admitted no desire to move back to Virginia anymore because he had already "got used to this country" and fully adapted to the "ways of the people." Yet however

[1] James W.C. Pennington, *The Fugitive Blacksmith; Or, Events in the History of James W.C. Pennington, Pastor of a Presbyterian Church, New York, Formerly a Slave in the State of Maryland, United States* (London: Charles Gilpin, 1849), iv, vii–viii.

[2] Frederick Law Olmsted, *A Journey in the Seaboard Slave States in the Years 1853–1854, with Remarks on their Economy* (New York: Dix & Edwards, 1856), 676 (quotes). In the American context the term "Creole" refers to somebody born in Louisiana.

assimilated William may have seemed in the Louisiana slave society that had become his new home, cracks in his identity were clearly evident, as he proudly continued to identify himself first and foremost as an outsider, a Virginian, even confiding to Olmsted his opinion that "the Virginia negroes were better looking than those who were raised here" and that there "were no black people anywhere in the world who were so 'well made' as those who were born in Virginia."[3]

William was certainly not alone in his experiences as a slave migrant. Uprooted from his home, transported to another slave society, and cast as a stranger into a new community to which he was forced to assimilate, he was one of millions. Forced migration was a central experience in the lives of black slaves throughout the New World, as their labor and, by extension, their *bodies*, were continuously reallocated across space according to the demands of various slave economies. In the case of the American South, two major waves of forced migration occurred during the era of bondage. The first took place in the colonial and (post-)revolutionary periods, especially between 1680 and 1808, and was characterized by the importation of more than a half million slaves from Africa to North America. The second wave occurred in the antebellum period (roughly 1800–1860) and witnessed an even more massive reallocation of slave labor within the South itself. This latter wave of domestic forced migration was monumental – scholars such as Ira Berlin have even referred to slaves from this period as the "migration generations." Yet not all nineteenth-century newcomers experienced removal quite like William did. Indeed, antebellum slave migration was three-pronged: first, almost a million American-born slaves from the "older" slave states in the Upper South and Atlantic seaboard were, similar to William, forcibly transported to other states, especially in the expanding southwest; second, roughly twice as many slaves were scattered locally (within the same state) through estate divisions and local sales; and finally, innumerable slaves from rural areas were sold or hired out in the burgeoning towns and cities of the region.[4]

[3] Ibid., 676–77 (quotes).

[4] Ira Berlin, *Generations of Captivity: A History of African-American Slaves* (Cambridge, Mass.: Harvard University Press, 2003), 21–96, 159–244; Peter Kolchin, *American Slavery, 1619–1877* (New York: Hill & Wang, 1993), 18–24, 96–98. Steven Deyle, *Carry Me Back: The Domestic Slave Trade in American Life* (New York: Oxford University Press, 2005), 41–46, 157–60, 283–89; Robert William Fogel, *Without Consent or Contract: The Rise and Fall of American Slavery* (New York: Norton, 1989), 63; Peter McClelland and Richard Zeckhauser, *Demographic Dimensions of the New Republic: American Interregional Migration, Vital Statistics, and Manumissions, 1800–1860* (New York: Cambridge University Press, 1982), 118–19, 135; David L. Lightner, *Slavery and the Commerce Power: How the Struggle Against the Interstate Slave Trade Led to the Civil War* (New Haven: Yale University Press, 2006), 5–8; Walter Johnson, *Soul by Soul: Life Inside the Antebellum Slave Market* (Cambridge, Mass.: Harvard University Press, 1999), 6–7; Jonathan D. Martin, *Divided Mastery: Slave Hiring in the Antebellum South* (Cambridge, Mass.: Harvard University Press, 2004), 6; Walter Johnson, ed., *The Chattel Principle:*

How did American-born slaves experience forced migration in its various forms during the nineteenth century? How was their knowledge of forced migration characterized, and to what extent did they attempt to resist or negotiate the terms of their removal? To what extent and by what means did they adapt to new slave communities, work regimes, and master–slave relations? How were their relations with other forced migrants and local slaves characterized, and to what extent did domestic migration contribute to the development of broader slave-based identities? This book examines the nineteenth-century migration experiences of American slaves from a comparative perspective. Juxtaposing and contrasting the experiences of long-distance, local, and urban slave migrants born in the American South, it addresses three broad themes. First, it underscores the *different* experiences of slave migrants, especially according to type of migration but also according to age, sex, and regional background. As this book argues, antebellum slave migrants experienced forced removal in a variety of ways, and the boundaries and opportunities with which they were confronted – to negotiate the terms of their migration, for example, or adapt to new slave societies – often differed widely. Second, this study examines the ways in which slave migrants attempted to rebuild their lives upon arrival – the extent to which they assimilated or were integrated into new American slave cultures or communities; their experiences in adjusting to new work regimes; and the extent to which they implicitly or explicitly protested their migration, new environments, or new masters or clung tenaciously to overly romantic memories of home. Third, this study addresses the consequences of forced migration for identity formation among American-born slaves during the antebellum period. It points to the importance of regional and fluid identities as well as memories of place – both during the migration experience itself and after arrival at new destinations – and argues that for slave migrants,

Internal Slave Trades in the Americas (New Haven: Yale University Press, 2004). Calculating the extent to which interstate migrants were transferred to their new destinations by domestic slave traders has been the source of heated debate among historians. Fogel and Engerman estimated in their statistical study of slavery *Time on the Cross* (1974), for example, that of the hundreds of thousands of American slaves who were forcibly relocated across state lines between 1820 and 1860, only 16 percent were deported via the domestic slave trade. The rest supposedly accompanied their masters into the interior. Their sources and conclusions were fiercely criticized and discredited by a number of scholars, however, most aptly by Michael Tadman, who argued in his groundbreaking study *Speculators and Slaves* (1989) that between 60 and 70 percent of the total interstate slave migration could be attributed to the domestic slave trade. Since then, most scholars have tended to agree that approximately two-thirds of interstate slave migrants – well over half a million – were transported by traders, a significant percentage by any standard. See Deyle, *Carry Me Back*, 283–89; Robert William Fogel and Stanley L. Engerman, *Time on the Cross: The Economics of American Negro Slavery* (Boston: Little, Brown, 1974), 49; Herbert Gutman, *Slavery and the Numbers Game: A Critique of Time on the Cross* (Urbana: University of Illinois Press, 1975), 102–11; Michael Tadman, *Speculators and Slaves: Masters, Traders, and Slaves in the Old South* (Madison: University of Wisconsin Press, 1989), 44–45.

the process of adapting to new environments was an important factor in the development of personal and group identities.[5]

In contrast to the numerous studies that deal with transatlantic forced migration and the cultural assimilation of Africans in America in the colonial period, the internal migration experiences of American-born slaves in the antebellum South have received relatively little attention from historians. A handful of scholars – including Michael Tadman, Walter Johnson, Stephen Deyle, Robert Gudmestad, and David Lightner, to name only the most prominent – have examined the economic, demographic, and political aspects of domestic forced migration, but the actual experiences of forced migrants both during the migration process itself and after arrival in new communities have rarely been the focus of in-depth academic research. Historians who have delved into these topics – such as Ira Berlin's masterful examination of the assimilation experiences of domestic slave migrants in his seminal work *Generations of Captivity* (2003) – have moreover largely focused on the experiences of *interstate* migrants. Indeed, no studies have attempted to compare the experiences of interstate, local, and urban slave migrants, and virtually none have acknowledged that there were similarities and differences in the ways these groups experienced migration. These gaps in the historical literature are especially poignant when one considers that the ways in which enslaved people experienced and endured removal are of particular importance in understanding the centrality of forced migration to the slave experience.[6]

For the antebellum period, when few American slaves escaped the onslaught of forced migration, an analysis of the ways in which enslaved people anticipated, responded to, and experienced migration itself – from the first news of removal to arrival at new destinations – reveals volumes about how

[5] For more on fluid and group identities, see, for example, Hazel Rose Markus and Maryann G. Hamedani, "Sociocultural Psychology: The Dynamic Interdependence among Self Systems and Social Systems," *Handbook of Cultural Psychology* (New York: 2007), 7; Neil Campbell and Alasdair Kean, *American Cultural Studies: An Introduction to American Culture* (London: Routledge, 2006), 22–23; Tom Postmes & Nyla Branscombe, eds., *Rediscovering Social Identity* (New York: Psychology Press, 2010), Chapters 1 and 2.

[6] For the colonial period, see, for example, Philip D. Morgan, *Slave Counterpoint: Black Culture in the Eighteenth-Century Chesapeake & Lowcountry* (Chapel Hill: University of North Carolina Press, 1997); Richard Price and Sidney W. Mintz, *The Birth of African American Culture: An Anthropological Perspective* (Boston: Beacon, 1992); Mechal Sobel, *The World They Made Together: Black and White Values in Eighteenth-Century Virginia* (Princeton: Princeton University Press, 1987); Herbert Klein, *The Atlantic Slave Trade* (New York: Cambridge University Press, 2000); Ira Berlin, *Many Thousands Gone: The First Two Centuries of Slavery in North America* (Cambridge, Mass.: Harvard University Press, 1998). For the antebellum period, see, for example, Tadman, *Speculators and Slaves*; Fogel, *Without Consent or Contract*; Martin, *Divided Mastery;* Deyle, *Carry Me Back*; Johnson, *Soul by Soul*; Robert H. Gudmestad, *A Troublesome Commerce: The Transformation of the Interstate Slave Trade* (Baton Rouge: Louisiana State University Press, 2003); Lightner, *Slavery and the Commerce Power*; Berlin, *Generations of Captivity*, 159–244.

they understood and negotiated the commodification of their valuable bodies. Enslaved people were indeed often fully aware of the circumstances by which they could be removed from their homes, had clear ideas and opinions about proposed destinations, and often anticipated and prepared themselves for forced removal long before it actually occurred. Indeed, when forced removal appeared imminent, attempts to avoid, resist, or negotiate the terms of their migration were commonplace, as bondspeople strove to use various strategies to assert some agency over the reallocation of their bodies.[7]

During removal itself – whether hawked on a humiliating auction block, locked in a filthy slave pen, chained in a coffle headed south, or simply accompanying their masters to town to be disposed of – bondspeople were again confronted with both the commodification of their bodies and separation from their home communities. Their understanding of the nature of their removal and the destinations to which they were being removed informed their actions along the way. Although many urban migrants looked forward to life in the city, for example, and local migrants hoped to be able to maintain at least limited contact with loved ones, most interstate migrants perceived their removal to distant locations as a traumatic experience that severed their bonds with friends, family, and everything they knew (from crop regimes to masters). Indeed, social contact among interstate migrants during the journey south was extremely important because it helped them to cope with forced separation from loved ones and the daunting exodus into the unknown with which they were confronted. Resistance to forced removal also often took its most dramatic forms during this stage, as many slaves undertook last-ditch attempts to escape their captors' grasp and either flee slavery altogether or return to their home communities.[8]

Upon arrival at their destinations, migrants were confronted with the monumental task of rebuilding their lives, a theme that is acutely lacking in the current historiography. Indeed, from browsing the historical literature, one would be excused for believing that for American-born slaves in the nineteenth century, little or no adjustment was involved in moving from one place to another. An examination of slave migrants' experiences, however, reveals that they consistently experienced tension in at least three areas. First, they had to find their

[7] Gudmestad, *Troublesome Commerce*, 43; Deyle, *Carry Me Back*, 246; Phillip Troutman, "Grapevine in the Slave Market: African-American Geopolitical Literacy and the 1841 *Creole* Revolt," in Walter Johnson, ed., *The Chattel Principle: Internal Slave Trades in the Americas* (New Haven: Yale University Press, 2004), 204–208. See Chapter 2 of the present volume.

[8] Johnson, *Soul by Soul*, 63–77; Berlin, *Generations of Captivity*, 174; Robert Gudmestad, "Slave Resistance, Coffles, and Debates Over Slavery in the Nation's Capital," in Johnson, ed., *The Chattel Principle*, 80–82; Frederick Douglass, *Narrative of the Life of Frederick Douglass, an American Slave* (1845; New York: Dover, 1995), 16–17; Paul D. Lack, "An Urban Slave Community: Little Rock, 1831–1862," *The Arkansas Historical Quarterly* 41 (autumn 1982): 265; Seth Rockman, *Scraping By: Wage Labor, Slavery, and Survival in Early Baltimore* (Baltimore: Johns Hopkins University Press, 2009), 35–36.

place within new slave communities. This process has often eluded scholars because of a flawed approach to antebellum slave culture: in the past, many scholars erroneously assumed that domestic slave migrants were easily assimilated into their new communities because their cultural backgrounds (from religion to language to family life) were supposedly all more or less alike by the nineteenth century. Even Ira Berlin recently argued that in the Deep South, "slaves from the North, Chesapeake, and lowcountry mixed easily." Enslaved newcomers, however, often experienced considerable difficulties finding their place within new slave communities, mixing with local-born slaves, and even getting along with other forced migrants. This was especially true for long-distance slave migrants, who were often sent to parts of the South that they deemed inferior in every respect to their places of origin. Divisions also arose in the cities, where slave migrants from the countryside clashed with urban slave communities. The American slave population was not always as united as is often believed, and integration processes were often slow and full of setbacks, although under specific circumstances (especially when confronted with incidents of oppression), slaves from all backgrounds and origins – newcomers and locals alike – frequently came to identify with each other as a group, transcending regional and local identities.[9]

The assimilation and integration of American-born forced migrants were further complicated by new work patterns, cultivation methods, and economic arrangements. Scholars have expended much energy analyzing and comparing the various agricultural regimes of the antebellum South, including the consequences of various work patterns and economic arrangements for slave culture in different regions. The seasonal calendars and various methods of cultivating tobacco, wheat, rice, cotton, or sugar had far-reaching consequences for slaves' daily lives and, as I have argued elsewhere, even their family arrangements. For country slaves sold to or hired out in cities, work patterns were on another order altogether. Yet few scholars have examined the ways in which new work patterns were *learned* by forced migrants or the difficulties involved in adjusting to unfamiliar economic regimes. For example, slaves from the Upper South sold to work as field hands on cotton plantations often experienced extreme stress in learning to pick cotton and keep up with more experienced local hands. Slaves who were forced to learn to cultivate new crops or perform new tasks also appear to have been particularly vulnerable to work-related punishments. On the other hand, local migrants were often easily assimilated into new work

[9] Berlin, *Generation of Captivity*, 170–71 (quote). Many revisionist scholars have tended to portray slave culture as having been largely homogenous by the antebellum period. See (among others), for example, John W. Blassingame, *The Slave Community: Plantation Life in the Antebellum South* (New York: Oxford University Press, 1979); Eugene Genovese, *Roll, Jordan, Roll: The World the Slaves Made* (New York: Vintage, 1976); Fogel, *Without Consent or Contract*; Starling Stuckey, *Slave Culture: Nationalist Theory and the Foundations of Black America* (New York: Oxford University Press, 1987).

regimes, and many country slaves apprenticed to artisanal trades in the cities appear to have welcomed the opportunity to learn new skills.[10]

Third, slave migrants who changed owners (whether long distance, local, or urban) were confronted with new masters and therefore new master–slave relations. Rules, temperaments, and privileges often varied widely among southern slaveholders. Most slaves indeed believed that there were distinct regional differences in master–slave relations, with the Deep South in particular standing out for its cruel masters and overseers compared with the "mild" Upper South. City slaves, on the other hand, were usually granted a considerable degree of autonomy in their daily lives, and urban newcomers often enjoyed new arrangements, although they often unknowingly breached urban codes of segregation that resulted in severe reprimands. Furthermore, slaveholding size had important consequences for master–slave relations: whereas slaves sold to large plantations were often largely anonymous to their owners and governed through overseers and drivers, those who were sold to small farms usually had more personal relationships with their masters.[11]

The ways in which newcomers adjusted to new masters raise important questions about the treatment of slaves in general. Indeed, although the focus for this study is on the migrants themselves, an additional underlying aim of this book is to use the theme of forced migration as a springboard to engage in broader historical debates concerning the nature of master–slave relations in the antebellum South. To what extent was forced migration compatible with slaveholders' claims to the ideology of paternalism (as conceptualized by Eugene Genovese), in which they maintained that their slaves were natural extensions of their own families ("our family, black and white") and in which they loudly professed their commitment to the benign rule of the "childlike" bondspeople under their stewardship? How could the sellers of slaves reconcile the mutual obligations of paternalism (i.e., protection and care in exchange for absolute obedience and hard work) with forced migration and the forced separation of families? How could the buyers or hirers of slaves reconcile such beliefs with their purchase or hire of slaves who had been torn from their families or with their often brutal treatment of newcomers?

[10] For comparative studies of slave culture in various economic regions, see, for example, Berlin, *Generations of Captivity*; Daina Ramey Berry, *Swing the Sickle for the Harvest is Ripe: Gender and Slavery in Antebellum Georgia* (Urbana: University of Illinois Press, 2007); Damian Alan Pargas, *The Quarters and the Fields: Slave Families in the Non-Cotton South* (Gainesville: University of Florida Press, 2010).

[11] For paternalism, planter ideology, and the treatment of slaves, see, for example, Eugene D. Genovese, *The World the Slaveholders Made: Two Essays in Interpretation* (New York: Vintage, 1971), 195–234; Genovese, *Roll, Jordan, Roll*, 3–7, 5 (first quote); James Oakes, *Slavery and Freedom: An Interpretation of the Old South* (New York: Knopf, 1990), 137–94; Kolchin, *American Slavery, 1619–1877*, 111–32; Eugene D. Genovese and Elizabeth Fox-Genovese, *Fatal Self-Deception: Slaveholding Paternalism in the Old South* (New York: Cambridge University Press, 2011); David Brion Davis, *Inhuman Bondage: The Rise and Fall of Slavery in the New World* (New York: Oxford University Press, 2006), 193–200.

These questions have sparked considerable debate among historians. Eugene Genovese and Elizabeth Fox-Genovese argued in *Fatal Self-Deception* (2011), a publication that concluded nearly forty years of research on the subject, that despite its contradictions, antebellum slaveholders were essentially sincere in their commitment to paternalism, that they "said what they meant and meant what they said," and that they "managed to square" forced migration and family separations with their paternalist self-image by insisting that these were merely untimely and unforeseeable ruptures in an otherwise benign master–slave relationship. By formulating slave sales and forced separations as constituting only minor and irregular exceptions to the rule (mere last resorts in times of financial distress or grave consequences for unruly slaves who failed to meet their obligations to the master), slaveholders were able to execute forced migration yet still believe that they were exercising hegemony in Gramscian terms – imposing their worldview upon the slaves they owned and procuring a form of accommodation that even minor "apolitical" acts of day-to-day resistance did not fundamentally threaten – and sincerely retain their claim that they governed in the interest of the enslaved. Framing their peculiar institution as a form of human interdependence whose abolition would lead to the extinction of the black race, they stubbornly believed that their society was humane and superior to every other even when they contradicted themselves in their own behavior. They ultimately deceived themselves, the Genoveses argue, a claim that provides the title to their book. Yet, they maintain, "because the ground beneath their feet was unstable does not mean that they were insincere," claiming that slaveholders' commitment to their deceptive and faulty ideology was so strong that it propelled them and the nation into the civil war that ultimately destroyed their institution altogether.[12]

Critics of this view, most notably Walter Johnson, have dismissed paternalist justifications for slave sales and family separations as planter alibis rather than evidence of commitment to a deceptive ideology, contending that forced migration was such a logical result of a system that treated human beings as commodities that it was essentially impossible to reconcile with paternalism. These scholars argue that from participation in the slave market to treatment of newcomers, slaveholders undermined claims to paternalism, making them dishonest. The slaveholders did so because of their unwavering commitment to self-enrichment, their fundamental view of enslaved people as valuable bodies rather than human beings, and the brutally expropriative – rather than altruistically benevolent – nature of their class relations. Virtually none were willing to place paternalist responsibilities above financial self-interest. Although they

[12] Genovese and Fox-Genovese, *Fatal Self-Deception: Slaveholding Paternalism in the Old South* (New York: Cambridge University Press, 2011), 1 (first quote), 5 (second and third quotes); Genovese, *Roll, Jordan, Roll*, 25–49, 147–49, 587–97; Kathleen M. Hilliard, *Masters, Slaves, and Exchange: Power's Purchase in the Old South* (New York: Cambridge University Press, 2014), 2–5.

tried to defend their actions through a paternalist framework, Johnson argues, "the proslavery construction of slave-market 'paternalism' was highly unstable," constantly threatening "to collapse at any moment beneath the weight of its own absurdity." Aware that their ideology was based largely on fiction, slaveholders attempted to reconcile obvious contradictions "the same way they solved other problems," namely by constructing "ever more elaborate fantasies about the slave market," "bewilder[ing]" forced migration and paternalism, and concocting ridiculous and contradictory justifications that few could have possibly taken seriously. According to Johnson, paternalism can be seen more as "a pose that slaveholders put on for one another than as a praxis through which they governed their slaves." Indeed, the very existence of forced migration was crucial to creating that pose in the first place: the only way antebellum slaveholders were able to formulate a system of labor discipline that did not rely on torture – and thus outwardly appear even remotely benign – Johnson claims, was not by imposing cultural hegemony and procuring the accommodation of the enslaved but rather through the implicit (and often explicit) threat of forced migration and family separations. In other words, the slaveowners ruled through terror, a fact that stands in complete contradiction to their claims of benevolence and good intentions. The best way of "describing the relationship of slaveholders' effusive paternalism to the threats of family separation through which they increasingly governed their slaves," Johnson writes, "is this: the slaveholders were liars."[13]

This book aligns broadly with the latter view. Although there were surely exceptions throughout the South, this study argues that most southern slaveholders' commitment to paternalism was inconsistent at best and nonexistent at worst, and that their disregard for their own contradictory definitions of benevolent rule was most starkly revealed in the role they played in slave migration – when they rid themselves of bondspeople, casually orchestrated forced separations of slave families, skimped on newcomers' material conditions, and authorized (or inflicted) extreme physical abuse on new slaves. Slaveholders nobly claimed to outsiders that they encouraged and protected slave families but dangled forced separation in front of their slaves as a threat and executed forced separations without qualms; they loudly advocated a humane treatment of slaves but brutally "broke" newcomers who were believed to have been "spoiled" by their former owners or who unknowingly breached new rules; they wrote contracts in which they demanded that their hired slaves be treated well but often ignored (or even ridiculed) hirelings who ran home complaining

[13] Johnson, *Soul by Soul*, 107–15, 109–10 (first quote); Richard Follett, *The Sugar Masters: Planters and Slaves in Louisiana's Cane World, 1820–1860* (Baton Rouge: Louisiana State University Press, 2005), 151–94; Davis, *Inhuman Bondage*, Chapters 9–10; Hilliard, *Masters, Slaves, and Exchange*, 2–5; Walter Johnson, "A Nettlesome Classic Turns Twenty-Five: Re-Reading Eugene D. Genovese's *Roll, Jordan, Roll*," *Common Place* 1 (July 2001): http://www.historycooperative.org/journals/cp/vol-01/no-04/reviews/johnson.shtml (second and third quotes).

of abuse at the hands of their employers. As this book reveals, the contradictory spider web of justifications that slaveholders developed to perpetuate and sustain the forced removal of slave bodies in the antebellum period illuminates how difficult – indeed, impossible – it was for them to reconcile their claims to benevolence with the inconvenient reality of forced migration. The amount of force and violence necessary to successfully execute forced migration, moreover, suggests that slaveholders were aware that their attempts to impose hegemony over the people they bought, sold, willed, hired, and moved were unsuccessful. As Johnson has argued, all of the whips, chains, slave pens, threats, and lies "were made necessary by the fact that slaveholders knew that they weren't exercising hegemony but fighting something that sometimes looked a lot more like a war."[14]

Besides consulting secondary literature, the source material consulted for this study runs the full gamut of available primary evidence, with a particular emphasis on that left by slave migrants themselves. These include slave narratives, government interviews with former slaves, and antebellum interviews with slave refugees in the North and Canada. Moreover, primary source material left by nonslaves has also been consulted, such as slaveholders' records and memoirs, travelers' accounts of conversations with slaves, runaway slave advertisements, and government records of the slave population (including the marriage records of the Freedmen's Bureau).

Because much of this qualitative investigation into the fears and feelings of slave migrants relies on nineteenth-century narratives and interviews of former slaves – sources that historians in the past have shied away from – some remarks regarding source analysis are in order. During the first half of the twentieth century, historians generally rejected slave testimony for two reasons: first, because of their conviction that victims of oppression are its least credible witnesses, and second, because the transcription and publication of antebellum narratives (which predated emancipation) occurred in the North or Great Britain and served the cause of abolitionism, supposedly rendering the accounts of slaves who had fled the South to be so biased as to be unworkable. This changed in the 1970s, when revisionist historians gained a renewed interest in slave testimonies as offering alternative perspectives to a field of study that had hitherto been approached in a top-down manner and dominated by the sources left by biased white southerners. Since then, most slavery scholars have tended to consult slave narratives sparingly, although some continue to dismiss their validity. Nineteenth-century slave narratives and interviews do indeed pose some important challenges – they represent only a minority of bondspeople, especially those who fled slavery, and many were indeed transcribed and published by northern whites who strongly disapproved of slavery. Yet

[14] Genovese, *Roll, Jordan, Roll*, 598; Johnson, "Nettlesome Classic," (quote). For a recent discussion of the debates surrounding Genovese's use of Antonio Gramsci's concept of cultural hegemony and the nature of slave resistance, see Hilliard, *Masters, Slaves, and Exchange*, 3–5.

to dismiss them as complete fabrications is misleading. Several scholars have mined a variety of records to authenticate many of the most famous narratives. John Blassingame also found that in general, the white editors of antebellum narratives were well-educated professionals with no formal connection to abolitionism and whose procedures were virtually identical to those now used in contemporary oral history projects, including final crosschecks and approval by the interviewee before publication. Furthermore, many narratives were published *after* emancipation and thus did not serve the antislavery movement at all. Narratives published before emancipation are often supported by other evidence, including records left by white southerners and travelers, as well as post-emancipation slave testimonies. I agree with Walter Johnson's opinion that "though they require careful reading, the nineteenth-century narratives remain our best source for the history of enslaved people in the slave trade."[15]

For this study, I have followed Johnson's three-tiered strategy for using slave narratives to uncover the fears and reactions of enslaved people confronted with forced migration. First, the antebellum narratives are used alongside other sources, such as travelers' accounts, planters' records, newspapers, and post-emancipation testimonies of former slaves. Tales of slave migrants mutilating themselves to prevent deportation, for example, are revealed not only in narratives but also in antebellum newspaper articles, travelers' accounts, and even court records. Second, the narratives have been analyzed for facts that fall outside of the abolitionist cause. Although abolitionists had every reason to condemn the forced separation of families as painful and traumatic for enslaved people, for example, their interests were less clearly served by stories of slaves successfully negotiating to retain family bonds intact, yet such accounts are recorded in the narratives and interviews. There is also no reason to assume that forced separations were *not* painful and traumatic. Third, the narratives have been analyzed for what Johnson calls "symbolic truths" that transcend factual details. The metaphors and dialogues that antebellum slaves used to dictate their experiences to interviewers are more important for the feelings they convey – fear, sadness, confusion – than for exact quotes or numbers. By reading the narratives according to Johnson's strategy, this study seeks to illuminate the prospect and reality of internal migration from the perspective of the enslaved.[16]

[15] Johnson, *Soul by Soul*, 9–10, 10 (quote); John Blassingame, "Using the Testimony of Ex-Slaves: Approaches and Problems," *Journal of Southern History* 41 (Nov. 1975):473–492. The interviews of former slaves conducted by the Federal Writers' Project (FWP) in the 1930s pose far greater challenges to the historian than the nineteenth-century testimonies. The former slaves were elderly at the time of their FWP interviews and had moreover only experienced slavery as children. I have therefore limited my use of these interviews in general; the FWP interviews that are cited in this book only deal with elements of the slave migrant's experience that are overwhelmingly supported by other evidence.

[16] Johnson, *Soul by Soul*, 9–11. David Thomas Bailey found that antebellum slave narratives, which served the antislavery movement, match post-emancipation narratives published in the

This book is divided into two parts. Part I, titled "Migration," revolves around the central theme of forced removal. Chapter 1 examines the reasons for forced migration in its various forms in the antebellum South. It provides an overview of the economic factors that stimulated an intensification of slave labor mobility in the post-Revolutionary period and discusses the ways in which forced removal was formally and informally organized. Chapter 2 shifts the focus to the perspective of the enslaved, delving into the ways in which enslaved people anticipated and responded to the prospect of forced migration. It specifically underscores the importance of family and kinship ties in explaining slaves' fears and reactions to the possibility of removal. Chapter 3 illuminates how slaves experienced removal itself, including how they experienced holding chambers and auction blocks, journeys to their destinations, and what their first impressions of their new homes were like.

Part II is titled "Assimilation" and pays particular attention to the ways in which slave migrants adapted to their new environments. Chapter 4 examines the ways in which various migrant groups learned and adjusted to new work patterns, highlighting the advantages and disadvantages to new work regimes in interstate, local, and urban settings. In Chapter 5, the experiences of slave migrants regarding new masters, overseers, and employers are analyzed. The final chapter delves into migrants' social assimilation into new slave communities. It places particular emphasis on the development of migrants' identities, the "dual orientation" that many continued to manifest even years after removal, their memories of place, and the institutions that aided them in their integration process. Most important, it discusses the divisions within slave communities and underscores the fluidity of slaves' personal and group identities.

As a comparative study, this book largely (though not always) discusses interstate, local, and urban migrants in separate sections. Each chapter begins with an analysis of the migrant group that was subjected to the most extreme experiences vis-a-vis removal and assimilation: interstate migrants. Local and urban migrants are then discussed in relation to how their migration experiences compared with those experienced by interstate migrants. The intention is not to place undue weight on one migrant group over another; structuring the analysis in this way rather facilitates a comparative perspective. Interstate migrants did not necessarily always experience the most change of all antebellum migrants, but their experiences were often the most extreme, traumatic, and stressful. Only by comparing other migrants' experiences with the worst-case

late nineteenth century, when there was no antislavery agenda to pursue. These postbellum narratives have also been consulted for this study. See David Thomas Bailey, "A Divided Prism: Two Sources of Black Testimony on Slavery," *Journal of Southern History* 46 (Aug. 1980): 381–404, especially 402. Blassingame agreed. See Blassingame, "Using the Testimony of Ex-Slaves," 478–79.

scenario can students and scholars of slavery begin to appreciate the variations in the experiences of slave migrants. Although this study cannot provide a definitive analysis of slave migration in the antebellum South, its intention is to stimulate more comparative studies of domestic slave migration in the nineteenth century.[17]

[17] Peter J. Parish, *Slavery: History and Historians* (New York: Harper Collins, 1989), 97.

PART I

MIGRATION

1

Valuable Bodies

A darkey's worth a hundred dollars as soon as he kin holler – dat's what de white folks say bout here.

Virginia slave to James Redpath, 1854[1]

Recalling his life as a slave before the Civil War, William Henry Singleton closed his short autobiography (published in 1922) by expressing infinite gratitude to Abraham Lincoln for emancipating "me and all the rest of my race." The former bondsman considered all of the privileges and responsibilities that came with freedom a blessing, but above all else he was clearly most grateful for the acknowledgment by the United States government of his humanity – in his words, for the right "not to be bought and sold any more ... not to be treated as things without souls any more, but as human beings." Having been deported from his North Carolina home to Georgia as a young boy, Singleton knew firsthand what it was like to be bought and sold like a "thing" without a soul. That his definition of freedom entailed first and foremost the right not to be traded like an inanimate object is hardly surprising – for millions of African Americans, the commodification of slave bodies symbolized the atrocities of antebellum slavery.[2]

Such dehumanization was, of course, nothing new in the nineteenth-century South: the selling of bondspeople domestically from one slaveholder to another

[1] James Redpath, *The Roving Editor; or, Talks with the Slaves in the Southern States* (1859; New York: Negro Universities Press, 1969), 199.

[2] William Henry Singleton, *Recollections of My Slavery Days* (n.p., 1922), 9 (first quote). Maryland slave James Pennington blamed the constant disruption of slaves' identities through forced removal in the antebellum period on "the chattel principle," or the dehumanizing commodification of slave bodies. James W.C. Pennington, *The Fugitive Blacksmith: Or Events in the Life of James W.C. Pennington* (London, 1849), iv–vii. This concept has been further explored by Walter Johnson in his seminal study of the antebellum slave market, *Soul by Soul*. See Walter Johnson, *Soul by Soul: Life Inside the Antebellum Slave Market* (Cambridge, Mass.: Harvard University Press, 1999), 19–44.

had existed in the colonial period, and the immediate and (potentially) permanent reallocation of individual slaves' labor across space underpinned the very institution of chattel slavery in the first place. What did set the antebellum period apart, however, was the sheer *magnitude* of domestic forced removal. The frequency with which enslaved people were relocated increased dramatically in the early nineteenth century, and by the outbreak of the Civil War, the scale of forced migration in the southern states had truly skyrocketed. For a variety of reasons, more American-born slaves from the so-called "migration generations" – those who lived between the Revolutionary War and the Civil War – found themselves uprooted and removed from their homes than ever before. Few African Americans emerged unscathed when emancipation finally came; those who had not been forcibly removed themselves usually had family members or friends who had been.[3]

Why were enslaved people forcibly relocated in the antebellum South? How was the forced migration of American slaves organized and executed? And to what extent were interstate migrants, local migrants, and urban migrants moved for different reasons or by different means? This first chapter broadly illuminates the various reasons for the reallocation of slave labor (in all of its forms) in the nineteenth-century South, with a particular emphasis on the supply and demand for slave labor. It then examines the formal and informal organization of different types of forced migration.

I.

The economic undercurrents that propelled domestic slave migration in the antebellum period varied by region and especially type of migration. For most students and scholars of American slavery, the forced relocation of enslaved people in the nineteenth century is virtually synonymous with interstate migration: a one-way trajectory from east to west and from north to south. This is partly because of the stark contrast that interregional migration in that era posed with domestic migration in earlier periods. In the colonial period, slavery had mostly been confined to the eastern seaboard – especially the tobacco lands of the Chesapeake and the rice swamps of the lowcountry – and domestic slave trading had consisted mainly of local transactions. In antebellum America, however, the increasingly national market for slaves stimulated, as economic historian Lewis Cecil Gray once put it, a massive "shift of slave population from the older planting regions – particularly the border states – to the newer planting regions in the lower South." This "shift of population" both characterized and defined the explosive expansion of slavery in the nineteenth century

3 Steven Deyle, *Carry Me Back: The Domestic Slave Trade in American Life* (New York: Oxford University Press, 2005), 31; Ira Berlin, *Generations of Captivity: A History of African-American Slaves* (Cambridge, Mass.: Harvard University Press, 2003), 161–244.

and has therefore understandably received the most attention from scholars of American slave migration.[4]

The numbers alone are staggering. The most recent estimates suggest that between 1820 and 1860, at least 875,000 slaves were forcibly removed from the Upper South and sent to the Lower South – if starting from the end of the Revolutionary War estimates run as high as one million, or *double* the number of African slaves sent to North America in the years of the Atlantic slave trade. The Upper South was indeed drained of so many bondspeople in the nineteenth century that by the time the Civil War broke out, its slave population was only 60 percent of what it would have been if it had grown naturally. On the receiving end of this unprecedented wave of forced migration, the Lower South consistently experienced periods of unnaturally high growth rates among its slave population as drove after drove of enslaved newcomers permeated its borders. In the banner decade of the 1830s, for example, when interstate migration reached its peak, the slave population of the up-and-coming states of Georgia, Florida, Alabama, Mississippi, Tennessee, Arkansas, and Louisiana increased by an impressive 68 percent; that of Alabama alone more than doubled; and Mississippi's number of slaves almost tripled. In the same period, the slave population of Delaware, Maryland, the District of Columbia, Virginia, and the Carolinas not only failed to grow at all, but the number of slaves forcibly removed from these states as a whole was so great that the population there actually *decreased* in absolute terms by 2 percent.[5]

A number of factors were responsible for the "mighty torrent" that, in the words of Ira Berlin, "washed thousands of black men and women across the continent" in the half century preceding the outbreak of the Civil War. Most important, as the United States expanded west of the Atlantic tidewater after the Revolutionary War, the successful development of slave-based cotton, sugar, and tobacco economies in the newly settled territories, combined with

[4] Lewis Cecil Gray, *History of Agriculture in the Southern States to 1860* (Washington, DC: The Carnegie Institution of Washington, 1933), 2:650 (quote). For the most well-known studies of interstate slave migration, see, for example, Frederic Bancroft, *Slave-Trading in the Old South* (1931; reprint Columbia: University of South Carolina Press, 1996); Michael Tadman, *Speculators and Slaves: Masters, Traders, and Slaves in the Old South* (Madison: University of Wisconsin Press, 1989); Berlin, *Generations of Captivity*, ch. 4; Johnson, *Soul By Soul*; Deyle, *Carry Me Back*; David L. Lightner, *Slavery and the Commerce Power: How the Struggle Against the Interstate Slave Trade Led to the Civil War* (New Haven: Yale University Press, 2006); Robert H. Gudmestad, *A Troublesome Commerce: The Transformation of the Interstate Slave Trade* (Baton Rouge: Louisiana State University Press, 2003).

[5] Deyle, *Carry Me Back*, 41–46, 283–89; Berlin, *Generations of Captivity*, 161; Robert William Fogel, *Without Consent or Contract: The Rise and Fall of American Slavery* (New York: Norton, 1989), 63; Peter McClelland and Richard Zeckhauser, *Demographic Dimensions of the New Republic: American Interregional Migration, Vital Statistics, and Manumissions, 1800–1860* (Cambridge: Cambridge University Press, 1982), 118–19, 135; Lightner, *Slavery and the Commerce Power*, 5–8.

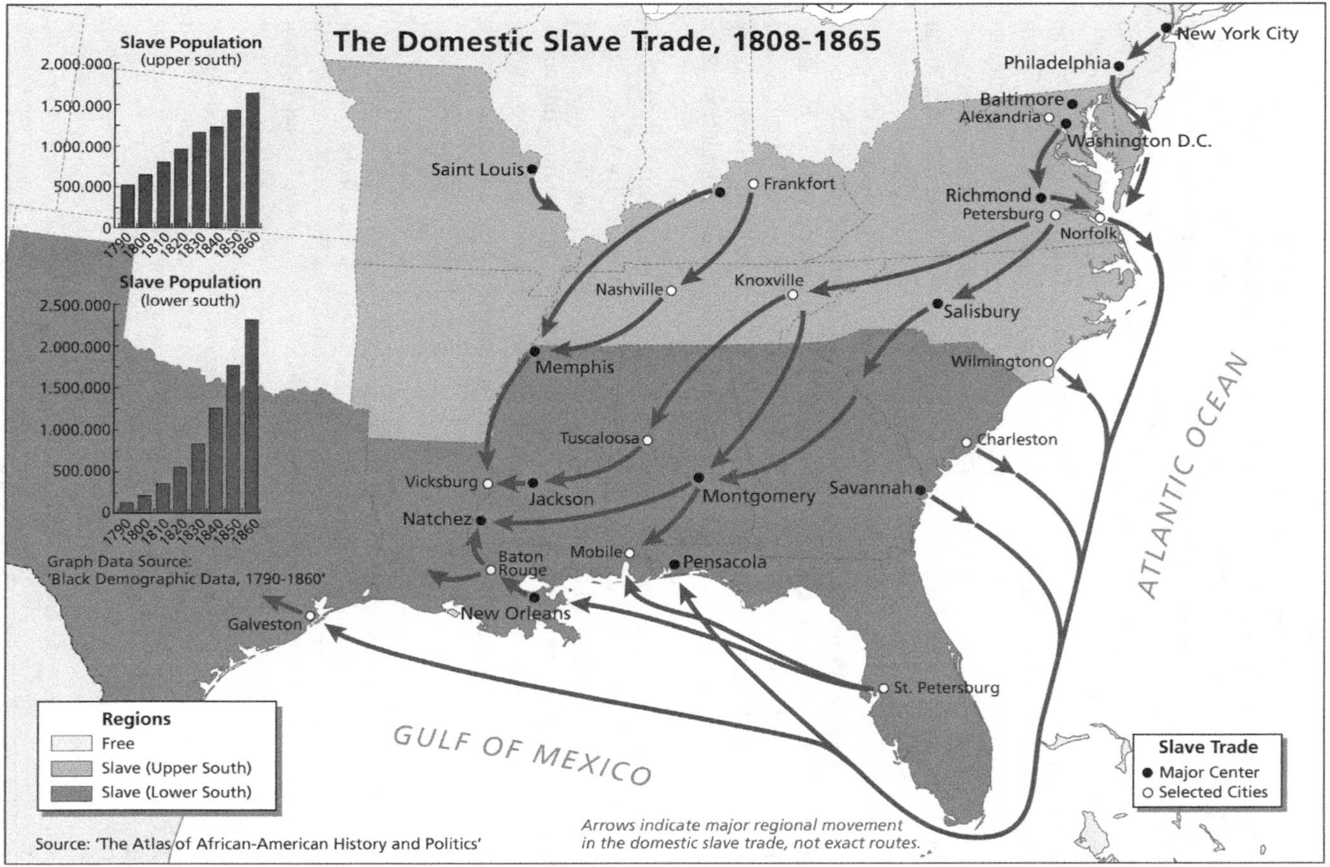

FIGURE 1.1. "Map of the domestic slave trade, 1808–1865." *Graphic design: Armand Haye.*

the decline of slave-based agriculture in parts of the Upper South, pulled slaves from the eastern seaboard to the southern interior like a giant magnet.[6]

More than anything else, the rise of cotton revitalized the institution of slavery in the new republic and stimulated a massive reallocation of slave labor to the Lower South. As early as the late eighteenth century, there arose an explosive demand for American cotton in Great Britain, a demand that could never fully be met by the geographically limited production of long-staple ("sea-island") cotton that was cultivated as a secondary crop in the rice lands of the South Carolina and Georgia lowcountry. American planters along the eastern seaboard were keenly aware of the potentially lucrative production of the short-staple variety, but experience had shown this to be ultimately too expensive because of the difficulties in separating its seeds. The invention of the cotton gin in 1793 and subsequent improvements thereof, however, solved this problem, increasing productivity exponentially and paving the way for the "cotton fever" that gripped the American South in the antebellum period.[7]

The interstate movement of American slaves both followed and fueled the geographic expansion of cotton. Due to climatic conditions, the short-staple variety was best cultivated in the vast and as yet sparsely settled lands of the interior rather than the coastal plains where most planters and slaves lived at the time of the Revolution. Gradually moving inland, the piedmont regions of South Carolina and Georgia were the first to be cleared and converted to cotton at the turn of the nineteenth century, but the westward expansion quickly spilled into the new territories of the Deep South. To contemporaries, opportunities to convert new frontiers into profitable cotton plantations seemed limitless because the land itself seemed limitless. The close of the Revolutionary War had resulted in the acquisition of most of the lands east of the Mississippi, and the subsequent purchase of the Louisiana Territory in 1803 increased the territory in which cotton could potentially be cultivated by millions of acres. Following their new cash crop into the beckoning "cotton kingdom," settlers from the eastern seaboard – both solitary prospectors and entire slaveholding families – rushed to establish themselves in a broad belt of upcountry that ultimately stretched from the South Carolina piedmont through Texas. "My object is to make a fortune here as soon as possible," wrote one planter emigrant to Alabama back home to his brother in Virginia in 1835. Southern cotton production soared (from 178,000 bales in 1810 to more than four million in 1860), becoming the nation's primary export product, generating unfathomable wealth, and sustaining an almost insatiable demand for slave labor

6 Berlin, *Generations of Captivity*, 163 (quote); Walter Johnson, *River of Dark Dreams: Slavery and Empire in the Cotton Kingdom* (Cambridge, Mass.: Harvard University Press, 2013).

7 Fogel, *Without Consent or Contract*, 64–65; Peter Kolchin, *American Slavery, 1619–1877* (New York: Hill & Wang, 1993), 94–95; Deyle, *Carry Me Back*, 20–22; Gray, *History of Agriculture*, 2:678–95; Joyce E. Chaplin, "Creating a Cotton South in Georgia and South Carolina, 1760–1815," *Journal of Southern History* 57 (May 1991): 171–200.

in the states of the Deep South. As early as the 1820s, visitors to Mississippi reported that local cotton planters were netting "from ten to forty thousand dollars a year," most of which they reinvested in more land and more slaves, paying truly exorbitant prices for the latter. In 1835, one Natchez resident exclaimed in a letter to his father-in-law in Maryland that "Negroes are selling here at $1000 for women and $1500 for men!" By the late antebellum period, southerners had become so obsessed with "niggers and cotton – cotton and niggers" that they spoke of little else, according to traveler James Stirling, who visited the region in 1857. The resulting geographic shift of the American slave population into the cotton regions fundamentally altered the southern allocation of slave labor: whereas at the beginning of the nineteenth century only 11 percent of American slaves lived on cotton plantations, by 1860 some 64 percent did. The Mississippi Valley, rather than the eastern seaboard, became the new center of gravity for American slavery.[8]

Paralleling the expansion of the cotton industry in the Lower South, the sugar revolution in southern Louisiana simultaneously increased demand for American slave labor in the Lower Mississippi Valley even further. This development came as something of a surprise because the region's unpredictable climate frustrated initial attempts in the eighteenth century to cultivate sugarcane on a commercial scale, resulting in an inferior product that failed to granulate properly and therefore could not compete with West-Indian production. The lack of a lucrative cash crop kept Louisiana's slave population relatively small during most of the eighteenth century, but that changed in the 1790s. The slave revolt on Saint-Domingue in 1791 reduced North America's sugar supply, raised its price, and sent hundreds of skilled sugar makers fleeing to Louisiana, leading to renewed and ultimately successful efforts to establish a commercial cane industry along the Mississippi River. New cultivation methods, granulation techniques, and technological advances around the turn of the nineteenth century further increased productivity and improved the quality of Louisiana sugar. The final victory for North American proponents of cane production, however, came with the acquisition of Louisiana by the United States in 1803 and its subsequent admission as a state in 1812, which provided

[8] Johnson, *Soul by Soul*, 5–6; Fogel, *Without Consent or Contract*, 30, 64–65; Kolchin, *American Slavery*, 94–96; Deyle, *Carry Me Back*, 20–21; Gray, *History of Agriculture*, 2:678–95; Timothy Flint, *Recollections of the Last Ten Years* (New York: De Capo Press, 1968), 296 (first quote); Henry A. Tayloe to B.O. Tayloe, Jan. 5, 1835, Tayloe Family Papers, RASP, Series E., Part 1 (microfilm), JFK Institute, Freie Universität, Berlin (second quote); John Knight to Wm. M. Beall, Sept. 10, 1835, John Knight Papers, RASP, Series F, Part 1 (microfilm), JFK Institute, Freie Universität, Berlin (third quote); James Stirling, *Letters from the Slave States* (1857; New York: Negro Universities Press, 1969), 179 (fourth quote); Anthony Gene Carey, *Sold Down the River: Slavery in the Lower Chattahoochee Valley of Alabama and Georgia* (Tuscaloosa: University of Alabama Press, 2011), 14–70; Adam Rothman, *Slave Country: American Expansion and the Origins of the Deep South* (Cambridge, Mass.: Harvard University Press, 2005), 37–72. See also Daniel S. Dupre, *Transforming the Cotton Frontier: Madison County, Alabama, 1800–1840* (Baton Rouge: Louisiana State University Press, 1997).

planters with a lucrative domestic market and attractive tariff protection from West-Indian competition. Both established Creole farmers and profit-seeking "American" migrants in southern Louisiana (many of whom were slaveholders from the eastern states) needed no other incentives to take up cane cultivation. By the first decade of the nineteenth century, southerners were declaring in awe that "those who have attempted the cultivation of Sugar Cane are making immense fortunes." Estwick Evans, who visited the sugar country in 1818, reported that "immense profits" of "20,000 to 30,000 dollars" had become almost standard on southern Louisiana cane plantations.[9]

Although the cotton boom was by far the most important pull factor in the reallocation of American slave labor from the eastern seaboard to the southern interior, the expansion of Louisiana's enormously profitable sugar plantations disproportionately increased the number of displacements, as the sugar masters did absolutely everything in their power to supply their plantations with an adequate slave labor force. In 1805, an act passed by Congress that banned the importation of slaves into Louisiana who had been brought from Africa after 1798 was conveniently interpreted by local authorities to permit the importation of slaves from any other part of the United States (including those born in Africa), opening the floodgates to a flourishing slave trade that continued on a large scale until the Civil War. Indeed, New Orleans became the South's busiest slave market. Ever dependent on importation from other states, the slave population in the sugar parishes – which uniquely failed to grow naturally – mushroomed from less than 10,000 in 1810 to more than 88,000 in 1860.[10]

The cotton and sugar regions received a majority of interstate slave migrants in the antebellum period – the four largest importers, Alabama, Mississippi, Louisiana, and Texas alone received more than 75 percent. A minority of long-distance slave migrants, however, were transferred to the frontier states that lay just north of the "cotton kingdom," states such as Kentucky, (most of)

9 J. Carlyle Sitterson, *Sugar Country: The Cane Sugar Industry in the South, 1753–1950* (Lexington, Ky.: University of Kentucky Press, 1953), 1–14; Richard Follett, *The Sugar Masters: Planters and Slaves in Louisiana's Cane World, 1820–1860* (Baton Rouge: Louisiana State University Press, 2005), 10–11, 17–18; John C. Rodrigue, *Reconstruction in the Cane Fields: From Slavery to Free Labor in Louisiana's Sugar Parishes* (Baton Rouge: Louisiana State University Press, 2001), 10–11; Rothman, *Slave Country*, 73–118; René J. Le Gardeur, Jr, "The Origins of the Sugar Industry," in *Green Fields: Two Hundred Years of Louisiana Sugar*, compiled by the Center for Louisiana Studies, University of Southwestern Louisiana (Lafayette, La.: The Center, 1980), 4–22; Gray, *History of Agriculture*, 2:739–40; V. Alton Moody, *Slavery on Louisiana Sugar Plantations* (New Orleans: Cabildo, 1924), 8–10; J.A. Leon, *On Sugar Cultivation; in Louisiana, Cuba, & the British Possessions* (London, 1848), 10; T.B. Thorpe, "Sugar and the Sugar Region of Louisiana," *Harper's New Monthly Magazine* 42 (Nov. 1853): 747–48; *Louisiana Gazette*, Aug. 8, 1806 (first quote); Estwick Evans, *A Pedestrious Tour of Four Thousand Miles Through the Western States and Territories during the Winter and Spring of 1818* (Concord, NH: Joseph C. Spear, 1818), 326 (second quote).

10 Berlin, *Generations of Captivity*, 179; Sitterson, *Sugar Country*, 10; Rodrigue, *Reconstruction in the Cane Fields*, 11; Fogel, *Without Consent or Contract*, 30; Johnson, *Soul by Soul*, 2.

Tennessee, and Missouri. Kentucky's slave population grew from just more than 40,000 in 1800 to more than 225,000 in 1860; Tennessee's mushroomed from 13,500 in 1800 to almost 276,000 on the eve of the Civil War; and Missouri's grew from only 3,000 in 1810 to almost 115,000 in 1860. Indeed, many early slave migrants from Virginia and Maryland accompanied their masters to these territories and states in the opening decades of the nineteenth century, often in search of better opportunities to cultivate and manufacture tobacco. As Missouri historian Diane Mutti Burke has argued, white Upper South migrants were first and foremost "enticed westward by the promise of reasonably priced fertile land in the bottomlands of the Missouri and Mississippi Rivers and their tributaries," but they were also attracted by the possibility of replicating "a farming and slaveholding experience much like the one that they left in the East." Slaves living in states such as Virginia and Maryland were therefore constantly confronted with the prospect of moving west into the expanding frontier.[11]

To some extent, the large-scale westward movement to the border states was a chain migration, with slaveholding families and neighbors from specific counties following each other into the territories of the new frontier. Between 1810 and 1830, for example, several leading slaveholding families from struggling Fairfax County, Virginia, departed for Kentucky, and a number of them pressed on and ended up in Callaway County, Missouri. Henry Clay Bruce, a former slave from Virginia, claimed that his master moved west because his brother-in-law was going west. According to Bruce, his owner "became greatly dissatisfied with his home and surroundings... and being persuaded by his brother-in-law, W.B. Bruce, who was preparing to go to the western country, as Missouri and Kentucky were called, he decided to break up his Virginia home, and take his slaves to Missouri, in company with Mr. W.B. Bruce." By the 1830s and 1840s, settlers in Kentucky, Missouri, and Tennessee were also importing slaves from the eastern seaboard, albeit in lower numbers than their counterparts in the cotton and sugar regions.[12]

The rise in demand for slave labor in the ever expanding plantation South during the early decades of the nineteenth century coincided with the

[11] Fogel, *Without Consent or Contract*, 65; McClelland and Zeckhauser, *Demographic Dimensions*, 118–19; Kolchin, *American Slavery*, 96–97; Gray, *History of Agriculture*, 2:754–59; Gudmestad, *Troublesome Commerce*, 8–9; Joan Cashin, *A Family Venture: Men and Women on the Southern Frontier* (Baltimore: Johns Hopkins University Press, 1991), 32–52; Diane Mutti Burke, *On Slavery's Border: Missouri's Small-Slaveholding Households, 1815–1865* (Athens: University of Georgia Press, 2010), 26–29, 27 (first quote); William Greenleaf Eliot, *The Story of Archer Alexander: From Slavery to Freedom* (Boston: Cupples, Upham, & Co., 1885), 27; Francis Fedric, *Slave Life in Virginia and Kentucky; or, Fifty Years of Slavery in the Southern States of America* (London: Wertheim, MacIntosh, and Hunt, 1863), 14.

[12] Nan Netherton, et al, *Fairfax County, Virginia: A History* (Fairfax, Va.: Fairfax County Board of Supervisors, 1978), 156; Henry Clay Bruce, *The New Man: Twenty-Nine Years a Slave, Twenty-Nine Years a Free Man* (York, Pa.: P. Anstadt & Sons, 1895), 15 (quote).

abolition of the transatlantic slave trade in 1808, so it was clear that the new slave labor force in the southern interior would have to be recruited mainly from the American slave population of the eastern seaboard rather than Africa. As stated earlier, the Upper South – especially the Chesapeake – was the major supplier of forced migrants to the rest of the South, but the rise of cotton (or sugar or western tobacco) alone does not fully explain the mass exodus of slaves from that region in the nineteenth century. Planters in Virginia and Maryland would have had little reason to want to export their slaves (or emigrate with their slaves) if Chesapeake tobacco had remained the primary staple of the South, as it had been in the colonial period; successful planters, after all, rarely felt pressured to emigrate or cash in on their human property. Indeed, this is evident in some of the most successful parts of the South Carolina lowcountry – Georgetown District, for example – where the sustained profitability of rice production not only largely protected antebellum slaves from long-distance sales but actually made the rice country a net *importer* of slaves from elsewhere. As the cash crops of the new southern territories grew relative to other southern commodities such as Chesapeake tobacco, however, "efficiency dictated a reallocation of [slave] labor... to the best western lands," in the words of Robert Fogel.[13]

The geographic expansion of plantation agriculture in the Lower South in fact neatly dovetailed with the interests of slaveholders in struggling parts of the "Old South" such as the Chesapeake. Economic developments in the nineteenth century encouraged – even forced – thousands of Chesapeake slaveholders to either emigrate with their bondspeople or get rid of surplus slaves. Put simply, the supply of slaves in that region came to far outweigh the demand. Throughout Virginia and Maryland, the second half of the eighteenth century witnessed the crumbling of tobacco monoculture and, subsequently, a dramatic shift away from the slave-based cash crop that had once been so vital to the region. Excessive soil exhaustion had taken its toll on the land, diminishing productivity and profits with each passing year. Indeed, as early as the 1760s, it had become clear that tobacco cultivation was depleting the once fertile soil of Virginia and Maryland to a point of such sterility that progressive planters – such as George Washington – began to switch to other crops and gradually phase out their production of tobacco altogether. The economic malaise facing local tobacco planters was compounded by the Revolutionary War, which, as economic historian Avery Odell Craven once put it, "acted as a powerful force in bringing disaster to much that was already on its way to ruin, and

[13] Fogel, *Without Consent or Contract*, 65 (quote); Larry E. Hudson, Jr., *To Have and to Hold: Slave Work and Family Life in Antebellum South Carolina* (Athens: University of Georgia Press, 1997), 175; Deyle, *Carry Me Back*, 296. I examined Georgetown District as a net importer of slaves, rather than an exporter, in an earlier work. See Damian Alan Pargas, *The Quarters and the Fields: Slave Families in the Non-Cotton South* (Gainesville: University Press of Florida, 2010), 188–91.

gave added impulse to many of the changes already begun." With tobacco production already waning, the war dealt Chesapeake planters a death blow by cutting them off from their most important markets (especially Great Britain) for seven years.[14]

By the turn of the nineteenth century, many planters in the Chesapeake had largely abandoned tobacco monoculture and switched to mixed farming, increasingly relying on the cultivation of small grains such as wheat, corn, rye, and oats to keep their plantations afloat. They also expanded their truck farming activities, supplying urban markets with meat, dairy products, and vegetables. Although tobacco production certainly did not disappear – in some areas, it even expanded – it ceased providing most slaveholders with their sole source of income. Tobacco became at best one of several low-paying cash crops, and in practice small mixed farms rather than large tobacco plantations came to dominate the landscape of Virginia and Maryland. Crucially, none of the other agricultural enterprises were typical slave crops – on the contrary, most of the crops grown in the Chesapeake during the antebellum period were also grown in the northern (especially mid-Atlantic) states with free labor. The shift from tobacco to mixed farming thus fundamentally changed the need for, and employment of, slave labor in the Upper South.[15]

As the profitability of employing slaves in local agriculture plummeted, the natural growth of the Chesapeake's slave population increasingly became a burden to the region's farmers and planters. This was evident even to outsiders. Ethan Allen Andrews, while investigating the domestic slave trade to the Deep South, observed during a trip to northern Virginia in 1835 that "the land-holders in parts of Virginia are becoming poorer nearly in direct proportion to the number of their slaves." With the explosive demand for slave labor from the southern interior driving up the prices for able-bodied slaves to dizzying amounts, however, planters in Virginia and Maryland found themselves sitting on a potential gold mine. "Your negroes would bring here about $120- to $130,000," wrote one Alabamian to a large slaveholding family member in Virginia in 1835. "If [prices] continue high I would advise you to sell them in this country." Indeed, speaking with an employee of the infamous slave trading firm Franklin & Armfield in Alexandria, Ethan Allen Andrews was told that

[14] Avery Odell Craven, *Soil Exhaustion as a Factor in the Agricultural History of Virginia and Maryland, 1606–1860* (Urbana: University of Illinois Press, 1926), 72–73 (quote); Gray, *History of Agriculture*, 2:589–92; Lorena S. Walsh, "Plantation Management in the Chesapeake, 1620–1820," *Journal of Economic History* 49 (June 1989): 400–401; Allan Kulikoff, *Tobacco and Slaves: The Development of Southern Cultures in the Chesapeake, 1680–1800* (Chapel Hill: University of North Carolina Press, 1986), 157–58; Netherton, et al., *Fairfax County*, 161–70; James Silk Buckingham, *The Slave States of America* (London: Fisher & Son, 1842), I:182. See also Pargas, *Quarters and the Fields*, 188–91.

[15] Kulikoff, *Tobacco and Slaves*, 157–58; Berlin, *Generations of Captivity*, 211–13; Gray, *History of Agriculture*, 2: 602–608; David Klingaman, "The Significance of Grain in the Development of the Tobacco Colonies," *Journal of Economic History* 29 (June 1969): 275.

because of the success of cotton and sugar in the Deep South, the prices for Virginia slaves had become "*monstrous* high, and that, in fact, is the very reason so many are willing to sell." And sell they did. According to the Virginia state legislature's own estimates in 1832, at least 6,000 slaves were "yearly exported [from Virginia] to other states." Virginians openly admitted that theirs was "a negro-raising state for other states" and that the interstate slave trade was an important "source of wealth" to their struggling economy. J.D. Paxton, a Virginia reverend, tellingly declared that "the best blood in Virginia flows in the blood of the slaves." Selling slaves south became so common in the Chesapeake that the local white population became virtually desensitized to it, something that never failed to amaze northern visitors. One Virginia overseer, charged with bringing one of his employer's slave girls to Richmond to be sold to traders in the 1850s, was astonished to be asked by a northern visitor *what* his employer was selling her for. "Sell her for!" he exclaimed. "Why shouldn't he sell her? He sells one or two every year; wants the money for 'em, I reckon." By the late antebellum period, even the other tobacco and mixed grain states of the Upper South, such as Kentucky and Missouri, were starting to export slaves to the Deep South, following the same boom-and-bust cycle as their eastern counterparts.[16]

II.

The specific occasions for selling slaves south varied, but upon estate divisions especially, sales to interstate slave traders (either directly or through public auctions) were the order of the day in the Upper South, as the heirs of struggling slaveholders struggled to pay off the debts of the estate or simply cashed in on their inheritance. Planters in the region had a reputation for hiding their de facto poverty and "not paying their debts until they died," as one Virginian put it. Consequently, the death of every slaveholder attracted swarms of creditors, and slaves were often among the first to be sold off to settle open

[16] Berlin, *Generations of Captivity*, 211–13; Ethan Allen Andrews, *Slavery and the Domestic Slave-Trade in the United States, in a Series of Letters Addressed t the Executive Committee of the American Union for the Relief and Improvement of the Colored Race* (1836; reprint Freeport, NY: Books for Libraries Press, 1971), 117 (first quote), 137 (third quote); Henry A. Tayloe to B.O. Tayloe, Jan. 5, 1835, Tayloe Family Papers, RASP, Series E, Part 1 (microfilm), JFK Institute, Freie Universität, Berlin (second quote); Thomas Weld, *American Slavery As It Is: Testimony of a Thousand Witnesses* (New York: American Anti-Slavery Society, 1839), 182 (fourth quote); British and Foreign Anti-Slavery Society, *Slavery and the Internal Slave Trade in the United States of North America* (London: Thomas Ward and Co., 1841), 33–70, 33 (fifth quote); Frederick Law Olmsted, *A Journey in the Seaboard Slave States, with Remarks on Their Economy* (New York: Dix and Edwards, 1856), 56–57 (sixth quote); Allan Kulikoff, "Uprooted Peoples: Black Migrants in the Age of the American Revolution, 1790–1820," in Ira Berlin and Ronald Hoffman, *Slavery and Freedom in the Age of the American Revolution* (Charlottesville: University of Virginia Press, 1983), 143–71; Deyle, *Carry Me Back*, 42–43; Bancroft, *Slave-Trading*, 124–44; Gudmestad, *A Troublesome Commerce*, 67.

accounts. Newspapers regularly printed advertisements like the following one from Virginia: "Valuable Slaves for Sale... to secure certain debts due the administrator debonis non of George Hunter, deceased, will be sold on Saturday... *Sixteen Valuable Slaves*... or so many thereof as will be sufficient to raise the sums required." Traders flocked to such auctions, but planters' records also reveal numerous instances in which the heirs of heavily indebted estates actively sought out traders. In 1835, for example, the five heirs of Francis Lightfoot Lee, master of Sully plantation in northern Virginia, decided to sell the slaves attached to his estate to the Deep South to pay off debts. They instructed an agent to "see if it will be possible to get any or all of those negroes off. The sooner the arrangements are made, the better." Estate sales to local traders indeed often resulted in lawsuits as bickering heirs – impatient to convert their human property into cash – quibbled over the proceeds. Eleanour Berry, the trustee of one Benjamin Berry of Prince Georges County, Maryland, was taken to court by her relatives in 1830 for illegally taking it "upon herself to sell and dispose of various... negro slaves," including one bondswoman named Rachel, whom she "bargain[ed] and contract[ed] with Franklin and Armfield" for deportation to the Deep South.[17]

Such occurrences became standard in the nineteenth century, but slaveholders in the Upper South did not always have the luxury of waiting for death to settle their accounts – court-ordered sales were often executed when creditors called their loans, and many masters voluntarily culled their labor forces when financial distress compelled them to do so. Despite claims that their slaves were natural extensions of their own families, slaveholders viewed their bondspeople first and foremost as capital investments that could be liquidated when they – the white part of the plantation "family" – needed money. Indeed, as agricultural productivity declined, even the oldest and most established slaveholding families in the Chesapeake were forced to sell slaves south for cash, a situation they often found embarrassing if necessary. Bushrod Washington, the nephew of George Washington and master of Mount Vernon plantation in northern Virginia, sold fifty-five of his slaves to a Louisiana planter in 1821 for the sum of $10,000, an act that broke up several families. Finding it necessary to publicly explain his decision, he claimed to a local newspaper that he had struggled for twenty years to turn a profit from the "products of their own labor," but his slaves being "worse than useless," and his plantation losing between $500 and $1000 per year, he thought he had no choice.[18]

[17] Joseph Packard, in Bancroft, *Slave-Trading*, 89 (first quote); *Alexandria Gazette & Advertiser*, Dec. 31, 1822 (second quote); Robert S. Gamble, *Sully: The Biography of a House* (Chantilly, Va.: Sully Foundation, 1973), 65 (third quote); "Robert Beale to the Circuit Court, Washington County, District of Columbia, 1830," in Loren Schweninger, ed., *The Southern Debate over Slavery: Volume 2, Petitions to Southern County Courts, 1775–1867* (Urbana: University of Illinois Press, 2008), 148–51 (fourth quotes).

[18] Walter Johnson has argued that at the heart of the slave market, a contest was played out over meaning: whether slave sales were untimely ruptures in an otherwise benign system of slavery, as slaveholders claimed, or whether they were "the inevitable and predictable result of a system

Washington's justification is interesting. Eugene Genovese and Elizabeth Fox-Genovese have argued that in the antebellum South, economic exigency was not only considered a legitimate reason to sell slaves, but that it was also considered fully compatible with slaveholders' claims to paternalism because to them "it seemed more humane to sell a young slave or two rather than risk foreclosure and the breakup of the plantation household." In other words, sacrificing *some* slaves was alright as long as doing so saved the *rest* of the master's "black family" during periods of financial crisis. Although some cunning masters may have indeed justified their actions in this way, however, Washington said nothing about "saving" the slaves who remained, nor did he express sorrow at parting from fifty-five of his black "family members" or even at orchestrating his slaves' forced separation from loved ones, which clearly stood in contradiction to his paternalist duty to protect slave families. Instead, he seemed interested only in absolving himself of guilt by flipping the paternalist tenet of mutual obligations between masters and slaves on its head, arguing that his *slaves* had dissolved the paternalist bond by failing to meet *their* end of the bargain – namely, dutiful labor. According to him, the sale was the result of the slaves' own slovenly work habits, which had sabotaged the profits necessary for their master to sustain them. Surely Washington – a progressive and "scientific" planter – was aware that the exhausted soil was the real culprit of his financial losses, far more than the work ethics of his slaves. And indeed, a good paternalist master was supposed to command such respect from his slaves that they were supposed to work for him with the utmost efficiency anyway. Washington's attempt to stretch the elasticity of his paternalist ideology to incorporate forced migration was at best clumsy and contradictory. The fact that he went to such lengths to justify this sale at all, moreover, suggests that he was implicitly aware that his actions were incompatible with the paternalist image he wished to convey to his peers. Washington was far from alone, however, even in his own neighborhood of Chesapeake grandees. His neighbor, Lawrence Lewis, master of Woodlawn plantation, became equally fed up with his slaves and eventually felt compelled to do the same. In 1837, Lewis wrote to an agent in Louisiana about the "prospect . . . of either selling [the slaves] or hireing [sic] them out; the loss I have met with will make me prefer the former rather than the latter." "Indeed," he continued, "my income is nothing . . . Woodlawn is worse than nothing . . . it is best to sell the negroes as early as possible." Whether to settle estate accounts or to cash in when times got rough, many Chesapeake slaveholders were keen to "put their slaves in their pocket" – in other words, convert them into cash by selling them to the Deep South.[19]

that treated people as property," as slaves claimed. See Johnson, *Soul by Soul*, 29–30. Bancroft, *Slave-Trading*, 15 (quote).

[19] Eugene Genovese and Elizabeth Fox-Genovese, *Fatal Self-Deception: Slaveholding Paternalism in the Old South* (New York: Cambridge University Press, 2011), 38 (first quote). According to Johnson, "invok[ing] the mutuality of the broken promise" was a common justification for

Although most slave migrants from the eastern seaboard who were deported to the Deep South were removed purely for financial reasons, a minority were sold long distances for more personal motives by both wealthy and struggling slaveholders alike. The insatiable demand for slaves in the southern interior afforded antebellum slaveholders the opportunity to rid themselves of bondspeople who caused them trouble, whom they simply did not like, who embarrassed them, or whose presence in any way disturbed their daily lives. Individual slaves were regularly disposed of for poor work or misbehavior or even to cover up the sexual affairs of their masters; many were deliberately sold to interstate traders by masters who wanted them sent as far away as possible. Indeed, southerners frequently accused slaveholders from the eastern seaboard of sending them their "refuse." One Louisiana plantation mistress, livid over the flight of a newly purchased slave from Virginia, expressed a common sentiment when she complained in a letter to her mother in 1856 that the runaway's "conduct for the last three months shows that he is a grand old scoundrel & was probably sold in Virginia for some rascality."[20]

Although often exaggerated, such accusations were not always entirely unfounded because slaveholders from the eastern seaboard often openly admitted to selling recalcitrant slaves out of state simply to be rid of them. One Delaware slave owner petitioned the court in 1826 for a "Permit or License to export, sell or carry out for Sale from this State into the State of Maryland or any other of the United States of America" his slave girl named Julia Ann, who was deemed too "dangerous" to remain in Delaware after she attempted to poison the baby of the man to whom she was hired and subsequently tried to burn her master's house to the ground. Although this was an exceptional case, many slaves were deported as punishment for less serious crimes such as running away or talking back to their masters. The extremely successful and wealthy South Carolina rice planter Robert F.W. Allston, for example, sold a recalcitrant slave to New Orleans in 1847 as punishment for "gross and wicked misconduct" – one of the only times he ever sold a slave. In 1863, Georgia planter Charles Manigault sold one slave named Jack Savage "away from this place" to a Savannah-based interstate trader for $1,800 for being "quite impertinent" and showing a "general disposition to run away." Richard Marshall Scott, Jr., a struggling wheat planter from Virginia, made a habit of selling surplus slaves whenever they misbehaved, doubtless so as to reconcile his financial troubles with any moral difficulties he may have had concerning sale. On one such occasion in October 1850, he "sold our man Aaron ... to

selling slaves. Johnson, *Soul by Soul*, 29–30, 35; Lawrence Lewis to Major G.W. Butler, Jan. 18, 1837, Custis-Lee Family Papers, Library of Congress, Washington, DC (second and third quotes).

20 Berlin, *Generations of Captivity*, 169–70; Johnson, *Soul by Soul*, 35; Tryphena Blanche Holder Fox to her mother, Aug. 31, 1856, in Wilma King, ed., *A Northern Woman in the Plantation South: The Letters of Tryphena Blanche Holder Fox, 1856–1876* (Columbia: University of South Carolina Press, 1997), 61 (quote).

[slave trader] B.O. Shekell... on condition that said Shekell would remove him from the state." Slaveholders outwardly justified such sales – when they justified them at all – by arguing, like Washington, that their slaves had broken the paternalist bond of mutuality by failing to obey their master.[21]

Yet some slaves were sold long distances quite obviously for no fault of their own, revealing just how thin the veil was between slaveholders' outward claims to paternalism and mutual obligations on the one hand and the real character of the slave system on the other. Louisa Picquet was sold from central South Carolina to Georgia as a small child, along with her mother, because her mistress discovered the sexual affair her master had been having with Louisa's mother and subsequently demanded the removal of both the slave woman and her illegitimate daughter. At first attempts were made to cover up the affair: Louisa's mother was simply "forbid to tell who was my father." But, the former bondswoman declared, "I looked so much like Madame Randolph's [her mistress] baby that she got dissatisfied, and mother had to be sold." William Henry Singleton, a slave who was the offspring of an affair between his master's brother and a slave woman, was sold from North Carolina to Georgia for the same reason. "My presence on the plantation was continually reminding them [his master and his master's brother] of something they wanted to forget," Singleton declared in his memoir. As a consequence, his "master sold me to get me out of the way." In such cases, it was much more difficult for slaveholders to fall back on any claims to paternalism to justify their actions. Unless they resorted to outright lying (which some, of course, did), they could not easily blame their slaves for misbehavior, nor the masters' financial woes, nor claim to be benefitting anybody but themselves when they executed such sales. Instead, most slaveholders dealt with these awkward situations in a much easier way – by not justifying themselves at all.[22]

Whatever the reasons for their removal, most long-distance slave migrants thus found themselves being drawn from the Upper South to the Lower South and from the Atlantic tidewater to the southern interior. Indeed, even *within* the Lower South and the southern interior, the direction of forced migration was ever westward, following the highest prices for slave labor and the newest

[21] "Peregrine Hendrickson to the Court of General Quarter Sessions, New Castle County, Delaware, 1826," in Schweninger, ed., *Southern Debate over Slavery*, 130–31 (first quote); William Dusinberre, *Them Dark Days: Slavery in the American Rice Swamps* (New York: Oxford University Press, 1996), 403 (second quote); Ulrich B. Phillips, ed., *Plantation and Frontier: Documents, 1649–1863, Illustrative of Industrial History of the Colonial and Ante-Bellum South* (Cleveland: The Arthur H. Clark Co., 1909), 2:32–33 (third quote); Richard Marshall Scott, Jr., Diary, Oct. 5, 1850 (typescript), Fairfax City Regional Library, Fairfax, Va. (fourth quote). See also Frank Bell, in Charles L. Perdue, Jr., et al, eds., *Weevils in the Wheat: Interviews with Virginia Ex-Slaves* (Charlottesville: University of Virginia Press, 1976), 27.

[22] Louisa Picquet, *Louisa Picquet, the Octoroon: Or, Inside Views of Domestic Slave Life* (New York: The Author, 1861), 6 (first quote); Singleton, *Recollections*, 1–2 (second quote).

slave territories. Slaves from Alabama were moved to Mississippi and Texas; bondspeople from Kentucky were moved to Missouri and Arkansas. By the 1850s, Georgia was a net slave-exporting state. One British visitor to the South found that the cotton planters of Georgia "could not have pursued a more fatal course than they have done for the last thirty years," exhausting the soil and forcing many to sell out or relocate to more fertile lands in the West. Scottish traveler Charles Lyell reported sharing a steamship from Mobile to New Orleans in 1846 with a number of cotton planters from Alabama, who were "going to Texas with their slaves. One of them confessed to me that he had been eaten out of Alabama by his Negroes." Such interstate relocations within the interior almost certainly occurred with less frequency than the massive removal of slaves from the Upper South to the Lower South, but they were nevertheless far from unique – as slavery continued to expand during the antebellum period, thousands of bondspeople from the interior found themselves being taken even farther west.[23]

III.

Not all migrants were transferred across state lines, however; slaves from all southern regions were indeed more likely to be moved locally – within the same state – than long distances. Local transactions in the antebellum period have until recently largely eluded the attention of historians, overshadowed by interstate migration. Yet, as Walter Johnson has noted, although local sales "do not show up in the statistics that have been used to measure the extent and magnitude of the slave trade," they were "as much a feature of the antebellum economy as interstate slave trading." He estimates that roughly twice as many American slaves were in fact sold locally in the antebellum period. Historian Steven Deyle has recently argued that some two-thirds of all slaves professionally sold between 1820 and 1860 were sold to local buyers.[24]

Certain regional variations must be considered when analyzing the local removal of enslaved people. In the Upper South, hard-pressed planters and farmers (and their heirs) had incentives enough to sell slaves, and despite the facility with which slaves could be deported via interstate traders, many were satisfied to sell locally if it could be done conveniently and if a decent price could be attained. Virginia slave Henry Banks was sold from Stafford County to neighboring Spotsylvania County when his master "broke up – sold the farm and all his people." Hastily auctioned off to purchasers from the immediate vicinity, Banks and his family "were scattered, but not very far apart – some six or seven miles," he told interviewers in 1856. Local exchanges in slaves were

[23] Carey, *Sold Down the River*, 52; Buckingham, *Slave States*, I:173 (first quote); Charles Lyell, in Allan Nevins, ed., *America Through British Eyes* (New York: Oxford University Press, 1948), I:234 (second quote).

[24] Johnson, *Soul by Soul*, 6–7 (quote); Deyle, *Carry Me Back*, 157–60.

also frequent between slaveholding neighbors and family members, for whom attaining the highest prices for their bondspeople may not have been a primary concern. Numerous slaves were given away as wedding presents, for example, or sold to friends or family members for discounted prices. William Grimes, a slave born in King George County, Virginia, was abruptly sold at the age of ten years to his master's brother-in-law in Culpepper County. Grimes's owner had not even originally intended to sell him, but the slaveholder's brother-in-law had come "down from the mountains... to buy negroes," and he felt obliged to supply a family member with a surplus slave. Culpeper was not Grimes' last destination in Virginia – before long he was given as a gift to his new master's son, who in turn sold him to his brother in Port Royal, who in turn moved him to Richmond. By the time he was a young man, William Grimes had lived on farms and in towns all over the state (eventually he was sold to Georgia).[25]

The decision to sell locally rather than long distance was usually one of convenience, but some slaveholders in the Upper South, sensitive to the idea of their slaves being forcibly separated from friends and family members, specifically sold their bondspeople on the sole condition that they remain in the general area. One advertisement for "sundry negroes" in the *Alexandria Gazette* in northern Virginia specified that they were "not to be sold to anyone not residing in the district of Columbia, or the county of Fairfax." The seller of a twenty-eight-year-old man in Alexandria in 1820 also sought a buyer who lived in the District of Columbia (which at that time included Alexandria), in consideration of the man having a "wife [who] resides in town." Another advertisement from the same newspaper in 1853 for a young woman with her two-year-old son explicitly stated: "Not to be sold to traders." Slaveholders who specified such conditions were certainly exceptions to the rule, and on the surface they appeared to make sincere attempts to reconcile forced migration with paternalism. But in reality, it is unlikely that the decision to sell locally was merely a reflection of benevolence. It is indeed important to consider the role that slaves themselves played in negotiating local sales in the Upper South. As will become clear in Chapter 2, slaves threatened with forced separation from family members through long-distance sale frequently attempted to compromise with their masters, begging or negotiating (by threatening to run away or otherwise sabotage sale, for example) to be sold locally instead. Sometimes the efforts were successful. For these and a variety of other reasons, thus, local sales were frequent in the Upper South despite the insatiable demand for slaves in the states of the Deep South.[26]

[25] Henry Banks, in Benjamin Drew, ed., *A North-Side View of Slavery. The Refugee, or Narratives of Fugitive Slaves in Canada* (Boston: John P. Jewitt & Co., 1856), 73 (first quote); William Grimes, *Life of William Grimes, the Runaway Slave* (New York: n.p., 1825), 8 (second quote), 16–22.

[26] *Alexandria Gazette and Advertiser*, Nov. 8, 1822 (first quote); Ibid., July 20, 1820 (second quote); Ibid., Jan. 11, 1853 (third quote).

In the booming slave societies of the southern interior, local removals were also common, but often for different reasons than those in the older slave states of the eastern seaboard. During estate divisions in the Lower South, for example, slaves were far more likely than their counterparts in the Upper South to change hands locally rather than be deported through the interstate slave trade. The main reason for this had to do with the high demand for slave labor within the region itself, which often served to prevent deportation. When slaves in the interior were bequeathed to local family members, most heirs kept them – barring any major debts – rather than try to cash in on their inheritance. When they were sold at estate auctions, slaves in the Lower South were very likely to be purchased by local slaveholders. Indeed, established planters in the southern interior were constantly on the lookout for local bargains, and slaves could often be obtained more cheaply at their neighbors' estate auctions than from traders. According to one study, Mississippians, especially, "bought many slaves from other states but exported relatively few" because slaves put up for sale there were usually snatched up by local cotton planters. Other states of the Lower South followed the same trend. Local purchases were indeed even widely considered to be good business practice among the most successful grandees. When South Carolina rice baron Robert Allston heard of his nephew's intentions of starting a plantation, for example, Allston – who accumulated more than six hundred slaves during his career, mainly through local purchases – took the young man under his wing, advising him to buy slaves in bulk from local estate auctions. "I would not buy negroes at cotton prices," he wrote his nephew, referring to interstate traders. In the cotton upcountry of the same state, Francis Pickens giddily informed John Calhoun in 1841: "I hear about 500 negroes are soon to be sold from deaths [of slaveholders] not far off, from different estates," an opportunity not to be missed. Turner Reavis, the owner of Cedar Bluff plantation in Sumter County, Alabama, purchased all of his thirty-one slaves locally, twenty-eight of whom he bought in bulk at two separate auctions in 1859 and 1861.[27]

[27] Charles S. Sydnor, *Slavery in Mississippi* (1933; Baton Rouge: Louisiana State University Press, 1966), 133 (first quote); George Bratton to James Polk, May 31, 1839, in Katherine M. Jones, *The Plantation South* (Indianapolis: Bobbs-Merrill Co., 1957), 286; Robert F.W. Allston, in J.H. Easterby, ed., *The South Carolina Rice Plantation as Revealed in the Papers of Robert F.W. Allston* (Chicago: University of Chicago Press, 1945), 30 (second quote); Francis W. Pickens to John C. Calhoun, Oct. 2, 1841, in Jones, ed., *Plantation South*, 148–49 (third quote); Turner Reavis Account Book, 1842–1890, RASP, Series C, Part 1 (microfilm), JFK Institute, Freie Universität, Berlin. For slaves' accounts of local sales in the Deep South, see, for example, William H. Heard, *From Slavery to the Bishopric in the A.M.E. Church: An Autobiography* (Philadelphia: A.M.E. Book Concern, 1928), 24; Charles Thompson, *Biography of a Slave; Being the Experiences of the Rev. Charles Thompson, a Preacher of the United Brethren Church, While a Slave in the South, Together with Startling Occurrences Incidental to Slave Life* (Dayton, Ohio: United Brethren Publishing House, 1875) 17–21, 21; William Gant, in Federal Writers' Project, Slave Narratives from the Federal Writers' Project, 1936–1938 (typescript), vol. III, pt. 2, 11.

Local sales in the southern interior were also frequent because, as Ira Berlin has argued, "the frontier plantation was extraordinarily unstable." Although plenty of planters became unbelievably wealthy in the new cotton, sugar, and tobacco regions, many others "failed because of undercapitalization, unproductive land, insect infestation, bad weather, or sheer incompetence." With each setback, slaves were sold and scattered across the landscape, bought up at bargain prices by more successful slaveholders. When the owner of one cotton plantation near Natchez, Mississippi, returned home from a summer excursion to the North in 1843, he found his plantation in such a disastrous state, owing to the "bad management of my overseer," that he feared heavy losses for the coming harvest season. Four weeks later he "sold to Mr. Shelly ... two negro boys[,] Charles Cooler & Hallory[,] for one thousand dollars" to cover anticipated losses. Some regions, such as the southern Louisiana cane region, where set-up costs were so high that planters often began their careers heavily in debt, even had something of a reputation for their volatile nature. A single crop failure, a conflict between partners, or the untimely death of a young planter could lead to the liquidation of all or part of a sugar estate. Newspaper sale advertisements and probate records abound with such cases. In New Orleans, thirty-year-old Tom, his wife Molly, and their three children were all sold off to local planters at the Exchange Coffee House on June 2, 1827, to "close the affairs of a late partnership." The widow of sugar planter Auguste Gaudet, from St. James Parish, petitioned the parish court in 1832 to sell the plantation and all of the slaves belonging to her late husband's estate to "pay the debts left by him." The widow of Jean Baptiste Chastant, also from St. James Parish, similarly found her husband's estate "burthened with debts to a considerable amount," making it "absolutely ... necessary to sell the greater part (if not the whole)," including most of the slaves and the plantation itself.[28]

The frontier plantation was not only unstable because of financial setbacks, however, but also because of the restless character of many southern slaveholders – even successful ones – who were often quick to decide that the grass was greener in another district. More than a few slaves were removed locally in the antebellum period simply because their masters decided to upgrade their holdings within the same state, dragging all of their bondspeople with them. Mississippi slave Charles Thompson was moved from his native Attala County

[28] Berlin, *Generations of Captivity*, 190–91 (first quote); Carey, *Sold Down the River*, 62–66; Georgena Duncan, "'One negro, Sarah ... one horse named Collier, one cow and calf named Pink': Slave Records from the Arkansas River Valley," *The Arkansas Historical Quarterly* 69 (Winter 2010): 336–37; Moses Roper, *A Narrative of the Adventures and Escape of Moses Roper, from American Slavery* (Philadelphia: Merrihew & Gunn, 1838), 60–61; Journal of Araby Plantation, Nov. 1, 1843, Nov. 2, 1843, Nov. 28, 1843 (second quote), RASP, Series F, Part 1 (microfilm), JFK Institute, Freie Universität, Berlin; *Louisiana Advertiser*, May 29. 1827 (third quote); Succession of Auguste Gaudet, Apr. 18, 1832, Probate Records, St. James Parish Courthouse, Convent, La. (fourth quote); Succession of Jean Baptiste Chastant, Jan. 10, 1832, ibid (fifth quote).

when his master decided to move to another plantation in Pontotoc County, "about a hundred miles from [his master's] Atala County plantation." Joe Clinton recalled a similar story: he was born in Penola County, Mississippi, but when he was a child, his "ole mars sold out his land and took us all to de delta where he had bought a big plantation bout two or three miles wide in Coahoma County, not far from Friar Point."[29]

IV.

The local removal of slaves was common throughout the South, but such moves were not always of a permanent nature. Temporal, seasonal, and annual migration were also widespread. Thousands of southern slaveholders profited from their slaves' labor by hiring them out for long periods of time, usually to merchants, factories (e.g., cotton mills or tobacco factories), and business establishments in and around urban centers, but also to local farmers who lacked the capital or desire to purchase slaves. The scale of slave hiring in the nineteenth century has proved difficult to quantify, but historian Jonathan Martin has argued that the practice was "nothing short of monumental." Although some hirelings managed to secure permission to hire their own time, the vast majority of slaves who were hired out by the year did not leave their homes of their own accord. Their masters entered into agreements and signed contracts with third parties that lasted for fifty-one weeks, allowing them only the week between Christmas and New Year to spend at home with their families before being forcibly hired out again. As historian Donald Sweig aptly put it: "For the slaves . . . hiring must have seemed little better than outright sale."[30]

There are several reasons why slaveholders often preferred to hire out their surplus slaves rather than sell them. Some historians have suggested that in the Upper South, where slave hiring was most prevalent, many slaveholders were "educated men, sensitive to abolitionist pressure, who had a strong revulsion against selling their slaves." Hard put to rid themselves of surplus bondsmen in a failing slave economy, they found hiring – especially in urban centers such as Baltimore, Washington, and Richmond – a more humane way of doing so than sale. This explanation clearly emphasizes slaveholders' commitment

[29] Charles Thompson, *Biography of a Slave; Being the Experiences of Rev. Charles Thompson, a Preacher of the United Brethren Church, While a Slave in the South* (Dayton, Ohio: United Brethren Publishing House, 1875), 21 (first quote); Joe Clinton, in Slave Narratives, vol. II, pt. 2, 30 (second quote).

[30] Jonathan D. Martin, *Divided Mastery: Slave Hiring in the Antebellum South* (Cambridge, Mass.: Harvard University Press, 2004), 6 (first quote); Bancroft, *Slave-Trading*, 145–46; Robert S. Starobin, *Industrial Slavery in the Old South* (New York: Oxford University Press, 1970), 11–13; E.M. Lander, Jr., "Slave Labor in South Carolina Cotton Mills," *Journal of Negro History* 38 (Apr. 1953): 161–73; Donald Sweig, "Northern Virginia Slavery: A Statistical and Demographic Investigation" (PhD dissertation, College of William & Mary, Williamsburg, Va., 1982), 161 (second quote).

to paternalism, suggesting that slave hiring was a way for struggling masters to avoid the dreaded slave market for their "black family members." Other scholars have underscored the importance of the "social economy," in which productive relations were determined by social obligations rather than the quest for profit. According to this explanation, slaveholders with surplus slaves rented out their bondspeople to labor-strapped small farmers out of a sense of obligation to their fellow white southerners. These arguments are problematic, however. The social economy explanation ignores the fact that slave hiring was immensely profitable in the antebellum South. And although sensitivity to abolitionist pressure may have certainly induced some "educated" slaveholders to avoid sale by hiring their slaves to third parties, plenty of evidence indicates that the most respected and educated gentlemen of the Upper South, including those such as the above-mentioned Bushrod Washington, sold their slaves to the Deep South when the going got rough. Indeed, slaveholders in the Upper South often expressed little interest whether their slaves were hired out or sold, as newspaper advertisements like the following one from Virginia attest: "FOR SALE OR HIRE – A likely WOMAN 43 to 45 years of age." The idea was simply to profit from a surplus slave in the most convenient manner possible, not necessarily bow to abolitionist pressure. Valiant paternalist determination to avoid the slave market rarely came into consideration at all in justifying slave hiring, and indeed because hiring separated slave families during most of the year and often elicited resistance from hirelings themselves, the institution could not easily be squared with slaveholders' commitment to acting in the interest of slave families.[31]

For slaveholders, there were a number of advantages to hiring out surplus slaves rather than selling, the most important of which were financial rather than ideological. First, it provided slaveholders with a regular income from bondspeople who were otherwise superfluous or unproductive. Those who hired slaves were responsible for housing, feeding, and clothing them during fifty-one weeks of the year, which spared slave owners the financial burdens of having to care for them (a fact that in and of itself conflicted with slaveholders' paternalist obligation to provide for their slaves' material wants). On top of that, slaves were often hired out for as much as 10 to 20 percent of their market value – in other words, a slaveholder could often earn more money by hiring out a slave for five to ten years than he could if he sold the same slave. Many slaveholders hired out their slaves for a number of years and then sold them, thereby increasing their profits even more. The system also brought

[31] Sweig, "Northern Virginia Slavery," 158–61, 158 (first quote); *Alexandria Gazette & Virginia Advertiser*, May 25, 1857 (second quote); Martin, *Divided Mastery*, 17–44; Eugene Genovese, "Yeoman Farmers in a Slaveholders' Democracy," *Agricultural History* 49 (Apr. 1975): 338; Keith C. Barton, "'Good Cooks and Washers': Slave Hiring, Domestic Labor, and the Market in Bourbon County, Kentucky," *Journal of American History* 84 (Sept. 1997): 439–40; Johnson, *Soul by Soul*, 34–35.

with it certain social advantages, however. It allowed owners to rid themselves of surplus slaves yet without losing their status as slaveholders, and it allowed nonslaveholders to put on airs of the slaveholding class. In the case of industrial employers, hired slaves were reputedly more efficient and dependable than hired whites (especially Irish immigrants) because they could be coerced in ways that hired whites could not. For all of these reasons, as Jonathan Martin has argued, "hiring became a slaveholding cure-all" in struggling states such as Virginia and Maryland, and participation in the slave hire economy in the Upper South was therefore great indeed. In Loudoun County, Virginia, an estimated 20 percent of the slave population was hired out in 1860; in neighboring Fairfax County in the same year, the proportion of hired slaves approached 25 percent. Most hirelings from these northern counties were sent to nearby Alexandria or Washington to work at the docks or as domestics in hotels and private residences, but for slaves living in the central or southern part of the state, the iron and tobacco-manufacturing centers of Richmond or Lynchburg were the most likely destinations. Some 40 percent of slaves employed at tobacco factories in Virginia in 1850 were hired from their masters, and by the eve of the Civil War, more than half of the slaves in eastern tobacco manufacturing plants as a whole were hirelings.[32]

Not only in the Upper South, however, but throughout the slave states – including the southern interior – markets for hired slaves thrived. Major cities such as Charleston, Savannah, Mobile, St. Louis, New Orleans, Natchez, and Montgomery became "hotbeds of slave hiring," as did even the smallest county seats and crossroads. Northern traveler Joseph Ingraham reported that "many of the negroes who swarm in the cities" of the Deep South, including New Orleans and Natchez, were "what are called 'hired servants.'" Several southern industries depended in large part on hired slave labor. In Talbot County,

[32] Martin, *Divided Mastery*, 74–86, 75 (first quote); Bancroft, *Slave-Trading*, 145–48; Sarah S. Hughes, "Slaves for Hire: The Allocation of Black Labor in Elizabeth City County, Virginia, 1782 to 1810," *William & Mary Quarterly* 35 (Apr. 1978), 260–86; Barbara Jeanne Fields, *Slavery and Freedom on the Middle Ground: Maryland during the Nineteenth Century* (New Haven: Yale University Press, 1985), 27; Barton, "'Good Cooks and Washers,'" 439–40. Richard C. Wade, *Slavery in the Cities* (New York: Oxford University Press, 1964), 28–54; Brenda E. Stevenson, *Life in Black and White: Family and Community in the Slave South* (New York: Oxford University Press, 1996), 184; Starobin, *Industrial Slavery*, 129–30. Mitchell Garnett, a slaveholder from Essex County, Virginia, hired out most of his 39 slaves in the 1830s, keeping meticulous accounts of the profitability of each slave's hire during the years 1830–1834. He averaged between 7 and 8 percent profit per year. See Mitchell Garnett Ledger Book, RASP, Series E, Part 1 (microfilm), JFK Institute, Freie Universität, Berlin. For urban slavery in the antebellum Upper South, see also Calvin Schermerhorn, *Money over Mastery, Family over Freedom: Slavery in the Antebellum Upper South* (Baltimore: Johns Hopkins University Press, 2010); Seth Rockman, *Scraping By: Wage Labor, Slavery, and Survival in Early Baltimore* (Baltimore: Johns Hopkins University, 2008); Midori Takagi, "*Rearing Wolves to Our Own Destruction": Slavery in Richmond, Virginia, 1782–1865* (Charlottesville: University of Virginia Press, 1999).

Georgia, for example, two hundred hirelings were recruited in 1851 to work on the Muscogee Railroad, the railroads even promising slaveholders that their slaves would "be insured against accidents arising on the work." In New Orleans, hirelings were recruited by employers as diverse as the municipality (for public works), sawmills, hotels, and even the Southern Shoe Manufacturing Company. From domestic servitude in urban centers to unloading cargo at ports along the Ohio and Mississippi Rivers, hired slaves were a common sight in virtually every sector in the southern interior.[33]

The southern interior's frontier nature made the necessity of hiring all the more pressing. Settlers relied heavily on slave hiring both as a source of labor (for those setting up plantations or businesses but as yet unable to afford to purchase all the slaves they needed) and as a source of income (for those who intended to save up enough money to expand their operations or purchase a plantation). Henry Bruce, whose master took him from Virginia to Missouri, then to Mississippi, and then back to Missouri, was hired out several times before his owner became established; slave hiring indeed provided his owner with an important means of income. During their second stay in Missouri in the 1850s, Bruce was hired out to a tobacconist for four years, then to a local farmer for a year, and finally to another tobacco factory for a year. Similarly, when Israel Campbell's Kentucky master "took a notion to go to Mississippi," Campbell found himself being forcibly moved south. Upon arrival, however, his "old master Crookesty did not commence operations... immediately, but hired all his slaves except one woman." Campbell was hired out to a local cotton plantation, the owner of which was in need of a few extra hands. William Wells Brown, who moved with his master from Kentucky to Missouri, recounted in his autobiography how he was continuously hired out in St. Louis at a number of different trades – his employers included a public house, a steamboat, a hotel, a newspaper publisher, and even a slave trader. In none of these cases did the slaveholders claim to be acting on behalf of the interest of their slaves but rather only seemed interested in profiting financially from the superfluous bodies in their possession.[34]

33 Martin, *Divided Mastery*, 7 (first quote), 34–43; Joseph Holt Ingraham, *The South-West. By a Yankee* (New York: Harper & Bros., 1835), 2:250 (second quote); *Georgia Journal and Messenger*, Dec. 17, 1851 (third quote); Wade, *Slavery in the Cities*, 44–45; Burke, *On Slavery's Border*, 107–18.

34 Burke, *On Slavery's Border*, 107–18; Bruce, *The New Man*, 64–70; Israel Campbell, *An Autobiography. Bond and Free: Or, Yearnings for Freedom, from My Green Briar House. Being the Story of My Life in Bondage, and My Life in Freedom* (Philadelphia: C.E.P. Brinkloe & Co., 1861), 32 (quote), 33; William Wells Brown, *Narrative of William Wells Brown, a Fugitive Slave* (Boston: The Anti-Slavery Office, 1847), 21–41. Richard Follett also found that sugar planters in southern Louisiana regularly hired extra hands from neighboring cotton districts to augment their labor forces. See Follett, *Sugar Masters*, 82–83; Andrew W. Foshee, "Slave Hiring in Rural Louisiana," *Louisiana History* 36 (Winter 1985): 63–73; Solomon Northup, *Twelve Years a Slave: Narrative of Solomon Northup, a Citizen of New York, Kidnapped in*

V.

Whatever their destination and whatever the reasons for their forced migration, antebellum slave migrants could be relocated in a variety of formal and informal ways, ranging from a chained coffle to a casual walk down the road to a neighboring plantation. Arguably the most well known, feared, and complex method of forced removal was via the domestic slave trade, which historians now agree was the fate of an overwhelming majority of slave migrants who were relocated across state lines. Calculating the extent to which interstate migrants were transferred to their new destinations by domestic slave traders has in the past been the source of heated debate among historians. Fogel and Engerman estimated in their statistical study of slavery *Time on the Cross* (1974), for example, that of the hundreds of thousands of American slaves who were forcibly relocated across state lines between 1820 and 1860, only 16 percent were deported via the domestic slave trade. The rest supposedly accompanied their masters into the interior. Their sources and conclusions were fiercely criticized and discredited by a number of scholars, however, most aptly by Michael Tadman, who argued in his groundbreaking study *Speculators and Slaves* (1989) that between 60 and 70 percent of the total interstate slave migration could be attributed to the domestic slave trade. Since then, most scholars have tended to agree that approximately two-thirds of interstate slave migrants – well more than half a million – were transported by traders, a significant percentage by any standard.[35]

The sheer scale of interstate slave trading in the antebellum period underscored its importance to the southern economy. As plantation agriculture expanded into the southern interior, African-American slaves became the most valuable form of property in the South. Consequently, the interstate slave trade was big business, even becoming the most important form of commerce in the southern states and the largest economic sector outside of plantation agriculture itself. Shifting the supply of American slave labor to the demand, the slave trade "held together the various [southern] states... in a mutual dependent relationship," in the words of Steven Deyle.[36]

Slave traders – commonly called "speculators," "Georgia traders," or "nigger traders" – came in various shapes and sizes, from large-scale dealers to farmers and planters who occasionally dabbled in a little speculation. Most traders fell into the midrange and small-scale category. Whatever the size of their operations, however, traders all shared a commitment to engaging in the "the

Washington City in 1841, and Rescued in 1853 (Auburn, NY: Derby & Miller, 1853), 208; Martin, *Divided Mastery*, 34–43.

35 Deyle, *Carry Me Back*, 283–89; Robert William Fogel and Stanley L. Engerman, *Time on the Cross: The Economics of American Negro Slavery* (Boston: Little, Brown & Co., 1974), 49; Herbert Gutman, *Slavery and the Numbers Game: A Critique of Time on the Cross* (Urbana: University of Illinois Press, 1975), 102–11; Tadman, *Speculators and Slaves*, 44–45.

36 Berlin, *Generations of Captivity*, 168; Lightner, *Slavery and the Commerce Power*, 7–8; Deyle, *Carry Me Back*, 42–46, 41 (quote).

dirty work" of turning people into prices and "making a living in the space between the prices they paid and those they received" for human chattels, as Deyle put it. Indeed, they did more than that. Not only did traders mediate and profit from the transfer of human chattels across space, but, as a number of scholars have argued, they even changed how southerners *thought* and *spoke* about their bondspeople. As the trade grew and its place within southern society became more and more institutionalized, the business began to take on its own cultural language – a language intended to further dehumanize and commodify the people being bought and sold. Although paternalist masters in the antebellum period tried to convince themselves and outsiders that their slaves were really just extended members of their own families – "our family, black and white" – traders unabashedly spoke of "prime hands, bucks, breeding wenches, and fancy girls," terms that eventually trickled down into the vocabularies of southern planters as well. Indeed, slaves were most often referred to as simply "head" or "hands." A.J. McElveen, a South Carolina trader, for example, boasted to his partner in Charleston in 1852 that he "bought only ten head yesterday and give thundering prices for them." Outsiders and the uninitiated frequently took offense to such terms. When Virginian John Wise attended his first slave auction in Richmond as an adolescent in the 1850s, he found the auctioneer's language vulgar. "The sale was begun with some 'bucks,' as he facetiously called them," Wise noted. "They were young, unmarried fellows from eighteen to twenty-five." Later on a "rattlin' good breeder" was auctioned off. Although offensive to Wise's young ears, his elders expressed great excitement at the slaves being advertised: "bidders drew near to them [the slaves], examined their eyes, spoke with them to test their hearing and manners, made them open their mouths and show their teeth, ran their hands over the muscles of their backs and arms, caused them to draw up their trousers to display their legs, and, after fully satisfying themselves on these and other points, bid for them what they saw fit." Interestingly, purchasers outwardly often attempted to reconcile their participation in the slave market with their paternalist ideology by claiming that they were "redeeming" unfortunate bondspeople who had been tragically exposed to the slave trade, reframing the act of slave buying into a charitable enterprise in southern culture. Yet the ways they went about inspecting and prodding the human merchandise on hand suggest that in reality they were less interested in the tragic lot that had befallen these slaves than they were in their physiques. Whatever the image they wished to convey to themselves or the outside world, both slave traders and by extension the slaveholders to whom they sold their commodities viewed bondspeople as bodies in the nineteenth century – valuable bodies whose prices reflected their ability to work and reproduce. The records that speculators kept and the terms they used to describe their commodities were therefore "chillingly economical," in the words of Walter Johnson.[37]

[37] Deyle, *Carry Me Back*, 46 (first quote), 94–141; Berlin, *Generations of Captivity*, 168 (second quote); Edward E. Baptist, "'Cuffy,' 'Fancy Maids', and 'One-Eyed Men': Rape, Commodification, and the Domestic Slave Trade in the United States," *The American Historical Review*

Southern slave traders were unparalleled not only in their ability to turn people into products but also in their general organization of forced migration in the nineteenth century. As Ira Berlin has argued, the interstate slave trade was "the most advanced [southern enterprise] in its employment of modern transportation, finance, and publicity." Whereas domestic trading in slaves had existed on an ad hoc basis since colonial days – often the work of individual traders – the transcontinental transfer of slaves in the antebellum period was a massive, rational, and lucrative capitalistic endeavor, its tentacles creeping into several sectors of America's market economy. According to Steven Deyle, southern slave traders were "the agents of the emerging market world. In addition to taking advantage of all of the new innovations in transportation and communications, these men also introduced many of the new business practices that were revolutionizing American society at that time." They developed complex business organizations with offices and agents in several states, became adept at calculating profits and gauging market trends, and stimulated demand through creative advertising and marketing techniques. In short, these were "hard-headed businessmen, seriously dedicated to the pursuit of profit," as Michael Tadman put it.[38]

The most successful interstate slave traders developed a web of important business relationships (often, but not always, along family lines) and established themselves in urban centers in both the Upper South (the supply region) and the Lower South (the demand region). Franklin and Armfield, who between 1828 and 1836 were far and away the largest traders in the South, provide an interesting example of how these networks operated. The two men wisely established their main headquarters on Duke Street in Alexandria, Virginia – according to one scholar, the "very seat and center" of the domestic slave trade because of the willingness of slaveholders in northern Virginia and southern Maryland to sell. Their enterprise was also well established in the hottest markets of the Deep South, however, including New Orleans, Baton Rouge, and Natchez. Indeed, the two business partners worked opposite ends of the domestic slave trade. Armfield lived in Alexandria and was responsible for buying slaves and forwarding them to the Deep South; Franklin received the "shipments" of slaves and sold them on the Louisiana and Mississippi markets. The infamous slave dealers also collaborated with several brokers and petty traders who worked for them on commission in a number of towns and cities. In the Upper South, for example, the firm recruited slaves not only through Armfield's headquarters in Alexandria but also through local "agents" in Richmond and Warrenton

106 (Dec. 2001): 1619–50; A.J. McElveen to Z.B. Oakes, Jan. 6, 1852, in Edmund Drago, ed., *Broke by the War: Letters of a Slave Trader* (Columbia: University of South Carolina Press, 1991), 43 (third quote); John S. Wise, in Jones, *Plantation South*, 72–73 (fourth quote); Johnson, *Soul by Soul*, 14 (fifth quote), 108–11.

[38] Berlin, *Generations of Captivity*, 168 (first quote); Deyle, *Carry Me Back*, 94–141, 96 (second quote); Tadman, *Speculators and Slaves*, 47 (third quote); Lightner, *Slavery and the Commerce Power*, 7–10.

(in Virginia) and Fredericktown, Baltimore, and Easton (in Maryland). With agents scouring the countryside and tapping into supply lines throughout the Chesapeake, Franklin and Armfield became extremely successful: by the mid-1830s, they were reportedly deporting more than a thousand slave migrants a year to the Lower Mississippi Valley.[39]

The men who traded in African-American slaves knew their markets and consequently speculated on the most desirable laborers for their southern customers, which in turn had important repercussions for the demographic composition of interstate forced migration. Countless advertisements in Upper South newspapers promised distressed slaveholders cash for healthy, young, fertile hands – not small children or older slaves – because these bondspeople were in the best position to perform hard labor and to reproduce and therefore brought the highest prices in the cotton and sugar districts. Franklin & Armfield, for example, offered sellers "Cash for one hundred likely YOUNG NEGROES of both sexes, between the ages of 8 and 25," adding that since the "negroes are wanted immediately," they would "give more than any other purchasers that are in the market or may hereafter come into the market." William Harkin, an interstate trader based in southern Maryland, advised local sellers of "all likely negroes from 8 to 40 years" to inquire at his office. R.W. Lucas, working out of Lexington, Kentucky, offered "the highest price in cash" for "a large number of sound and health [sic] Negroes of both sexes." Speculators almost always offered their sellers cash on the spot for these slaves rather than entering into terms of extended credit, mainly to avoid interest payments. Cash also gave traders an advantage over local purchasers by promising struggling sellers immediate payment in full. Enticing local slaveholders with hard currency, dealers deported hundreds of thousands of healthy, young slaves between the ages of eight and forty to the Deep South, thereby significantly draining some parts of the Chesapeake of an important age cohort.[40]

Intuitively, southern speculators responded to localized market trends. The sugar country of southern Louisiana, where planters exhibited a strong preference for able-bodied men above women, provides an interesting case in point. The reason for Louisiana slaveholders' preference for men had to do with the especially labor-intensive nature of sugar cultivation, which planters believed was most aptly performed by a predominately male labor force. Interstate slave traders therefore imported twice as many men to the region, leading to a severe sexual imbalance and even negative population growth rates. Many traders, specialized in supplying the sugar region with slaves, specifically advertised

39 Deyle, *Carry Me Back*, 99–100; Bancroft, *Slave-Trading*, 58–59; Wendell Holmes Stephenson, *Isaac Franklin: Slave Trader and Planter of the Old South* (1938; Gloucester, Mass.: P. Smith, 1968), 22–93; Lightner, *Slavery and the Commerce Power*, 8–9. See also Andrews, *Slavery and the Domestic Slave Trade*, 80, 134–153.

40 *Phenix Gazette*, Dec. 25, 1828 (first quote); Bancroft, *Slave-Trading*, 120 (second quote), 305 (fourth quote); *Kentucky Statesman*, Jan. 13, 1860 (third quote); Tadman, *Speculators and Slaves*, 46–55.

their desire to purchase "for the New Orleans market," and some even explicitly stated that "fellows will be preferred." Historians such as Michael Tadman and Richard Follett have calculated that approximately 70 percent of slaves exported to New Orleans by interstate traders were male.[41]

The methods that interstate slave traders adopted to purchase, hold, and transport their "goods" to the southern interior testify to their organizational skills, their connections, their knowledge of the market, and their psychological dehumanization of the people in whom they were trading. In supply regions, slaves were purchased from local sellers both passively (by advertising and attending to sellers who stopped by the office in town) and aggressively (by actively seeking out potential sellers). Indeed, according to one Virginian, it was not uncommon to see speculators or their brokers roaming "from house to house plucking the flower from every flock." Maryland slave Charles Ball was sold to one such aggressive Georgia trader, who came up to the house one day and began "speaking with my master." Before Ball realized what was happening, the trader seized him "by the collar, [and] shook me violently, saying I was his property, and must go with him to Georgia." In Knox County, Tennessee, a lawsuit was filed in 1836 against two traders who stopped to see a local slave owner and proceeded to intoxicate the man until he agreed to sell nine valuable slaves at a pittance, "so intoxicated with spirituous liquor, that he did not know what he was doing." Even when they remained at their headquarters, however, traders hung out their shingles in prominent urban locations and made sure that sellers knew where to find them. Dealers were indeed often located in the same street or neighborhood, so that sellers could easily "shop around" for the best prices. One northern visitor to Richmond in the 1850s was appalled to see the offices of Dickinson, Hill & Company, "body-sellers and body-buyers," located "within pistol shot of the capitol of Virginia," and directly across the street "the office of another person engaged in the same inhuman traffic." Both had large signs painted above the doors.[42]

After a deal was struck and money exchanged hands, slaves were temporarily kept in dreary "slave pens" or "jails," usually attached to the headquarters of the slave-dealing firm. There they were held until there were enough slaves to

[41] Michael Tadman, "The Demographic Cost of Sugar: Debates on Slave Societies and Natural Increase in the Americas," *The American Historical Review* 105 (Dec. 2000): 1538; Berlin, *Generations of Captivity*, 179–80; Follett, *Sugar Masters*, 46–54; Tadman, *Speculators and Slaves*, 64–71, 65–66 (second quote); Jonathan B. Pritchett, "The Interregional Slave Trade and the Selection of Slaves for the New Orleans Market," *Journal of Interdisciplinary History* 28 (summer 1997): 57–85.

[42] Tadman, *Speculators and Slaves*, 46–55; Deyle, *Carry Me Back*, 145–46; M.D. Conway, *Testimonies Concerning Slavery* (1864; New York 1969), 21 (first quote); Charles Ball, *Fifty Years in Chains; Or, the Life of an American Slave* (New York: H. Dayton, 1859), 28 (second quote); "George Peery to the Chancery Court, Knox County, Tennessee, 1836," in Schweninger, ed., *Southern Debate over Slavery*, 180–81 (third quote); James Redpath, *The Roving Editor; or, Talks with the Slaves in the Southern States* (1859; New York: Negro Universities Press, 1969), 245–46 (fourth quote).

FIGURE 1.2. Front of a "slave pen," Alexandria, Va., 1861–1865. "Photograph showing a Union army guard and other men in front of a building designated Price, Birch & Co., dealers in slaves." This slave pen on Duke Street in Alexandria, Va., served as headquarters for several successful slave traders, including Franklin & Armfield, in the 1830s. By the Civil War, it was in possession of Price, Birch and Co. Inscribed on the photograph was the text: "Building contained numerous cells and a whipping post." *Source:* Russell J. Andrew, 1861–1865. Courtesy of the Library of Congress, Prints and Photographs Division, LOT 11486-H, no. 10.

be transported as a group to the South; depending on the circumstances, this could take a couple of days or a couple of months. When the decision was finally made to depart, most speculators transported their slaves by means of overland coffles, consisting of droves of slaves chained together. The journey to the South was usually made on foot along dusty dirt roads and could take several weeks or months. Although by the 1850s, some traders were reportedly transporting their slaves by train, taking advantage of a new and much quicker means of travel, there were well-calculated reasons for slave traders to organize their trips in overland coffles. Coffles allowed traders to roam the countryside, from county to county, purchasing extra slaves directly from local slaveholders or at estate auctions as they went – the domestic slave trade's equivalent of "coasting." As Michael Tadman has argued, slave purchasing in the exporting states was of a "roving nature" by design, partly as a way of developing local knowledge of the supply in a particular area and partly as a way of offering sellers an easy way of disposing of their slaves. For convenience, traders frequently stopped by plantations to "speculate" for likely bondspeople, often returning before dawn the next morning to pick up purchased slaves when such transactions would be unlikely to cause a scene to the rest of the slave community. Leonard Harrod, a bondsman from Maryland who eventually managed to escape to Canada, told interviewers that at "about six o'clock one morning, I was taken suddenly from my wife; she knew no more where I had gone than the hen knows where the hawk carries her chicken. Fifteen hundred miles I wore iron on my wrist, chained in a gang from Georgetown [Washington, D.C.] to Port Gibson [Mississippi]. There I was sold and put to receive and pack cotton, etc., for six years." Benjamin, a fugitive slave from Virginia, testified to interviewer William Still in 1868 that "frequently slaves would be snatched up, handcuffed and hurried off south on one of the night trains without an hour's notice."[43]

The coffles' many stops along the way to the Deep South connected several regions in the trade, from the northernmost reaches of the Upper South, through the piedmont and mountain districts, and into the southern interior. The coffle in which Charles Ball was chained passed through parts of Virginia that were "the picture of sterility," then on through Richmond and Bowling Green, traversing North Carolina, finally crossing into South Carolina near Camden, and continuing on to Columbia, where the speculator disposed of his first load. John Brown, a Virginia slave transported to Georgia, was marched through Roanoke, from there to Raleigh, and on to Augusta, Georgia, where the first few slaves were sold. After Augusta, the rest of the gang continued to the cotton plantation of one Ben Tarver in Jones County, where they stopped for two weeks. Tarver was an acquaintance of the speculator, who employed several of the newly arrived slave migrants in his fields while Finney, the slave trader, went out selling groups of slaves to the plantations in the neighborhood. Brown was finally taken to Milledgeville, where he and the remainder of the coffle were

[43] Tadman, *Speculators and Slaves*, 46–50; Deyle, *Carry Me Back*, 146–47; Lightner, *Slavery and the Commerce Power*, 10; David Brion Davis, *Inhuman Bondage: The Rise and Fall of Slavery in the New World* (New York: Oxford University Press, 2006), 183; William J. Anderson, *Life and Narrative of William J. Anderson, Twenty-Four Years a Slave* (Chicago: Daily Tribune Book and Job Printing Office, 1857), 11; Henry Bibb, *Narrative of the Life and Adventures of Henry Bibb, an American Slave* (New York: The Author, 1849), 91–99; John Brown, *Slave Life in Georgia: A Narrative of the Sufferings, and Escape of John Brown, a Fugitive Slave, Now in England*, edited by Louis A. Chamerovzow (London: L.A. Chamerovzow, 1855), 13–14; Leonard Harrod, in Drew, ed., *North-Side View*, 339–40 (first quote); William Still, *The Underground Railroad: A Record of Facts, Authentic Letters, &c.* (1872; New York: Negro Universities Press, 1968), 479 (second quote). Frederick Law Olmsted reported seeing groups of slaves being transported by train to the Deep South. Olmsted, *Seaboard Slave States*, 55, 308, 377. John Springs III, one of the largest slave importers to South Carolina in the 1820s, also routinely visited several parts of the Chesapeake during slave-buying trips (including Maryland's Eastern Shore, Richmond, and Norfolk), seeking to fill his coffle before starting off for South Carolina. Michael Tadman, "The Hidden History of Slave Trading in Antebellum South Carolina: John Springs III and other 'Gentlemen Dealing in Slaves,'" *South Carolina Historical Magazine* 97 (Jan. 1996): 21–28.

sold at auction. The journey that Virginia slave William Anderson was made to endure included travel by land and by boat. Anderson was marched off in a coffle consisting of sixty-five or seventy slaves, who were chained two by two and transported overland into the southern interior. Departing from Richmond, their route went "straight up the James River," through "many towns which it would be useless to mention," finally arriving in Nashville. There the speculator delivered the entire coffle to another trader, who huddled the slaves onto a boat and shipped them down the river to Mississippi. "In due time we arrived safely at a slave-pen at Natchez," Anderson recalled in his autobiography.[44]

The transportation of slaves to the Natchez and New Orleans markets often provided an exception to the rule of overland coffles. Speculators for these markets regularly "shipped" slaves from the exporting states to New Orleans by way of the Ohio and Mississippi Rivers or even by way of the Atlantic Ocean and Gulf of Mexico. Similar to overland coffles, the slave trade between the Chesapeake and New Orleans connected several cities in different parts of the South, in all of which speculators had contacts and agents. Steamships traveling the river route, for example, called in at other slave-trading hubs such as Louisville, St. Louis, Memphis, Vicksburg, and Baton Rouge, picking up and disposing of slaves along the way. William Hayden, a slave from Frankfort, Kentucky, was picked up by one of these Virginia river dealers in 1817, who had stopped in Kentucky while making his way to the lower Mississippi markets. Employed by the speculator as an assistant and steersman, Hayden traveled with his new master down the Ohio and Mississippi Rivers to the slave markets in Natchez, afterward continuing on to Bayou Sara in Louisiana and then finally to Plaquemines, where "the balance were easily sold." Ships traveling the coastal route, meanwhile, turned Chesapeake cities such as Baltimore, Alexandria (from which Franklin & Armfield shipped their slaves), Richmond, and Norfolk into major slave-collecting hubs for the New Orleans market.[45]

Upon arrival in slave markets throughout the southern interior, speculators and their agents enticed buyers with well-worded circulars, handbills, and advertisements in local newspapers. Traders in Montgomery, Alabama, hawked "young likely negroes to suit any purchaser," while in Natchez, they promised "a large and well-selected stock of Negroes" with "fresh arrivals weekly." In New Orleans, speculators could barely contain their excitement, with newspaper ads regularly blaring the headline "VIRGINIA NEGROES!" Shipments from Virginia were often openly advertised as such because

[44] Tadman, *Speculators and* Slaves, 46–50; Ball, *Fifty Years in Chains*, 32 (fourth quote), 32–38; Brown, *Slave Life in Georgia*, 17–21; Anderson, *Life and Narrative*, 12–14 (fifth quote).

[45] Davis, *Inhuman Bondage*, 183; Tadman, *Speculators and Slaves*, 64–65; Deyle, *Carry Me Back*, 147–48; Johnson, *Soul by Soul*, 50; Rockman, *Scraping By*, 235–36; William Hayden, *Narrative of William Hayden, Containing a Faithful Account of His Travels for a Number of Years, Whilst a Slave, in the South* (Cincinnati: W. Hayden, 1846), 51–58, 56 (first quote).

bondspeople from that state had gained a good reputation for hard work and good health and were therefore especially in demand in the Deep South. The Mississippi cotton planter who bought Virginia slave Louis Hughes at auction in 1844 expressed a common sentiment when, during the inspection period before the bidding commenced, he declared that "Virginia always produces good darkies." Hughes explained that "Virginia was the mother of slavery, and it was held by many that she had the best slaves. So when Mr. McGee found I was born and bred in that state he seemed satisfied."[46]

After their grueling journey, the droves of interstate slave migrants were once again lodged in "pens," many of which were legally bounded by high walls so that they could not be seen from the street, where they awaited sale. At these sites, slave traders prepared their human commodities for market, often greasing their skin, dying their hair, giving them new suits of clothes to wear for the auction, and prepping them on how to answer questions from potential buyers (advising many to lie about their ages and tell buyers that they had never run away). One Virginia slave claimed that upon arrival in Natchez in 1827, he was thrown into a slave pen with a number of other slaves. "The slaves [were] made to shave and wash in greasy pot liquor, to make them look sleek and nice; their heads must be combed, and their best clothes put on; and when called out to be examined they are to stand in a row." Henry Watson, also sold at Natchez, explained in his autobiography that "just before the doors are opened [for the auction], it is usual for the keeper to grease the mouths of the slaves, so as to make it appear that they are well and hearty, and have just done eating meat." Slave women were often made to undergo an extra humiliation: a private inspection of their naked bodies to gauge their reproductive potential. James Redpath, a northern journalist who attended one such auction in 1855, was sickened to see a young woman "taken into the inner room, after the bidding commenced, and there indecently '*examined*' in the presence of a dozen or fifteen brutal men." Northern traveler Philo Tower observed auctioneers publicly exposing slave women's breasts on the stand during a sale at New Orleans in 1854. Even the *purchasers* of slaves were sometimes "prepared" for auction – one attendant to a slave market in Charleston in the 1830s reported that alcohol was gratuitously distributed among prospective buyers "to stimulate the spirit of jockeying."[47]

[46] Bancroft, *Slave-Trading*, 294–311; *Montgomery Confederation*, Dec. 8, 1859 (first quote); *Natchez Courier*, Jan. 26, 1853 (second quote); *Louisiana State Gazette*, Jan. 20, 1826 (third quote); Louis Hughes, *Thirty Years a Slave: From Bondage to Freedom* (Milwaukee: South Side Printing Co., 1896), 11 (fourth quote).

[47] Johnson, *Soul by Soul*, 24; Deyle, *Carry Me Back*, 148–49; Anderson, *Life and Narrative*, 14 (first quote), 15; Henry Watson, *Narrative of Henry Watson, a Fugitive Slave* (Boston: Bela Marsh, 1848), 12 (second quote); Redpath, *Roving Editor*, 252 (third quote); Philo Tower, *Slavery Unmasked: Being a Truthful Narrative of a Three Years' Residence and Journeying in Eleven Southern States* (1856; New York: Negro Universities Pres, 1969), 305–307; Weld, *American Slavery As It Is*, 167 (fourth quote).

VI.

Although a majority of interstate slave migrants were transported across state lines by domestic slave traders and sold at public auctions in the receiving societies, a significant percentage (around one-third) were moved south and west by their masters. These slaves usually fell into one of two categories. First, there were those bought by new masters who were visiting from other states and who subsequently brought them (or had them brought) "home" to their residences in the Lower South. These migrants often experienced deportation in much the same way as those delivered to traders – they were sent to local dealers, sometimes kept in slave pens, and put up on the auction block to be sold away. Rather than being deported by speculators, however, they were bought by southerners from the interior who wished to circumvent the expensive interstate slave trade and import their slaves themselves, often traveling great distances to do so. This practice appears not to have been uncommon. Northerner Joseph Ingraham found during a residence in Mississippi in 1835 that the phrase "he is gone to Virginia to buy negroes" was as common among cotton planters there as "he is gone to Boston to buy goods" was among country merchants in New England.[48]

The method of transport by these slave purchasers was arranged privately rather than in coffles. Such was the experience of Virginia slave Jourden Banks, for example, who, along with one other slave, was "struck off" to an Alabama cotton planter at a Richmond auction in 1857. Wishing to stay in Virginia a few weeks longer, Banks' purchaser decided not to bring his new bondsmen home himself but rather delivered them into the hands of his nephew, who acted as conductor and accompanied the slaves "through North Carolina, South Carolina, and Georgia, into Alabama, all by rail, till we got to Montgomery." From there the three men "took a steamer and went 110 miles" to a small landing; the last thirty miles to their new home were traversed on foot. No roving was involved in this journey – Banks was sent south via the quickest and most direct route. It is indeed likely that many of the slaves transported across state lines by rail and steamer in the 1850s were in fact already purchased by southern planters, who had no reason to roam around the countryside in overland coffles. One Louisiana sugar planter, advertising in a South Carolina newspaper in 1859 for "50 to 150 good plantation negroes" to be shipped directly to him, even explicitly asked sellers to forward him details of the "most accessible route from Charleston or whereabouts," so as not to lose time in transit. Certainly not all were transported by train or boat, of course; many such migrants found themselves marched on foot into the southern interior. One Virginia slave who, along with several other bondsmen, was knocked off at a Richmond auction to a Mississippi planter in 1844 claimed that he and

[48] Gudmestad, *A Troublesome Commerce*, 11–12; Davis, *Inhuman Bondage*, 183; Ingraham, *South-West*, 2:234 (quote).

the other newly purchased slaves were led south "on foot, or in a wagon," while their new master traveled home by train. Mississippi planter William McNeill, who purchased a number of slaves in Nashville during a similar trip, brought them back to his plantation by land "without any difficulty," despite the fact that "none of the gang were ironed or shackled in any way," as newly purchased slaves often were.[49]

The remainder of slave migrants who moved west and south with their masters were not auctioned off but rather moved with owners whom they knew personally (sometimes their whole lives); in most cases, they moved with their owners' other slaves as well. Unlike migrants transported by strangers – whether speculators or new masters from other states – migrants who accompanied their existing masters west were rarely chained or shackled because their owners seldom feared any violent uprisings, and many did not even fear escape attempts. And unlike those deported by speculators, no roving was involved in these journeys. One Virginia slave accompanied his master to Missouri without chains and by the quickest means possible – his owner even purchased "three large wagons" for the journey, "one for the whites and two for the slaves." The last leg of the trip, from Louisville to St. Louis, was made by steamboat. Some slaveholders made the entire journey by river rather than overland. Israel Campbell's Kentucky master, who decided to move to Mississippi, transported both the white family and all of the slaves by means of a flatboat, which he had specifically bought for the purpose. In this case, the slaves were not only moved south but were responsible for moving their masters south as well. Campbell recalled that "after we had all embarked we [the slaves] rowed down the Ohio and Mississippi rivers."[50]

VII.

Local slave migrants in the antebellum South were spared such exhausting journeys over hundreds and hundreds of miles. However, similar to their interstate counterparts, enslaved people who were sold locally were often disposed of at formal auctions organized by professional slave dealers. Indeed, the organization of local slave trading – the pens, transactions, and auctions – was in fact very similar to that of interstate trading, minus the trip itself. The experiences of Kentucky bondsman Isaac Johnson are illustrative. When Johnson's master wanted to sell his slaves and leave the state, he arranged for the sheriff to

49 Gudmestad, *A Troublesome Commerce*, 15; James W.C. Pennington, *A Narrative of the Events of the Life of J.H. Banks, an Escaped Slave, from the Cotton State, Alabama, in America* (Liverpool: M. Rourke, 1861), 48–49 (first quote); Picquet, *Louisa Picquet, the Octoroon*, 18; *Charleston Courier*, Sept. 17, 1859 (second quote); Hughes, *Thirty Years a Slave*, 12–13 (third quote); Watson, *Narrative of Henry Watson*, 22 (fourth quote).

50 Burke, *On Slavery's Border*, 29–30; Bruce, *The New Man*, 16 (first quote); Campbell, *Bond and Free*, 32 (second quote).

come and take "us all to Bardstown in Nelson county, about two days journey eastward," where the group was "placed in the negro pen for the night." Rather than depart in a coffle, however, Johnson and his family members were disposed of the next morning at the slave pen itself. A crowd gathered for the sale, and the slaves were put up on the auction block, while the auctioneer shouted: "Time is precious, gentlemen, I must sell them all before night; how much do I hear for this nigger?" Knocked off to a local planter who was in no rush to depart immediately, Johnson was "chained to a post as though I had been a horse" until his new master was ready to leave town. Finally, in the late afternoon, his "new master put me into a wagon and took me over very rough and hilly roads to his home about five miles distant."[51]

Estate auctions, through which a significant percentage of local slave migrants in the antebellum South were sold, strongly resembled professional auctions like the one Isaac Johnson experienced, the main difference being that estate auctions were often (but not always) held at the local court house, town marketplace, or even the plantation itself. A perusal of southern newspapers reveals that such auctions occurred with regularity. In Gadsden County, Florida, "thirteen negro slaves" were sold "for Cash, before the Court door in the town of Quincy" to settle an estate division in 1830. In Lynchburg, Virginia, "17 valuable slaves" were auctioned off "before the front door of the market house" in a similar settlement. The thirty-six slaves attached to one James Island cotton plantation in South Carolina were sold by the executor of the estate "at the Mart" in Charleston in 1860; and in Mississippi, advertisements such as the following were a frequent sight: "Will be exposed at public sale on the Plantation of the undersigned, in Jefferson county . . . the personal estate of the late John H. Hoggatt, deceased, consisting of 16 Negroes (different sexes), a pair of cart wheels, and one rifle gun." Local migrants sold off in this manner never had to spend the night inside – or indeed even see – a filthy slave pen or jail because they were usually taken out to be auctioned off on the same day. The rest of the transaction, however, from the prodding inspections of potential buyers to the auctioneer's hammer, was virtually identical to that of an auction at a slave dealer's establishment. Former North Carolina slave John Jacobs recounted that the estate auction at which he and his family members were sold even had an actual auction stand. "The hungry heirs ordered us slaves to mount the auction-block," he recounted in an autobiographical essay in 1861. "They began to sell off the old slaves first, as rubbish," but swiftly

[51] Isaac Johnson, *Slavery Days in Old Kentucky* (n.p., 1901), 9 (first quote), 10 (second quote), 11 (third quote); Johnson, *Soul by Soul*, 6–7; Deyle, *Carry Me Back*, 157–60. Historian Georgena Duncan has noted that some remote areas of the southern frontier, such as Pope and Conway County, Arkansas, had no organized slave markets and no newspapers to announce sales. News about slave sales spread by word of mouth, transactions were casual affairs, and estate sales often took place on the courthouse steps. See Duncan, "'One negro, Sarah,'" 327–28.

moved on to the more valuable slaves; Jacobs was sold "under the auctioneer's hammer" to a local slaveholder.[52]

A number of local migrants were disposed of more informally without having to mount the humiliating auction block or withstand the intrusive glares of buyers. For example, the division of slaves during estate settlements – when they did not result in auctions – was often organized in the form of a private lottery. One former bondsman claimed that upon the death of his master, "allotments were regulated so as to equalize the value of each division." Then "when the lots had been told off, the names of the men, women, and children composing them were written on three slips of paper, and these were put into a hat," to be drawn by the respective heirs. Another Virginia slave recounted in 1861 that during an estate settlement, an "appraiser proceeded to set us [the slaves] apart into five lots of equal value; and each name being written upon a card, the cards were placed in a hat, and each one of the children drew from the hat a card, and the names written on the card were theirs."[53]

Some local transactions were indeed so informal and casual that they came as a complete surprise to the slaves being traded. The second time that Georgia slave William Heard was sold was without any warning at all; the principal of a nearby boarding school, who stopped by the plantation one day, decided to negotiate with Heard's master for a few slaves to be employed at domestic work. Oblivious to the negotiations, Heard and his family were rounded up and sent off to their new home in Elberton without delay. The earlier mentioned William Grimes, who was moved locally several times within the state of Virginia before being deported to Georgia, recalled a similar experience. The first time he was sold was also without any warning – his master's brother-in-law arrived one day looking to buy slaves, and a deal was swiftly struck. Abruptly compelled to leave his mother, the ten-year-old slave found himself being taken down the road to Culpeper County. While still living in Maryland as a young man, Charles Ball was also forced to change masters without a moment's notice. "At work in the cornfield one day," he was suddenly approached by one Mr. Ballard, who "came and told me I was his property; asking me at the same time if I was willing to go with him." Entering the big house to confirm the transaction, Ball was told by his mistress that "I must go with Mr. Ballard."[54]

Antebellum slave migrants who were hired out to third parties for extended periods of time were disposed of in ways very similar to slaves who were sold

[52] *Floridian & Advocate* (Tallahassee, FL), Feb. 23, 1830 (first quote); *Lynchburg Virginian*, Nov. 22, 1832 (second quote); *The Charleston Courier, Tri-Weekly*, Jan. 12, 1860 (third quote); *The Natchez Gazette*, Dec. 29, 1830 (fourth quote); John S. Jacobs, "A True Tale of Slavery," *The Leisure Hour: A Family Journal of Instruction and Recreation*, Feb. 14, 1861, 86 (fifth quote).

[53] Duncan, "One negro, Sarah," 333–36; Brown, *Slave Life in Georgia*, 7 (first quote); Pennington, *Life of J.H. Banks*, 36 (second quote).

[54] Heard, *From Slavery to the Bishopric*, 24–25; William Grimes, *Life of William Grimes, the Runaway Slave. Written by Himself* (New York: n.p., 1825), 8; Ball, *Fifty Years in Chains*, 25 (quote).

or moved locally: many were hired through formal channels (at auctions and through hiring brokers), and others became hirelings through more informally brokered deals. Because hiring revolved around annual terms of employment, formal hiring auctions throughout the South tended to be concentrated at the end of the calendar year; most took place on (or in the week of) New Year's Day. Contracts were then signed for fifty-one weeks in the ensuing year, stipulating not only the price but also the conditions of hire, the most general being that the person hiring must furnish the slave with clothes and board and that excess abuse would result in immediate termination of the contract and forfeiture of payment. Such occasions were well advertised in local communities; during the month of December, southern newspapers abounded with advertisements for "hiring days" at local auction houses or court houses. Benjamin Rogers, a hiring agent from North Carolina, ran a notice in Raleigh's *Daily Register* for three weeks in December 1859, advertising to local residents that "my usual day of hiring Negroes will take place on Monday, the 3rd day of January next, when a parcel of likely servants will be hired, consisting of men, boys, women, and girls." In northern Virginia, newspaper advertisements informed locals in December 1851 that "the days for hiring servants in Fairfax Co. are as follows – Fairfax Court House on Monday, December 30; Dranesville on Tuesday, December 31; Centreville on Wednesday, January 1." Hiring auctions were sometimes held at private residences, rather than auction halls or the courthouse. In Little Rock, Arkansas, for example, an auction in 1830 was held "at the residence of Mrs. Hannah T. Brown" to "hire out the Slaves belonging to the estate of... John Brown, deceased." In Missouri "several Negro Men" were hired out in 1821 "at the plantation of Mr. Carrico."[55]

At public auctions of this sort, slave hirelings were placed on an auction block and struck off to the highest bidder in almost exactly the same way as a slave sale. As North Carolina slave Allen Parker recalled after emancipation, "it was customary in those days for those having slaves to let, to take them to some prominent place, such as where two roads crossed, on the first day of the New Year, and at a given hour of the day the slaves would be put up at auction, and let to the highest bidders for one year." He added that "there was generally quite a gathering on these occasions." William Webb, regularly hired out in Mississippi, remembered on one particular occasion that when "hiring out day came around again" he was "placed on the block," his heart "trembling, for fear I should be hired to some hard master." Indeed, such occasions were often intimidating to slaves. Employers or their agents gathered around to gauge slaves' laboring potential – handling them like merchandise

[55] Martin, *Divided Mastery*, 93–102; Bancroft, *Slave-Trading*, 147–50; Wade, *Slavery in the Cities*, 38–40, 46–47; Takagi, *"Rearing Wolves,"* 22–23; *The Daily Register* (Raleigh, NC), Jan. 1, 1859 (first quote); *Alexandria Gazette & Virginia Advertiser*, Dec. 30, 1851 (second quote); *The Arkansas Gazette* (Little Rock, Ark.), Dec. 22, 1830 (third quote); *St. Louis Enquirer*, Dec. 15, 1821 (fourth quote).

and asking them questions – and bid on them as they saw fit. Whites spoke of hirelings as cogs in a machine at these auctions, rarely mentioning slaves' names and often referring to men as "boys," their focus almost exclusively on extracting the most labor at the least cost. One agent to a North Carolina railroad magnate wrote his employer after attending one such auction: "I had a boy without a wife, about 20 years of age strong and likely that I will hire for fifty dollars with the usual clothing. If you will take him at that price I will send him to you next Monday."[56]

Informally brokered deals outside of the traditional hiring days were also common, however. Southern newspapers served as a medium that brought slaveholders and prospective employers in contact with one another, and advertisements for hirelings consequently ran throughout the year, often leading to less public arrangements than formally organized auctions. In May of 1841, St. Louis factory owners Childs & Carr advertised that they wished "to hire for the balance of the year, 10 or 12 negro men and 12 or 15 boys, from to 10 to 15 years of age, to work in our bagging and rope factory." Slaveholders with bondsmen to hire, especially slaves with experience, were simply advised to inquire at the factory. In Jackson, Mississippi, newspapers advertised in May of 1853 for "50 negroes" wanted to hire "on the Vicksburg and Jackson Railroad," the owners requested to contact the railroad company for further information. Some transactions necessitated no advertising at all. When bondsman William Hayden was hired out to a ropemaker in Georgetown, Kentucky, one year, the transaction occurred not only unbeknownst to him, but – as his mistress's brother negotiated the deal – initially even unbeknownst to his mistress. William Wells Brown was similarly hired out behind his back to a slave trader based in St. Louis. The trader had originally approached Brown's master seeking to purchase him, but his master compromised by allowing the trader to hire him out by the year. "When I learned the fact of my having been hired to a negro speculator . . . no one can tell my emotions," Brown bitterly recalled.[57]

Whether relocated across state lines, locally, or hired out in southern towns and cities, enslaved people were removed for a variety of reasons and in a variety of ways in the decades preceding the Civil War. Broad economic undercurrents dictated the supply and demand for slave labor at both the local and national levels and were thus directly and indirectly responsible for sweeping millions of American slaves from their homes during the antebellum period. The logistics

[56] Allen Parker, *Recollections of Slavery Times* (Worcester: Chas. Burbank & Co., 1895), 9–10 (first quote); William Webb, *The History of William Webb, Composed by Himself* (Detroit: Egbert Hoekstra, 1873), 11 (second quote); W.H. Jozned to John D. Hawkins, Franklinton, Dec. 31, 1845, Hawkins Family Papers, Subseries 1.1: Correspondence, Records of Ante-Bellum Southern Industries, Series B (microfilm), JFK Institute (third quote).

[57] *Daily Missouri Republican* (St. Louis), May 13, 1841 (first quote); *Mississippian and State Gazette* (Jackson, MS), May 20, 1853 (second quote); Hayden, *Narrative of William Hayden*, 24; Brown, *Narrative of William W. Brown*, 39 (third quote).

of this massive wave of forced removal, meanwhile, could be as formal as the meticulously organized interstate slave trade or as informal as an estate lottery consisting of slips of paper drawn from a hat. Yet even as their valuable bodies were commodified and their labor reallocated across space by southern slaveholders, speculators, and auctioneers, slave migrants grappled as human beings with the threats and realities of forced removal. As the next chapters will show, the ways in which various types of migrants experienced and reacted to forced removal – both emotionally and physically – bore both subtle similarities and striking differences.

2

The Gathering Storm

There is . . . a constant dread felt by the whole slave population, that they shall be torn from their families and friends.

Professor E.A. Andrews, 1836[1]

During a newspaper assignment in Alabama in 1910, progressive civil rights activist and journalist Mary White Ovington asked an elderly ex-slave named Kitty to tell her about her experiences in bondage. Similar to many former slaves asked the same question, Kitty began by recalling the horrors of forced removal. "De hardes' part ob dose days," she told Ovington, "were being sold. It done seem as tho yer couldn't to bear it. When I was sold away by de speculators it seem like I griebe ter death." Ben, another former slave whom Ovington interviewed, emphasized not only forced removal itself but also bondspeople's constant anxiety that they would one day be forced to move. Where he lived, the threat recurred annually. "Every fall they sell people jes' like cattle," he explained. "They go from place to place drivin' us along as ef we was mules or cows. Sons 'ud be taken from their mothers, women from their husbands." He himself had been put "on the block" twice as a young man – first to be forcibly hired out for two years and then to be sold. "I brought a good price. A heap o' people done want me fer I could do a sight o' work. Um, Um."[2]

[1] Portions of this chapter were previously published in adapted form in Damian Alan Pargas, "The Gathering Storm: Slave Responses to the Threat of Interregional Migration in the Early Nineteenth Century," *Journal of Early American History* 2 no. 3 (Fall 2012): 286–315. E.A. Andrews, *Slavery and the Domestic Slave-Trade in the United States. In a Series of Letters Addressed to the Executive Committee of the American Union for the Relief and Improvement of the Colored Race* (Boston: Light & Stearns, 1836), 107.

[2] Ovington's interview with former slaves in Alabama, which she argued were "typical of the recollections of hard-worked field hands who were early sold away from their families into the Gulf States," was originally published in the *Independent* on May 26, 1910. It is reprinted in

Although economic trends and market labor demands turned enslaved people into commodities in the account books of white slaveholders and traffickers, African-American slave migrants such as Kitty and Ben experienced the reallocation of their valuable bodies as human beings rather than products. For them, forced removal from the plantations, farms, and residences where they had been born or where they had lived for long periods of time was *the* central event in their lives; as such, it was frequently the very first episode they recalled in interviews and autobiographies, both during slavery and after the institution's demise. Indeed, an analysis of antebellum slave narratives and testimonies suggests that no other aspect of bondage occupied such an important part of enslaved people's memories as forced relocation. To some a welcome escape from harsh masters or monotonous work patterns, to innumerable others a shattering separation from loved ones and a daunting exodus into the unknown, slave migrants throughout the South perceived leaving home as a life-altering turning point in their personal histories – one that wrought fundamental changes in their communities, family relationships, and even identities.[3]

How did enslaved people react to the initial prospect of being removed across state lines, locally, or to urban areas? What ideas did they have about the proposed destinations? To what extent did they attempt to resist or negotiate the terms of their migration, and what were their prime motivations in doing so? Shifting the perspective from the broad undercurrents and organizational aspects of forced migration to the slave migrants themselves, this chapter considers how migrants (and their loved ones) experienced and dealt with the news of forcible removals, with particular emphasis on the fear of family separation as a motivating factor behind many bondspeople's actions and reactions.

I.

The ways in which enslaved people in the antebellum South responded to the prospect of moving stood in stark contrast to slaveholders' frequent claims to outsiders that their slaves neither understood nor cared about forced relocation, one of many arguments proffered to help southerners reconcile their commitment to paternalism with the existence of the domestic slave trade. Georgian proslavery theorist Thomas R.R. Cobb voiced a common stance

John W. Blassingame, ed., *Slave Testimony: Two Centuries of Letters, Speeches, Interviews, and Narratives* (Baton Rouge: Louisiana State University Press, 1977), 533–43, 535–46 (first quote), 534–35 (second quote).

[3] Walter Johnson, *Soul by Soul: Life Inside the Antebellum Slave Market* (Cambridge, Mass.: Harvard University Press, 1999), 19; Anthony Gene Carey, *Sold Down the River: Slavery in the Lower Chattahoochee Valley of Alabama and Georgia* (Tuscaloosa: University of Alabama Press, 2011) 69–70. Susan O'Donovan argues that forced relocation was "nothing short of catastrophic" for slaves. See Susan Eva O'Donovan, *Becoming Free in the Cotton South* (Cambridge, Mass.: Harvard University Press, 2007), 20–21.

when he argued in 1858 that slaves exhibited a "prominent defect in the mental organization" that completely incapacitated them from understanding cause and effect. According to Cobb, slaves were unable to comprehend the consequences of forced migration for their personal lives, and so they did not fear it. He maintained moreover that bondspeople's "natural affections are not strong" anyway, so they "suffer little by separation" from loved ones. Indeed, Frederick Law Olmsted reported during his travels through the South that "it is frequently remarked by Southerners, in palliation of the cruelty of separating relatives, that the affections of negroes for one another are very slight." By claiming that forced relocations were *not* cruel and did *not* cause anxiety or grief in the slave quarters, slaveholders were implicitly subscribing to the view that they could execute forced relocations and still be considered "humane" masters. As we shall see, this train of thought not only contradicted slaveholders' own behavior (the way they dangled forced migration in front of their slaves as a threat or duped their slaves on false errands to lure them into the hands of traders for fear of resistance) but also their paternalist image of themselves as benevolent protectors of slave families (what exactly were they protecting if they believed their slaves did not even love their own family members or miss those from whom they had been torn away?). Even Genovese and Fox-Genovese admit that "few slaveholders swallowed that cant" and concede that proslavery apologetics "sometimes descended to the ludicrous."[4]

[4] Adam Rothman, "The Domestication of the Slave Trade in the United States," in Walter Johnson, ed., *The Chattel Principle: Internal Slave Trades in the Americas* (New Haven: Yale University Press, 2004), 32–54; Thomas R.R. Cobb, *An Inquiry Into the Law of Negro Slavery in the United States of America* (Philadelphia: T. and J.W. Johnson & Co., 1858), 35 (first quote), 39 (second quote); Frederick Law Olmsted, *A Journey in the Seaboard Slave States in the Years 1853–1854, with Remarks on Their Economy* (New York: Dix & Edwards, 1856), 555–56 (third quote); George M. Frederickson, *The Black Image in the White Mind: The Debate on Afro-American Character and Destiny, 1817–1914* (Middletown, Conn.: Wesleyan University Press, 1987), 57–58; David L. Lightner, *Slavery and the Commerce Power: How the Struggle to End the Interstate Slave Trade Led to the Civil War* (New Haven: Yale University Press, 2006), 13; Steven Deyle, *Carry Me Back: The Domestic Slave Trade in American Life* (New York: Oxford University Press, 2005), 246–48; Heather Andrea Williams, *Help Me to Find My People: The African American Search for Family Lost in Slavery* (Chapel Hill: University of North Carolina Press, 2012), ch. 3. Genovese and Fox-Genovese admit that few southerners believed that slaves did not suffer from forced separations but allow for the possibility that slaveholders truly believed that forced separations occurred only "for fault" of the slave (i.e., misbehavior) or when economic exigency compelled them to sacrifice one or two slaves to prevent foreclosure and save the rest of the slaves from sale. See Eugene D. Genovese and Elizabeth Fox-Genovese, *Fatal Self-Deception: Slaveholding Paternalism in the Old South* (New York: Cambridge University Press, 2011), 38 (fourth quote), 39 (fifth quote). Other scholars have argued that southerners resorted to outright fabrication when they overtly justified forced separations in these ways. Robert Gudmestad has argued that southerners "created reality and insisted that it be honoured," for example. See Gudmestad, *A Troublesome Commerce*, 48. Walter Johnson has shown that slaveholders were fully aware that forced separations caused anguish among their slaves and therefore often resorted to "outright lies" or "surprise" to lure them into the hands of traders. See Johnson, *Soul by Soul*, 38–39.

Whatever their desperately confused and contradictory reasoning, slaveholders knew that slaves usually viewed the prospect of forced removal as catastrophic. Bondspeople, for their part, usually knew a great deal more than they let on, routinely feigning ignorance or disinterest about many matters that directly affected them but that they felt were too dangerous to openly acknowledge in front of their masters. Despite charges that they were too ignorant to understand the supply and demand for slave labor in the plantation South and too devoid of feelings to care, bondspeople were generally all too aware of the financial state of affairs on their plantations and of the consequences thereof for their domestic arrangements. Holding a deep interest in economic developments that directly affected the stability of their communities, they often silently anticipated the possibility of forced removal long before any decisions were formally announced (if they were announced at all). When removal seemed imminent, enslaved people shed any signs of ignorance or disinterest; many attempted – though rarely successfully – to resist or negotiate the terms of their migration. Interstate, local, and urban migration confronted slaves with different kinds of threats and opportunities, however; the urgency and ways that they and their loved ones responded to the prospect of relocation therefore differed by degrees.

With the exception of only the very smallest children, most interstate slave migrants – especially those from the Upper South – were far from oblivious to the prospect of forced removal by the time they were actually confronted with it. With speculators' droves roaming the countryside, rumors and knowledge of the slave trade spread through slave communities like wildfire, a process that strengthened slave communities and underscored what Phillip Troutman has called the "geopolitical literacy" of enslaved people. Indeed, coffles of chained migrants on their way to the Lower South were often plainly visible to slaves living in both rural counties and urban areas. Former slave Thomas Johnson, who grew up in northern Virginia, recalled after emancipation that "Georgia Traders" were such a common sight in his area that "whenever we [slave children] saw a white man looking over the fence as we were at play, we would run and hide, sometimes getting near our mothers, thinking they could protect us." William Anderson, also born a slave in Virginia, first witnessed the traffic in human chattels to the Deep South as an adolescent, making a lasting impression on him and driving home to him the risk that confronted slave communities in his region. Employed at a tavern situated at a crossroads in Hanover County in the 1820s, he saw "hundreds of slaves pass by for the Southern market, chained and handcuffed together by fifties." Even at his young age, Anderson found the mere sight of a coffle one of "the horrors of slavery," for he knew exactly what was to become of these interstate migrants: "they were driven away to Georgia, and Louisiana, and other Southern States, to be disposed of."[5]

[5] Gudmestad, *Troublesome Commerce*, 43; Deyle, *Carry Me Back*, 246; Phillip Troutman, "Grapevine in the Slave Market,: African-American Geopolitical Literacy and the 1841

The Deep South gained a dreadful reputation among slaves in the Upper South, as bondspeople developed an alternative vision of the southern interior to that conjured up by their masters. When slaveholding whites imagined the new territories of the southwest, they saw a dreamscape of agricultural prosperity – a vast kingdom of cotton (and sugarcane) stretching toward the horizon, dotted here and there by orderly mansions; lush gardens; and neat, whitewashed slave cabins. Slaveholding whites who emigrated west during the antebellum period even desperately wanted to believe that their bondspeople were just as excited as they were to remove to the southern interior. Charles Tait, a Georgia planter who decided to relocate to Alabama in 1819, tried to convince himself that his slaves were "cheerful" at the prospect of moving, expressing "strong hopes that every one will go without a murmer." Another Maryland slaveholder who was planning to emigrate to Mississippi in 1809 haughtily contended in a letter to his brother that all he had to do to spark his slaves' enthusiasm about moving was to simply convince them that their living conditions – work, food, and housing – in the Deep South would be far superior to those in the Chesapeake: "for the blacks, the idea of contentment and the assurance of good living is everything." Both doubtless knew that they were wrong: when most slaves envisioned the southern interior – whether as a destination to which their masters intended to emigrate or as the receiving end of the interstate slave trade – they saw a nightmare. British traveler James Buckingham reported in 1842 that "all the slaves have a great horror of being sent to the south or the west, – for the farther they go in either of these directions, the harder they are worked, and the worse they are used." George Johnson, a bondsman from Harper's Ferry, Virginia (now West Virginia), recalled to interviewers in 1855 that enslaved people in his area were "always afraid of being sold South." According to the stories that circulated in the quarters, fieldwork on the cotton and sugar plantations never ceased, and southern masters were reportedly "much worse than those about us." Deportation to the Louisiana cane country, in particular, was virtually synonymous with a death sentence. As one northerner observed during a journey through the South in the 1850s, "none of the states are so much dreaded by the slaves as Louisiana." Former South Carolina slave Jacob Stroyer contended that Louisiana was "considered by the slaves as a place of slaughter."[6]

Creole Revolt," in Johnson, ed., *The Chattel Principle*, 204–208; Thomas L. Johnson, *Africa for Christ: Twenty-Eight Years a Slave* (London: Alexander & Shepherd, 1892), 10 (second quote); William J. Anderson, *Life and Narrative of William J. Anderson, Twenty-Four Years a Slave* (Chicago: Daily Tribune Book and Job Printing Office, 1857), 11 (third quote).

6 Charles Tait, quoted in James David Miller, *South by Southwest: Planter Emigration and Identity in the Slave South* (Charlottesville: University of Virginia Press, 2002), 5 (first quote); L. Covington to A. Covington, July 22, 1809, in Phillips, ed., *Plantation and Frontier*, 212 (second quote); Gudmestad, *Troublesome Commerce*, 43; James Silk Buckingham, *The Slave States of America* (London: Fisher & Son, 1842), I:248 (third quote); George Johnson in Benjamin Drew, ed., *A North-Side View of Slavery. The Refugee: or, Narratives of Fugitive Slaves in Canada*

Slaves' fears of deportation to the southern interior were often exploited and sometimes even sparked by slaveholders who sought to thwart misbehavior among their bondspeople, contradicting both their own vision of the new South and their claims that slaves neither understood nor cared about forced removal. As historian Anthony Gene Carey has argued, "sale or threat of sale was a major disciplinary tool for slaveholders." One former bondsman charged his Virginia master and mistress with igniting his fear of the Lower South, recounting that they "often threatened to sell me to the negro buyer from Georgia, for any trifling offence, and in order to make me dislike to go there, they would tell me I should have to eat cotton seed, and make indigo, and not have corn bread to eat as I did in Virginia." Joseph Ingraham, a northerner who resided in the South during the 1830s, concurred that Virginia slaves, especially, would do anything to prevent deportation to the cotton regions. In his words they were "full of the impression . . . that the south is emphatically the grave of their race," a fear that their masters openly took advantage of by "daily [holding it] up before their imaginations at home, *in terrorum*, to keep them in the line of duty, if insubordinate." Jesse, a Maryland slave who often "grossly misbehaved himself," was regularly threatened by his master with sale "out of the state," a scenario so terrifying that Jesse eventually ran away. If southerners had truly believed that their slaves did not understand the consequences of interstate migration or that their affections were not strong enough for them to care about forced separations from family members, surely they would not have resorted to such threats to maintain discipline. Such tactics also suggest that slave discipline was based less on a sincere belief in bondspeople's accommodation to their masters' worldview – in other words, less on their deceptive image of themselves as hegemons, as Genovese claimed – than it was on terror, as Johnson has argued.[7]

(Boston: John P. Jewett & Co., 1856), 52 (fourth quote); Philo Tower, *Slavery Unmasked: Being a Truthful Narrative of a Three Years' Residence and Journeying in Eleven Southern States* (1856; New York: Negro Universities Press, 1969), 286–87 (fifth quote); Jacob Stroyer, *Sketches of My Life in the South* (Salem: Salem Press, 1879), 30 (sixth quote); Seth Rockman, *Scraping By: Wage Labor, Slavery, and Survival in Early Baltimore* (Baltimore: Johns Hopkins University Press, 2009), 236–37; Charlotte Brooks, in Octavia V. Rogers Albert, *Charlotte Brooks and Other Slaves* (1890; New York: Oxford University Press, 1998), 4; Robert Gudmestad, "Slave Resistance, Coffles, and Debates over Slavery in the Nation's Capital," in Johnson, ed., *The Chattel Principle*, 78–79.

7 Carey, *Sold Down the River*, 60 (first quote); Gudmestad, *Troublesome Commerce*, 43; William Grimes, *Life of William Grimes, the Runaway Slave* (New York: n.p., 1825), 22 (second quote); Joseph Holt Ingraham, *The South-West. By a Yankee* (New York: Harper & Bros., 1835), 2:235 (third quote); "James L. Davis to the County Court, Frederick County, Maryland, 1838," in Loren Schweninger, ed., *The Southern Debate over Slavery: Volume 2, Petitions to Southern County Courts, 1775–1867* (Urbana: University of Illinois Press, 2008), 189–90 (fourth quote); Gudmestad, "Slave Resistance," 78–79; Eugene Genovese, *Roll, Jordan, Roll: The World the Slaves Made* (New York: Pantheon, 1974), 597–98; Walter Johnson, "A Nettlesome Classic Turns Twenty-Five," *Common-Place* 1 (July 2001), http://www.common-place.org/vol-01/no-04/reviews/johnson.shtml.

Vague threats of deportation to the dreaded Deep South were very different from actually being confronted with it face to face, however. Specific circumstances, such as financial setbacks or the death of a slaveholder, greatly heightened enslaved people's anxiety of forced removal, often sparking wild rumors of potential deportation that threw slave communities in the supply regions of the interstate slave trade into a general panic. When Josiah Henson's Maryland master "fell into difficulty" in 1825, his slaves became paralyzed with the fear that the "sheriff would seize every one who belonged to him, and that all would be separated, or perhaps sold to go to Georgia, or Louisiana – an object of perpetual dread to the slave of the more northern States." One Virginia slave recalled in 1861 that when his master hit a rough patch – one that would eventually result in the deportation of most of his slaves – all of the bondspeople "were fully aware that we were passing through a crisis," with even neighboring slave communities keeping anxiously abreast of the arresting developments on his plantation. In Maryland in 1833, the administrators of the estate of one deceased slaveholder even had the slaves "placed in the custody of Warden of Baltimore County Jail" for fear that "some of them would run away" to avoid the prospect of deportation.[8]

The threat of family separation made forced migration across state lines – even when the destination was not the dreaded Deep South – especially terrifying to antebellum slaves because it meant permanent separation from loved ones. Herein lay the main difficulty in reconciling paternalism with long-distance sale. An important tenet of southerners' paternalist ideology required benevolent masters to make a genuine effort to protect slave families from dissolution. White southerners often claimed to outsiders that "a good master never sells the husband from the wife"; one visitor to the South was even assured by a Mississippi man that "it is a rule seldom deviated from [in the South], to sell families and relations together, if practicable, and if not, at least to masters residing in the neighbourhood of each other." Genovese and Fox-Genovese have argued that the desire to prevent forced separations was usually sincere, writing that "almost no one defended the separation of husbands and wives" but that slaveholders ostensibly believed that forced separations were legitimate (if tragic) as long as they were deemed absolutely necessary, such as when a slave misbehaved or when pressing financial matters left them no other choice, as discussed in Chapter 1. In reality, however, as historian Robert Gudmestad has argued, the claim of preserving or even attempting to preserve

[8] Deyle, *Carry Me Back*, 246–48; John Hope Franklin and Loren Schweninger, *Runaway Slaves: Rebels on the Plantation* (New York: Oxford University Press, 1999), 17–23; Josiah Henson, *The Life of Josiah Henson, Formerly a Slave, Now an Inhabitant of Canada, as Narrated by Himself* (Boston: Arthur D. Phelps, 1849), 21–22 (first quotes); James W.C. Pennington, *A Narrative of the Events of the Life of J.H. Banks, an Escaped Slave, from the Cotton State, Alabama, in America* (Liverpool: M. Rourke, 1861), 20 (second quote); The Administrators of the Late Thomas H. Gist, Baltimore County, Maryland, 1833, in Schweninger, *Southern Debate over Slavery*, 165 (third quote).

family relations was at best "a bit of sophistry" on the part of white southerners, designed to allow buyers and sellers to "disregard reality in favor of a patronizing illusion of benevolence."[9]

Indeed, southern records abound with examples of slaveholders callously separating family members without even the slightest sense of remorse. When one man – a reverend, no less – who separated a slave woman from her child was asked why he did not take the woman's child as well, he replied: "Do you think I would have [that] black bratt in my house with my children?" An acquaintance remarked that his indifference would cost him "at the Judgment." Non-southern eyewitnesses to the slave trade consistently reported that family separations were common. Ethan Allen Andrews, a university professor charged with investigating the domestic slave trade in 1835 and 1836, found that "family ties are often disregarded in this traffic." Visiting Franklin & Armfield's slave pen in Virginia in 1836, he discovered that "in almost every case, family ties have been broken in the purchase of these slaves." Another Alexandria slave trader assured Andrews that "he never separates families" upon sale (a lie intended to legitimize his business to the northerner) but admitted "that in purchasing them he is often compelled to do so, for that 'his business is to purchase, and he must take such as are in the market!'" When Andrews asked whether the traders often bought wives without their husbands, the reply was: "Yes, very often; and frequently, too, they sell me the mother while they keep her children. I have often known them to take away the infant from its mother's breast and keep it, while they sold her." African Americans living in the supply regions of the interstate trade emphatically corroborated such charges, both during and after slavery. In 1854, James Redpath learned from a northern Virginia slave that the separation of slave families through deportation there was as "common as spring water runs." Another bondsman from North Carolina reported after emancipation that in the region where he lived, the "breaking up of families and parting of children from their parents was common . . . and one of the things that caused much bitterness among the slaves."[10]

Historical scholarship has confirmed that charges of forced separation through the interstate slave trade were no exaggeration. In the 1970s and

9 Donald P. McNeilly, *The Old South Frontier: Cotton Plantations and the Formation of Arkansas Society, 1819–1861* (Fayetteville: University of Arkansas Press, 2000), 45–46; Francis and Theresa Pulszky, *White, Red, Black* (1853; New York: Johnson Reprint Co., 1970), 102 (first quote); Ingraham, *South-West*, 2:203 (second quote); Genovese and Fox-Genovese, *Fatal Self-Deception*, 38 (third quote); Gudmestad, *Troublesome Commerce*, 13–14 (fourth quote).

10 J.H. Mortyn to Rev. Daniel Newell, June 1, 1838, John Knight Papers, RASP, Series F, Part 1 (microfilm), JFK Institute, Freie Universität, Berlin (first quote); Ethan Allen Andrews, *Slavery and the Domestic Slave Trade, in a Series of Letters Addressed to the Executive Committee of the American Union for the Relief and Improvement of the Colored Race* (1836; Freeport, NY, 1971), 49, 137–39 (second quotes); James Redpath, *The Roving Editor: Or, Talks with the Slaves in the Southern States* (1859; New York: Negro Universities Press, 1968), 199 (third quote); William Henry Singleton, *Recollections of My Slavery Days* (n.p., 1922), 2 (fourth quote).

1980s, the extent of family separations through interregional sale was the subject of considerable debate among historians, sparked by controversial conclusions drawn by Fogel and Engerman in *Time on the Cross* (1974), that the domestic slave trade accounted for only 2 percent of dissolved marriages among slaves living in the Upper South. Their calculations, however, have long since been refuted as a gross underestimate by historians such as Herbert Gutman and Michael Tadman, among others. Indeed, family separation in fact made economic sense in the interregional slave trade; as Tadman has argued, its very structure was "custom-built to maximize forcible separations." Because the antebellum slave trade was highly selective (in age, ability, and sex) according to the demands of specific markets, speculators usually preferred – even openly advised their agents – to purchase desirable slaves individually, tearing husbands from wives, as well as children and young adults from their parents and younger siblings. A survey of New Orleans slave ship manifests confirms that most interstate migrants indeed arrived in the Deep South as individuals and not in family units. The Brig Tribune, for example, a ship chartered by the infamous traders Franklin & Armfield in 1833, carried 68 slaves from Alexandria and Norfolk, Virginia, to New Orleans, most of whom were in their teens and twenties and only three of whom were in their thirties (the oldest was thirty-eight). Of the ship's enslaved passengers, six young women were transported with one infant child each. The rest of the slaves in the customs manifest were listed individually, all with different surnames, implying that they were not related. Even when family members were deported together, they were often sold separately in the receiving societies because it was more profitable to do so. Scholars have estimated that forced separations probably destroyed one of every three first marriages among slaves in the Upper South; at least half of all slave families in the region were ruptured through the deportation of either a spouse or child during the antebellum period. The westward migration of slaveholders from the eastern seaboard to the southern interior, moreover, severed cross-plantation marriages as well as extended family bonds in countless slave communities.[11]

[11] Robert William Fogel and Stanley L. Engerman, *Time on the Cross: The Economics of American Negro Slavery* (Boston: Little, Brown, & Co., 1974), 49; Herbert Gutman and Richard Sutch, "The Slave Family: Protected Agent of Capitalist Masters or Victim of the Slave Trade?" in Paul A. David, et al, *Reckoning with Slavery: A Critical Study in the Quantitative History of American Negro Slavery* (New York: Oxford University Press, 1976), 94–133; Herbert G. Gutman, *The Black Family in Slavery and Freedom, 1750–1925* (New York: Vintage, 1976), 144–52; Michael Tadman, *Speculators and Slaves: Masters, Traders, and Slaves in the Old South* (Madison, Wisc.: University of Wisconsin Press, 1989), 133–78, 141 (quote); Ira Berlin, *Generations of Captivity: A History of African-American Slaves* (Cambridge, Mass.: Harvard University Press, 2003), 169; Andrews, *Slavery and the Domestic Slave Trade*, 49–50; "Report and Manifest of the Cargo of Slaves on Board the Brig Tribune of New York," Jan. 22, 1833, transcription at http://files.usgwarchives.net/va/shiplists/slavship.txt, consulted Mar. 6, 2012; Gudmestad, *Troublesome Commerce*, 42; Deyle, *Carry Me Back*, 246–47. Traders Franklin & Armfield, to their credit, began to purchase more slaves in family groups after 1834 in an effort

Enslaved people throughout the South lived in continual apprehension of such separations, especially as the often total lack of knowledge about migrants' destinations left slaves uncertain about the fate of their loved ones for the rest of their lives. Drawing from family psychology, historian Heather Andrea Williams has described such separations as "ambiguous loss," a loss that is "uncertain, a disappearance in which those left behind or those taken away remain unaware of the whereabouts or status of loved ones." One literate slave woman named Juliet from Virginia, for example, illustrated this uncertainty when she wrote in a letter to her sister in 1846 that she felt "lonely... when I think how our family is scattered, my father I know not where nor how he is whether dead or alive, one sister in Alabama.... This is enough to make me low spirited is it not?" For Juliet's family, it was too late, but the threat of ambiguous loss haunted slave families and communities throughout the South. A group of Virginia slaves told traveler Adam Hodgson in 1820, for example, that "their liability to be sold... and to be separated from their families, was a cruel part of their condition" and one of the main causes of stress and anxiety in slave quarters throughout the state. One North Carolina slave spoke for his fellow bondsmen when he claimed to a northern visitor that he lived in constant anxiety that his wife would be sold away from him, as indeed his first two wives had been. The fear of separation "was always impending over him, and threatening every moment to crush him beneath its weight," wrote a visitor who spoke with the slave. Even white southerners admitted perceiving trepidation among their slaves about the prospect of interstate migration. Mary Stratton, a Virginia slaveholder's wife, recorded in her diary on the eve of the family's emigration to Missouri in 1855 that one of her slave women named Patience was especially "uneasy about what will become of her [and] dreads a separation from her children," who were owned by another master and from whom she was indeed eventually separated.[12]

to blunt criticism of the slave trade. Other traders, however, spread "fairy tales," claiming to keep families together when confronted with charges of inhumane practices by outsiders. See Gudmestad, *Troublesome Commerce*, 160–61. Such was the extent of family separation through interstate migration that it even began to affect families' ability to reproduce, especially in the Upper South. In the 1830s, when forced migration reached its peak, the natural growth rate among slaves fell to 24.0 percent after having risen in the previous decades. See Calvin Schermerhorn, *Money Over Mastery, Family over Freedom: Slavery in the Antebellum Upper South* (Baltimore: Johns Hopkins University Press, 2011), 14–15.

12 Gudmestad, *Troublesome Commerce*, 43; Rockman, *Scraping By*, 238–40; Williams, *Help Me to Find My People*, 122 (first quote); Juliet Grimshaw, quoted in Richard S. Dunn, "Winney Grimshaw, a Virginia Slave, and Her Family," *Early American Studies: An Interdisciplinary Journal* 9 (Fall 2011): 508 (second quote); Adam Hodgson, *Remarks During a Journey through North America in the Years 1819, 1820, and 1821, in a Series of Letters* (1823; Westport, Conn.: Negro University Press, 1970), 102 (third quote); Andrews, *Slavery and the Domestic Slave Trade*, 103–104 (fourth quote), 107; Mary Stratton, quoted in Diane Mutti Burke, *On Slavery's Border: Missouri's Small-Slaveholding Households, 1815–1865* (Athens: University of Georgia Press, 2010), 18 (fifth quote).

Because young people made up a large component in the interstate trade, slave parents in particular often psychologically prepared themselves for the loss of a child to forced migration, particularly in supply states such as Virginia and Maryland. One Virginia slave recalled that when his master died, the slave mothers on his plantation began to prepare themselves for the worst: they all "cried very much," and his own mother, in anticipation of losing her children forever, "took to kissing us [children] a good deal oftener." Another former slave from Stafford County, Virginia, even claimed that his mother had been openly anxious of losing him from the moment he was born; according to him, she had always had "a presentiment, that she was not the one designed by Providence to rear me." By convincing herself that God had other plans for her son, the slave woman began to cope with the idea of losing him long before she actually did. Similarly, Virginia slave Henry Brown claimed that from "an early age," his mother would take him "on her knee, and point to the forest trees," explaining to him that "the children of slaves [are] swept away" like autumn leaves. In the precious time that she had with her children, Brown's mother attempted to teach them as much about morality and religion as she could in the hope that – should they ever be taken away from her – they would lead righteous lives and meet her in heaven.[13]

The theme of family separation through interstate migration ran so deep in the daily experiences of enslaved people that it was even infused into their religious and musical culture, especially in the Upper South. Slave preachers in cities such as Richmond and Louisville regularly called upon God to "hab mercy on our poor flicted, *scattered*, pressed people." Several popular slave songs also recalled the forcible break-up of families, giving voice to the sentiments of thousands who had lost loved ones to the slave trade. In the song "I'm Gwine to Alabamy," for example, a young man sings about his desire to travel to Alabama to "see my mammy," who was sold there "from Ole Virginny"; in the popular tune "Motherless Child" a slave woman whose baby, mother, and sister have been sold to unknown destinations grieves her loss by getting "down on my knees and pray[ing]." The "Coffle Song" was more explicit and took the perspective of the migrant:

> "I'll send you my love by the whoop-o'-will
> The dove shall bring my sorrow
> I leave you a drop of my heart's own blood
> For I won't be back to-morrow."

[13] Deyle, *Carry Me Back*, 247–49; John Brown, *Slave Life in Georgia: A Narrative of the Sufferings, and Escape of John Brown, a Fugitive Slave, Now in England*, edited by Louis Alexis Chamerovzow (London: L.A. Chamerovzow, 1855), 6 (first quote); William Hayden, *Narrative of William Hayden: Containing a Faithful Account of his Travels for a Number of Years, Whilst a Slave, in the South* (Cincinnati: n.p., 1846), 17 (second quote); Henry Box Brown, *Narrative of Henry Box Brown* (Boston: Brown & Stearns, 1849), 15 (third quote). See also Heather Andrea Williams, *Help Me to Find My People: The African American Search for Family Lost in Slavery* (Chapel Hill: University of North Carolina Press, 2012), 21–46.

Yet another popular slave song describes (in the third person) the sadness of an enslaved man's wife and children upon losing him to a slave trader:

> "William Rino sold Henry Silvers;
> Hilo! Hilo!
> Sold him to de Georgy trader;
> Hilo! Hilo!
> His wife she cried, and children bawled;
> Hilo! Hilo!
> Sold him to de Georgy trader;
> Hilo! Hilo!"[14]

II.

In contrast to their interstate counterparts, local slave migrants were not threatened with removal across thousands of miles to a dreaded part of the continent; on the contrary, they were frequently removed within the vicinity of their old homes, thereby often allowing for limited contact with their families and old communities. Antebellum slaves preferred local moves over interstate ones to such an extent that some local moves were actually initiated by bondspeople. As we shall see, many slaves negotiated to move locally to prevent themselves or their loved ones from having to move across state lines. Others attempted to get sold locally to get away from hard masters or even unite cross-plantation families. Samuel Taylor, born a slave in Arkansas, related to interviewers of the Federal Writers' Project that his mother had been sold locally twice before freedom came, both times because she stubbornly resisted corporal punishment, fully aware of the consequences; her third master "was good to her," however, "so she wasn't sold no more after that." Another bondsman from Virginia told abolitionist Benjamin Drew in 1855 that he had once run away "in order that my master might sell me running, – I didn't care much whose hands I fell into, if I got out of his." The slave, whose family members all lived in the immediate vicinity, clearly anticipated being purchased by another local slaveholder, for when he was eventually caught and delivered to an interstate slave trader – a situation he had not counted on – he panicked, eventually escaping the slave pen in which he was held and successfully fleeing to Canada. Enslaved people's preference for a local move over an interstate one was so strong that white southerners audaciously even claimed that slave families actually "prefer being

[14] Tower, *Slavery Unmasked*, 253 (first quote; italics mine); "I'm Gwine to Alabamy," reprinted in William Frances Allen, *Slave Songs of the United States* (New York: Simpson & Co., 1867), 92 (second quote); "Motherless Child," in Bernard Katz, ed., *The Social Implications of Early Negro Music in the United States* (New York: Arno Press, 1969), 91 (third quote); "The Coffle Song," recounted by Sella Martin, in Blassingame, ed., *Slave Testimony*, 705–706 (fourth quote); "Henry Silvers," in Dena J. Epstein, *Sinful Tunes and Spirituals: Black Folk Music to the Civil War* (Urbana: University of Illinois Press, 1977), 179 (fifth quote). See also Williams, *Help Me to Find My People*, 121.

sold to different masters in the same neighborhood" rather than remaining together, a preference they attributed to "the roving propensity of the race." This was yet another lie designed to patch over the contradictions in their paternalist ideology – masters *tried* to keep families together, but because of slaves' "slight affections" for each other, they *did not want to remain together*. By such logic, slaveholders were acting according to the wishes of their slaves when they separated families locally. In reality, of course, the opposite was true – slaves indeed frequently negotiated local sales to *unite* divided families. In Anne Arundel County, Maryland, for example, a divided couple named Cato and Nancy successfully negotiated for Cato's master to purchase Nancy and their infant son in 1860. Although rarely successful, such appeals were not uncommon in the antebellum South.[15]

For those who were *forced* to leave their homes, however, the initial prospect of a possible move, whether through sale or estate divisions, frequently instilled the same fears in local slave migrants as it did in interstate ones because in the early stages it was often unclear to slaves whether they would be moved within the area or across state lines. Many anticipated the worst, and the first rumors of sale or removal were thus usually met with the same panic and terror of permanent separation from family and friends. When as a twelve-year-old boy Kentucky slave Israel Campbell was told by his master one day "that he was going to sell me before long," for example, neither he nor his mother knew whether he would be deported or whether he would remain within the state. Because Kentucky had by the late antebellum period begun to deport slaves regularly to the Deep South, they expected a permanent separation, and, similar to many interstate slave migrants, Israel turned to God, praying "earnestly every day that the Lord would not let my master sell me; pleading that if I was sold my mother would be bereft of her only help." But the "Lord had other ends," and as Israel departed with his master one day to go on a "mission," his mother, "comprehending that I was going to be sold, came to me and bade me good-bye, urging me to be a good boy... and, if she never saw me again in this world, to meet her in heaven." In the end, however, Israel was sold to a planter in a neighboring county, close enough that he attempted to go back and see his mother several times.[16]

Yet it was clear to many slaves that even removals within the same state could result in the permanent (or virtually permanent) separation of families,

[15] Samuel S. Taylor, in Slave Narratives of the Federal Writers' Project, 1936–1938 (typescript), vol. II, pt. 2, 336–37 (first quote); Henry Banks, in Drew, ed., *North-Side View*, 75 (second quote); Ingraham, *South-West*, 2: 203 (third quote); Genovese and Fox-Genovese, *Fatal Self-Deception*, 38; John Franklin Accounts, RASP, Series D (microfilm), JFK Institute, Freie Universität, Berlin. Similar appeals moved Cato's master, John Franklin, to purchase the wife of another one of his slaves in 1848.

[16] Israel Campbell, *An Autobiography: Bond and Free: Or, Yearnings for Freedom, from My Green Briar House. Being the Story of My Life in Bondage, and My Life in Freedom* (Philadelphia: C.E.P. Brinkloe & Co., 1861), 24 (quotes).

simply because distances were sometimes too great for any possibility of regular contact. Depending on the pass system for weekend visiting and traveling on foot, antebellum slaves found that even a distance of twenty or thirty miles could permanently separate them from their family members. William Grimes, for example, was sold locally as a boy – from King George County, Virginia, to Culpeper County – but the distance between his old home and his new one was so great that it entailed a two-day journey on horseback, making it impossible for William to see his family on weekends. Understanding this, his mother took the news that her son was going to Culpeper badly. Grimes claimed, "it grieved me to see my mother's tears at our separation," but his mother's grief certainly proved to be justified. Despite residing within the same state, Grimes would not see his mother or brothers again until ten years later, when, traveling with yet another master to Northumberland County, he coincidentally passed by his old plantation. Former slave Isaac Johnson's family was also dispersed throughout Kentucky when his master decided to give up slaveholding and sell off his human property at a slave auction in Nelson County. Johnson recalled that his "family was scattered, without even the privilege of saying 'Good by' to each other, and never again to be seen." Slaves who were sold or removed locally more than once – as many slaves were – sometimes only gradually lost contact with their family members, as the distance between themselves and their loved ones increased with each move. Former bondsman Lewis Charlton was sold several times throughout the state of Maryland, always managing to maintain contact with his family members until his fifth change of masters, when he finally "lost sight of my mother" altogether.[17]

Such cases of permanent family separations occurred with frequency in the antebellum South; nevertheless, the chances of at least some family members remaining together in local removals were certainly higher than in interstate sales. During estate divisions, especially, slaves were often bequeathed to new masters along with one or more family members but rarely as entire nuclear family units. Such occasions could be traumatic nonetheless – depending on where their new owners lived, separation from other friends and family could be permanent or not on such occasions – but many slaves at least did not depart their homes alone. John Brown, a former slave originally from Virginia, recalled that when his master passed away the slaves became nervous about "whether the husbands would go with their wives" and the extent to which families would be forcibly separated. When lots were drawn, virtually every family was broken up to some extent, but both Brown and his mother were bequeathed

[17] For more on the pass system, see Stephanie M.H. Camp, *Closer to Freedom: Enslaved Women and Everyday Resistance in the Plantation South* (Chapel Hill: University of North Carolina Press, 2004), 13–20. Grimes, *Life of William Grimes*, 8 (first quote), 16; Isaac Johnson, *Slavery Days in Old Kentucky* (n.p., 1901), 10–11 (second quote); Lewis Charlton, *Sketch of the Life of Lewis Charlton, with Reminiscences of Slavery* (Portland, Me.: Daily Press Print Co., n.d.), 1–4, 4 (third quote).

to the same man, who lived forty-five miles away. Even then, however, his mother's separation from her other children and relations entailed "parting for life," a prospect that nearly broke her will to live. Brown recalled that he "really thought my mother would have died of grief," for she knew that forty-five miles was simply too far to visit her loved ones. Similarly, one slave from Mississippi claimed that he was bequeathed along with two sisters to the same master upon an estate division, yet he and his siblings were all separated from their mother and father, whom he never saw again and who thus became "dead to me forever."[18]

In some parts of the South, it was even the custom to keep some family members together during a local move. In South Carolina and lowcountry Georgia, especially, slaves were routinely (though not always) sold and bequeathed in nuclear family groups, a rarity that has caught the attention of other historians. Larry Hudson, for one, found that "as the antebellum period wore on, it was clear that slave masters in South Carolina were making efforts to keep slave families together," a claim that plantation documents and newspaper advertisements amply confirm. Estate inventories from South Carolina and the Georgia lowcountry usually listed slaves in family groups with a collective price, for example, indicating that they were to be transferred together rather than individually. In the records of rice planter Paul D. Weston, an inventory of 145 slaves "to be sold" in 1859 listed and appraised them all in family groups – and such inventories were the norm rather than the exception. An appraisal of Duncan Clinch's lowcountry Georgia estate in 1859 likewise listed all 257 slaves in 49 family lots. Sale advertisements in South Carolina newspapers also often announced slaves in family units. The auction house of John Shackleford & Son in Georgetown advertised in 1819 the sale of "Nine valuable Negroes," adding that "these negroes being one family, cannot be separated." William Belluney offered for sale "a family of eight Negroes" in the same newspaper. Fifty-three Waccamaw slaves offered for sale in 1857 were also advertised and sold in families, and Richfield plantation in Georgetown District was advertised for sale along with "a gang of about 111 Negroes ... to be sold in Families." Local purchasers advertised to buy slaves in family groups as well. One planter wanted "a family of 6 or 8 Negroes." Another promised "cash ... for a family of 8 to 10 healthy negroes." Surely here was a region in which slaveholders

[18] Georgena Duncan has found that in the Arkansas River Valley, many young slaves who were given as gifts or bequeathed to members of their masters' families were indeed separated from some or all of their family members, but because heirs often lived in the immediate vicinity, they were able to maintain some contact with loved ones. See Georgena Duncan, "'One negro, Sarah ... one horse named Collier, one cow and calf named Pink': Slave Records from the Arkansas River Valley," *The Arkansas Historical Quarterly* 69 (Winter 2010): 332–34. Brown, *Slave Life in Georgia*, 7–8 (first quote); Charles Thompson, *Biography of a Slave; Being the Experiences of Rev. Charles Thompson, a Preacher of the United Brethren Church, While a Slave in the South, Together with Startling Occurrences Incidental to Slave Life* (Dayton, OH: United Brethren Publishing House, 1875), 18 (second quote).

were sincerely committed to the protection of slave families, as Genovese and Fox-Genovese argued? Not necessarily; as we shall see, the lowcountry tradition of keeping families intact during relocations was more a response to the threat of slave resistance than a reflection of underlying paternalist social relations (although it was certainly justified as such).[19]

The state of Louisiana also provided an exception to the rule. In local sales throughout the South, slave women were often sold along with their infants, but in Louisiana, the law prescribed for slave children up to the age of ten to be sold or transferred along with their mothers; the only exceptions were orphans or children who had been brought to Louisiana from another state without their mothers. First adopted during the Spanish colonial period (and thus not a construction of antebellum slaveholders at all), the law appears to have been generally respected in the antebellum period, as court records amply confirm. When the heirs of sugar planter Jean Baptiste Keller sold the slaves attached to the estate in 1833, for example, they demanded a down payment of "fifty dollars on each of them, not reckoning the children under ten years of age who may be sold along with their mothers." William Spears of Union Parish sold "Amanda aged sixteen years & her child Malinda about nine months" to one Humphrey Ramsey in 1857. Louisiana law allowed slaveholders to claim that slave sales in their state were executed in a humane manner, but in practice, keeping mothers and small children together was a minor concession for an illusion of benevolence. The treatment of families during sales and transfers still reflected more self-interest than paternalist sympathies. Children older than the age of ten were routinely separated from their parents with little care for the grief it imposed on slave families, and children whose mothers had died were also casually sold apart from their fathers, siblings, and other family members. From the perspective of the slave mothers, however, the Louisiana law was better than no law at all. Local sales in certain parts of the South, therefore, tended to confront slaves with partial separation from family and friends but often not the full and definitive ruptures that most interstate migrants were faced with.[20]

19 Larry E. Hudson, Jr., *To Have and to Hold: Slave Work and Family Life in Antebellum South Carolina* (Athens: University of Georgia Press, 1997), 175 (first quote); Rosser H. Taylor, *Antebellum South Carolina: A Social and Cultural History* (New York, 1970); Slave Inventory of the Paul D. Weston Estate, 1837, Paul D. Weston Papers, in RASP, Series B (microfilm), Hill Memorial Library, Louisiana State University, Baton Rouge, La.; Duncan Clinch Slave List, 1859, RASP, Series C, Part 1 (microfilm), JFK Institute, Freie Universität, Berlin; *Winyah Intelligencer*, Mar. 31, 1819 (second quote); Ibid., Jan. 12, 1819 (third quote); Slave Sale Broadside, Jan. 27, 1857 and Slave Sale Broadside, Mar. 1, 1854, James Ritchie Sparkman Papers, RASP, Series A, pt. 2 (microfilm), Hill Memorial Library, Louisiana State University, Baton Rouge, La. (fourth quote); *Winyah Intelligencer*, Nov. 10, 1819 (fifth quote); Ibid., Nov. 24, 1819 (sixth quote); Genovese and Fox-Genovese, *Fatal Self-Deception*, 38.

20 The law made it illegal to "sell the mother of any slave child or children, ten years of age or under, separate from said mother." Acts of the Legislature of the State of Louisiana, 1828–1829, cited in Wendell Holmes Stephenson, *Isaac Franklin: Slave Trader and Planter of the*

III.

Enslaved people faced with the prospect of moving to cities and towns responded in ways both similar and different from their interstate and local counterparts. Similarities are to be expected, of course, for removal to an urban area could be long distance or local, depending on the circumstances, and virtually all slaves anticipated the worst-case scenario when their masters died or suffered financial reversals. Interestingly, however, an analysis of slave testimonies from various sources reveals that one of the most striking differences between the various classes of migrants was that many slaves responded to the news of urban migration with optimism and sometimes even excitement. As a rule, antebellum slaves were of the impression that life in cities and towns was adventurous and that it carried with it enormous advantages that might relieve them of the heaviest burdens of slavery. Indeed, the lure of the city enticed many rural slaves to flee *to* urban environments, and city slaves frequently resisted removal to the *countryside*, where they feared a deterioration in their work and living conditions. One Charleston slave family positively refused to move to their new master's rice plantation on the Santee in 1826, arguing that they were "accustomed to Town Work and unfit for the Labor of the Field." Young slaves from the country, on the other hand – especially young men – hoped for more attractive work (with the possibility of earning extra money in their off-time), more privileges, better treatment, and a more lively social life in urban environments. One slave told Frederick Law Olmsted that the slaves who were sent to New Orleans were better off than those who remained in the country "because they make more money, and it is 'gayer' there, and there is more 'society.'" Frederick Douglass was happy – he used the word "ecstasy" to describe his feelings – to hear that he was to be removed from a rural wheat plantation in eastern Maryland to the city of Baltimore, where he was ordered to work for his master's son-in-law. "I received this information about three days before my departure," Douglass recalled in his autobiography. "They were three of the happiest days I ever enjoyed." As he had "the strongest desire to see Baltimore," he left the plantation "without a regret, and with the highest hopes of future happiness."[21]

Old South (1938; Gloucester, Mass., 1968), 77; Richard Follett, *The Sugar Masters: Planters and Slaves in Louisiana's Cane World, 1820–1860* (Baton Rouge: Louisiana State University Press, 2005), 53; Succession of Jean Baptiste Keller, Jan. 14, 1833, Probate Records, SJPC (first quote); William Spears to Humphrey Ramsey, Union Parish Deed Book I, p. 332, Spearsville, La. (second quote).

21 Paul D. Lack, "An Urban Slave Community: Little Rock, 1831–1862," *The Arkansas Historical Quarterly* 41 (autumn 1982): 265; Seth Rockman, *Scraping By: Wage Labor, Slavery, and Survival in Early Baltimore* (Baltimore: Johns Hopkins University Press, 2009), 35–36; Franklin and Schweninger, *Runaway Slaves*, 124–48; "William R. Maxwell to the Equity Court, Charleston District, South Carolina, 1826," in Loren Schweninger, ed., *The Southern Debate over Slavery: Volume 2, Petitions to Southern County Courts, 1775–1867* (Urbana: University of Illinois Press, 2008), 130 (first quote); Olmsted, *Seaboard Slave States*, 677 (second quote); Frederick

Such elation at the prospect of moving to the city must be placed within its proper context to be fully understood, however. In contrast to many migrants, Douglass had no family ties to bind him to his plantation: "my mother was dead, my grandmother lived far off, so that I seldom saw her," and he barely had any relationship with his brother or sisters. He was therefore not confronted with family separation but simply with a welcome change of scenery, work, and – he hoped – treatment. Douglass admitted that he "found no severe trial in my departure" and that he "could not feel that I was leaving any thing which I could have enjoyed by staying." Similarly, Henry Watson, a slave born in Virginia but deported to Mississippi at a young age, was delighted to learn one day that his new Mississippi master intended to train him and his fellow bondsmen "for a hotel, which he intended opening in a neighboring city." Watson admitted that the news that he would be moved to work in the city "pleased me much; for I thought the larger the city I was in, the smaller the chance would be of my getting on a farm," where, according to him, labor amounted to mere drudgery. Similar to Douglass, Watson was in no danger of a family separation because he had already been separated from all his relatives when he was moved from Virginia.[22]

Douglass and Watson had little to lose from a move to the city, but even when confronted with a temporary separation from family, slave migrants often responded positively to the prospect of urban migration. Many urban migrants were hired slaves from the countryside, for example, and as hirelings were hired out for fifty-one weeks out of the year they could at least look forward to the one-week holiday between Christmas and Near Year, when they were often permitted to return home and visit with loved ones before being hired out again for the ensuing year. Noah Davis, born a slave in Madison County in Virginia's Shenandoah Valley, was forced to leave his loved ones when he was hired out in the city of Fredericksburg at the age of fourteen. "For the first time in my life,

Douglass, *Narrative of the Life of Frederick Douglass, an American Slave* (1845; New York: Dover, 1995), 16–17 (third quote).

22 Douglass, *Narrative*, 17 (first quote); Watson, *Narrative of Henry Watson*, 26 (second quote). Maryland slave Charles Ball was confronted with virtually the same situation as an adolescent: when his master "told me that he had hired me out for a year at the city of Washington," he "felt very happy." His family members had by that time all been sold South, however, so a year in Washington never threatened to tear him away from his loved ones. Ball, *Fifty Years in Chains*, 18. North Carolina slave John Jacobs, brother of the infamous Harriet Jacobs, was faced with a move to the nation's capital when his master was elected to Congress one year, taking John with him as a body servant. "I was ordered to get ready for Washington," Jacobs told an interviewer in 1861, a city "which I so much wanted to see" because it was reputedly "much enjoyed by the slaves, their privileges being greatly extended." The move would separate Jacobs from his grandmother and sister (who by then was already in hiding) by hundreds of miles, but that did not take away from his excitement, partly because he knew the move was temporary and that he would return home when his master's term was up. John S. Jacobs, "A True Tale of Slavery," *The Leisure Hour: A Family Journal of Instruction and Recreation*, no. 478 (Feb. 21, 1861): 125.

I left my parents, to go a distance from home," he related in 1859. Although Davis was "sad at the thought of parting" with his family, he admitted that "the expectation of seeing Fredericksburg, a place which, from all I had then learned, I supposed must be the greatest place in the world, reconciled me somewhat with the necessity of saying Good-bye to the dear ones at home." As a hireling, Davis was not confronted with the threat of permanent separation from family and friends; like many local migrants, he expected to be able to retain contact with his parents (as indeed he did).[23]

It was not uncommon for slaves to be hired out along with one or more family members to the same city or even to the same employer, allowing family members to keep track of one another and retain a degree of personal contact. In 1874, former Virginia slave Lizzie Gibson claimed to an interviewer that when her master died and the slaves were told that they would have to be hired out in Hampton to pay the debts of the estate, most of her friends and family members responded to the news with optimism. The idea of being hired out "was not so grievous at first," Gibson claimed. Indeed, the slaves "would get together and talk to each other about it, and about how we were going to eat good things when we got to our new homes." As they were all to be hired out in the same town, few apparently feared a permanent separation from loved ones. Henry Bruce, an ex-slave from Virginia who was dragged by his master to Missouri, claimed that upon arrival, he and his entire family were hired out "to J.B. Barrett, a tobacconist" in the town of Brunswick. His mother and sisters worked in their employer's household, and Bruce and his brothers worked in the factory, so family contact remained frequent. William Wells Brown, whose master moved all his slaves from Kentucky to Missouri, also claimed to have remained close to his mother when he was hired out in St. Louis. "My mother was hired out in the city," he recalled in his narrative, "and I was also hired out there to Major Freeland, who kept a public house," so he was able to maintain regular contact with his mother during the term of his hire.[24]

Slaves who did not fear permanent separation from family members thus often responded optimistically to urban moves, which allowed slaveholders to mask their financial self-interest with an illusion of benevolence. Satisfying themselves that they were protecting families from forced dissolution and that their slaves were grateful for their new situations, southern masters could easily claim to be meeting their paternalist obligations. The mask was discarded

[23] Noah Davis, *A Narrative of the Life of Rev. Noah Davis, a Colored Man* (Baltimore: John F. Weishampel, 1859), 13 (third quotes). See also Isaac Mason, *Life of Isaac Mason, a Slave* (Worcester, Mass.: n.p., 1893), 18–19; John S. Jacobs, "A True Tale of Slavery," *The Leisure Hour: A Family Journal of Instruction and Recreation*, Feb. 21, 1861, 125.

[24] Lizzie Gibson's interview was taken in 1874 while she was a teacher at a school in Hampton, Virginia. Reprinted in Blassingame, ed., *Slave Testimony*, 738–39 (first quote); Henry Clay Bruce, *The New Man: Twenty-Nine Years a Slave, Twenty-Nine Years a Free Man* (York, Penn.: P. Anstadt & Sons, 1895), 64–65 (first quote); William Wells Brown, *Narrative of William W. Brown, a Fugitive Slave* (Boston; The Anti-Slavery Office, 1847), 21 (second quote).

altogether if slaves made it clear that they did not want to go, however, and that occurred often enough. Even the prospect of limited contact with loved ones did not reconcile all slaves' fears of changing masters and residences when hired out to urban employers. Many slaves who were repeatedly hired out from year to year felt anxiety at the approach of New Year's Day, the traditional day for hiring in the South, because they did not know whether or how far they would be separated from friends and kin or whether or not they would fall into the hands of a good or bad employer. Harriet Jacobs, for one, claimed that on New Year's Eve, hirelings gathered together "their little alls, or more properly speaking, their little nothings, and wait anxiously for the dawning of the day." One Louisville slave named Nathan, whose wife was a hireling from the countryside, begged his master in December 1841 to write his wife's master to inquire about her fate for the ensuing year, fearing that she would be hired out somewhere where he would not be able to visit her with regularity. "Nathan has come to me and begged me to write you in his name," the Louisville slaveholder wrote. "He says now that a new year is about to commence he is anxious to know what disposition is to be made of his wife. He says to avoid the necessary changing about, as hired servants have to do, he would look out for a good master and prevail on some of his friends to buy his wife if you are willing to sell her."[25]

When urban removal confronted slaves with permanent separations from their loved ones or when they feared permanent separations, a move to the city not only seemed less exciting but downright catastrophic, evoking the same disbelief, sorrow, and resistance that interstate migration did. Indeed, the prospect of urban migration across state lines was identically feared as rural migration across state lines was and for the same reasons. One Virginia slave – a husband and father – responded with anything but excitement in 1828 when he heard a rumor that his master intended to sell him to Charleston, South Carolina, to an acquaintance of his who wished to purchase "a fancy nigger" for his urban residence there. His son recalled after emancipation that his father received the news in shock, even dismissing the idea as absurd: "Massa ain't a-goin' to do it, nudder," he claimed. Days later the rumor was confirmed when the slave was deceitfully lured into the hands of a trader's agent and deported to Charleston, separating him from his wife and children. Similarly, one Alabama slave woman who was sold at auction to a resident of New Orleans told an interviewer in 1861 that she was much grieved about having to leave her mother, who dropped "right on her knees, with her hands up,

[25] Calvin Schermerhorn, *Money over Mastery, Family over Freedom: Slavery in the Antebellum Upper South* (Baltimore: Johns Hopkins University Press, 2011), 80; Barbara Jeanne Fields, *Slavery and Freedom on the Middle Ground: Maryland in the Nineteenth Century*, 27–28; Jonathan Martin, *Divided Mastery: Slave Hiring in the American South* (Cambridge, Mass.: Harvard University Press, 2004), 44–45; Harriet Jacobs, *Incidents in the Life of a Slave Girl* (1861; Mineola, NY: Dover, 2001), 16 (first quote); Garnett Duncan to Orlando Brown, Dec. 19, 1841, in Blassingame, *Slave Testimony*, 28–29 (second quote).

prayin' to the Lord for me. She didn't care who saw her: the people all lookin' at her." City life was only attractive to antebellum slaves if it did not destroy their family bonds.[26]

IV.

Desperate attempts by enslaved people to negotiate or resist all types of removal usually revolved around the central goal of keeping family ties intact. For interstate migrants, who were almost unanimously confronted with permanent separations, both resistance and negotiation attempts took their most extreme forms. With the most to lose, many slaves singled out to be deported (or their loved ones) personally confronted their masters, attempting to convince them that family separation was immoral, unchristian, or both. Indeed, according to historians such as Calvin Schermerhorn and Phillip Troutman, appeals to emotion, sentiment, and religion were essential – if unreliable – components of bondspeople's strategies to protect domestic arrangements that were threatened with separation. Holding up a mirror to slaveholders' paternalist ideology, slaves endeavored to reveal the hypocrisy in permanently breaking up families that were supposed to be protected by benevolent masters who proudly claimed that their "Christian slavery" was the most humane and compassionate social system on earth. Most failed. During such confrontations, slaveholders feebly fell back on promises to do what they could to soften the blow of separation, but at the end of the day, financial self-interest trumped the tenets of paternalism. Former North Carolina slave William Robinson claimed that when his mother heard her husband (William's father) had been sold to an interstate slave trader in 1858, she panicked. Thinking that "she would reach [her master] through his religious views," the enraged slave woman barged into her master's bedroom, where he was sleeping, demanding to know whether he had "forgotten your religion" and whether he had "the heart" to sell her children's father away from them. Her last-minute attempt at striking a Christian nerve in her master's conscience was unsuccessful; the best Robinson's mother could get was a vague promise that he would "see that [her husband] is not taken out of this state," a promise the slaveholder never even attempted to keep. Anna, a Maryland slave threatened with deportation to Georgia, similarly told an interviewer in 1836 that when she heard that she was sold, she went "upon her knees to her young master, and begged him that she and her children might not be separated from her husband and their father." Her appeal generated "a great oath" from her master, "that they should not be separated," but in the end, her master "did not find it convenient to adhere to the promise."[27]

[26] William Greenleaf Eliot, *The Story of Archer Alexander, From Slavery to Freedom* (Boston: Cupples, Upham & Co., 1885), 21–22 (first quote); Louisa Picquet, *Louisa Picquet, the Octoroon: or, Inside Views of Southern Domestic Life* (New York: Hiram Mattison, 1861), 18 (second quote).

[27] Franklin and Schweninger, *Runaway Slaves*, 49–74; Edward E. Baptist, *Creating an Old South: Middle Florida's Plantation Frontier Before the Civil War* (Chapel Hill: University of North

When appeals to slaveholders' religious views or moral conscience failed, as they often did, some slaves made open threats to their masters. Aware of the monetary values placed on their bodies, they threatened to flee, sabotage sale attempts, or even commit violence to frustrate business transactions that would destroy their domestic lives. British traveler James Buckingham related during a trip through the South that a slave woman from Georgia who, along with her son, was singled out to be sold in Alabama, made "great objection" to her being removed from the state, even declaring to her master that "she would 'sulk' [on the auction block], so that nobody should buy her, and she would rather kill her brown boy than let him go to Alabama." In the end "the matter was compromised" by the woman being sold within the state of Georgia and her son being sold to a buyer in the city of Charleston, an environment the slave woman at least thought better for her child than the cotton fields of Alabama. Similarly, when Virginia slave Jourden Banks' eldest sister was singled out to be sold to settle some outstanding debts, his father attempted to prevent it by appealing to his master's conscience, reminding him "how faithful he had been to him in all his days," and beseeching him that such a loyal servant did not deserve to have his children sold away from him. When that failed, however, Banks' father boldly pleaded to be sold in his daughter's place, and when *that* failed, he threatened to go truant, declaring that he would rather "go and live in the woods" than witness the deportation of his loved ones. Indeed, slaves' negotiating power rested to no small extent on the mere threat of running away because it frightened slaveholders with the loss of a valuable investment. Even fugitives who were apprehended declined in value, simply for being prone to running away.[28]

Because of the prevalence of cross-plantation marriages, especially in regions with small slaveholdings such as the Upper South, planter migration threatened slave families just as much as the interstate slave trade did; consequently, news of emigration often led to similarly frantic negotiation attempts to buy spouses and children or sell slaves to the owners of their family members. When Virginia slaveholder Pendleton Adams concluded in 1850 to "sell out this spring & Moove," he was admonished by one of his slave women to try to sell her to her husband's owner. "My Girl Evoline is anxious to be as near George as she can,"

Carolina Press, 2001), 67–68; Calvin Schermerhorn, *Money over Mastery, Family over Freedom: Slavery in the Antebellum Upper South* (Baltimore: Johns Hopkins University Press, 2011), 105–107; Phillip Troutman, "Correspondences in Black and White: Sentiment and the Slave Market Revolution," in Edward E. Baptist and Stephanie M.H. Camp, eds., *New Studies in the History of American Slavery* (Athens: University of Georgia Press, 2006), 214; Genovese and Fox-Genovese, *Fatal Self-Deception*, 1; William H. Robinson, *From Log Cabin to Pulpit, or, Fifteen Years in Slavery* (Eau Claire, Wisc.: James H. Tifft, 1913), 23 (first quote); Andrews, *Slavery and the Domestic Slave Trade*, 130 (second quote).

28 Buckingham, *Slave States*, I:248 (second quote); Pennington, *Life of J.H. Banks*, 19–24, 22 (second quote); Seth Rockman, *Scraping By: Wage Labor, Slavery, and Survival in Early Baltimore* (Baltimore: Johns Hopkins University Press, 2009), 64. Research by Calvin Schermerhorn reveals how slaves' threats and appeals to their masters' emotions sometimes backfired, resulting in sale for causing trouble. See Schermerhorn, *Money over Mastery*, 106–108.

Adams wrote to George's owner. "I am disposed to sell her . . . to accomadate them." A few days later, he was even visited by George, who, Adams claimed, "insists on Me to Send you a few lines as he is very anxious for Me to sell you Evoline." Literate slaves sent their own letters. When Missouri slaves Sukey and Ersey heard that they were to be carried to Texas by members of their master's extended family in 1842, they wrote their master – who was living in Virginia – a letter, explaining that they "can't bear to go to Texas" because "to be separated from our husbands forever in this world would make us unhappy for life." The slave women pleaded for their master to sell them locally, promising that there would not "be the least difficulty in getting ourselves sold" and even suggesting a few slaveholders in the neighborhood who might be interested. Many slaves resorted to outright begging when confronted with separation through emigration. Francis Fedric remembered in 1863 that when his Virginia master decided to move to Kentucky, he witnessed "men and women down on their knees begging to be purchased to go with their wives or husbands, who worked for my master." Their pleas were to no avail, and all cross-plantation family ties were broken in the move. Emily, a literate North Carolina slave whose husband was "torn from me, and carried away by his master" in 1836, wrote a letter to her mother in which she claimed to have done absolutely everything in her power to prevent the separation, including begging and even arranging for a local slaveholder to buy her husband for $800. But "all my entreaties and tears did not soften his [her master's] hard heart. They availed nothing with him. . . . So in a few short months we had to part."[29]

Attempts to keep families together were usually futile under such circumstances, but success stories were not unknown. Some masters genuinely respected their slaves' feelings and allowed them to stay with loved ones. Crucially, however, such acts of "kindness" were never initiated by slaveholders, who apparently failed to consider their slaves' desire to stay with family members until they were confronted by distraught slaves themselves. America, a slave of Lettie Watkins Walton from Carroll County, Mississippi, made it abundantly clear to her mistress that she did not want to emigrate with her mistress to Texas. Walton consented to give America to a local family member and let her remain in Mississippi. When John Baylor, a Kentucky slaveholder, announced his intentions to remove to Arkansas territory in 1824, one of his slave women became so hysterical for her husband Williams, who lived on another farm owned by Lucien Fiemster, that the owners of both slaves struck a deal with

[29] Ronald L. Lewis, "Slave Families at Early Chesapeake Ironworks," *The Virginia Magazine of History and Biography* 86 (Apr. 1978): 174 (first quotes); Sukey & Ersey to Nathaniel Beverley Tucker, Oct. 24, 1842, in Blassingame, *Slave Testimony*, 13 (second quote); Francis Fedric, *Slave Life in Virginia and Kentucky, or, Fifty Years of Slavery in the Southern States of America* (London: Wertheim, MacIntosh, and Hunt, 1863), 14–15 (third quote); Emily to mother, Feb. 12, 1836, reprinted in Blassingame, *Slave Testimony*, 22–23 (fourth quote); Johnson, *Soul by Soul*, 41.

each other. Because the slaves "seemed very much attached to each other, and it seemed cruel and inhuman to separate them" when their owners could not agree on a sale of either slave, Fiemster agreed to let Williams accompany his wife out to Arkansas and see her settled in, Baylor to return him to Kentucky later that year. In the end, "months and years rolled round" and Williams never returned, making clear his intention to remain with his wife in Arkansas rather than go back to Kentucky. After an absence of five years and several entreaties, Williams's master finally resorted to filing a lawsuit against Baylor for theft of his slave. Other emigrating slaveholders who accommodated their slaves acted more openly out of self-interest rather than sympathy. Caring only to attain a financially attractive settlement and indifferent to whom their slave was sold, some masters succumbed to the facility of giving in to their bondspeople's desires to stay behind. Again, such transactions were always initiated by the slaves themselves. Maryland slave William Green's mother successfully prevented her son from being taken to Louisiana by preemptively negotiating a local sale herself. William had been bequeathed apart from his mother in an estate division, having fallen into the hands of his master's youngest son, who "took it into his head to go to New Orleans." Fearing that if her son "went to the far South that she would [n]ever see me again," William claimed that his mother decided to confront his master, begging him "not to take her poor child away from her" and ultimately striking a deal with him. The slaveholder promised William's desperate mother that "if she would find any person who would buy me, in one week, he would sell me and not take me away." Scouring the area, she wasted no time in finding a new master for her boy, a local farmer "who said he would purchase me to save me from going to the South."[30]

Even successful negotiation attempts and open threats were dependent on the final judgment of slaves' masters, however, and if they failed, slaves frequently took it into their own hands to try to prevent deportation and forced separation. The most common course of action, as John Hope Franklin and Loren Schweninger have argued, was running away. Some did so preemptively, when deportation was not yet imminent but seemed unavoidable. One Virginia bondsman named Randolph, for example, fled to the North in the 1850s after "three of his brothers [were] sold South." Oscar Payne, also from Virginia, did likewise after "three brothers and one sister [were] sold South." Hesitant to leave their homes behind, however, most runaways waited until news of their removal was confirmed before fleeing or going into hiding. Maryland slave

30 Arthur E. Grey Dimond and Herman Hattaway, eds., *Letters from Forest Place: A Plantation Family's Correspondence, 1846–1881* (Oxford, Miss.: University Press of Mississippi, 1993), 491; "Lucien Fiemster to the Circuit Court, Bourbon County, Kentucky, 1829," in Loren Schweninger, ed., *The Southern Debate over Slavery: Volume 2, Petitions to Southern County Courts, 1775–1867* (Urbana: University of Illinois Press, 2008), 140–43, 141 (first quote); William Green, *Narrative of Events in the Life of William Green* (Springfield, Ill.: L.M. Guernsey, 1853), 3–4 (second quote). See also Henry Bibb, *Narrative of the Life and Adventures of Henry Bibb, an American Slave* (New York: The author, 1849), 41.

Isaac Mason hastily fled to Philadelphia when he heard of his master's plan to sell him to Louisiana; "to New Orleans I did not intend to go if I could prevent it," he recalled in his autobiography, preferring the precarious life of a fugitive to that of an interstate slave migrant. In 1837, a Virginia slave named Wilson, whose wife and children were owned by a different master and lived on a nearby plantation, absconded when his master made up his mind to move to Alabama. Wilson's master sold him running, and when he was eventually retaken, he was fortuitously bought by a local slaveholder, thus remaining in the vicinity of his family. When the owner of Rody, a Kentucky slave woman from Barren County, made plans to "sell her to some Natchez men," she "got wind of it & laid out until they were gone & then came home," employing truancy as a means to preventing her deportation. Eventually, her master sold her locally.[31]

Fleeing the South altogether – whereby potential migrants rejected commodification and reclaimed their humanity – was dangerous and often seen as a last resort. Although many slaves attempted or planned flight when confronted with interstate migration, relatively few were successful, and southern records are full of stories of failed or aborted escape attempts. For some, the fear of being caught was simply too powerful to ultimately go through with running away. Such was the case with North Carolina slave Ambrose Headen, whose desire to flee was agonizingly tested when he was sent to walk alone to the auction house where he was to be sold, a distance of fourteen miles without any supervision. On the way he "tried to lay some plans to run away," even securing the help of a white woman who promised to feed him if he went to live in the swamp. In the end, however, Headen was too "afraid of the dogs and men that would catch me," and he resigned himself to his lot. Delivering himself into the hands of the auctioneer, he was knocked off to an Alabama planter and deported. Headen's anxieties were certainly not without base because many fugitives were indeed caught in the act of fleeing. When Virginia slave Bethany Veney learned that her husband, Jerry, had been sold to an interstate trader to absolve his master's debts, for example, the couple frantically concocted a plan that "Jerry should take to the mountains, and... I [Bethany] would join him there, and we would make for the North together." But the plan ultimately failed, as Veney related after emancipation; in the end, the two were discovered by an agent of the slave trader, and Jerry was deported. Slaves who used truancy as a means to avoid deportation ran even greater risks of being caught. A Virginia field hand named Sharper resorted to a common strategy when he unsuccessfully opted for long-term truancy upon hearing that he was going

[31] Franklin and Schweninger, *Runaway Slaves*, 49–74; Randolph and Oscar Payne, in Still, *The Underground Railroad: A Record of Facts, Authentic Narratives, Letters, &c.* (1872; New York, 1968), 391 (first quote), 396 (second quote); Mason, *Life of Isaac Mason*, 35 (fourth quote); *Richmond Whig*, July 25, 1837; "Henry Dickerson to the Circuit Court, Barren County, Kentucky, 1821," in Schweninger, ed., *Southern Debate over Slavery*, 109 (fourth quote).

to be deported in 1831. He fled to his wife's residence, who kept him hidden and fed, remaining at large for seven weeks, but he was eventually caught and deported.[32]

Even physical violence and self-mutilation were tactics used by some slaves to avoid deportation or to exact revenge on the slaveholding whites who had sold them or their loved ones. As historian Steven Deyle has argued, slave violence toward whites on the occasion of sale or deportation was not uncommon; some of the most extreme confrontations even resulted in death or serious injury. In North Carolina in 1822, a "shocking occurrence" befell the family of General G.L. Davidson: they were all poisoned by their slaves, who were "unwilling to go to Alabama with the General and his family." One Maryland slave shot and killed a trader who came to pick up his wife and children, and another slave in Kentucky stabbed to death an agent who had been sent for him. Trotter and Bolton, two interstate slave traders based in Virginia, were murdered – nearly decapitated – by slaves en route to the Deep South in 1848. Also in Virginia, an enslaved man who had been sold along with his wife to a trader went back and attacked his wife's former owner with knives and an ax – intentionally cutting himself in the process – and burned his house down. This he did not only to take revenge on the slaveholder but also to render himself worthless for deportation. Indeed, many interstate slave migrants maimed themselves upon the prospect of removal, robbing their bodies of their commodity value in an attempt to sabotage their salability in southern markets. When Virginia slaveholder Elizabeth Tyler died, for example, estate records reveal that one of her slaves named Henry fled immediately to escape sale to the Deep South by the heirs. He was caught in Baltimore and sent back to Virginia, upon which he chopped off his own hand, apparently to render himself worthless for sale. Even this did not save Henry – he was sold anyway, presumably at a great loss. Swedish traveler Fredrika Bremer met a slave in a Richmond slave jail in 1851 who had chopped off the fingers of his right hand with an ax, slashing his body's value to exact revenge on his master for separating him from his wife. In 1858, a young slave woman put up at auction in Richmond reportedly had a lame right hand, which was missing a forefinger because she had chopped it off "to keep her from being sold down South."[33]

32 Interview with Ambrose Headen originally published in the *American Missionary* 32 (Dec. 1878):388–89. Reprinted in Blassingame, ed., *Slave Testimony*, 743–44 (first quote); Bethany Veney, *The Narrative of Bethany Veney, a Slave Woman* (Worcester, Mass.: n.p., 1889), 21–24, 21 (second quote), 24 (third quote); Franklin and Schweninger, *Runaway Slaves*, 53 (fourth quote), 149–181.

33 Steven Deyle has examined several cases in which desperate slave migrants used physical violence against their owners or traders. See Deyle, *Carry Me Back*, 254. News of the murder of the Davidson family was published in the Baton Rouge newspaper *Republic* on July 23, 1822. Reprinted in Ulricht B. Phillips, ed., *Plantation and Frontier: Documents, 1649–1863, Illustrative of Industrial History in the Colonial and Ante-Bellum South* (Cleveland: Arthur H. Clark & Co., 1909), 2:120–21 (first quote); Carey, *Sold Down the River*, 53; Estate Account of

Many slaves continued to resist from within the slave pens, desperately seizing every opportunity to escape their lot before their coffle departed. Twenty-one-year-old Virginia slave David Musy broke out of an Alexandria slave pen in 1859, "doubtless making his way to a free state." Some slave migrants had messages to their home communities smuggled out of traders' jails, seeking the help of family members and even abolitionists to arrange for local purchases. In January of 1850, one literate young slave woman named Emily Russell wrote a chilling letter to her mother from a slave pen in Alexandria, Virginia, begging her to do something because "I am in [Joseph] Bruin's jail, [along with] aunt Sally and all her children, and aunt Hagar and all her children, and grandmother is almost crazy." She closed with the lines: "Do not forsake me; for I feel desolate! Please come now." Emily's mother arranged for abolitionist William Harned to offer to buy her daughter from the well-known slave trader, but Bruin demanded the exorbitant sum of $1800 because "she was the finest-looking woman in this country." Within a week, Emily was deported in a coffle going south; she died en route in Georgia. Another slave woman, held in a slave pen in Richmond, Virginia, begged her husband in a letter in 1840 to "try to see if you can get any one to buy me up... if you don't come down here this Sunday, perhaps you wont see me anymore." Similarly, James Phillips, a fugitive slave in Pennsylvania who was captured and carried back to his native Virginia, informed his wife in a letter in 1852 that he was "in a trader's hands" in Richmond, adding that he would "rather die than to go South. Tell all of the people that if they can do anything for me, now is the time to do it. I can be bought for $900."[34]

As Phillips stated in his letter to his wife, some enslaved people felt that life was simply not worth living if it meant permanent separation from their homes and loved ones; suicide attempts were therefore not unknown, even among slaves who were removed with their masters. One Tennessee slave named Jane "expressed great unwillingness to remove to the State of Missouri" with her master in 1820, ultimately drowning herself in a nearby pond just a few days before departure. Most suicides appear to have been the result of the domestic slave trade, however, a disturbing trend that "spoke volumes as to how the trade ruined slaves' lives," in the words of historian Robert Gudmestad. Adam Hodgson noted while traveling through the South in 1820 that "instances are not rare of Slaves destroying themselves, by cutting their throats, or other violent measures, to avoid being sent to Georgia or New Orleans." Many such

Elizabeth Tyler, Will Book O-1, 424 (microfilm), Fairfax City Regional Library, Fairfax, Va.; Fredrika Bremer, *The Homes of the New World: Impressions of America* (New York: Harper & Bros., 1853), 2:533; Redpath, *Roving Editor*, 252–53 (second quote).

34 *Alexandria Gazette & Virginia Advertiser*, Dec. 26, 1859 (first quote); Emily Russell to mother [Nancy Cartwright], Jan. 22, 1850, originally reprinted in *Monthly Illustrations of American Slavery*, May 1, 1850. Subsequently reprinted in Blassingame, ed., *Slave Testimony*, 87 (second quote); Sargry Brown to Mores Brown, Oct. 27, 1840, reprinted in ibid., 46 (third quote); James Phillips to Mary Phillips, June 20, 1852, reprinted in ibid., 95 (fourth quote).

cases were committed after being delivered to slave traders, when other means of escape seemed impossible. In a widely publicized incident that ignited fierce debates about abolishing slavery in the nation's capital, for example, a Maryland slave woman named Anna, having been separated from her husband and children and sold to traders in Washington, jumped out of an upper window of the jail where she was being held in an attempt to kill herself. She survived but broke her limbs "in a shocking manner," leaving her a "helpless cripple" but ultimately preventing her deportation. Another slave flung herself into the Potomac River and drowned during an escape attempt from a Washington slave pen in the 1850s. Across the river in Alexandria, Virginia, an instance was reported in the winter of 1838 of a "poor colored man [who], overcome with horror at being sold to the South, put an end to his life by cutting his throat" in one of the city's many slave pens. Even Lemuel Sapington, a "reformed" slave trader, admitted to the American Anti-Slavery Society in 1839 that he had once handcuffed a slave in Louisville to be shipped down to New Orleans, "but choosing death rather than slavery, he jumped overboard and was drowned," his valueless body left floating in the river for weeks. The hopelessness felt by deportees is chillingly illustrated by accounts of slave mothers resorting to infanticide when they were informed of a forcible separation from their babies, an act committed not only to prevent forced separation but also to enact revenge on the slaveholding whites who would attempt to steal their babies from them. In Yorkville, South Carolina, a slave woman was executed in 1828 for killing her own baby when her master attempted to sell her away from her child, a situation that "drove her to madness." A similar occurrence was reported in Maryland in 1821, when a slave woman, "on being informed that she was sold, first cut the throat of her child, and then her own, – by which both of them immediately died." Rather than "apolitical" and localized forms of resistance that reflected accommodation to slavery instead of revolutionary aspirations (as Genovese characterized slave resistance in general in *Roll, Jordan, Roll*), extreme acts such as suicide and infanticide can more aptly be seen as outright rejections of the dehumanization and commodification of slave bodies on which the institution of slavery itself was based.[35]

[35] "Gideon Thompson and Robert McCombs to the Circuit Court, Rutherford County, Tennessee, 1823," in Schweninger, *Southern Debate over Slavery: Volume 2*, 121 (first quote); Gudmestad, *Troublesome Commerce*, 35–37, 47 (second quote); Hodgson, *Remarks During a Journey*, 178 (third quote); Andrews, *Slavery and the Domestic Slave Trade*, 112–13 (fourth quote), 128–132; Tower, *Slavery Unmasked*, 48–49; John G. Whittier, et al, *Voices of the True-Hearted* (Philadelphia: Merrihew & Thompson, 1846), 66 (fifth quote); Testimony of Lemuel Sapington, in Thomas Weld, *American Slavery as It Is: Testimony of a Thousand Witnesses* (New York: American Anti-Slavery Society, 1839), 50 (sixth quote); Deyle, *Carry Me Back*, 256; E.S. Abdy, *Journal of a Residence and Tour in the United States of North America, from April 1833 to October 1834* (1835; New York: Negro Universities Press, 1969), 91 (seventh quote), 93 (eighth quote); Genovese, *Roll, Jordan, Roll*, 597–98; Walter Johnson, "A Nettlesome Classic Turns Twenty-Five," *Common-Place* 1 (July 2001), http://www.common-place.org/vol-01/no-04/reviews/johnson/shtml.

IV.

Attempts to prevent deportation were, of course, the exception rather than the rule, and – with the exception of suicide and infanticide – were usually unsuccessful. Confronted with overwhelming force and often insurmountable boundaries, most interstate migrants had little choice but to accept their fate. Last goodbyes to loved ones were often traumatic occurrences accompanied by practical advice, prayers, and reassurances that they would meet again in the next life. Indeed, forced separation reinforced slaves' religious convictions, as parting took the form of a social death that would be overcome in spiritual form in heaven. One slave claimed that "in parting with their friends... the poor blacks have the anticipation of meeting them again in the heavenly Canaan, and sing: 'O fare you well, O, fare you well/God bless you until we meet again/Hope to meet you in heaven, to part no more." Virginia slave Elizabeth Keckley recounted in 1868 how the departure of her father, who was forced to move west with his master, struck her household "like a thunderbolt." Her parents' final leave of one another took place amid "tears and sobs," strong embraces, and a "solemn prayer to Heaven." The Keckley family found solace in the Christian message that "at the grave, at least," they would be reunited. Friday Jones, enslaved in North Carolina, recalled that when his mother was told that she would soon be deported to Alabama, she made it a point to teach her eleven children how to pray, undoubtedly in the hope that if they put their faith in God, they would all be reunited in heaven. Knowing he would never see his mother again during his lifetime, Jones claimed that "the morning she left I could not bear to shake her hand and bid her good bye," but after that day, he indeed became much more religious.[36]

Slave families such as the Joneses and Keckleys at least had the time to prepare and formally take leave of each other. In many cases, however, separations were so swift that there was no time for prayers, embraces, or anything other than a hasty goodbye. William Grose, born a slave in Virginia, was so abruptly marched off with interstate traders one day that he experienced profound shock and disbelief. "How I felt that day I cannot tell," he related to an interviewer in 1855. "I had never been more than twenty miles from home, and now I was taken away from my mother and wife and children." William's wife had even run after him and was allowed to accompany him down the road, but he claimed that he "was so crazy, I don't know what [she] said. I was beside myself to think of going south. I was as afraid of traders as I would be of a

[36] Williams, *Help Me to Find My People*, 120–21; Peter Randolph, *From Slave Cabin to the Pulpit. The Autobiography of Rev. Peter Randolph: The Southern Question Illustrated and Sketches of Slave Life* (Boston: James H. Earle, 1893), 188 (first quote); Elizabeth Keckley, *Behind the Scenes, or, Thirty Years a Slave, and Four Years in the White House* (New York: G.W. Carleton & Co., 1868), 23–24 (second quotes); Friday Jones, *Days of Bondage. Autobiography of Friday Jones. Being a Brief Narrative of His Trials and Tribulations* (Washington, DC: Commercial Publishing Co., 1883), 1 (third quote).

bear." When ten-year-old Virginia slave John Brown was sold off without a moment's notice to a passing speculator and marched off of his plantation, he "looked round and saw my poor mother stretching out her hands after me." The slave woman ran up to her son and "begged and prayed to be allowed to kiss me for the last time, and bid me good-bye," but the trader pushed her away and shut the gate in her face. In shock, Brown was "so stupefied with grief and fright, that I could not shed a tear, though my heart was bursting." He never saw or heard from his mother again.[37]

The misery that long-distance family separations inflicted on slave communities was indescribable. Because of white southerners' frequent claims that slaves were too devoid of feelings and family attachments to care about separations, visitors to the region often made it a point to comment on the agony they witnessed during sales and departures while traveling through the South. One traveler concluded that "from all the information I could obtain on this subject, the negroes feel these separations as acutely as any whites could do, and are unhappy for years afterwards." Touring the South by train in the 1850s, another northern visitor named C.G. Parsons witnessed a parting scene that became etched in his memory and made a deep impression on him. While the cars were stopped one day in North Carolina, he looked out the window and saw

> a group of twenty-four slaves near the car, – some of them crying, – some weeping silently, – others running to and fro, as if in the excitement of incipient mania, or of approaching delirium, – while *one* sat mute in despair. The whole scene was so wild and unnatural that I did not comprehend it, and I asked the slaveholder [who was seated beside him in the train] what was going on there. "Nothing, only some of these niggers are sold, I suppose, and the others are making a fuss about it," he replied, in a cold, formal manner, as he raised up his chin and gave a stoical, stupid look, and then he attempted to resume conversation with me. . . .

Parsons was not only surprised at the extent of suffering exhibited by the slaves at leaving their loved ones behind, which contradicted what he had been told by white southerners, but also at the callous indifference of the other white passengers in the train, which underscores the extent to which many southerners became desensitized to family separations. Indeed, some of them found the whole situation humorous:

> There were thirty-five passaengers in that car, but no sympathy was expressed for the wretched victims. . . . Young ladies – daughters of slaveholders, well educated, connected with refined families – were in that car, but they did not seem to pity the poor, despairing slaves. They laughed at them, and ridiculed their expressions of grief. "Look out here!" said one of the ladies at a window, to a school mate opposite, "just see those niggers! What a rumpus they are making! Just as if niggers cared anything about their babies!

37 William Grose, in Drew, ed., *North-Side View*, 83 (first quote); Brown, *Slave Life in Georgia*, 15 (second quotes).

See Cuffee kiss Dinah! What a taking on! Likely as not he will have another wife before another week."[38]

However inhumanely white southerners interpreted such scenes – awkwardly drawing from their unstable conviction that slaves cared little for their own families – last goodbyes between slave migrants and their loved ones were, of course, far from exaggerated "takings-on." They even often made white southerners uncomfortable, their assertions to outsiders notwithstanding. When Plowden Weston – one of the wealthiest rice planters in the South Carolina lowcountry – decided to sell one hundred of his slaves to Georgia in 1856, separating many slaves from cross-plantation and extended family members, he stoically maintained an appearance of indifference to his slaves' fate as they were transported by boat to Charleston for deportation. But his wife Emily was obviously moved by the sight of families taking leave of one another, as she recorded in her diary: "The vessel steamed along for a little while very slowly. Tears filled my eyes as I *looked* and *listened* to the wail from those on shore echoed by those on board."[39]

As white southerners knew all too well, slaves unanimously responded to family separations with tears, bitterness, anger, and dejection. Indeed, even physiological and psychological illnesses were a frequent complaint among slaves whose family bonds had been forcibly separated by interregional migration, as the trauma and stress of losing loved ones took a heavy toll on their bodies and minds. When Virginia slave Henry Watson's mother was secretly sold away one night, the news that he would never see her again "brought on a fit of sickness, from which they did not expect I would recover... I felt as if all hope was gone; that I was forsaken and alone in this world." Paulina, a pregnant Virginia slave woman who was sold to a trader based in North Carolina in 1847, became so physically ill after the sale that doctors were consulted, and the trader decided to return her to her original owner. "I am very much afraid that she is diseased," the trader wrote Paulina's old master, "so that I shall have her to return back to you." In the end, her sickness was deemed psychosomatic and did not save her from deportation, however, and Paulina was returned to the trader. Another Virginia slave woman reportedly died six months after her husband was sold to South Carolina. "There was no special disease," her son told interviewer William Greenleaf Eliot in 1885. "She kind-a fell off... She didn't take no hand in nothin', like she used to [but] seemed to be a thinkin' about somethin', and *prayed powerful.*" In the end, she "just grieved herself to death." Bouts of depression and shot nerves were more common. One North

38 Buckingham, *Slave States*, I:182–83 (first quote); C.G. Parsons, *An Inside View of Slavery* (1855; Savannah: The Beehive Press, 1974), 85 (second quote), 86–87 (third quote). For more on white attitudes toward the separation of slave families in the antebellum South, see Williams, *Help Me to Find My People*, 90–116.

39 Emily Weston, quoted in William Dusinberre, *Them Dark Days: Slavery in the American Rice Swamps* (New York: Oxford University Press, 1996), 402 (quote).

Carolina slave woman broke down completely after her fourteen-year-old son was sold to speculators. "Her reason fled, and she became a perfect *maniac*, and had to be kept in close confinement," a white neighbor later reported to the Anti-Slavery Society. Historians such as Steven Deyle have found that slaves who lost family members to the interstate trade often showed signs of mental breakdown, with symptoms ranging from refusing to eat to conversing out loud with loved ones who had been sold away.[40]

V.

Slaves' resistance and negotiation attempts during local moves differed slightly in aim and motivation from that of interstate migrants. Specifically, their actions tended not to center around *preventing* removal and were seldom motivated by a paralyzing fear of the proposed destination, as was usually the case with migrants sent to the dreaded Deep South. Few local migrants longed to die as their interstate counterparts often did. Rather, enslaved people's negotiation attempts and resistance during local moves focused mainly on keeping families as close as possible after the move, with varying degrees of success. Some attempted to get sold to specific slaveholders who lived in the vicinity of their loved ones, for example. John Little, born a slave in North Carolina, claimed that when he was informed that he was to be sold at a local auction, his mother tried to preemptively find a purchaser for her son who lived as close as possible. She "ran all about among the neighbors trying to persuade one and another to buy me; which none of them would promise to do." Eventually, Little was sold only ten miles away – close enough to (illicitly) retain contact with his mother, who nevertheless "felt miserably" that her son did not live closer. At local auctions and estate divisions throughout the South, it was also common for slaves to beg to be sold along with one or more family members. As historian Daina Ramey Berry has argued, slaves "developed a keen understanding of their value, going to great lengths to negotiate their [local] sale in such a way as to maintain family ties." When one Mississippi slave woman and her child were sold together at a Natchez auction in 1835, for example, the woman humbly "solicited" her new mistress to purchase her able-bodied and hard-working husband as well, which the mistress subsequently agreed to do, thereby sparing the young family from having to live apart.[41]

40 Watson, *Narrative of Henry Watson*, 6 (first quote); Joseph Pointer to William Bailey, June 7, 1847 (second quote), C.H. Jordan to William Bailey, Oct. 5, 1847, William Bailey to Joseph Pointer, Oct. 6, 1847, Receipt of Joseph Pointer for return of Paulina, June 29, 1847, William Bailey Papers, RASP, Series E, Part 1 (microfilm), JFK Institute, Freie Universität, Berlin; Eliot, *Story of Archer Alexander*, 29 (third quotes); Testimony of Francis Hawley, in Anti-Slavery Society, *Slavery as It Is*, 97 (fourth quote); Deyle, *Carry Me Back*, 246–47.

41 John Little, in Drew, ed., *North-Side View*, 198 (first quote); Daina Ramey Berry, "'We'm Fus' Rate Bargain': Value, Labor, and Price in a Georgia Slave Community," in Johnson, ed., *The Chattel Principle*, 55–56 (second quote); Ingraham, *South-West.*, 2:200 (third quote).

Regional strategies of negotiation during local removals are striking, especially in South Carolina. As stated earlier, many slaves living in South Carolina were more likely to be transferred in family units during local removals than slaves living in most other parts of the South. Interestingly, enslaved people themselves played an important role in maintaining this element of family stability during local sales and estate divisions, more than any paternalist sympathies. Far from passive victims in the buying, selling, and trading of human property, South Carolina slaves created opportunities to keep simple families intact by making it unattractive to acquire them otherwise, a tactic that had been widely used there since the eighteenth century. Historian Leslie Schwalm found that in the lowcountry, especially, "the pending sale and separation of members of a slave community created a 'general gloom' that settled on the plantation slaves 'at the idea of parting with each other.'" Their reaction had a negative effect on plantation labor and indeed "so disrupted the peace and efficiency of the slave workforce that it became common wisdom among nineteenth-century rice planters that slaves should be purchased and sold in intact family groups." Doing otherwise could have disastrous consequences. According to one planter, if slaves were bought individually and thrown "all together among strangers, they don't assimilate, & they ponder over former ties, of family, &c., & all goes wrong with them." Adjusting to the demands of the market, South Carolina auctioneers and sellers of slaves offered them in family groups when possible. South Carolina slave trader A.J. McElveen, for example, even took into consideration an enslaved man's family ties after his master explicitly ordered him to sell him out of the state, which would have separated him from his loved ones. Forwarding the slave from Sumterville to his business partner in Charleston, McElveen explained that the slave "is not Gilty off no criminal offence" and that he had begged him to be allowed to stay in Charleston because "his wife is there." For South Carolina slaves, the central goal was not necessarily to prevent removal altogether, which was usually futile, but to prevent family separations during removals.[42]

Remarkably, some slaves turned local hiring into vehicles for uniting families separated by local sales or cross-plantation marriages. When one Alabama slave named Demps was sold to a local slaveholder named Turner Reavis in 1859, for example, he successfully arranged for his wife Judy and their four children to be hired out to Reavis as well for $100, thereby uniting a divided family. An elderly Virginia slave named Jeffrey and his cross-plantation wife Jane "made urgent appeals" to their owners "that they might be allowed to spend the remainder of their lives together." In the end, the matter was settled when Jeffrey was hired

[42] Robert F. W. Allston, in J.H. Easterby, ed., *The South Carolina Rice Plantation as Revealed in the Papers of Robert F.W. Allston* (Chicago: University of Chicago Press, 1945), 30 (first quote); Leslie A. Schwalm, *A Hard Fight for We: Women's Transition from Slavery to Freedom in South Carolina* (Urbana: University of Illinois Press, 1997), 56 (second, third and fourth quotes); A.J. McElveen to Z.B. Oakes, Aug. 9, 1853, in Edmund Drago, ed., *Broke by the War: Letters of a Slave Trader* (Columbia: University of South Carolina Press, 1991), 48 (fifth quote).

to his wife's owner indefinitely. In Fairfax County, Virginia, where hiring was especially prevalent during the late antebellum period, estate documents and planters' records contain several illuminating examples of slaves negotiating to be hired out to free family members or to the owners of family members. Henry Hubert, a free black man, was able to hire his enslaved sons from the estate of Harrison Allison between 1835 and 1840. One Letty, owned by John J. Frobel of Wilton Hill plantation, was hired out to Thomas Janney, the owner of her husband, at the outbreak of the Civil War. At Bush Hill plantation, a woman named Ellen Ann, the wife of a free black man named David Grey, managed to get hired out to her husband in 1848, a year she spent mostly pregnant and in which she was delivered of a child. This arrangement was probably only permitted because she was pregnant, however, because the following year she was hired out "to Murray Mason... not to husband," undoubtedly because the former could offer more money.[43]

For all local slave migrants, the need to resist or negotiate became more pressing when local removals threatened to result in permanent or semipermanent separations from loved ones. Hasty last-minute attempts to prevent such separations were frequently made from the auction block itself, as the distances that would separate family members during local sales often only became clear to slaves while the bidding was going on. In the Louisiana sugar country in 1855, a slave mother and her seventeen-year-old daughter were unsuccessful in their attempt to prevent a permanent separation during a local auction at New Orleans, the mother being sold within the city limits while her daughter was bought by a cotton planter up on Red River, much too far to ever allow for any visiting. Faced with the threat of a permanent separation, the daughter resorted to pleading with her mother's new master: "pray, massa, please do, massa, buy me too," but the man replied that he could not, and, an eyewitness reported, the two women "took a last and final embrace of each other... both weeping aloud." During a similar scene witnessed at a slave auction in Richmond, Virginia, the husband of a slave woman named Martha Ann, who had been put up for local sale, attempted to preemptively prevent a permanent separation by beseeching potential purchasers: "I kin do ez much ez ennybody; and, marsters, ef you'll only buy me and de chillum with Martha Ann, Lord knows I'll wuk myself to deth fur you." The family was separated, however. Martha Ann was knocked off to a man who lived near the North Carolina border, too far to visit her husband or children. Implicitly acknowledging feelings of guilt, her new master implored her to "cheer up; you'll find me a good master, and I'll

[43] Martin, *Divided Mastery*, 138–60; Turner Reavis Account Book, 1842–1890, RASP, Series C, Part 2 (microfilm), JFK Institute, Freie Universität, Berlin; W. Craddock to William Bailey, n.d., RASP, Series E, Part 1 (microfilm), JFK Institute (first quote); Redpath, *Roving Editor*, 188; Donald M. Sweig, "Northern Virginia Slavery: A Statistical and Demographic Investigation," (PhD dissertation, College of William & Mary, Williamsburg, Va., 1982), 161; Anne S. Frobel, *The Civil War Diary of Anne S. Frobel of Wilton Hill in Virginia* (Birmingham, Ala., 1986), 215; Richard Marshall Scott, Jr., Diary (typescript), Mar. 1, 1848, Jan. 1, 1849 (second quote), Fairfax City Regional Library, Fairfax, Va.

get you a new husband," an awkward promise designed to compensate for the forced separation he had just executed.[44]

Similar to their interstate counterparts, many slaves threatened with permanent separations from family members during local moves resorted to more drastic measures to prevent it, including running away. One Mississippi slave named Ben, for example, took to the wilderness when he learned of his master's intentions to move to another plantation about a hundred miles away so that he would not be separated from his wife, who lived on another plantation. He "stayed under cover in the woods, in such lurking places as the nature of the country provided, in the day time, and at night would cautiously approach his wife's cabin, when, at an appointed signal, she would let him in and give him such food and care as his condition required." Failing to track him down with his bloodhounds, his master finally caved in and bought Ben's wife, whereupon the truant reemerged from the woods and agreed to move with the rest. Townsend Derricks, a Virginia slave who fled the South in 1857, taking "in his company with him his wife Mary, the property of the estate of Caldwell Carr," was less fortunate in his attempt to prevent a permanent separation. A northern abolitionist society received Derricks as a refugee but reported that "the wife was captured and carried back," adding that it "was particularly with a view of saving [her] that Townshend was induced to peril his life, for she (the wife) was not owned by the same party who owned Townshend, and was on the eve of being taken by her owners some fifty miles distant into the country, where the chances for intercourse between husband and wife would no longer be favorable." Clearly, the importance of maintaining family relationships across space motivated local slave migrants (and their loved ones) to often take the same risks as bondspeople confronted with interstate removal.[45]

VI.

Slave migrants who were hired out to urban areas were often afforded more opportunities to negotiate around long-term family separations than other forced migrants because both owners and hirers knew that "the profitability of hiring transactions rested to a great extent on the consent, however grudging, of the slaves involved," in the words of Jonathan Martin. Slaves hired out to Virginia ironwork factories, for example, often successfully convinced their masters to seek formal guarantees that would allow them one or two family visits during their terms of hire. One master wrote an ironmaster in 1828 that he would only hire out his slave on the condition that he be permitted

[44] Tower, *Slavery Unmasked*, 307–308 (first quote); John S. Wise, in Katherine M. Jones, ed., *The Plantation South* (Indianapolis: Bobbs-Merrill, 1957), 73 (second quote), 75 (third quote).

[45] Thompson, *Biography of a Slave*, 21–22 (first quote), 25. The runaway advertisement for Townsend Derricks and his wife was published in the *Alexandria Gazette*, Oct. 7, 1857 (second quote). After arrival in the North, Derricks was interviewed by William Still, where he related that his wife had been captured and taken back. See Still, *Underground Railroad*, 442–43 (third quote).

to "come home once in the course of the year to see his wife." Less formal arrangements whereby family members were kept together or in close proximity upon being hired out were also often the result of slaves' own negotiations with their masters and prospective employers. Nanny, a North Carolina slave, exhibited such aversion to being hired out to employers who lived far from her husband that her owner was "compelled to hire her out for a very small sum to such persons only [Nanny] preferred or she would immediately run away" with her husband to the Great Dismal Swamp, a tactic she used several times. Alonzo Jackson, a slave from Georgetown County, South Carolina, secured permission to hire himself out in the county seat every year for eighteen years; his master even allowed him the privilege of taking care of his own family with his earnings. Jackson proudly told interviewers of the Southern Claims Commission in 1873 that before freedom, "I hired all my time from my master... I paid every year $140 for my time and supported myself and family from my own earnings – working only for whom I chose." Similarly, Georgia slave Elbert Head related to an interviewer in 1889 that for more than ten years before freedom, he had been allowed to hire himself out as a carpenter in the small town of Americus, using his earnings to in turn hire his own wife from his master as well.[46]

Indeed, slaves confronted with the prospect of being hired out in towns and cities often negotiated (or attempted to negotiate) with their masters to be allowed to choose their own employers. For some – such as Jones, Jackson, and Head – the chief motivation was to bend urban migration into a vehicle for uniting cross-plantation family relations or keeping co-residential families intact. But for others, the idea was mainly to secure the most lucrative labor arrangement – in other words, to ensure that they would be hired to a decent master or be allowed to work at a job that was likely to earn them some extra money or privileges. Although officially frowned upon and legally dubious – as historian Jonathan Martin has argued, self-hire arrangements could only rest on tacit agreement because slaves were prohibited from making binding contracts – more than a few slaveholders gave in to the wishes of their slaves, indifferent to the details surrounding their bondspeople's urban employment

46 See Martin, *Divided Mastery*, ch. 2, 51 (first quote); Schermerhorn, *Money over Mastery*, 105–106; Lewis, "Slave Families at Early Chesapeake Ironworks," 173 (second quote); Midori Takagi, *"Rearing Wolves to Our Own Destruction": Slavery in Richmond, Virginia, 1782–1865* (Charlottesville: University of Virginia Press, 1999), 50; "William Coppersmith and Elisha S. Nash to the Court of Pleas and Quarter Sessions, Pasquotank County, North Carolina, 1851," in Schweninger, ed., *Southern Debate over Slavery*, 265–66 (third quote); Testimony of Alonzo Jackson, in Ira Berlin, et al, eds., *Freedom: A Documentary History of Emancipation, 1861–1867, Series I, Volume I* (New York: Cambridge University Press, 1985), 813 (fourth quote). Elbert Head was interviewed in 1889 in Georgia by Levi J. Coppin. His interview was first published in the *A.M.E. Church Review* 6 (July 1889), 104–106. Reprinted in Blassingame, ed., *Slave Testimony*, 501 (fifth quote). Slaves such as Elbert Head, who hired both themselves and their wives, had to pay two masters just to keep their families together. Such arrangements occurred most often in the Upper South. See Schermerhorn, *Money over Mastery*, 28. See also Brown, *Narrative of Henry Box Brown*, 49–50.

as long as they earned an attractive return. One northern traveler who visited the South in the 1830s was astonished to learn that "some steady slaves are permitted to 'hire their own time;' that is, to go into town and earn what they can, as porters, labourers, gardeners, or in other ways, and pay a stipulated sum weekly to their owners, which will be regulated according to the supposed value of the slave's labour." Because the arrangement usually ensured a steady profit for the slaveholder and allowed the slave the relative "quasi-freedom" of choosing a master, however, he admitted that it was probably "mutually advantageous to both."[47]

Urban migration could turn out to be tolerable or even a blessing in disguise, especially for hirelings who were lucky enough to be able to choose their own masters and remain in close contact with loved ones. The most open forms of resistance to moving to the city were evoked when – similar to other slave migrants – urban migrants were confronted with a permanent or semipermanent separation from friends and family. Some negotiated for spouses and family members to remain together, sometimes successfully. One mechanic purchased by Oxford Iron Works in Virginia convinced his new master to buy his wife and two children shortly after arrival in 1812; the newcomer was so persuasive that his owner even sold another slave to finance the transaction. Flight was the most common course of action, however. Daniel, a West-Florida slave "raised in Jackson County," ran away in 1853 when he was hired out to an employer in the town of Pensacola, more than one hundred miles west from where he grew up. However exciting the lure of a port town such as Pensacola might have seemed to some slaves, Daniel apparently found the prospect of moving to an urban environment that would separate him from his native Jackson County for fifty-one weeks out of the year an unattractive proposition despite the near certainty that he would be able to see his loved ones during the last week of the year. And compared with some slaves' lot, Daniel's being hired out to Pensacola almost sounds attractive. Far worse was being sold or moving with a master to a town far away because then the separation from loved ones was more likely to be permanent, with no Christmas holiday at home to catch up with friends and family. In 1835, a forty-five-year-old slave woman named Mary, from Charleston District in the South Carolina lowcountry, fled her master when confronted with the prospect of moving more than one hundred miles to the state capital. A runaway slave advertisement in the *Charleston Courier* openly claimed that "the cause of her running away was her dislike to be brought to Columbia." Likewise, an Alabama slave named Alonzo fled when his mistress sold him – against the general flow of interstate migration – to a resident of Raleigh, North Carolina. William, a North Carolina slave, absconded from Columbia, South Carolina, almost immediately after arriving, endeavoring to make his way back to his home region. Other

[47] Martin, *Divided Mastery*, 161–87; Schermerhorn, *Money over Mastery*, 107–109; Takagi, "*Rearing Wolves*," 49–50 Ingraham, *South-West*, 250–51 (quote).

slaves even threatened extreme consequences if forced to move to towns that were too far away from loved ones. One slave from rural Louisiana threatened suicide if forced to be hired out to Baton Rouge and separated from his wife. Similar to their local and interstate counterparts, thus, urban slave migrants' opinion of a possible forced relocation was strongly influenced by the extent of family separation that such a move would entail.[48]

Despite white southerners' charges of ignorance and indifference, enslaved people living throughout the South in the nineteenth century were fully aware of the threat of forced migration and its potential consequences for their work and social lives. The agency demonstrated by so many slave migrants to escape or negotiate their lot bespeaks both the importance of their social relationships and the limits of their power to exert influence over their lives. More than anything else, the threat of forced separation from family members motivated antebellum slaves to take action when confronted with the prospect of migration in its interstate, local, and urban forms. Far from passive victims in the massive reallocation of slave labor within the ever expanding South, bondspeople resisted interstate deportation in every possible manner, sometimes even violently; they attempted to soften the blows of local moves by attempting to keep their families as close as possible; and they even resisted or attempted to renegotiate urban removal when it threatened to separate them permanently from their loved ones. That their actions were often unsuccessful does not take away from their *attempts* – nor does it necessarily suggest, as some scholars have, that historians' traditional claims of slave agency are therefore exaggerated. Slave migrants demonstrated agency every time they attempted to resist or negotiate their lot even if their actions failed because of external factors or overwhelming force.[49]

[48] David Ross to Edmund Sherman, Richmond, Feb. 9, 1812, Mar. 17, 1812, David Ross Letterbook, Slavery in Ante-Bellum Southern Industries, Series C (microfilm), JFK Institute; *Pensacola Gazette*, June 4, 1853 (first quote); *Charleston Courier*, Sept. 3, 1835 (second quote); *Weekly Flag & Advertiser* (Montgomery, Ala.), May 11, 1849; *Charleston Courier*, Nov. 2, 1830; Martin, *Divided Mastery*, 55.

[49] Valid charges of an overemphasis on slave agency in the works of revisionist scholars underscore the mistakes of approaching slave culture as having developed in a vacuum, underestimating the power of white slaveholders over their bondspeople, and attributing too much power and success to the enslaved. See, for example, Peter Kolchin, *American Slavery, 1619–1877* (New York: Hill & Wang, 1993), 137; Peter J. Parish *Slavery: History and Historians* (New York: Harper & Row, 1989), 76; Mark M. Smith, *Debating Slavery: Economy and Society in the Antebellum South* (New York: Cambridge University Press, 1998), 46–51; Wilma Dunaway, *The African-American Family in Slavery and Emancipation* (New York: Cambridge University Press, 2003), 4–5. Agency should not be confused with success, however. See Damian Alan Pargas, *The Quarters and the Fields: Slave Families in the Non-Cotton South* (Gainesville: University Press of Florida, 2010), 8; Schermerhorn, *Money over Mastery*, 24; Walter Johnson, "On Agency," *Journal of Social History* 37 (Autumn 2003): 113–24.

3

Changing Places

During certain seasons of the year... all the roads, steam-boats, and packets, are crowded with troops of negroes on their way to the great slave markets of the South.

Captain Basil Hall, 1829[1]

Ceceil George, an ex-slave born in South Carolina in 1846, had never been outside of Charleston District before her master died and the heirs sold her and her family members "like a gang of chickens" to a sugar planter in St. Bernard Parish, Louisiana. "We all cried [when we had to] leave de old country," she told interviewers from the Louisiana Writers' Project. "But we had more tears to shed." The journey itself was a traumatic experience; the former bondswoman recalled how she and the other slaves were transported by their new master to Louisiana "on de ship," cruising around Florida and up the Gulf of Mexico to New Orleans. She distinctly remembered the sight of the ocean, which to her represented not simply a route of travel but also a vast and impenetrable barrier that separated her old home from her new one. Although shipping newly purchased slaves from East Coast slave markets to Louisiana along the coastal route was considered by late-antebellum slaveholders to be an expedient and efficient method of transport, Ceceil and her relatives were convinced that the underlying motive for traveling by sea was primarily to disorientate bondspeople to discourage future escape attempts. "Dey made us go by de sea because den we can't go back," she explained. With each nautical mile, the only world Ceceil's family had ever known slipped further and further away, the steamship leaving no physical points of reference in its wake for the slaves to ever be able to retrace their journey back to South Carolina again. Arrival at

[1] Captain Basil Hall, *Travels in North America, in the Years 1827 and 1828* (Edinburgh: Cadell & Co., 1829), 3:197 (quote).

their destination only compounded their anxiety because the enslaved migrants' first impressions of their new home in the Deep South were, to put it mildly, negative. "God help us," Ceceil exclaimed to her interviewers. "We come to de most wicked country dat our God's Son ever died for. De old people used to cry; dear Lawd, how dey grieved. Dey never thought dey'd have to live in a heathern country."[2]

Although slave migrants such as Ceceil George and her family often had a general idea of what awaited them when they were singled out for forced removal, their experiences during the physical move itself, as well as their first impressions of their new homes, bespoke the hopes, fears, and feelings of otherness or alienation with which all migrants were to some extent confronted. As their physical horizons were forcibly broadened, slave migrants grappled with their anxieties, reevaluating the course of their lives, the nature of their slave status, and the core of their identities. This chapter explores the ways in which slave migrants experienced removal itself, including their feelings in slave pens and on auction blocks, their journeys to their new homes (especially those of long-distance migrants), and their first impressions of new environments.

I.

For most antebellum slave migrants, removal was experienced not all at once but in a series of different stages that could last anywhere from one day to several months. Each stage confronted bondspeople with unique experiences, but a strong argument could be made that for a large number of slaves, the first day or two – especially the initial departure from home and subsequent arrival at urban marketplaces to be sold or hired to new owners – formed the most daunting phase of forced migration. During this stage, countless numbers of bondspeople were subjected to dehumanizing measures aimed at securing their commodified bodies and safely transferring them between sellers and buyers or hirers – measures that evoked feelings of fear, grief, and shame. More than anywhere else, this process of dehumanization was driven home to migrants who found themselves at the markets, in the holding chambers, and on the auction blocks that formed the first stop in the *formal* transfer of human property in the antebellum South.

Slaves who were sent to auction houses or dealers' pens – whether to be sold locally or long distances – were frequently collected by traders' agents at crossroads, city wharves and train stations, subjected to overwhelming force and treated like prisoners or livestock by those who organized and executed their migration. "I saw droves of the poor fellows driven to the slave markets kept in different parts of the city," reported Silas Stone, a civil servant from New York, while visiting Charleston in 1807. "The arrangements ... appeared something

[2] Ceceil George, in Ronnie W. Clayton, ed., *Mother Wit: The Ex-Slave Narratives of the Louisiana Writers' Project* (New York: Peter Lang Publishing, 1990), 83–84 (quotes).

like our northern horse-markets." Already overwhelmed about having to leave their homes, such treatment exacerbated the stress of removal for countless migrants. One Virginia slave claimed to an interviewer in 1861 that when he was collected by a trader in Harrisonburg, he was "seized by the collar" by two men and dragged away in chains like "a stubborn horse." He complained: "Had I been a mad man, or some wild animal, there could not have been a greater ado made over me." Henry Bibb likewise claimed that when he and his family were transported to a slave pen in Louisville, Kentucky, the traders who came for him handcuffed him "with heavy irons, and two men guarded me with loaded rifles." In this manner, he was "driven through the streets of the city with my little family on foot, to jail."[3]

Indeed, the shock and trauma of deportation often arose from the fact that many slaves were *unknowingly* lured into the hands of slave traders, duped by their masters – who knew that their slaves would attempt to resist forced removal if overtly confronted with it – into going on false errands in town and then snatched up by dealers' agents. Their livid reactions when they realized that they were sold made physical force often necessary simply to restrain them. In a case that came before the circuit court of the District of Columbia in 1825, Helen, a nineteen-year-old slave woman from Washington, who had been promised her freedom, was enticed by her master to accompany the family on an errand to Fredericksburg. When she boarded the steamboat, however, she was collected by "traders in this species of property," who had purchased her to carry her "Southardly." The "agony which then overcame [Helen] was evinced by the violence of her conduct," and her reaction was so "frantic" that she was literally "dragged out of the water" by force and thrown into a wagon "to wheel her away."[4]

The aim of these migrants' captors – hard-headed businessmen all – when they secured enslaved people's bodies in this way was to prevent the escape of very valuable property, a common concern of antebellum slave dealers. As stated in Chapter 2, resistance to forced removal during initial transfers

[3] Silas Stone, in Thomas Weld, *American Slavery as It Is: Testimony of a Thousand Witnesses* (New York: American Anti-Slavery Society, 1839), 167 (first quote); J.C. Pennington, *A Narrative of Events of the Life of J.H. Banks, an Escaped Slave, from the Cotton State, Alabama, in America* (Liverpool: M. Rourke, 1861), 39–43, 40 (second quote), 42 (third quote); Henry Bibb, *Narrative of the Life and Adventures of Henry Bibb, an American Slave* (New York: n.p., 1849), 89–91 (fourth quotes).

[4] Walter Johnson has argued that "along with outright lies, slaveholders used surprise to avoid negotiating with the slaves they were selling," behavior that implicitly acknowledged their expectation of resistance to forced migration. See Johnson, *Soul by Soul*, 39; Ibid., "A Nettlesome Classic Turns Twenty-Five," *Common-Place* 1 (July 2001), http://www.common-place.org/vol-01/no-04/reviews/johnson.shtml. "Helen to the Circuit Court, Washington County, District of Columbia, 1825," in Loren Schweninger, ed., *The Southern Debate over Slavery: Volume 2, Petitions to Southern County Courts, 1775–1867* (Urbana: University of Illinois Press, 2008), 128 (quote).

occurred frequently enough that traders were kept constantly on guard, especially when conveying migrants through public spaces. When one South Carolina slave trader, for example, wrote to his business partner in 1853 that he had bought "the likeliest Girl I Ever Saw" and a "boy 17 or 18 years old," promising to forward them to the Charleston market by train as soon as possible, he warned him to "send to the cars for them" because "the Boy will Runaway at times," implicitly advising his colleague to prepare to have to physically constrain the two slaves upon arrival. Yet in practice, such treatment amounted to more than simple precautionary measures to ensure against escape attempts, for it simultaneously subjected migrants to a process of "othering," by which the white population publicly distinguished itself from captive enslaved blacks. Chained, roped, humiliatingly marched through crowded town squares, and preyed upon by the appraising glares of potential purchasers, slave migrants were quite visibly marked as inferior beings when they arrived at urban places of market.[5]

New arrivals who found themselves at the mercy of strangers and marched through urban centers like prisoners or cattle were often observed to be melancholy, dejected, angry, moody, and frightened. In December 1815, Dr. Jesse Torrey, a northern physician, saw a group of slaves opposite the Capitol in Washington, DC, "bound together, some with ropes, and some with iron chains (which I had hitherto seen only for restraining beasts)," the expressions on the slaves' faces so morose that the procession "resembl[ed] that of a funeral." Young slaves, especially, often expressed shock at being sent to town to be sold, being fully confronted with the "reality of [the] powerlessness" of their parents to protect them, as historian Heather Andrea Williams has argued. The sudden awareness that they were helpless and that even their parents could not prevent their removal caused many to become angry and depressed. In Virginia in the 1850s, one slave girl who was sent by train to Richmond to be sold was observed by white passengers to look like "a criminal," her "expression of face indicat[ing] dread and grief." Frederick Law Olmsted likewise reported several such scenes during his stay in Alexandria, Virginia, in 1854. On one particular occasion, he witnessed the arrival of three slaves – a middle-aged man; a twenty-year-old woman; and a boy, "considerably younger" – who had been sent by their master in the countryside to a slave dealer in town to be sold. They had "come in a canal boat" and been subsequently collected by the dealer's

[5] Robert Gudmestad, "Slave Resistance, Coffles, and Debates over Slavery in the Nation's Capital," in Walter Johnson, ed., *The Chattel Principle: Internal Slave Trades in the Americas* (New Haven: Yale University Press, 2004), 80–82; A.J. McElveen to Z.B. Oakes, Aug. 25, 1853, in Edmund Drago, ed., *Broke by the War: Letters of a Slave Trader* (Columbia: University of South Carolina Press, 1991), 52 (first quote). "Othering" is a process by which a dominant group distinguishes itself from another group, thereby maintaining its hegemony. For the classic works on othering and critical race theory, see Kimberlé Crenshaw, et al, eds., *Critical Race Theory: The Key Writings that Formed the Movement* (New York: New Press, 1995).

agent, who roped them together and led them through the streets to his office. The manner in which the slaves were marched through downtown Alexandria marked their status as chattel property: "the arms of all three were secured before them with hand-cuffs, and the rope by which they were led passed from one to another." People stopped to stare, and one white man quipped: "That ar's a likely gall." Olmsted remarked that the three slaves seemed miserable: "The boy looked most dolefully, and the girl was turning around, with a very angry face, and shouting, 'O pshaw! Shut up!'"[6]

Country slaves sent to the city to be hired out were not necessarily exempt from intimidation upon arrival at hiring markets, which sometimes even muffled their initial excitement about moving to an urban environment. Although most slaveholders personally brought their slaves to hiring auctions, southern cities also teemed with specialized hiring agents who operated like slave traders, often collecting slaves upon arrival and bringing them back to their offices, from where they negotiated hiring contracts with potential employers. Hirelings delivered to such agents experienced arrival in the city with much the same anxiety as those who were sent to town to be sold. Olmsted, for one, reported seeing a "singular group of negroes" in Alexandria, all men and boys, holding small bundles of extra clothes and blankets in their arms, who had been sent to a dealer in town to be hired out as factory hands. Having just arrived and standing in a row before a "villainous looking white man" (one of the hiring agents), the slaves were kept in line by the intimidating authority of their white broker. Clearly chagrined, "some of them, were quarreling, or reproving one another," Olmsted noted. Finally, a wealthy white man "with a large, golden-headed walking stick" came out of an office and, "without saying a word, walked briskly up the street" to the hiring office. The slaves "immediately followed, in file; the other white man bringing up the rear."[7]

These urban migrants obviously felt intimidated upon being collected by the hiring agents, yet such experiences probably tended to be the exceptions to the rule for slave hirelings. Indeed, many hirelings arrived at southern cities for

6 Jesse Torrey, *American Slave Trade; Or, An Account of the Manner in Which the Slave Traders Take Free People* ... (London: J.M. Cobbett, 1822), 54–55, 54 (first quote); Heather Andrea Williams, *Help Me to Find My People: The African American Search for Family Lost in Slavery* (Chapel Hill: University of North Carolina Press, 2012), 28 (second quote); Frederick Law Olmsted, *A Journey in the Seaboard Slave States, with Remarks on Their Economy* (New York: Dix & Edwards, 1856), 56 (third quote), 30 (fourth quote).

7 Jonathan Martin, *Divided Mastery: Slave Hiring in the Antebellum South* (Cambridge, Mass.: Harvard University Press, 2004), 33, 48–49; Frederic Bancroft, *Slave-Trading in the Old South* (Baltimore: J.H. Furst & Co., 1931), 149–51; Midori Takagi, *"Rearing Wolves to Our Own Destruction": Slavery in Richmond, Virginia, 1782–1865* (Charlottesville: University of Virginia Press, 1999), 38–39. Some urban employers specifically demanded hirelings to be brought by their owners and not through third parties. One establishment in Halifax, Virginia, advertised for "one hundred able bodied laborers," adding that "the hands will be required to be delivered in Halifax by the *owners*" (italics in the original). *Norfolk Beacon*, Mar. 21, 1838, reprinted in Weld, *American Slavery as It Is*, 137. Olmsted, *Seaboard Slave States*, 31 (quote).

the purpose of finding their own employers for the ensuing year. One resident of Richmond recorded a common sight when he wrote to a family member in Boston: "The city is full of niggers from all parts of the country to let themselves for the coming year." Northerner Nehemiah Adams observed during a three-month residence at the South in 1854 that "at the Christmas holidays, some of the southern cities and towns are alive with the negroes, in their best attire, seeking employment for the year to come, changing places, and having full liberty to suit themselves as to their employers." In contrast to their counterparts who were hired out through agents or who were sent to town to be sold, these relatively privileged hirelings arrived at urban marketplaces – often carrying notes of introduction from their owners to facilitate hiring negotiations – with optimism and an urgent sense of purpose. It is less likely that they felt reduced to mere chattel as they made their way through the city streets in search of a master. One North Carolina slave from a farm only fifteen miles from Raleigh, who negotiated with his master to give him a note and let him choose his own employer, arrived in town optimistic that he was improving his lot, claiming in an 1883 testimony that he had "many friends" in Raleigh and was cheerful at the prospect of finding a decent master.[8]

Part of the anxiety felt by slave migrants who arrived in cities to be delivered to traders and dealers – especially those sent to town to be sold – surely had to do with the fact that they were collected by complete strangers, who felt it necessary to intimidate or physically bind their chattels while transferring them to holding chambers or places of sale. Such was not the fate of all migrants, however, for most southern slaveholders personally delivered their bondspeople at auction houses and traders' offices, seldom resorting to chains or shackles to prevent escape along the way. As argued earlier, slaveholders frequently felt it necessary to disguise their intentions to sell their slaves, even duping them into accompanying them on false errands in town and then delivering them to traders. But many other slave migrants arrived at traders' offices or auctions fully aware that they were to be sold, their masters eager to convert their "people" into hard cash. Literally marched into town by their masters to be disposed of, slaves must have found the journey to urban marketplaces a physically and emotionally draining experience. "Chile, it gives you de creeps up yo' spine to think 'bout it," claimed one Virginia ex-slave who lived near a slave pen in Richmond. Having witnessed the arrival of hundreds of slaves whose masters had brought them to town to be sold, she lamented that slaves

[8] John Gault to Samuel Gault, cited in Gregg D. Kimball, *American City, Southern Place: A Cultural History of Antebellum Richmond* (Athens: University of Georgia Press, 2000), 30 (first quote); Nehemiah Adams, *A South-Side View; or, Three Months at the South, in 1854* (Boston: T.R. Marvin and B.B. Mussey & Co., 1854), 76 (second quote); Takagi, *"Rearing Wolves,"* 38–39; Friday Jones, *Days of Bondage: Autobiography of Friday Jones, Being a Brief Narrative of his Trials and Tribulations in Slavery* (Washington, DC: Commercial Publishing Co., 1883), 5–6 (third quote).

often seemed tired upon arrival, but "de ole masters didn't keer." In reality, even slaveholders often felt awkward and uncomfortable about delivering their bondspeople to sellers and auctioneers, however. Although they tried to convince themselves that their slaves did not care about forced migration, the visible expressions of fear or grief on their slaves' faces during the journey to town evoked genuine feelings of guilt among many masters. One struggling Virginia planter recorded in his diary on August 11, 1846: "Sold my woman Catherine very much against my feelings, for $480 to Joseph Bruin," an interstate slave trader based in Alexandria. Although he added that Catherine had to be sold because of her "improper conduct for some time past," the fact that he needed to justify the decision at all – especially in a private diary – suggests that he was clearly driven to guilt as he rode with her to town and dropped her off at Bruin's office. Others expressed remorse in a more selfish way. Thomas Chaplin scribbled in his journal after selling ten slaves in 1845: "I cannot express my feelings on seeing so many faithful Negroes going away from me forever, not for any fault of their own but for my extravagance. It is a dearly bought lesson, and I hope I will benefit by it." Whatever their feelings at departing from their "black family members," however, in the end, there was recognition that their slaves were valuable bodies that could be liquidated at market.[9]

II.

As explained in Chapter 1, slave migrants who were sent to urban markets to be sold through dealers – whether locally or long distances – were usually forced to await either deportation or sale in the dealers' private jails or slave pens. Traders tended to describe these holding chambers as flatteringly as possible, assuring sellers that their slaves would be "safely and comfortably taken care of." One trader in the 1830s advertised that he had "commodious buildings" for slaves awaiting sale or transit, while another referred to his pen as "a kind of hotel or boarding house." Indeed, even hiring agents afforded slaves "places to stay at night during the hiring," bragging in newspaper advertisements of "comfortable" apartments with "a good fire" and "sufficient shelter." For dealers in slaves, these were places of business, where merchandise was "stored" and showcased to potential buyers. For slaves in transit, they were sites of dehumanization. Whether they had to spend one night or several weeks in these dreary buildings, slave migrants who found themselves confined within

[9] Pennington, *Life of J.H. Banks*, 39–40; Charles L. Perdue, Jr., et al, eds., *Weevils in the Wheat: Interviews with Virginia Ex-Slaves* (Charlottesville: University of Virginia Press, 1976), 15 (second quote); Richard Marshall Scott, Jr., Diary, Aug. 11, 1846, (typescript) Fairfax City Regional Library, Fairfax, Va. (third quote); Thomas Chaplin, in Williams, *Help Me to Find My People*, 140 (fourth quote); Johnson, *Soul by Soul*, 39.

FIGURE 3.1. Slave pen, Alexandria, Va., 1861–1865. "Photograph shows interior view of a slave pen, showing the doors of cells where the slaves were held before being sold." This photograph of the interior of the slave pen used by slave dealers Price, Birch & Co., located on Duke Street in Alexandria, Virginia, was taken during the Civil War. Travelers to the South such as E.S. Abdy and Ethan Allen Andrews, who visited this slave pen when it was still used by Franklin & Armfield in the early 1830s, found that it resembled a prison. *Source:* Gift of Col. Godwin Ordway. Courtesy of the Library of Congress, Prints and Photographs Division, LOT 4161-H, no. 2.

the brick walls of a slave pen were truly confronted with their captivity and symbolic reduction to chattel property in the eyes of white sellers and buyers.[10]

Antebellum visitors to the slave states frequently commented that the pens attached to dealers' offices resembled at best prisons – some even doubled as

[10] Steven Deyle, *Carry Me Back: The Domestic Slave Trade in American Life* (New York: Oxford University Press, 2005), 115 (first quotes); Robert H. Gudmestad, *A Troublesome Commerce: The Transformation of the Interstate Slave Trade* (Baton Rouge: Louisiana State University Press, 2003), 14; Bancroft, *Slave-Trading*, 151 (second quote); Takagi, "*Rearing Wolves*," 38; Walter Johnson, *Soul by Soul: Life Inside the Antebellum Slave Market* (Cambridge, Mass.: Harvard University Press, 1999), 136–61.

city jails – and at worst stalls for livestock. One Ohio newspaper reporter who visited the slave pen of one Colonel Williams, "a dealer in human chattels" who operated within "full view of the Capitol" in Washington, DC, wrote in 1849 that the building seemed designed for the express purpose of confining valuable bodies. Built of solid brick, it contained an internal courtyard, where slaves were lined up "for inspection" whenever a potential purchaser called. The front of the building, which faced the street, was heavily fortified to prevent any means of escape: the "windows [are] grated and prison-like, and an iron gate opens to take in and let out the unfortunate occupants." E.S. Abdy, who visited a "wretched hovel" of a slave pen in the same neighborhood in 1833, described the jail in much the same way. "The outside alone is inaccessible to the eye of a visitor," Abdy reported, "what passes within being reserved for the exclusive observation of its owner... and his unfortunate victims. It is surrounded by a wooden paling fourteen or fifteen feet in height, with the posts outside to prevent escape." A few days later he visited Franklin & Armfield's pen in Alexandria, across the river, which he at least found "clean and in good order" if prison-like in appearance. "The sexes are separated by a passage, into which the iron gratings of their doors look. These last are doubly locked, and strongly secured. The yards, which are sufficiently spacious, are surrounded by high walls." Ethan Allen Andrews, who also visited Franklin & Armfield's jail in 1836, wrote that it reminded him "of the penitentiary" in Washington, with its "apparatus of high walls, and bolts, and bars, to secure the prisoners." He learned that the slaves were even "chained at night... lest they should overpower their masters." The only difference between the slaves and the convicts at the penitentiary, Andrews claimed, was that "the situation of the convicts was far less deplorable than that of these slaves, confined for the crime of being descended from ancestors who were forcibly reduced to bondage."[11]

Slave pens not only physically resembled penitentiaries, but they also functioned in much the same way, with particular emphasis placed on the threat or application of overwhelming force to curb resistance and misbehavior. One Washington dealer confided to Swedish traveler Fredrika Bremer in 1854 that the way to maintain order in the pens was to threaten migrants with the whip: "they would be unruly enough if they were not afraid of a flogging," he claimed. Holding chambers also resembled penitentiaries in the sense that "inmates" experienced extreme confinement and isolation from the outside world, were lodged in rude and dark cells, and were fed inferior victuals. References to

[11] *The Cleveland Herald*, Apr. 14, 1849 (first quotes); E.S. Abdy, *Journal of a Residence and Tour in the United States of North America, from April 1833 to October 1834* (1835; New York: Negro University Press, 1969), 2:96–97 (second quote), 179 (third quote); Ethan Allen Andrews, *Slavery and the Domestic Slave-Trade in the United States in a Series of Letters Addressed to the Executive Committee of the American Union for the Relief and Improvement of the Colored Race* (Boston: Light & Stearns, 1836), 141–43 (fourth quotes). The walls surrounding one New Orleans slave pen were reportedly so high that they could "keep out the wind." See Johnson, *Soul by Soul*, 2–3.

traders' pens in slave testimonies from both before and after emancipation illuminate bondspeople's feelings of imprisonment, powerlessness, and anger. "The jail was one of the most disagreeable places I ever was confined in," recalled Kentucky slave Henry Bibb in 1849. The pen where he and his family were held was filthy – "there were bed-bugs, fleas, lice and musquitoes in abundance" – and the slaves had to sleep on the floor because there were no beds. He also complained that the "food was very scanty, and of the most inferior quality. No gentlemen's dog would eat what we were compelled to eat." Bethany Veney, a former Virginia bondswoman who recorded her memories of slavery in 1889, lamented that when she arrived in Richmond to be sold as a young woman, she was "shut up in jail, all around which was a very high fence, so high that no communication with the outside world was possible." Like a prisoner, she was confined inside this holding chamber until she was put up at auction the next day. Solomon Northup, a free black man from New York who was kidnapped in Washington in 1841 and thrown into a slave pen to await deportation to the Deep South, recalled that the jail in which he was held had windows with "great iron bars," an "iron-bound door" leading to dark cells, and an internal courtyard that was invisible from the street and "surrounded by a brick wall ten or twelve feet high." "It was like a farmer's barnyard in most respects," Northup claimed, "save it was so constructed that the outside world could never see the human cattle that were herded there."[12]

For women, slave pens constituted not only sites of dehumanization but also sexual exploitation. Several scholars have noted that sexual abuse of slave women occurred frequently in slave markets throughout the South. Visitors to the southern states also regularly commented on such practices – indeed, their testimonies of prostitution and rape strengthened abolitionists' arguments regarding the immorality and atrocities of the domestic slave trade. One northern minister was appalled to find that in the "slave-brokers' offices" at New Orleans, "whole barracoons of beautiful slave-women are... kept in any quantity, to let to gentlemen for sleeping companions." Another sojourner was horrified to hear that in Washington slave pens, "good-looking mulatto girls in the gang" were sometimes prostituted by "the traffickers in this horrid business."[13]

[12] Fredrika Bremer, *The Homes of the New World: Impressions of America* (New York: Harper & Bros., 1858), 1:493 (first quote); Bibb, *Narrative*, 91 (second quote); Bethany Veney, *The Narrative of Bethany Veney, a Slave Woman* (Worcester, Mass.: n.p., 1889), 29 (third quote); Solomon Northup, *Twelve Years a Slave: Narrative of Solomon Northup, a Citizen of New York, Kidnapped in Washington City in 1841, and Rescued in 1853, From a Cotton Plantation Near the Red River, in Louisiana* (London: Sampson Low, Son & Co., 1853), 41–42 (fourth quotes).

[13] E. Baptist, "'Cuffy,' 'Fancy Maids', and 'One-Eyed Men': Rape, Commodification, and the Domestic Slave Trade in the United States," *The American Historical Review* 106 (Dec. 2001): 1619–50; Schermerhorn, *Money over Mastery*, 110–11; Deyle, *Carry Me Back*, 126–27; Tower, *Slavery Unmasked*, 316 (fist quote); Abdy, *Journal of a Residence*, 100 (second quote).

When slave pens or jails were full or of inadequate size to accommodate the number of slaves being sold, crude alternative holding chambers were devised that underscored the chattel nature of the merchandise on hand. Savannah's prime slave broker Joseph Bryan, for example, held a gang of 140 slaves "at Laroche's Brickyard, one mile east of the city" in 1859, advising interested purchasers "who have money to invest in that species of property" to call upon him there. Bryan also organized and executed the famous sale of Georgia planter Pierce Butler's 436 slaves that same year, the largest sale of a single lot of slaves to take place in the antebellum South. According to one newspaper reporter who attended the widely publicized event, no depot in Savannah was anywhere near large enough to house over four hundred people, so the slaves were marched three miles outside of town "to the Race Course, and there quartered in sheds erected for the accommodation of the horses and carriages of gentlemen attending the races." Literally crammed into horse stables, the migrants were observed "huddled together on the floor, there being no sign of a bench or table," and they were forced to eat and sleep on bare boards. The reporter further noted: "On the faces of all was an expression of heavy grief; some appeared to be resigned to the hard stroke of Fortune that had torn them from their homes, and were sadly trying to make the best of it; some sat brooding moodily over their sorrows, their chins resting on their hands, their eyes staring vacantly, and their bodies rocking to and fro." Interestingly, he observed, "few wept," because "the place was too public and the drivers too near."[14]

Butler's slaves were at least "quartered" together with friends and family members who could console them while they awaited sale and removal, but most migrants who were transferred through formal channels were sold individually and crammed among strangers into relatively small spaces. Even for slaves who were initially total strangers to one another, however, social isolation was nearly impossible under such circumstances. Besides sober holding chambers where dealers confined slaves until they could be deported or sold, slave pens also constituted sites of contact for slave migrants from the surrounding areas in which the pens were located. Enslaved people sent to traders' yards inevitably found themselves surrounded by fellow bondspeople who were going through the same ordeal that they were, who had also been forcibly removed from their homes and who awaited an unknown fate. The fact that they usually came from the same general region and shared a common culture, moreover, facilitated feelings of connectedness. One Virginia slave, who was sold to Alabama as a young man but later fled north, expressed a common sentiment when he told interviewer James Pennington in 1861 that

[14] Bancroft, *Slave-Trading*, 223–36, 224 (first quote). Report of the sale of Butler's slaves originally written by Mortimer Thomson and published in the *New York Tribune*, Mar. 9, 1859 (second quote). Later reprinted under the title: *Great Auction Sale of Slaves*. See also Deyle, *Carry Me Back*, 142–43.

when he was initially thrown into a Richmond "Trader's Gaol," he found himself strongly indentifying with his fellow inmates, whose suffering "made a deep impression" on him. Talking with the other slaves about where they were from and how they had fallen into their current predicament even helped the enslaved man to endure confinement: "My attention was diverted from myself by sympathy with others," he recalled. Indeed, the stress and anxiety shared by fellow migrants caused many to bond together in ways that psychologically alleviated their suffering or even sparked a glimmer of hope in the future, whatever it may bring. Benjamin Holmes, a slave who found himself thrown into a slave pen in Charleston at the start of the Civil War, claimed in an interview in 1872 that the prisoners joined together in regular prayer meetings. "One old man," Holmes remembered, "held a prayer meeting right there in the mart," in full view of both traders and customers. Former slave William Robinson, originally from North Carolina, recalled secretly visiting his father in a slave pen early one morning and finding the inmates all singing. "Some religious songs, such as 'God has delivered Daniel,' and other melodies, while others were singing the songs of the world," Robinson claimed. The migrants were all "seemingly rejoicing in their own way. Some were rejoicing because they were sold, hoping to fall into the hands of better masters, while others were rejoicing because of the hope of meeting their mother, father or child" who had already been sold before them.[15]

However squalid bondspeople found the jails in which they were confined, their dealers had a keen interest in keeping their human merchandise presentable whenever potential purchasers came around. Dejected and morose specimens hardly stood a chance of being sold quickly, so traders instructed their employees to make their prisoners presentable for interested customers. Frequently, this included lifting slaves' morale, or at least trying to do so when customers walked in. When E.S. Abdy visited a Virginia slave pen in 1834, he learned that the owner did everything he could to keep the slaves "in good humor" because "a 'sulky one' is not likely to find a buyer." Another visitor to a slave pen in Washington claimed that when he arrived, the slave boys were all lined up for inspection, but thereafter they were encouraged to play marbles, "apparently as contented and happy as so many schoolboys." Ethan Allen Andrews, who was openly opposed to the domestic slave trade, was initially surprised to encounter a group of "cheerful and contented" slaves at Franklin & Armfield's slave pen in Alexandria, Virginia. Some were "amusing themselves with rude sports, and others engaged in conversation, which

[15] Steven Greenblatt, et al, eds., *Cultural Mobility: A Manifesto* (New York: Cambridge University Press, 2009), 250–51; Johnson, *Soul by Soul*, 68–69; Pennington, *Life of J.H. Banks*, 47 (first quote); Benjamin Holmes, in John W. Blassingame, ed., *Slave Testimony: Two Centuries of Letters, Speeches, Interviews, and Autobiographies* (Baton Rouge: Louisiana State University Press, 1977), 618 (second quote); William H. Robinson, *From Log Cabin to the Pulpit, or, Fifteen Years in Slavery* (Eau Claire, Wisc.: James H. Tifft, 1913), 23–24 (third quote).

was often interrupted by loud laughter." He quickly learned, however, that this theatrical spectacle had been orchestrated by the traders themselves to impress him. An employee of the establishment explained to Andrews that these particular slaves were happier in the slave pen than they had been on their home plantations, "a discourse apparently intended for the joint benefit of the slaves and their northern visitor." But one of the young men in the trader's yard "looked earnestly" at Andrews and "shook his head," seemingly "desirous of having me understand, that he did not feel any such happiness as was described, and that he dissented from the representation made of his condition." For slave migrants throughout the South, being for sale entailed putting on a show for interested buyers. Historians have argued that migrants in slave pens experienced a "double consciousness": an externally fashioned outward self presented to white customers and an inward self often kept hidden from the white population.[16]

Even more important than their morale, dealers in human chattels made sure that slaves' bodies were made presentable to purchasers while awaiting sale in the pens. Walter Johnson has convincingly argued that this entailed a process of racialization: the selling qualities of black bodies were "marked" and hawked to potential buyers, who were less interested in how new slaves would fit into their extended households – as their paternalist ideology claimed – than they were in how new slaves would fit into their account books. Slaves' physical appearances – their youth, strength, and perceived "breeding" qualities – were *the* factors that determined their salability. More than anything else, white southerners looking to buy slaves asked for "likely negroes," by which they meant attractive, polite, healthy bondspeople who would provide a welcome addition to their work forces. A slave in the market, in other words, had to catch a purchaser's eye, and traders knew it. They greased slaves' skin and dyed their hair. The practice of adorning slave merchandise in attractive apparel was frequently commented on by both travelers and forced migrants alike. Joseph Ingraham, a northerner who visited a Natchez slave market in the 1830s, encountered a group of forty local slaves, each "dressed in the usual uniform of slaves, when in market, consisting of a fashionably shaped, black fur hat, roundabout and trowsers of coarse corduroy velvet." He further observed that "good vests, strong shoes, and white cotton shirts, complemented their equipment." Lined up for inspection, the slaves "stood perfectly still, and in close order, while some gentlemen were passing from one to another examining for the purpose of buying." Bethany Veney claimed that the day after she arrived at a Richmond jail, some hours before her auction was to commence, the dealer sent her and two other slaves to a nearby dressmaker with instructions to "fix us up fine." She was attired with a "white muslin apron" and a "large cape" with

[16] Johnson, *Soul by Soul*, 6–7, 163–64; Abdy, *Journal of a Residence*, 180 (first quote); *The Cleveland Herald*, Apr. 14, 1849 (second quote); Andrews, *Slavery and the Domestic Slave-Trade*, 137–38 (third quote).

bows on the shoulders and forwarded to the auction site. Virginia slave Louis Hughes also remembered that "it was expected that all the slaves in the yard for sale would be neatly dressed and clean before being brought into the show-room," it being "the foreman's business to see that each one was presentable." Whenever a potential customer arrived, the slave men were lined up on one side of the room and the women on the other, and the interested person "passed up and down between the lines," inspecting their bodies and questioning them about their work experience. "Sometimes," Hughes recalled, "the slave would be required to open his mouth that the purchaser might examine the teeth," an inspection intended to judge the slave's "physical soundness."[17]

III.

Slaves who did not sell from the jails or pens in which they were confined were often made to endure the auction block – the "most outrageous, most abominable, most heart-rending, and most anti-human [scene] that a civilized man can look upon," according to one New England visitor to New Orleans – from which they were publicly bartered to new masters, dealers, or employers. Indeed, many local slaves who were sent to urban marketplaces to be transferred to new owners or employers were spared the slave pen altogether and immediately auctioned off on the same day that they arrived, while some who were transferred during estate auctions were "cried off" right on their home plantations. As discussed in Chapter 2, the auction block provided many migrants with a last-ditch opportunity to exert agency over the nature of their removal. Numerous slaves attempted to get sold along with family members, for example, sometimes successfully. Others "spoke up," openly expressing their desire to be sold within a certain region or to specific bidders. Adam Hodgson observed a "sale of human flesh" in Charleston in 1820, during which a "poor woman" stepped onto the platform with her small children and attempted to negotiate the terms of her sale. She "spoke a few words in a faltering voice to the auctioneer, who repeated them aloud, in which she expressed a strong desire to be purchased by some one who lived near Charleston, instead of being sent to a distant plantation." With even less to lose, hirelings who were transferred via the auction block had a reputation for speaking up in an attempt to avoid being hired to potentially bad employers. Nancy Williams, a Virginia ex-slave who was hired out in Norfolk, recalled to interviewers of the Virginia Writers' Project that while on the stand, she once made a vain attempt to avoid being hired out to a dreaded poor white man. "When dey put me on de block to 'cry

17 Walter Johnson has argued that "at no site was race more readily given daily shape than in the slave market." See Johnson, *Soul by Soul*, 136–61; Gudmestad, *A Troublesome Commerce*, 96; Joseph Holt Ingraham, *The South-West. By a Yankee* (New York: Harper & Bros., 1835), 2:193 (first quote); Veney, *Narrative*, 29–30 (second quote); Lewis Hughes, *Thirty Years a Slave: From Bondage to Freedom* (Milwaukee: South Side Printing Co., 1893), 7–9 (third quotes).

me off', all de po' white bacy-chewin' devils [were] stanin' 'roun waitin' to get me," she claimed. "Den I yells out loud's I could, 'I don' wan no po' white man git me! Ain' wanna wuk for no po' white man!' As de devil would have it, one got me." Ben, an ex-slave from Alabama who was regularly hired out by his master, confirmed that such negotiations from the stand were common during hiring auctions but claimed that they seldom had the desired effect. He related to an interviewer that "ef yer didn't want to go to the man that bid for yer they'd tell yer to talk an' say so, but it done make no difference. He'd hire yer, jes' the same."[18]

Some slaves even appeared slightly amused while on the stand. A British journalist from the *Illustrated London News*, who attended a slave auction in Richmond in 1861, observed how one slave walked straight through the crowd and "put himself in a most dignified attitude" as he mounted the platform, while another "seemed in no way to feel pain at being sold, but endeavoured to make himself out as fine a fellow as possible," even grinning as a customer opened his mouth and inspected his body. Such behavior – and there are countless examples – suggests that many migrants attempted to assert a sense of human dignity during the humiliating experience of public sale. Standing up straight and appearing cheerful as their bodies were bid upon and inspected by customers may have also constituted a carefully calculated strategy to make themselves as presentable as possible, hopefully attracting only the best purchasers. L.M. Mills, a Missouri slave who was once sold at a St. Louis auction house, claimed to an interviewer in 1892 that even though "they made us strip and examined us for broken bones and deformities" and "opened our mouths and looked at our teeth, just as a horse buyer does," slaves had to remain polite and positive, for "when a negro was put on the block he had to help sell himself."[19]

[18] Philo Tower, *Slavery Unmasked: Being a Truthful Narrative of a Three Years' Residence and Journeying in Eleven Southern States* (1856; New York: Negro University Press, 1969), 306–307 (first quote); Adam Hodgson, *Remarks During a Journey through North America in the Years 1819, 1820, and 1821, in a Series of Letters* (1823; Westport, Conn.: Negro University Press, 1970), 125 (second quote); Nancy Williams, in Perdue, et al, eds., *Weevils in the Wheat*, 318 (third quote); Blassingame, ed., *Slave Testimony*, 535 (fourth quote); Martin, *Divided Mastery*, 48–49. One woman who was put up at auction in St. Louis – while pregnant – even claimed in an 1892 interview to have bitten the hand of a customer while he attempted to inspect her teeth, upon which she was severely beaten and miscarried. See Blassingame, ed., *Slave Testimony*, 507.

[19] *The Illustrated London News*, Feb. 16, 1861 (first quotes); L.M. Mills, in Blassingame, ed., *Slave Testimony*, 502–503 (second quote). For other instances of slaves appearing slightly amused or proud to white visitors while on the stand, see, for example, Olmsted, *Seaboard Slave States*, 37; John Wise, in Katherine M. Jones, ed., *The Plantation South* (Indianapolis: Bobbs-Merrill Co., 1957), 73; Tower, *Slavery Unmasked*, 309; Hall, *Travels in North America*, 3:144–45. Francis Pulszky also noted during a visit to a slave market in New Orleans that slaves attempted to help sell themselves. One girl, who mistook him for a buyer, "seemed to like my countenance, and did her best to please me," assuring him that she could do "a little of everything." See Pulszky, *White, Red, Black*, 100.

Others simply attempted to hide their emotions while on the stand, however, refusing to speak up and appearing virtually expressionless to observers as their bodies went under the hammer. Peter Randolph, a Virginia slave, declared after emancipation that while slaves on the auction block were being "handled and examined like any piece of merchandise," it was of little use but to simply "bear it." Historians such as Walter Johnson have argued that expressions of apparent indifference while on the stand may have been a sign that slaves were suffering from shock or even "psychic death," a mental breakdown that diminished their will to resist or negotiate the terms of their transfer. Northern and European visitors were often baffled by such scenes. One attendant to a Virginia slave auction in 1853, for example, reported "an entire absence of emotion" among the slaves on the stand, adding that "none [of the slaves] showed any signs of resistance; nor did any one utter a word. Their manner was that of perfect humility and resignation." Northern traveler Philo Tower attended a slave auction at New Orleans during which a young man on the block was physically probed and examined like an animal, but curiously "bore it with silent patience." Francis and Theresa Pulszky, who traveled through the South in the early 1850s, witnessed a local slave auction at New Orleans in which "the slaves looked very sullen" but remained absolutely silent and made no attempts to negotiate their sale. Accepting their fate, all of these migrants attempted to turn off their emotions and stoically weather the storm of forced removal.[20]

Countless slave migrants who were removed through formal traders, dealers, and auctioneers were thus made to endure this first transitional phase in their forced migration, as their bodies were sent to urban markets to be transferred to new owners or employers. Enslaved people who were collected by passing coffles already in transit or forced to leave their homes through less formal means (e.g., through private transactions or removal with their masters), however, were usually spared the holding chambers and auction blocks so dreaded by slave migrants throughout the South. Even slaves who were sold in private transactions, however, were often forced to endure a humiliating inspection of their bodies. In a case fairly typical for the South, one Kentucky man whose father sold a slave privately from his own house described that the purchaser, one Dickerson, "went into my Kitchen with my father who told him there was the girl, to examine her . . . and told the girl to pull off her stocking[.] Dickerson told her to get up and walk first, and she walked across the floor and he the [said] Dickerson observed she did not limp," after which a deal for $600 was hastily struck. Such ordeals were surely tense and embarrassing, but

20 Peter Randolph, *From Slave Cabin to the Pulpit. The Autobiography of Rev. Peter Randolph: The Southern Question Illustrated and Sketches of Slave Life* (Boston: James H. Earle, 1893), 184 (first quote); Johnson, *Soul by Soul*, 64; W.C., quoted in Olmsted, *Seaboard Slave States*, 35, 37 (second quotes); Tower, *Slavery Unmasked*, 309 (third quote); Francis and Theresa Pulszky, *White, Red, Black* (1853; New York: Johnson Reprint Co., 1970), 96 (fourth quote).

at least these slaves, along with those who removed with their masters, were not subjected to dank holding chambers and chaotic auction platforms. For them, the first real phase of the migration process entailed the journey itself, an experience that constituted the second phase for many of their counterparts.[21]

IV.

Timothy Flint, a Presbyterian missionary, witnessed a "pleasing and patriarchal scene" of masters and slaves moving west to Mississippi, in which he believed to denote a "delight in [the slaves'] countenances, for their labours are suspended and their imagination excited." He was even convinced that the slaves were "quite as much delighted and interested in the immigration, as the master." Although his optimism surely tended toward exaggeration, it must be noted that many testimonies of slaves who emigrated west with their masters are indeed full of excited descriptions of travel, landscapes, and cityscapes. Most slave migrants had seldom, if ever, been permitted to travel more than a few miles from their home plantations, and a vast journey across the continent naturally subjected them to new sights, sounds, and experiences. As bondspeople's horizons were broadened, their sense of place – indeed their understanding of the South as a geographical and cultural region – became radically transformed, arousing wonder and a sense of adventure among some migrants. To make sense of such excitement, however, historians must be careful to consider the personal circumstances of slaves who were moved by their masters. Certainly not all bondspeople experienced westward migration with "delight," and indeed general perceptions of interstate moves appear to have differed markedly among age cohorts. A perusal of slave testimonies, for example, suggests that those most excited about traveling west into the unknown were children and adolescents, who perhaps did not fully understand the long-term consequences of forced removal for their extended families and communities and for whom the novelty of long-distance migration doubtless overshadowed any painful thoughts about leaving home.[22]

"I shall never forget the great preparations made for our start to the West," recalled former slave Henry Bruce in his 1895 autobiography. Bruce's master moved his entire slave force from Virginia to Missouri when Bruce was a young boy. Three wagons were filled to capacity for the journey, and from the very start, Bruce admitted, his attention was focused almost exclusively on the trip itself and on the completely foreign scenery to which his young eyes were exposed. "I remember that I was delighted with the beautiful sceneries, towns,

[21] "Henry Dickerson to the Circuit Court, Barren County, Kentucky, 1821," in Loren Schweninger, ed., *The Southern Debate over Slavery: Volume 2, Petitions to Southern County Courts, 1775–1867* (Urbana: University of Illinois Press, 2008), 111 (quote).

[22] Timothy Flint, in Diane Mutti Burke, *On Slavery's Border: Missouri's Small-Slaveholding Households, 1815–1865* (Athens: University of Georgia Press, 2010), 27 (quote). See also William Greenleaf Eliot, *The Story of Archer Alexander: From Slavery to Freedom, March 30 1863* (Boston: Cupples, Upham, & Co., 1885), 32–34.

rivers, people in their different styles of costumes, and so many strange things that I saw on that trip from our old home to Louisville," he related. "But the most wonderful experience to me was, when we took a steamer at Louisville for St. Louis. The idea of a house floating on the water was a new one to me." Arrival in Missouri was equally fascinating to Bruce, as he was introduced to a frontier society that appeared far different from his native Virginia. "[F]inally we reached our destination . . . about June or July, 1844 . . . about seven or eight miles from Keytesville, Missouri," he remembered. "At that time the country was sparsely settled; a farm house could be only seen in every eight or ten miles. I was greatly pleased with the country, for there was plenty of everything to live on, game, fish, wild fruits, and berries." Bruce's innocent excitement and expressions of wonder about traveling to new lands were common among young interstate migrants who moved west with their masters. Unable to fully appreciate the difficulties that lay ahead or to pine for extended family left behind, the slave boy experienced the journey to his new home in the West as an adventure rather than a traumatic experience.[23]

Even slaves who were old enough to understand the gravity of permanent separation from family and friends often reported curiosity and fascination with the new landscapes and regions through which they passed en route to the frontier. Francis Fedric, a Virginia slave whose master moved all of his bondspeople west to Kentucky when Fedric was fourteen years old, had few good words to say about the long-term consequences of interstate removal when he dictated his experiences in bondage in 1863. Many of the slaves on his plantation had been married to slaves from other plantations, and all of these cross-plantation families were separated when Fedric's master departed "with several wagons and a sorrowful cavalcade on our way to Kentucky." Yet despite the "heart-rendering" separations that loomed over the slave migrants as they left Virginia, Fedric admitted being struck by feelings of "amazement and wonder" when passing over the Allegheny Mountains, which he had never seen before. Traveling through "what appeared to be a long, winding valley," he found himself often gazing up at the "huge, blue-looking rocks" that rested precariously on ledges up the steep sides of the mountains, and the "torrents of water, arising from the ice and melting snow, [that] were rushing down in hundreds of directions." Every "now and then," his attention was distracted "by immense droves of pigs, which are bred in Kentucky" and were driven to markets along the very roads that Fedric's party traveled. The completely new scenery to which Fedric was exposed during his journey west introduced him to the vast scale and frontier character of southern Appalachia, a region he had hitherto known nothing about.[24]

[23] Henry Clay Bruce, *The New Man: Twenty-Nine Years a Slave, Twenty-Nine Years a Free Man* (York, Pa.: P. Anstadt & Sons, 1895), 16–17 (quotes).

[24] Francis Fedric, *Slave Life in Virginia and Kentucky; or, Fifty Years of Slavery in the Southern States of America* (London: Wertheim, MacIntosh, and Hunt, 1863), 14–16 (quotes).

Unlike Bruce, however, Fedric also remembered the move west as a trying experience, both because of the "hard and wild" landscape – with its "screaming" black birds, "howling... wolves, and other wild animals" – and the anxiety expressed by his master and overseers as they traveled into the densely forested frontier, which added to the party's stress and fatigue. Journeys into the frontier were full of danger and hardship, and Fedric's master appeared to be especially fearful of resistance among his slaves. "Two or three times during the night, when we were encamped and fast asleep," he recalled, "one of the overseers would call our names over, every one being obliged to wake up and answer." Compounding the slaves' frequent lack of sleep was a lack of adequate food, the bondspeople subsisting on little more than cakes made of "Indian meal on griddles... together with salt herrings." Finally arriving in Mason County, where Fedric's master had bought a farm, the slaves were confronted with a scene similar to Bruce's descriptions of "sparsely settled" Missouri, save for their dreadful realization that they were going to have to carve a plantation out of the wilderness by the sweat of their brows. "When we arrived... we found a great deal of uncultivated land belonging to the farm," Fedric recollected, all of which would have to be transformed into a proper agricultural enterprise in the months and years to come.[25]

Genovese and Fox-Genovese recently claimed that the trying nature of frontier conditions served to bring slaves and slaveholders closer together, solidifying southern paternalism and in the process strengthening master–slave relations. In reality, however, arrival at remote destinations in the southern interior often served to pit slaves against their masters even more. Indeed, slaves who migrated west with their masters were often struck by the unsettled, wild, and "poor" appearance of the territories to which they were forced to move. Many pioneer slaves who were removed to the frontier "found nothing in place but some surveyor's markers," as historian Ira Berlin aptly put it. Susan O'Donovan has suggested that "the scene that greeted [young migrants] when they arrived at their new homes could hardly have filled them with hope." As academic proponents of standpoint theory have argued, masters and slaves perceived different geographies in the antebellum South, and although white slaveholders viewed wild tracts of land in the southern frontier as virgin dreamscapes of financial opportunity, slaves often perceived them as daunting projects that promised little more than drudgery and primitive living conditions for years on end. "This country was wild," recalled former bondswoman Josephine Barnett, whose master emigrated with his slaves from Tennessee to Arkansas before the Civil War. "It was different from Tennessee... where we come from. None of the slaves liked it but they was brought." Elizabeth Keckley, whose master moved west from Virginia to Missouri and later sent for his family and slaves to come and join him, was dispirited by the poor look of her master's new plantation when she arrived. Recalling the move in 1868, she claimed that

[25] Fedric, *Slave Life*, 15–17 (quotes).

when she and her fellow bondspeople "joined him in his new home on the banks of the Mississippi, we found him so poor that he was unable to pay the dues on a letter advertised as in the post-office for him." One slaveholder's daughter, whose father took his family and slaves from Virginia to a new plantation in Mississippi in 1835, admitted that arrival at their remote new home, which was tens of miles from the nearest town, brought "many difficulties" and was no joyous occasion for the slaves. "One of the first [problems] was the unavoidable delay in getting supplies of meat for the servants. For two weeks after their arrival they had none." William Nuttall, a young southerner whose father dragged his slaves from Virginia to Florida in 1828, conceded in a letter to his brother that the slaves hated their new home. "If Father had have known the discontent of the negroes, he certainly would have had them brought back."[26]

Like Fedric, most adult slaves who migrated across state lines with their masters found the arduous journey through the South above all an exhausting and even traumatic experience. They grieved over separations from family and friends as they traveled farther and farther from their old homes, but they also suffered from the tensions and hardships involved in the trek itself, a situation exacerbated by their nervous and impatient masters. While anchored in Cincinnati en route to the Deep South in 1809, for example, Leonard Covington, a Maryland slaveholder who dragged thirty-six of his slaves to a new cotton plantation in Mississippi, seethed with frustration about the journey as he dashed off a hastily written letter to his brother, who was waiting for him in Mississippi. Covington complained that the river voyage from Wheeling had been "most tedious, difficult and laborious," adding that "to drag through shoals, sandbars and ripples is my dreaded fate." The boat upon which he and

[26] Eugene Genovese and Elizabeth Fox-Genovese, *Fatal Self-Deception: Slaveholding Paternalism in the Old South* (New York: Cambridge University Press, 2011), 1; Clifton Ellis and Rebecca Ginsburg argued in a recent study that "enslaved Africans and elite whites literally viewed the world differently and... these differences influenced the way they inhabited shared environments." See Clifton Ellis and Rebecca Ginsburg, eds., *Cabin, Quarter, Plantation: Architecture and Landscapes of North American Slavery* (New Haven: Yale University Press, 2010), 6. Ironically, white mistresses often expressed similarly disappointed first impressions of their new homes in the frontier as their slaves. One Virginia mistress whose husband dragged her and their slaves to Missouri in 1855 reported in her diary upon arrival that her new home "looked so lonesome and desolate I cryed like a child for sometime." Burke, *On Slavery's Border*, 18; Ira Berlin, *Generations of Captivity: A History of African-American Slaves* (Cambridge, Mass.: Harvard University Press, 2003), 174 (first quote); Susan O'Donovan, *Becoming Free in the Cotton South* (Cambridge, Mass: Harvard University Press, 2007), 21 (second quote); Josephine Ann Barnett, in Slave Narratives of the Federal Writers' Project, 1936–1938 (typescript), vol. II, pt. 1, 109–10 (third quote); Elizabeth Keckley, *Behind the Scenes, or, Thirty Years a Slave, and Four Years in the White House* (New York: G.W. Carleton & Co., 1868), 44 (fourth quote); Susan Dabney Smedes, in Katherine M. Jones, ed., *The Plantation South* (Indianapolis: Bobbs-Merrill Co., 1957), 275 (fifth quote); John David Smith, ed., *Florida Plantation Records from the Papers of George Noble Jones* (University Press of Florida, 2006), 28 (sixth quote).

his slaves traveled was so small that he had to limit himself in the way of provisions to only "a few hundred pounds of pork and a few bbls of flour." Assuring his brother that the entire party remained healthy thus far, Covington nevertheless hinted at his slaves' exhaustion when he beseeched his brother to "make some preparations for the wearied travellers" when they all arrived. Visitors to the South and slave migrants themselves recalled similar scenes. British traveler George Featherstonhaugh encountered "a great many families of planters emigrating to Alabama and Mississippi" during his journey through the South in 1844. The slaves, he found, "suffer[ed] very much in these expeditions," both from the rainy weather through which they were forced to trudge and because the wagons were continually breaking down. One Kentucky bondsman whose master moved his slaves to a new plantation in Mississippi recalled in 1861 that the journey south was especially trying because of his irritating mistress. His master had purchased a flatboat to row down the Ohio and Mississippi Rivers with, for the slaves an exhausting endeavor in and of itself, but their mistress added to the tension on board by flying into hysterics every time a steamboat passed, demanding that the slaves row harder, "as she was sure [the steamboats] would kill them." By the time the party reached Vicksburg, their mistress had died, but "for this event the slaves did not feel sorry, for she had treated them very meanly."[27]

V.

Slave migrants who were moved west by their masters at least had the advantage of traveling as a group consisting of friends and family members who had known each other all of their lives and whose sense of community no doubt alleviated some of the harsher aspects of travel. Group solidarity manifested itself in various ways, as slaves comforted one another, socialized at campsites, cooked for each other, and worked together to overcome countless obstacles en route to their new destinations, from fording streams to repairing wagon wheels. Indeed, this particular aspect of the migration experience set them apart

[27] Leonard Covington to Alexander Covington, Dec. 1, 1809, in Ulrich B. Phillips, ed., *Plantation and Frontier Documents: 1649–1863* (Cleveland: Arthur H. Clark Co., 1909), 2:216 (first quotes); G.W. Featherstonhaugh, *Excursion through the Slave States* (London: John Murray, 1844), 317 (second quote); Israel Campbell, *An Autobiography. Bond and Free: Or, Yearnings for Freedom, from My Green Briar House. Being the Story of My Life in Bondage, and My Life in Freedom* (Philadelphia: C.E.P. Brinkloe & Co., 1861), 32–33 (third quotes). For more on the westward journeys of migrant planters with their slaves, see, for example, Joan Cashin, *A Family Venture: Men and Women on the Southern Frontier* (Baltimore: Johns Hopkins University Press, 1991), 53–77; Edward E. Baptist, *Creating an Old South: Middle Florida's Plantation Frontier Before the Civil War* (Chapel Hill: University of North Carolina Press, 2001), 66–87; James David Miller, *South by Southwest: Planter Emigration and Identity in the Slave South* (Charlottesville: University of Virginia Press, 2002), 60–79; Richard S. Dunn, "Winney Grimshaw, a Virginia Slave, and Her Family," *Early American Studies: An Interdisciplinary Journal* 9 (Fall 2011): 512–13.

from the overwhelming majority of interstate migrants, who traveled into the southern interior with complete strangers. Slaves who moved with their masters usually solidified *existing* relationships during their journeys rather than build new ones. They tended to express sympathy for and even an abstract sense of unity with other slaves, such as those they found on the plantations they passed along the way, but little personal contact took place between migrants and strangers en route to new destinations.

Most interstate migrants, however, experienced the trek to new states very differently – their journey was characterized by *continual* contact with strangers. Separated from loved ones and even the faintest acquaintances, slaves who were "propelled across the continent" in what Ira Berlin has dubbed the "Second Middle Passage" – such as those transferred in the domestic slave trade or those who were bought and transported across state lines by new owners – were confronted with the daunting task of completely rebuilding social relationships that had been forcibly torn apart, a process that often began in the slave pens, as stated earlier, but truly accelerated during the journey itself.[28]

More than their counterparts who were moved west by their masters, migrants who were transferred by and with strangers appear to have felt a more pressing need to develop strong social ties en route because their migration experience was in many ways more stressful, traumatic, and dangerous. The transfer of human property across state lines in the domestic slave trade – "the most detestable feature in the system of slavery," according to abolitionists – especially subjected enslaved people to arduous travel conditions, as most were driven to markets not in small cavalcades and family groups, but, as one migrant put it, "in droves like horses an' cows," involving perilous overland journeys that could last months. Encountering a coffle that was just arriving in Mississippi after seven weeks of marching, one northerner found the "whole horde" in a disgraceful state, wearing dirty and tattered garments and moving with a "slow pace and fatigued air" that gave the "whole train a sad and funeral appearance." Not only were such journeys long and physically draining, but they were also led by dealers who had little interest in slaves' feelings, caring only to deliver their chattel to distant anonymous customers in the most convenient manner possible. Chains were frequently used to prevent escape and, by extension, loss of investment. Ethan Allen Andrews discovered that the policy of traders Franklin & Armfield was to march their slaves south "chained together in pairs, to prevent their escape; and sometimes, when greater precaution is judged necessary, they are all attached to a long chain passing between them." The guards and conductors, Andrews remarked, were, "of course, well armed." Another sojourner from England reported witnessing "a singular spectacle" while traveling through the South in 1834, namely a "camp of negro slave-drivers, just packing up to start; they had about three

[28] Berlin, *Generations of Captivity*, 161 (quotes), 173.

FIGURE 3.2. "Slave Trader, Sold to Tennessee," from *Sketchbook of Landscapes in the State of Virginia* by Lewis Miller, Virginia, ca. 1853, accession # 1978.301.1, image # 87–1004. Courtesy of The Abby Aldrich Rockefeller Folk Art Museum, The Colonial Williamsburg Foundation. Gift of Dr. and Mrs. Richard M. Kain in memory of George Hay Kain.

hundred slaves with them, who had bivouacked the preceding night *in chains* in the woods; these they were conducting to Natchez. . . . "[29]

Slaves transported by ship or riverboat endured a shorter but not necessarily less exhausting journey to southern markets. Often packed tightly together on board, they suffered from uncomfortable accommodations and lack of sleep, motion sickness, and disorientation. Captain Basil Hall likened a brig he saw

[29] Berlin, *Generations of Captivity*, 171–72; *Genius of Universal Emancipation*, vol. 1, no. 12 (1830): 187 (first quote); Catherine Beale, in Blassingame, ed., *Slave Testimony*, 575 (second quote); Ingraham, *South-West*, 2:234 (third quote); Gudmestad, *Troublesome Commerce*, 45 (fourth quote); Andrews, *Slavery and the Domestic Slave-Trade*, 143 (fifth quote); Featherstonhaugh, *Excursion*, 120 (sixth quote).

in New Orleans, with two hundred slaves on board, to an Atlantic slave ship he had seen docked at Rio de Janeiro. Northern traveler Joseph Holt Ingraham sarcastically wrote that slaves from Virginia were frequently "shipped for New-Orleans, with as comfortable accommodations as can be expected, where one or two hundred are congregated in a single merchant vessel." One Kentucky slave confirmed that the bondspeople on board the ship that transported him from Louisville to New Orleans "got very little rest at night," the reason being that "all were chained together night and day, [and] it was impossible to sleep, being annoyed by the bustle and crowd of passengers on board, [and] by the terrible thought that we were destined to be sold in market as sheep or oxen.... " Another former slave who was shipped from the Upper South to Mobile, Alabama, and from there to New Orleans and finally Texas before being sold, claimed that she was on the ship "for weeks an' days. It were dark an' I were feared an' homesick an' seasick." Travel by ship could also be dangerous for interstate migrants. Ship manifests from New Orleans reveal plenty of cases of human cargo dying in transit. Jesse Botts, a twenty-five-old slave shipped from Virginia in 1833 was "not on board [and] said to be dead" when the ship reached Louisiana. Another "negro boy Henry died on the passage," as did several others. In June 1835, one schooner that transported slaves along the Ohio and Mississippi Rivers suffered such losses because of a cholera outbreak that the captain refused to depart Virginia until the epidemic had passed, to the frustration of dealers and southern purchasers.[30]

Bound, marched or shipped like cattle, forced to endure uncomfortable and often sleepless nights for weeks on end, *and* subjected to social deaths through separation from loved ones, most victims of the domestic slave trade traveled under conditions that were infinitely worse than those experienced by slaves who moved west with their masters. One result of the physically and emotionally grueling nature of their journey was that they often came to identify with their fellow bondspeople in transit despite starting out as total strangers

[30] Hall, *Travels in North America*, 190; Ingraham, *South-West*, 2:234 (first quote); Ceceil George, in Clayton, ed., *Mother Wit*, 83–84; Bibb, *Narrative*, 99 (second quote); Blassingame, ed., *Slave Testimony*, 536 (third quote); Wendell Holmes Stephenson, *Isaac Franklin: Slave Trader and Planter of the Old South* (Gloucester, Mass., 1968), 40–41 (fourth quote); David O. Whitten, "Slave Buying in 1835 Virginia as Revealed by Letters of a Louisiana Negro Sugar Planter," *Louisiana History* 11 (summer 1970): 238–39. Charles Lyell reported a case in which nine migrants were killed in a steamboat collision between St. Louis and Natchez in 1849. See Lyle, *Second Visit*, 2:126. Former slave William Anderson witnessed a similar accident in which a "gang of colored men" who were "chained together" on board a steamship were "drowned in the hull of the boat." Their wails were "horrifying and frightful in the extreme." See William J. Anderson, *Life and Narrative of William J. Anderson, Twenty-Four Years a Slave* (Chicago: Daily Tribune Book and Job Printing Office, 1857), 13. Robert Gudmestad writes that the infamous trader Isaac Franklin was once forced to secretly bury five slaves who had died on the steamboat from New Orleans to Natchez in a washed-out ravine, a job that he botched, the rains washing away the earth to "reveal a grisly scene." See Gudmestad, *A Troublesome Commerce*, 93.

to one another. As Walter Johnson has argued, this was a slow and subtle development, as slaves "set about the task of estimating one another" before allowing themselves to identify with or place their trust in other bondspeople. According to him, "the community of slaves in the trade had to be carefully built," a claim amply supported by slave testimonies. The narrative of John Brown, a Virginia slave who escaped slavery and dictated his experiences to British editor Louis Chamerovzow in 1855, provides an illuminating example of how this process worked in practice. Brown found himself abruptly sold to a passing trader one day, a man by the name of Finney who was en route to Georgia with a cargo of slaves. As he was torn away from his mother and led out to the road that passed in front of his plantation, he encountered a long coffle of slave migrants, "some of whom were hand-cuffed two and two, and fastened to a long chain running between the two ranks." He noted that "there were also a good many women and children, but none of these were chained," adding that he "soon learnt that they had been purchased in different places, and were for the most part strangers to one another and to the negroes in the coffle." Perceiving no means of escape, Brown "fell into the rank" as the gang "set off on our journey to Georgia." Interestingly, the former slave did not go into detail about landscapes or scenery, noting only that they "crossed the Roanoke river by ferry," but that he did "not recollect the names of all the places we passed through." He recounted only two incidents on the road, both of which highlighted the suffering of his fellow slave migrants. First, Brown recalled, a woman who had been purchased along the way, and who had expressed intense "anguish" about leaving home, died "in the night, whilst we were encamped in the woods." He claimed that "we set off in the morning, leaving her body there." The other incident was the kidnapping of an attractive young slave girl, who was added to the gang but "forced to get up in the wagon with Finney." The slave trader allegedly "ill-used her, and permitted his companions to treat her in the same manner." Brown claimed that "our women talked about this very much, and many of them cried, and said it was a great shame."[31]

Both incidents made a deep impression on Brown, and both caused him to identify with the other migrants in his coffle. He clearly felt sympathy for the woman who passed away in transit, underscoring in his testimony her feelings of grief in the days before she died, and implying a sense of guilt about leaving her body behind. His description of the rape of the slave girl revealed his identification with the other migrants even more explicitly, as Brown claimed that "*our* women" – suggesting a broad identification with the women in his coffle, all of whom had started out as strangers to one another and to him – discussed the incident frequently and denounced the abuse of a fellow bondswoman.

[31] Johnson, *Soul by Soul*, 64 (first quote), 67 (second quote); John Brown, *Slave Life in Georgia: A Narrative of the Life, Sufferings, and Escape of John Brown* (London: L.A. Chamerovzow, 1855), 16–19 (third quotes).

Brown's testimony underscores the fact that female migrants in transit were often subjected to different experiences than their male counterparts – they were not always chained, for example, and were moreover extremely vulnerable to sexual abuse at the hands of traders. But Brown's expressions of sympathy and feelings of attachment to the women in his coffle also suggest that social bonding among slave migrants in transit was *not* always segregated by sex, as some historians have argued, and indeed, this appears to have been the rule rather than the exception. North Carolina slave William Robinson, for example, who was marched off in a coffle as a young man, also recalled feeling sympathy for another migrant named Fannie Woods, who joined Robinson's coffle with her two children in tow, an eight-year-old boy and a baby at her breast. When Fannie's son proved to be a hindrance because he could not keep up, the slave trader became frustrated and "sold the little boy...to a man along the way," later selling her baby away from her as well. Fannie's "wails" and the "mourning of the other slaves on account of her sorrow" not only made a deep impression on Robinson but also served to forge bonds between the slaves in the coffle, who collectively mourned Fannie's loss and "prayed for God to have mercy upon us, and give us grace to endure the hard trials through which we must pass." Charles Ball likewise recalled identifying with migrants of both sexes when he was forced to march for four weeks from Maryland to South Carolina in a trader's coffle. The Maryland bondsman endured the entire journey "chained to my fellow-slaves," claiming that the man to whom he was chained often "wept like an infant." The slaves in the coffle became attached to each other en route, and when two women were sold along the way, they "both wept aloud" at "parting from us," Ball related, and the other slaves "all went to them, and bade them a last farewell." Charles Ball's references to the other members of the coffle as his "fellow slaves" and "companions" and his expressions of sadness at the separation of the group en route illuminate how slave migrants who began as strangers came to depend on one another during the traumatic journey south. As his testimony illustrates, interstate migrants frequently forged relationships that resembled those formed by shipmates in the transatlantic slave trade, establishing ties that often transcended gender and were based on mutual trust, which helped them to cope with the physical and emotional hardships of long-distance travel and separation from loved ones.[32]

Indeed, such relationships not only transcended gender but also age. As Steven Deyle has argued, children sold away from their parents and who thus lacked family protection were often looked out for by older migrants in the coffles. One eight-year-old Virginia slave marched off to the Deep South from Norfolk found himself chained to an older man, who attempted to relieve the

32 Walter Johnson has argued that sex segregation "shaped slaves' experience of the trade." Johnson, *Soul by Soul*, 68; Robinson, *From Log Cabin to the Pulpit*, 43–44 (first quotes); Charles Ball, *Fifty Years in Chains; Or, The Life of an American Slave* (New York: H. Dayton, 1859), 41–44 (second quotes); Berlin, *Generations of Captivity*, 173.

boy's suffering by making the "weight of the chain as light as he could." Mingo White, a slave born in South Carolina but sold to Alabama-bound traders when he was "jes' a li'l thang," related to interviewers of the Federal Writers' Project that during the journey south he was "taken care of" by a fellow migrant named John, who claimed to have known Mingo's father and took the boy under his wing. Laura Clark, a former bondswoman originally from North Carolina, likewise told interviewers that when a slave trader came and bought her to deport to Alabama, her mother hastily beseeched another woman in the coffle to "take keer my baby chile... and iffen I never sees her no mo' raise her for God."[33]

The social bonding among migrants that characterized interstate journeys helps to explain why slave coffles in transit sometimes even appeared cheerful to white observers. During his second visit to the United States in 1849, Scottish geologist Charles Lyell was surprised to see a coffle near Columbus, Georgia, consisting of slaves who appeared "very merry, talking and laughing" as his coach passed them on the road. On inquiry, Lyell was told that "it was a gang of slaves, probably from Virginia, going to the market to be sold." Lyell's observation was far from an isolated one. Another sojourner in the South in the 1830s observed a coffle of young slaves being marched through Mississippi who were "capering and practicing jokes upon each other." Olmsted likewise met with such a group of slaves on a boat from Alabama to Texas in 1854. "There was a fiddle or two among them, and they were very merry, dancing and singing," he noted, although a few "refused to join in the amusement, and looked very disconsolate." Three youngsters in particular caught his attention, the youngest of whom "seemed very sad, homesick and sulky" but who was plagued by two "very playful" shipmates, who were "continually teasing" him in what appeared to white passengers to be "mischievous fun." In all of these cases, the slave migrants were most likely not happy about being deported but rather attempting to cheer each other up on what was otherwise a grueling and emotionally traumatic journey. As Ira Berlin has argued, interstate slave migrants sometimes "exhibited a sort of manic glee, singing loudly and laughing conspicuously to compensate for the sad fate that had befallen them."[34]

[33] Deyle, *Carry Me Back*, 251 (first quote); *Mingo White, Slave Narratives*, vol. 1, 413–14 (second quote); *Laura Clark, in Slave Narratives*, vol. I, 72 (third quote).

[34] Charles Lyell, *A Second Visit to the United States of North America* (New York: Harper & Bros., 1850), 2:35 (first quote); Ingraham, *South-West*, 2: 239 (second quote); Olmsted, *Seaboard Slaves States*, 571 (third quote), 563 (fourth quote); Berlin, *Generations of Captivity*, 173 (fifth quote); Amos A. Parker, *Trip to the West and Texas* (Boston: Benjamin B. Mursey, 1836), 121–22. Walter Johnson has argued that the songs slaves sang during their journeys constituted "memorials for the communities the trade had destroyed." See Johnson, *Soul by Soul*, 68–69. Michael Tadman claimed that slaves sang because traders' forced them to in order to "reinforce among white observers the myth that blacks were a carefree people." See Michael Tadman, *Speculators and Slaves: Masters, Traders, and Slaves in the Old South* (Madison, Wisc.: University of Wisconsin Press, 1989), 72–73. The 1867 testimony of former slave Sella Martin also mentions that slaves en route to the Deep South were sometimes given "the order"

Many slaves continued to seriously consider resistance or escape en route to the southern interior, sometimes placing their trust in other slaves – strangers – to implicitly or explicitly assist them in doing so. In its most extreme and rare form, slave migrants resisted by collectively revolting, such as when nineteen bondsmen on board the *Creole* famously combined forces and revolted in transit from Norfolk to New Orleans in 1841, taking control and steering the ship to the British Bahamas, where slavery had been abolished. According to Walter Johnson, this incident more than any other illustrates the "generally invisible processes by which a group of strangers formed themselves into a resistant collective." Although unusual, the *Creole* revolt was by no means an isolated case. In both 1799 and 1826, slaves en route to the southern interior joined forces and killed their traffickers. But most traders were especially well armed and constantly on guard against such insurrections, even more so after the infamous *Creole* revolt. Former slave William Grose claimed, for instance, that when he was shipped from Baltimore to New Orleans along with seventy other migrants, "the captain... hurried us all below and closed the hatches" as the ship "came near an English island," obviously striving to avoid a repeat of the *Creole* until the ship had safely passed the Bahamas.[35]

With the chances of successful revolt so slim – whether on board a ship or in an overland coffle – slave migrants usually considered more subtle ways to escape their lot while in transit, such as running away. In 1833, traveler E.S. Abdy reported a case in which a slave woman who was carried south in a drove from Lexington, Kentucky, ran off 400 miles into the journey. Traveling "the whole way on foot" and "through unheard of difficulties," she made her way all the way back home to her husband, who kept her hidden for five weeks before she was discovered and returned to the trader. Four days later, the woman "eluded the vigilance of her keeper" again, this time for good. That same year, a coffle that departed from Alexandria, Virginia, also lost "a man with his wife and infant child," who escaped and "ultimately reached Philadelphia." In rare cases, runaways even resorted to violence to remain out of the hands of captors. Monday, a slave who belonged "to Lewis Gaylard, a negro trader from North Carolina," escaped his coffle and hid out in Walker County, Alabama, before being discovered and committed to jail. A newspaper announcement calling for the trader to come and claim him included in its description of the fugitive that he "fights like the Devil

to sing. Blassingame, ed., *Slave Testimony*, 705–706. It is unlikely that such dictates always underlay the singing observed in slave coffles in transit, however.

35 Berlin, *Generations of Captivity*, 174; Edward D. Jervey and C. Harold Huber, "The *Creole* Affair," *Journal of Negro History* 65 (summer 1980): 196–211; Johnson, *Soul by Soul*, 75–76 (first quote); David L. Lightner, *Slavery and the Commerce Power: How the Struggle Against the Interstate Slave Trade Led to the Civil War* (New Haven: Yale University Press, 2006), 10–11; Deyle, *Carry Me Back*, 255; William Grose, in Benjamin Drew, ed., *A North-Side View of Slavery. The Refugee; Or, the Narratives of Fugitive Slaves in Canada* (Boston: John P. Jewett & Co., 1856), 84 (second quote); Gudmestad, *A Troublesome Commerce*, 45.

when taken up." According to a sensational story reported in North Carolina's *Fayetteville Observer* in 1860, a white reverend named John E. Chambers was even "most inhumanely murdered" by one runaway while coming home from the town of Pekin. The murderer, a thirty-year-old slave who had escaped from a drove bound to the Deep South, presumably killed the white man to avoid being arrested. According to reports "he was originally from Virginia" but had been "sold to a Mr. Thomas or Thompson, a negro speculator [from whom] he escaped by being left behind in one train of cars, while his owner was hurrying a transfer from another." Finding himself miraculously left behind by the trader, the bondsman absconded and remained hidden by local slaves until Chambers stumbled upon him on the day of his death.[36]

As slaves were forced farther and farther from their homes, however, the daunting and risky prospect of traversing great distances as fugitives prevented a vast majority of slave migrants from even attempting to flee their captors' grasp. Charles Ball lost hope of escaping when his coffle, which had originated in Maryland, crossed the South Carolina border. Seriously contemplating suicide – "so great was my anguish" – Ball realized that he was "now a slave in South Carolina, and had no hope of ever again seeing my wife and children." Upon crossing the South Carolina border, the slave trader even "addressed us all, and told us we might now give up all hope of ever returning to the places of our nativity; as it would be impossible for us to pass through the States of North Carolina and Virginia, without being taken up and sent back."[37]

VI.

Resistance or escape en route to the Deep South was seldom successful, and, as historian David Lightner has argued, most interstate migrants "met their fate with tears and wails," pursuing their difficult journeys to their final destination. Arrival at southern places of market did not put an end to their ordeal, however, for there they were locked up in slave pens – most for the second time – and meticulously prepared for sale by traders and dealers, as discussed in Chapter 1. Newly arrived migrants often experienced priming and viewings by potential purchasers as an intimidating process, both because of the degrading commodification of their bodies for market and because traders – eager to turn a quick profit – frequently made overt threats to the slaves in their charge, ordering them to make themselves presentable and to do everything in their power to facilitate an easy sale. "Us was made to clean ourselves an' dress up," recalled Anne Maddox, who was sold from Virginia to Alabama at the

[36] Abdy, *Journal of a Residence*, 371–72 (first quote); Andrews, *Domestic Slave-Trade*, 152–53 (second quote); *Weekly Flag & Advertiser*, June 4, 1847 (third quote); *Fayetteville Observer*, July 2, 1860 (fourth quote). See also Franklin and Schweninger, *Runaway Slaves*, 55–57; Lightner, *Slavery and the Commerce Power*, 11.

[37] Lightner, *Slavery and the Commerce Power*, 11–12; Ball, *Fifty Years in Chains*, 35–36 (quote).

age of thirteen. "White peoples was dere from everywhere; de face of de earth was covered by dem." Henry Bibb claimed that the slaves in his drove were taken straight to the "trader's yard" upon arrival in New Orleans, where they were primed for potential purchasers. Every day at 10 o'clock, they were exposed for sale – their hair "had to be combed, and their faces washed, and those who were inclined to look dark and rough, were compelled to wash in greasy dish water, to look slick and lively." Bibb recalled that whenever a purchaser arrived, the slaves were "made to stand up straight, and look as sprightly as they could... and try to induce the spectators to buy them." If they "failed to do this, they were severely paddled after the spectators were gone." Bibb endured this grueling routine for months before he was finally sold. William Anderson, a former slave who was sold to a trader who took him from Virginia to Mississippi in 1826, felt most indignant about being treated like a "pig, or a hen, or merchandise," as customers meticulously examined his body in a Natchez slave pen. The women, he added, were inspected in ways "too wicked to mention." Henry Watson, who was likewise marched from Virginia to Natchez as a young man, claimed that upon arrival, the slaves in his coffle were treated like livestock and were kept in line with threats of corporal punishment for the slightest infraction. Reaching Natchez, Watson recalled, the slave trader took off the slaves' chains and changed their clothes, priming them for "visitors to examine the *flock*." If the slaves "displeased him in the least, he would order them to be stripped" and flogged with a paddle. Watson remained in the pen for weeks before finally being sold.[38]

Although most slaves were sold within a week of arrival, longer waiting periods such as those experienced by Bibb and Watson did not necessarily work to the trader's disadvantage because they allowed slaves to acclimate to the merciless southern climate, significantly increasing their value and salability. Indeed, cotton and sugar planters often explicitly asked for "acclimated" slaves because rumors of newly imported slaves succumbing to the heat and humidity of the Deep South made them especially wary of wasting their money on sickly bondspeople from the Upper South. One Mississippi planter was convinced that only especially dark slaves from Virginia and Maryland were worth purchasing. "The jet black negroes stand this climate the best, and no matter how ugly [their] faces, if they have large deep chests and... hips, stout limbs and active withal," then they were safe to buy. Another Louisiana sugar planter lamented in a newspaper editorial in 1830 that "the loss by death in bringing slaves from a northern climate" was far too high in the region; according to him "not

[38] Lightner, *Slavery and the Commerce Power*, 11 (first quote); Anne Maddox, in Slave Narratives, vol. I, 272 (second quote); Bibb, *Life and Adventures*, 103 (third quote); Anderson, *Life and Narrative*, 14 (fourth quote); Henry Watson, *Narrative of Henry Watson, a Fugitive Slave* (Boston: Bela Marsh, 1848), 10–12 (fifth quotes, italics mine). See also William Wells Brown, *Narrative of William W. Brown, a Fugitive Slave* (Boston: Anti-Slavery Office, 1847), 43; Brown, *Slave Life in Georgia*, 115–18.

less than twenty-five percent." Although often exaggerated, rumors of slaves expiring soon after arrival were not entirely unfounded. The city of Natchez reported in 1848 that the death toll for the previous year had amounted to "47 colored," most of whom were "strangers to the city or slaves owned by negro traders, besides those found drowned floating down the river." At Franklin & Armfield's stockade in New Orleans, slaves were sometimes returned by customers because they developed "maladies" since their arrival in Louisiana; others who fell ill upon arrival were sold at discounted prices. Acclimatization became such an important factor in determining slaves' value that most sellers of slaves found it advantageous to promote the length of their bondspeople's residence in the Deep South in sale advertisements. In Jackson, Mississippi, for instance, traders offered "from 60 to 75 likely, acclimated negroes, all Southern raised," while in New Orleans a twenty-seven-year-old woman named Elizabeth was hawked as an "acclimated" slave, "having been in the country eight years" and "fully guaranteed against vices and disease." Such sale tactics were the rule rather than the exception, and traders often went to great lengths to convince interested purchasers that their newly imported slaves had become sufficiently adjusted to the southern climate and thus did not constitute a risky investment.[39]

Whether sufficiently acclimated or not, bondspeople often wished to be sold as soon as possible. One visitor to a Mississippi slave pen surmised that this desire had to do with slaves' feelings of self-worth: "to be sold first is a great desideratum, for in their estimation it is an evidence of their superiority." But it is more likely that interstate migrants simply wished for their ordeal to be over with and not have to spend any more time in the pens than was absolutely necessary. Yet however quickly they were dispatched to new owners, sale brought with it challenges of its own, for when interstate slave migrants were purchased from pens or sold off at auctions at their final destinations, they were forced to endure a second separation, this time from the friends and acquaintances they had made in transit. One Virginia slave migrant claimed that upon sale at Natchez in 1827, there was much "crying and weeping when parting from each other." Indeed, similar to shipmates in the transatlantic trade, many antebellum migrants attempted to keep track of each other after sale or even negotiate to be sold together with one or more companions. A British traveler who attended a slave auction in Charleston, for example, reported seeing a slave woman knocked off to a rice planter, adding that "as soon as [she] came down from the platform, many of the Negroes crowded around

39 John Knight to Wm. Beall, Feb. 7, 1844, John Knight Papers, RASP, Series F, Part 1 (microfilm), JFK Institute, Freie Universität, Berlin (first quote); *New Orleans Argus*, Sept. 30, 1830, (second quote); Ingraham, *South-West*, 2:236; *Mississippi Free Trader and Natchez Gazette*, Feb. 1, 1848 (third quote); Stephenson, *Isaac Franklin*, 82–83 (fourth quote); *Semi-Weekly Mississippian*, Aug. 3, 1860 (fifth quote); *New Orleans Commercial Bulletin*, Aug. 24, 1833 (sixth quote); William Grose, in Drew, ed., *North-Side View*, 84.

[her], inquiring if she knew who had bought her, or whither she was going." Joseph Holt Ingraham attended an auction in Natchez in which he observed the slaves from a recently imported coffle cried off to various purchasers. Each time a slave was sold, "he returned and took leave of several of his companions."[40]

Final sale and arrival at their new plantations marked the end of a truly exhausting journey for most interstate migrants. One Louisiana slave claimed to interviewers that slaves who arrived in the Deep South always appeared "tired-looking" when they "just come off de auction block." She remembered that "dey would be sweatin' and lookin' sick." As they met their new masters and traversed the last few miles to their residences, newly imported bondspeople often acutely observed their environments in an attempt to mentally prepare themselves for a new life in a strange land. The chaos of transport finally over, they also began to fully grieve separations from loved ones, as the realization that they would never see them again began to truly sink in. "It was with great anxiety that I looked for the place, which was in future to be my home," recalled Charles Ball of being sold to a cotton planter in South Carolina. As a distraction during the twenty-mile trip to his new residence, he focused his attention on the landscape, noting the flatness of the countryside and the sight of magnolia trees and indigo plants, which he had never seen before. Finally reaching the plantation, he was somewhat relieved to be welcomed and treated kindly by his new master's family, who told him to rest and become acquainted with the grounds and the other slaves. Left to himself, however, Ball could not help but ponder the permanence of his situation. Memories of his wife and children haunted him, and as he contemplated his new life in South Carolina, he reached a low point, lamenting that he "was far from the place of my nativity," with "all my future one long, waste, barren desert, of cheerless, hopeless, lifeless slavery."[41]

Some migrants undoubtedly felt some sense of relief to finally arrive at their destination after the traumatic journey from their states of origin – one northerner dared suggest that slaves from the Upper South who were transported to Mississippi could not help but feel delighted "by the beautiful country to which they find themselves transplanted." Slave testimonies, however, suggest that most interstate migrants, like Ball, felt more overwhelmed than relieved when they first cast eyes upon their new homes. Not only did they grieve for loved ones left behind, but some also felt uneasy at the sight of new crops, the vast size of plantations in the Deep South, and what they perceived to be primitive or brutal living conditions. When after a "long and wearisome journey" Virginia slave Louis Hughes arrived at his new home in Mississippi, he claimed

40 Johnson, *Soul by Soul*, 7; Ingraham, *South-West*, 202 (first quote), 195–97 (fourth quote); Anderson, *Life and Narrative*, 14 (first quote); Hodgson, *Remarks During a Journey*, 126 (second quote).

41 Elizabeth Ross Hite, in Clayton, ed., *Mother Wit*, 103 (first quote); Ball, *Fifty Years in Chains*, 105–109 (second quotes), 115 (third quotes); Johnson, *Soul by Soul*, 190–91.

that "everything was strange to me." He was especially shocked by the sheer scale of his new masters' operations. "When I went out into the yard," Hughes recalled, "everywhere I looked slaves met my view. I never saw so many slaves at one time before. In Virginia we did not have such large farms. There were no extensive cotton plantations, as in Mississippi." Jourden Banks, a fellow Virginia slave who was deported to a plantation in Alabama, claimed that his "first impressions of my new home were extremely unpleasant." Not only did the slaves in the "dense cotton region" to which he was removed appear "poorly fed" and even "desolate in the extreme," but their housing left much to be desired as well. Banks was assigned a dilapidated, drafty cabin to live in and claimed that he felt like he had "fallen out of the frying-pan into the fire." Kentucky slave Henry Bibb similarly related that when he arrived at his new master's cotton plantation in Claiborne Parish, Louisiana, he "found his slaves poor, ragged, stupid, and half-starved." The sight immediately turned him against his new owner and overseer, whom he suspected of being cruel and inhumane masters. "My first impressions when I arrived on the Deacon's farm," Bibb recalled, "were that he was far more like what the people call the devil, than he was like a Deacon. . . . I really felt as if I had got into one of the darkest corners of the earth."[42]

VII.

Interstate slave migrants, whether removed by their masters or through the domestic slave trade, endured the most arduous journeys and the most radical changes in scenery as they were transferred to new residences. Bondspeople who were removed locally or to nearby urban areas, on the other hand, experienced much shorter, less exhausting, and less traumatic journeys to their new homes. The only slaves whose experiences even remotely resembled those of interstate migrants were those who were sold or bequeathed to distant counties or districts within their own states, thus rupturing some or all family ties and thrusting them into completely new settings. Resistance en route remained a real possibility for some of these migrants. George, a slave who lived in Tensas Parish in northern Louisiana, was purchased by a southern Louisiana slaveholder in 1850 and shipped on the "steamer Natchez no. 2 . . . to be sent to the country," a vessel from which he absconded around New Orleans. But most succumbed to their fate, undertaking their journeys with heavy hearts. When Virginia slave John Brown was removed about forty-five miles with some (but not all) of his family members after an estate division, for example, he recalled that the journey took two full days, that the slave cavalcade "went slowly" – grieving for loved ones left behind – and that they all "camped out

[42] Ingraham, *South-West*, 235 (first quote); Hughes, *Thirty Years a Slave*, 13–15 (second quotes); Pennington, *Life of J.H. Banks*, 49–51 (third quotes); Bibb, *Life and Adventures*, 110–114 (fourth quotes); Johnson, *Soul by Soul*, 190–91.

in the wood" at night. The following day their new master tried to pick up the tempo by promising his bondspeople "a feast of boiled black-eyed peas and bacon-rinds as soon as we got to Northampton," a promise he indeed kept upon arrival. "After supper we were driven to our quarters," the bondsman related, giving no further description of his new plantation. In 1853, Kentucky slave Isaac Johnson was likewise taken by the sheriff on a two-day journey from his plantation on the Green River to Bardstown, where he and his family members were thrown into jail for the night and sold separately at auction the following morning. Knocked off to a planter with an irritated and impatient countenance, Johnson was left tied to a hitching post while his new owner ran some errands in town before finally starting off for home. He arrived at his new plantation at around ten o'clock at night, where his master informed his wife that he had "a little boy here for you . . . one of those pumpkin seed niggers from the mountains." Johnson claimed that his new home was quite "a change," and he was disappointed with what he perceived to be primitive living conditions, his "bed being the floor." Similar to many of his interstate counterparts, he spent his first night sitting "for hours thinking of my mother, brothers and father until I was nearly wild with the change that had come."[43]

Even slaves who were sold long distances within the same state were spared the most extreme aspects of long-distance travel, however, and indeed, in interviews and testimonies, local slave migrants only rarely related details of their journeys or arrival at all. One fugitive slave who grew up twenty-five miles north of Charleston, South Carolina, and who dictated his experiences to a Massachusetts interviewer in 1838, related that when he was "about 14 years old," all the slaves on his plantation were divided among his mistress's children, he falling "to the oldest son," who "lived at Bethel, Sumpterville District, 8 miles from Sumpterville." No mention was made about the journey from his old plantation to his new one, and when he told his interviewer how he was subsequently sold to yet another planter, he stated simply that he was transferred "to Davy Cohen, a Jew who lived on Ashley River, about 12 miles from Charleston." William Grimes, a Virginia slave who was separated from his family when his master sold him from King George County to Culpeper County (he was later deported to Georgia), similarly skipped over most details of his journey, relating in his 1825 testimony that one morning he simply "started with [my new master] for Culpeper," adding that "after two days travel on horseback, we arrived at my new master's plantation, which was called Montpelier." Although he admitted that it grieved him to be separated from his mother, the bondsman's journey was in most respects incomparable to that of his interstate counterparts. Unchained, traveling on horseback, and only on the road for two days, he was spared the trials and hardships of a vast

43 *The Daily Picayune*, Mar. 3, 1850 (first quote); Franklin & Schweninger, *Runaway Slaves*, 55–57; Brown, *Slave Life in* Georgia, 9–10 (second quotes); Isaac Johnson, *Slavery Days in Old Kentucky* (n.p., 1901), 11–12 (third quotes); Gudmestead, *A Troublesome Commerce*, 45.

overland trek across the continent, made no contact with other migrants along the way, and was not struck by the novelty of new landscapes or scenery.[44]

Unlike bondspeople who were removed to other counties or districts, however, many local slave migrants remained within the general vicinity of their old homes, often within ten or twenty miles, their journeys entailing little more than a day's travel on foot or in a wagon. Interestingly, their first impressions of their new homes were strongly influenced by the extent of family separation during the move. If they were able to retain at least some family ties intact, their first impressions tended to be positive. Israel Campbell, who was bequeathed along with his mother and sister to a local man after the death of their master, made no mention of the short journey to his new home when he dictated his experiences of slavery in 1861. He did, however, emphasize that he was "very well pleased" with his home, "as I was with my sister and mother." Local slave migrants who were separated from loved ones, on the other hand, were more often unimpressed or pessimistic about their new homes. John Thompson, a former bondsman from Maryland who was bequeathed to "a cruel man" who lived in the same neighborhood when his mistress died, chose not to elaborate on either the journey or his first impressions of his new home when he dictated his life story in 1856. He reported simply that his new master told him to "come, go home with me," and that he "went home with him with a heavy heart." John Little, a North Carolina slave originally from Murfreesboro, related after escaping to Canada in the 1850s that at the age of twenty-three, he was sold at public auction to a planter who lived " about ten miles from the first place." As the deal was struck, Little's new owner gave him a pass and instructed him to "go down there to the quarters, with the rest of the niggers, and tomorrow I'll tell you what to do." Traveling alone, he simply walked down and "delivered myself up." Upon arrival, he encountered no new scenery or new crops but rather a large plantation with "seventy men, women, and children," who immediately warned the newcomer that their master "was a hard man." Frustrated about his new situation, Little spent his first evening at his new home reflecting on being separated from his mother and siblings – even such a short distance – admitting to interviewer Benjamin Drew that he "felt miserably bad."[45]

Former slave migrants who were relocated to cities similarly often failed to recall many details about their journeys when they talked or wrote about their experiences, but they did tend to comment more openly about their initial impressions of new environments. Many migrants from the countryside eagerly looked forward to moving to the city, as explained in Chapter 2, and upon

[44] "Recollections of Slavery by a Runaway Slave," *The Emancipator*, Aug. 23, 1838 (first quotes); William Grimes, *Life of William Grimes, the Runaway Slave* (n.p., 1825), 8 (second quotes).

[45] Campbell, *Bond and Free*, 20 (first quote); John Thompson, *The Life of John Thompson, a Fugitive Slave* (Worcester, Mass.: n.p., 1856), 29–30 (second quote); John Little, in Drew, ed., *North-Side View*, 199 (third quote).

arrival in urban areas, their anticipation was more often than not proved justified, as they were introduced to the excitement and hustle and bustle of towns and cities throughout the South. Isaac Mason, a Maryland slave from Kent County who was sent to the county seat Chestertown as an adolescent, recalled in 1893 that he had "to ride a distance of twenty-two miles" to his new home, "arriving there about night." The town, however, "was quite a thriving place, having five thousand or more inhabitants," and made an immensely positive impression on the young migrant. Mason clearly felt liberated from the isolation and economic retrogression that characterized the rural area in which he had been born, as he found himself in a proper town with "ready transportation to Baltimore" and "a large number of wealthy families." He concluded that he was "all right" and was "going to have a nice time at my new home." North Carolina slave John Jacobs, whose master took him to Washington to live after he was elected to Congress one year, remarked to interviewers in 1861 that "we were not many days on the way to [DC]," a city that he "very much wanted to see." Upon arrival, he found his excitement fully justified, as he confirmed that Washington was "a very lively place during the Session," with plenty of balls and parties, not only for the whites but also for the slaves. Virginia slave Noah Davis, who admitted feeling sad about the prospect of being separated from his family when he was hired out to Fredericksburg from his native Madison County in December 1818, recounted warming up to the idea of town life when he finally "arrived at Fredericksburg, after a day and a half's travel, in a wagon." The bondsman claimed that "having arrived in town, a boy green from the country, I was astonished and delighted at what appeared to me the splendor and beauty of the place." He spent a "merry Christmas" in his new home in town, "and for a while forgot the home on the farm."[46]

Yet many slaves also recalled feeling lonely or uneasy upon arrival at their new homes in the city. For some, separation from family members put a damper on their enthusiasm about moving to an urban environment. One Virginia slave reported that he felt "alone in the world" when his master transferred him from a plantation in Louisa County, Virginia, to the city of Richmond to work in a tobacco factory as an adolescent. Although he admitted sincerely believing that urban life would be "easy," he missed his mother terribly upon arrival, and it took him "some time before I became reconciled to my fate." Other slaves suffered from nervousness and anxiety as they traveled to their new homes, uneasy about what to expect of their new lives in urban areas. Frederick Douglass claimed that many slave hirelings were afflicted by "deep consternation" caused by a fear of the unknown, an uncertainty that hirelings

[46] Isaac Mason, *Life of Isaac Mason as a Slave* (Worcester, Mass.: n.p., 1893), 17–19 (first quotes); John S. Jacobs, "A True Tale of Slavery," *The Leisure Hour: A Family Journal of Instruction and Recreation* (Feb. 21, 1861): 125 (second quote); Noah Davis, *A Narrative of the Life of the Rev. Noah Davis, a Colored Man* (Baltimore: John Weishampel, 1858), 13 (third quote).

experienced "on a maddeningly regular basis," as Jonathan Martin has argued. Charles Ball, whose Maryland master hired him out to the Navy Yard in Washington before selling him to South Carolina, felt some insecurity when he accompanied his master "on foot" to town. "It was night when we arrived at the Navy Yard," Ball related, "and everything appeared very strange to me." Most confusing to the hireling was that he did not yet know what kind of work he would have to do, but shortly after arrival, his anxiety dissipated when he was "told by a gentleman who had epaulets on his shoulders, that I must go on board a large ship, which lay in the river... [and] that I had been brought there to cook," a task he looked forward to performing.[47]

The prospect of having to serve a "bad" or "cruel" master also appears to have influenced slaves' initial impressions of life in the city. Much like a self-fulfilling prophecy, slaves who were hired or purchased by urban masters whom they distrusted or especially did not like were often unimpressed upon arrival in southern cities. One slave who was purchased by a Savannah slaveholder became extremely "dissatisfied" with his new master during the journey to town, even getting into arguments with him along the way. As they entered the city, the migrant recalled after escaping slavery in 1825, he not only felt unimpressed by the bustle of Savannah but even intimidated, especially after passing a man on the street "who had a gun on his shoulder, loaded with shot [which] accidentally went off, the contents within a very few inches of me." The slave "began to despair" of ever living in Savannah "in peace." Louisa Picquet, a former slave who was purchased at an Alabama auction by a resident of New Orleans and transferred to that city by riverboat not only "felt pretty bad" about being separated from her mother as she started off for her new home but also became extremely uneasy when her new master "told me what he bought me for." On board the schooner, she explained to interviewer Hiram Mattison in 1861, her new owner told her that "he was getting old, and when he saw me he thought he'd buy me, and end his days with me." Realizing that she had been purchased by the Louisianan as a concubine, Picquet began to pray in vain "that he might die," even promising "the Lord one night... if he would just take him out of the way, I'd get religion and be true to him as long as I lived." For Picquet, arriving in New Orleans signaled only the beginning of a miserable existence with a hated new owner, and about her first impressions of the city, she indeed related nothing to her interviewer, indicating only that her new master was apparently not very wealthy and lived in a "rented house" in town.[48]

[47] Henry Brown, *Narrative of Henry Box Brown* (Boston: Brown & Stearns, 1849), 37 (first quote); Martin, *Divided Mastery*, 45 (second quotes); Ball, *Fifty Years in Chains*, 18 (third quote).

[48] Grimes, *Life of William Grimes*, 23 (first quote); Louisa Picquet and Hiram Mattison, *Louisa Picquet, the Octoroon: Or, Inside Views of Southern Domestic Life* (New York: Hiram Mattison, 1861), 18, 22–23 (second quotes).

Slave migrants transferred through formal or informal means, across state lines or to local towns or rural districts, all suffered both physically and emotionally during the physical removal of their bodies to new residences. Yet the experiences of different migrant groups varied by degrees, sometimes substantially. The most difficult and traumatic removals were undoubtedly experienced by victims of the domestic slave trade, most of whom were subjected not only to the most sterile and degrading methods of dehumanization on auction blocks and in traders' yards but also to the most grueling journeys across the continent. Even slaves who were forced by their masters into the southern interior were at least spared the chains, pens, and continual contact with strangers that characterized formal interstate removal. The extremely trying and drawn-out nature of deportation via the slave trade did encourage the forging of important social bonds among migrants, however, broadening slaves' identification with the southern slave population in general. Both local and urban slave migrants who were removed through formal means also often endured the humiliation of holding chambers and auction blocks, but because their journeys to their new homes rarely entailed traversing long distances, their travel experiences were characterized much less by hardship and physical exhaustion than the journeys of their interstate counterparts.

Depending on the nature of their removal, therefore, the forced transfer of slaves from old homes to new ones could be a short experience or a long and extended ordeal. Arrival at their final destinations brought entirely new challenges, however. The physical reallocation of their valuable bodies completed, slave migrants were next confronted with the need to assimilate to new work regimes, masters, and slave communities, a process that was not always as simple as many anticipated.

PART II

ASSIMILATION

4

Cogs in the Wheel

I found a great difference between the work in a steamboat cabin and that in a corn-field.

Former slave migrant William W. Brown, 1847[1]

When cotton planter Bennet H. Barrow, of West Feliciana Parish, Louisiana, decided to expand his operations in the early 1830s, he initially followed the conventional wisdom of the day and looked to the Upper South to provide him with the necessary augmentation to his slave labor force. Determined to circumvent the inflated prices of the domestic slave trade, Barrow departed his Highland plantation in 1834 to accompany his brother on an extended trip to Virginia to purchase slaves, returning home with a few able-bodied hands to work in his vast cotton fields. Much to his dismay, however, he discovered in the months that followed that his Virginia slaves – unaccustomed to the staple crops in the Deep South – were painfully slow learners at cotton cultivation. By the harvest season of 1836, Barrow's patience had worn out. Disgusted with his imported bondsmen, he recorded a note to himself in his diary on October 18, 1836: "I will never buy grown negros from Va. – or upper Country – small boys and girls may do, but grown ones are not worth as much – by at least one third as our creoles – one creole will pick as much as two of them." By the time he died in 1854, Bennet Barrow had amassed six plantations and nearly two hundred slaves but kept to his word and never bought another slave from outside Louisiana again.[2]

[1] Portions of this chapter were previously published in adapted form in Damian Alan Pargas, "In the Fields of a 'Strange Land': Enslaved Newcomers and the Adjustment to Cotton Cultivation in the Antebellum South," *Slavery & Abolition* 34 no. 2 (Apr. 2013): 1–17. William Wells Brown, *Narrative of William W. Brown, a Fugitive Slave* (Boston: The Anti-Slavery Office, 1847), 35.

[2] Bennet H. Barrow, Plantation Diary, Oct. 18, 1836, (typescript), Louisiana State University, Hill Memorial Library, Baton Rouge; Edwin Adams Davis, ed., *Plantation Life in the Florida*

Slave migrants were "nearly all bought and picked for work," as one southerner bluntly put it to Frederick Law Olmsted in 1854. The forcible removal of their bodies in the antebellum period constituted first and foremost a reallocation of their labor. Barrow's frustrated diary entry, however, illustrates some of the difficulties involved in transferring slaves' labor power from one place to another. Upon arrival at their new destinations, many slave migrants were confronted with the necessity of acquiring new skills and learning new tasks or adjusting to new work tempos, a process that could last weeks, months, or even years. Although some slaves genuinely enjoyed learning and performing new work – experiencing a boost in self-esteem as they mastered new trades and techniques and even profiting from work incentives and rewards – many others, such as Barrow's Virginia field hands, struggled to adapt to unfamiliar labor demands, disproportionately falling victim to work-related punishments and further compounding the trauma of forced removal.[3]

What kinds of work did antebellum slave migrants perform upon arrival at their new places of residence? How did they adapt to new work? What were the advantages and disadvantages of new work situations, and to what extent were long-distance, local and urban migrants confronted with similar work-related obstacles and opportunities? This chapter explores the assimilation process of migrants in the work sphere, delving specifically into the learning process with which slave newcomers were often confronted. It should be noted that migrants' experiences with new overseers and masters are more fully examined in Chapter 5; this chapter concerns itself rather with migrants' adaptation to new work itself.

I.

Of the three groups of antebellum slave migrants examined for this study, interstate migrants were not only subjected to the most extreme and severe *migration* experiences, but they also endured the most trying *assimilation* experiences. This was certainly the case when it came to adapting to new work patterns, although even then their trials differed by degrees depending on how, when, and to where they were deported.

The fate of an overwhelming majority of interstate migrants was to be transported across state lines in the domestic slave trade and put to field work on fully developed cotton plantations with an already existing slave labor force. These newcomers knew long before they were deported that work in the cotton South was hard, and upon arrival, they were burdened with extreme pressure

Parishes of Louisiana, 1836–1846, as Reflected in the Diary of Bennet H. Barrow (New York: AMS Press, 1967), 39; Edwin Adams Davis, "Bennet H. Barrow, Ante-Bellum Planter of the Felicianas," *Journal of Southern History* 5 (Nov. 1939), 439.

[3] Frederick Law Olmsted, *A Journey in the Seaboard Slave States in the Years 1853–1854, with Remarks on Their Economy* (New York: Dix & Edwards, 1856), 57 (quote).

to adapt quickly. Their situation was complicated by the fact that most found themselves placed under the authority of masters who were anxious to see them perform well from the start in order to justify the lofty prices they had paid for their valuable bodies. Indeed, southern slaveholders demanded nothing less, and although some masked their financial self-interest with entreaties of paternalist mutuality – it was the newcomer's *obligation* to work dutifully for the master in exchange for protection and care – others more openly claimed their right to profit maximization and unrestricted coercion. One former slave woman who was sold from the Upper South to Texas just before the Civil War claimed that upon arrival, her new master threatened her to "make dat money good what I pay for yer;" otherwise, he warned, "you know what I do to yer."[4]

To be sure, *some* slaveholders were considerate of the time needed for interstate migrants to adjust to cotton cultivation. One Mississippian, for example, who proposed to purchase "fifty or sixty first rate young negroes" from Virginia and Maryland for his plantation, admitted that they would have to be "moderately worked" during the first year or two in order "to become adept in the cotton business, especially in the most important branch of it: picking cotton, which they can only become efficient and quick in by considerable practice and experience." Most established cotton planters, however, like Bennett Barrow, were less patient and erroneously assumed that slaves from the Upper South would produce at full capacity in their first season. As one northerner discovered during a trip to the South in 1835, southern cotton planters demanded "fresh hands" who would be "immediately serviceable" on their plantations. Yet slaveholders' expectations regarding the rapidity with which their chattel investments would earn themselves back were often unrealistic, partly because they based their calculations solely on slaves' physical strength without taking into account the learning process involved in adapting to new crops. In other words, cotton planters reasoned that as long as newly imported slaves appeared "able-bodied" and physically sound, their productivity would match that of the other full hands. One Louisiana cotton planter who had just "bought three girls from Virginia, field-hands, strong enough . . . to split rails for fences," for example, boasted to Hungarian visitors in the early 1850s that he expected each of the girls to produce "between five and six bales of cotton a year," a tall order for slaves who had never cultivated cotton before. Indeed, many planters believed that cotton cultivation was so easy that enslaved newcomers from the Upper South would literally find it a breeze. As late as the Civil War, a

[4] Walter Johnson, *Soul by Soul: Life Inside the Antebellum Slave Market* (Cambridge, Mass.: Harvard University Press, 1999), 190–91; Susan E. O'Donovan, *Becoming Free in the Cotton South* (Cambridge, Mass.: Harvard University Press, 2007), 24–25; Walter Johnson, *River of Dark Dreams: Slavery and Empire in the Cotton Kingdom* (Cambridge, Mass.: Harvard University Press, 2013), 244–52; Eugene Genovese and Elizabeth Fox-Genovese, *Fatal Self-Deception: Slaveholding Paternalism in the Old South* (New York: Cambridge University Press, 2011), 2; John W. Blassingame, ed., *Slave Testimony: Two Centuries of Letters, Speeches, Interviews, and Autobiographies* (Baton Rouge; Louisiana State University Press, 1977), 536 (quote).

contributor to the agricultural journal *The Cultivator* swore that "cotton is not half so troublesome to raise as tobacco" and that slaves "from plantations in Maryland and Virginia," who already "understand the southern way of plowing, planting, hoeing, and chopping out crops," would adapt smoothly to work on a cotton plantation. During the harvest season, new migrants would even "find cotton picking as easy as picking blackberries." Similar claims regarding the relative facility of cotton cultivation have been made by some historians.[5]

Few slaves from the Upper South, however, had ever seen a cotton plant before their journey to the Deep South. And although cotton cultivation did not require the fine skill that some of the other staple crops of the South did, migrants' previous work experience often insufficiently prepared them for agricultural labor in the cotton kingdom. Most bondspeople who were raised in the Upper South grew up learning the specific intricacies of tobacco cultivation and were trained to cultivate mixed grains and other farm products during tobacco's downtime in the agricultural calendar. A "plant of perpetual difficulty" according to many Chesapeake planters, tobacco was a fragile and unpredictable staple crop that required close attention, skill, and delicate care throughout most of the year, from the time the seeds were sown and transplanted in the spring, to the repetitive hoeing, weeding, and deworming throughout the summer, to the tedious hand-harvesting, drying, rolling, and packing in the fall. During slack times, field hands' attention was shifted to wheat, corn, and other grains, which were straightforward enough to cultivate, if monotonous. But cotton was different. Despite certain obvious similarities, such as the use of virtually identical farm implements, cotton was less delicate than tobacco, more rushed, and more labor intensive. Hoeing and harvesting

[5] John Knight to Wm. Beall, Feb. 7, 1844, John Knight Papers, RASP, Series F, Part 1 (microfilm), JFK Institute, Freie Universität, Berlin (first quote); Andrews, *Slavery and the Domestic Slave Trade*, 50 (second quote). Even Ethan Allen Andrews, who was openly critical of the domestic slave trade, naively believed what slaveholders told him, that "the labor upon the cotton plantations is in general not very severe," and that Virginia slaves even preferred cotton to wheat and tobacco. See page 118. Francis and Theresa Pulszky, *White, Red, Black* (1853; New York: Johnson Reprint Co., 1970), 101 (third quote); D. Lee, "Cotton Culture in the United States," *The Cultivator*, vol. 12 (Nov. 1864): 348 (fourth quote). Maryland slave Charles Ball claimed that the slave trader who marched him to South Carolina promised the coffle that "he was going to sell us to gentlemen who would make us all very happy, and would require us to do no hard work, but only raise cotton and pick it." See Ball, *Fifty Years in Chains*, 94–95. Historian John Hebron Moore argued that when planters in late-eighteenth-century Natchez District abandoned experiments with tobacco and switched to cotton, they found the transition "easy" because the cultivation of the two crops was "the same," with cotton even "considerably easier" during certain stages than tobacco. Such convictions no doubt influenced their expectations of imported slaves from the tobacco regions. See John Hebron Moore, *The Emergence of the Cotton Kingdom in the Old Southwest: Mississippi, 1770–1860* (Baton Rouge: Louisiana State University Press, 1988), 77. Joyce E. Chaplin has also argued that the cultivation techniques of tobacco and cotton were "remarkably similar," adding that "both plants grew on freestanding stalks and could be tended in comparable ways." See Joyce E. Chaplin, "Creating a Cotton South in Georgia and South Carolina, 1760–1815," *Journal of Southern History* 57 (May 1991): 188.

cotton also required specific knowledge and handling that for newly arrived migrants would have seemed anything but straightforward.[6]

The cotton cycle began early in the year. In January and February, hands cleared the fields and performed odd jobs such as repairing fences, splitting rails, burning the stubble from the previous year's crop, and plowing to break up the earth for planting. In March and April, both cotton and corn were planted, ushering in a period during which slaves almost continually found themselves wielding a hoe from the time the seeds sprouted in the spring – "chopping" (thinning) and "scraping" (weeding) – until the harvest began in late August. Considerable skill was required to hoe down weeds within half an inch of the cotton plant without touching the leaves. When the plants were still small, weeding and thinning were even tediously performed by hand, a "painful process, because of the constant stooping," one Virginia slave in Georgia claimed. As in other parts of the South, brief slack periods offered little respite on a cotton plantation, as slaves shifted their attention back to the corn crop or the vegetable garden or performed a myriad of other tasks, most of which would have been familiar to newcomers. Harvesting cotton, however, seems to have constituted a major stumbling block for interstate migrants. Far from "easy as picking blackberries," picking cotton was backbreaking work. The number of pounds slaves were required to pick per day was often barely attainable, the prickly bolls lacerated slaves' hands and fingers – causing "great soreness," one migrant recalled – and the picking season lasted for months in often cold and miserable weather, usually until the end of December or beginning of January. And not only quantity but also quality was crucial in cotton picking: the highest returns went to the planters who were able to deliver "creamy white, clean, and expertly ginned cotton." As field hands hastily made their ways down the rows, they picked the fiber from the open bolls, made sure it was free of "trash," and shoved it into their sacks or baskets, which were regularly weighed by overseers before being sent to the gin house. There the cotton was dried, ginned, and packed for shipping. The harvest season was a

[6] For tobacco cultivation, see Philip D. Morgan, *Slave Counterpoint: Black Culture in the Eighteenth-Century Chesapeake & Lowcountry* (Chapel Hill, 1998), 164–70; Frederick Gutheim, *The Potomac* (New York, 1949), 70–74; Jack P. Greene, ed., *The Diary of Colonel Landon Carter of Sabine Hall, 1752–1778* (Charlottesville, Va.: University of Virginia Press, 1965), 346–47; T.H. Breene, *Tobacco Culture: The Mentality of the Great Tidewater Planters on the Eve of Revolution* (Princeton: Princeton University Press, 1985), 46–58; Brown, *Slave Life in Georgia*, 179–85; *Farm Journal*, 1850–1869, Tayloe Family Papers, RASP, Series E, Part 1 (microfilm), JFK Institute, Freie Universität, Berlin. For the cultivation of wheat, corn, rye, and oats, see David Wilson Scott, Diary, 1819–1821, Papers of David Wilson Scott, Manuscript Division, Library of Congress, Washington, DC. See also Morgan, *Slave Counterpoint*, 170–78; Brenda E. Stevenson, *Life in Black and White: Family and Community in the Slave South* (New York, 1996), 191; Harold B. Gill, Jr., "Wheat Culture in Colonial Virginia," *Agricultural History* 52 (1978): 380–93; Werner L. Janney and Asa Moore Janney, eds., *John Jay Janney's Virginia: An American Farm Lad's Life in the Early 19th Century* (McLean, Va., EPA Publications, 1978), 68–76, 72–73.

FIGURE 4.1. Cotton picking in Georgia. 1907. "Nine African Americans working in field." Taken at the beginning of the twentieth century, this photograph depicts field laborers picking cotton on a plantation in Decatur, Georgia. During slavery, cotton picking was often organized in gangs and supervised by masters or overseers. Newcomers frequently failed to meet their quotas at the end of the day, making them especially vulnerable to work-related punishments. *Source:* Marcus L. Brown, 1907. Courtesy of the Library of Congress, Prints and Photographs Division, LOT 4728.

labor-intensive time for slaves. Even after the sun went down, they were set to ginning, carding, spinning, and reeling, new tasks for those who had no experience with cotton before arriving in the southern interior.[7]

[7] For cotton cultivation, see Ira Berlin, *Generations of Captivity: A History of African-American Slaves* (Cambridge, Mass.: Harvard University Press, 2003), 176; J.A. Turner, *The Cotton Planter's Manual: Being a Compilation of Facts from the Best Authorities on the Culture of Cotton* (New York: Orange Judd & Co., 1857), 23–27; Joseph Jaynes Plantation Journals, Rankin County, Mississippi, 1854–1860, RASP, Series F, Part 1 (microfilm), JFK Institute, Freie Universität, Berlin; Journal of Araby Plantation, 1843–1850 (microfilm), ibid.; Louis Hughes, *Thirty Years a Slave: From Bondage to Freedom* (Milwaukee: South Side Printing Co., 1896), 26–40; John Brown, *Slave Life in Georgia: A Narrative of the Sufferings, and Escape of John Brown, a Fugitive Slave, Now in England*, edited by Louis A. Chamerozvow (London: L.A. Chamerozvow, 1855), 171–79, 174 (first quote), 172 (second quote); "Preparation of Cotton for Market," *Tri-Weekly Flag & Advertiser* (Montgomery, Ala.), Sept. 25, 1847; Anthony

Migrants who were put to work on a cotton plantation for the first time made earnest attempts to grasp the crop's cultivation techniques, but they struggled nonetheless, especially during the harvest season. Slave testimonies indeed contradict white southerners' claims that slaves adapted to cotton easily. The experiences of Maryland bondsman Charles Ball are indicative of the general trend. Ball endeavored to master cotton as quickly as possible when he arrived in South Carolina, even before he was formally sold and still in the custody of the slave trader who had carried him into the Lower South. One day, finding himself lodged on a plantation while the trader made local business transactions, Ball "determined to venture out into the fields... and see the manner of cultivating cotton." Knowing that his irrevocable fate was to toil at this new crop, he "felt anxious to know the evils, if any, attending it." He watched carefully and assisted a young girl at hoeing so he could get some practice in before he was finally sold. Yet even after he was purchased and put to work on his new plantation, Ball felt uneasy during his first season in the cotton fields. Hoeing posed no serious problems – he had hoed back in Maryland and quickly learned to hoe cotton without damaging the leaves – but the real challenge came during cotton-picking time, "a fatiguing labor" to the newly imported bondsman. "I had ascertained that at the hoe, the spade, the sickle, or the flail, I was a full match for the best hands on the plantation," Ball related in his autobiography. But "when it came to cotton picking I was not equal to a boy of fifteen." He worked hard the first day of picking, but by the time he had to weigh his basket, he still "had only thirty-eight pounds, and I was vexed to see that two young men, about my own age, had, one fifty-eight, and the other fifty-nine pounds." Finding that he could not measure up to the local field hands, "even the women," Ball admitted that he "felt very much ashamed" and frustrated. "The picking of cotton seemed to be so very simple a business," he complained, yet he could not master it; indeed, he even began to fear that he would "never be able to improve myself, so far as to become even a second rate hand." In the days and weeks that followed, the bondsman redoubled his efforts, and by the end of the month, he had made considerable progress, but even years later, after his escape from slavery, Ball claimed that he "never became reconciled" to cotton picking, a task that "may almost be reckoned among the arts." His self-esteem esteem suffered a serious blow; once a strong and able worker, he now ranked even behind the women and children in productivity, a clumsy newcomer entering the workforce at the very bottom of the ladder.[8]

Gene Carey, *Sold Down the River: Slavery in the Lower Chattahoochee Valley of Alabama and Georgia* (Tuscaloosa: University of Alabama Press, 2011), 89–94, 92 (third quote); Adam Rothman, *Slave Country: American Expansion and the Origins of the Deep South* (Cambridge, Mass.: Harvard University Press, 2005), 51–52.

[8] Johnson, *Soul by Soul*, 191–93; Berlin, *Generations of Captivity*, 176; Hughes, *Thirty Years a Slave*, 15; Ball, *Fifty Years in Chains*, 73–74 (first quotes), 147 (second and third quotes), 149 (last quote).

Ball's frustration was echoed by many slaves who were transported from the Upper to the Lower South, as several testimonies reveal. Some found virtually all aspects of cotton cultivation difficult to get used to during their first season, even planting and hoeing. Tom Bones, a Virginia slave sold to a cotton planter in Warren County, Mississippi, found that "for a long time he could not get used to cotton growing as he had been accustomed to wheat and tobacco." Moses Roper, a former slave sent from North Carolina to South Carolina in the early antebellum period, discovered that cotton cultivation was "very laborious work." His initial hoeing task he "could not get done, not having worked on cotton farms before." A bondswoman from Virginia who was sold to Alabama complained to Benjamin Drew in the 1850s that after only a few days of "hoeing cotton, a new employment," her "hands were badly blistered." Clearly, many newcomers found hoeing cotton trickier and more labor intensive than hoeing tobacco and grains, even if they did use the same instruments.[9]

Like Ball, however, most slaves specifically encountered trouble during the harvest season. As one Virginia newcomer in Georgia tellingly asserted in 1855, "many people may think [cotton picking] is a very light, pleasant occupation, but it is not." This was certainly a sentiment shared by many green hands, who found themselves lagging far behind the locals in the fields. Indeed, experienced cotton pickers who had grown up in the Deep South usually bagged well over a hundred pounds a day, sometimes much more. In one six-day work week at the beginning of the cotton harvest of 1834, for example, the best picker on John Randolph's plantation in Louisiana – a local woman named Betsy – *averaged* 184 pounds a day. Newcomers were rarely capable of picking even half that amount, and migrants thus frequently complained of stress and embarrassment for failing to pick as much as the rest. Henry Watson, a Virginia slave sold to Mississippi, immediately fell behind when he was introduced to cotton picking. Because he "had not been accustomed" to field work on a cotton plantation, Watson "found it impossible to keep up with the others." Israel Campbell, who had grown up working as a domestic servant and general farm hand in his home state of Kentucky, similarly experienced a drastic change when his master moved to Mississippi and hired him out to a local cotton planter. Describing the transition in 1861, Campbell claimed that he was told he had to pick a hundred pounds of cotton a day, an employment "too intense for my poor brain to describe." He "tried it for three days, but could not get over ninety pounds." Indeed, he admitted to have slipped a melon into his cotton basket

9 Christopher Morris, *Becoming Southern: The Evolution of a Way of Life, Warren County and Vicksburg, Mississippi, 1770–1860* (New York: Oxford University Press, 1995), 75 (first quote); Moses Roper, *A Narrative of the Adventures and Escape of Moses Roper, from American Slavery* (Philadelphia: Merrihew & Gunn, 1838), 14 (second quote); Mrs. John Little, in Benjamin Drew, ed., *A North-Side View of Slaver. The Refugee: or, the Narratives of Fugitive Slaves in Canada* (Boston: John P. Jewitt & Co., 1856), 225 (third quote).

on several occasions so that it would top a hundred pounds and save him a whipping. Inexperienced hands not only failed to keep up with local slaves in cotton picking, but they also failed to win monetary prizes that were frequently awarded to slaves who picked the most cotton, not having enough experience to compete with their counterparts in the fields.[10]

Many first-time cotton pickers moreover tended to pick cotton with trash still on the bolls, a source of frustration to innumerable plantation managers because trashy cotton sold for much less than clean cotton. Such was the extent of the problem that antebellum periodicals and cotton manuals regularly advised practical solutions. One planters' manual published in 1857 suggested that newly imported hands be given a "short training" in picking clean cotton, a procedure that would supposedly effect "wonders" and save much trouble. Although often necessary, planters usually considered the process of training new slaves in various aspects of cotton cultivation time consuming, however, and progress was sometimes painstakingly slow. One agriculturalist drew from racist stereotypes of blacks as unintelligent when he advised planters not to confuse new cotton hands but rather to simply train them at one task and keep them to it for as long as possible. "The difficulty of teaching the slave anything is so great, that the only chance of turning his labour to profit is, when he has once learned a lesson, to keep him to that lesson for life."[11]

To be sure, time and experience gradually molded the vast majority of newcomers from the non-cotton South into regular cotton hands and skilled cotton pickers, their rank slowly improving from the least productive workers to "first rate" hands. In Louisiana in 1827, one twenty-five-year-old interstate migrant named William was advertised as a "first rate field hand," having been "occupied on a cotton plantation in this state for the last five years." Another woman, age thirty-three, was advertised in Natchez in 1849 as "fully acclimated" and "a first rate cotton picker." Yet, as Bennet Barrow's diary entry illustrates, some planters clearly came to despair that their bondspeople from the Upper South would ever be as productive as the local slaves. Indeed, by the late antebellum period, imported bondsmen from other cotton states – the only interstate migrants who *did* arrive at their new destinations already adept at cotton cultivation – were often specifically advertised as such. In 1860, one Mississippi newspaper announced the sale of some sixty to seventy-five slaves, "all Southern raised and trained cotton pickers." Such advertisements

10 Brown, *Slave Life in Georgia*, 175–76 (fourth quote); John H. Randolph Papers, Cotton Record Book, vol. 1, Oct. 27–Nov. 1, 1834, RASP, Series I, pt. 1 (microfilm), JFK Institute, Berlin; Henry Watson, *Narrative of Henry Watson, a Fugitive Slave* (Boston: Bela Marsh, 1848), 20 (fifth quote); Israel Campbell, *An Autobiography. Bond and Free: Or, Yearnings for Freedom, From My Green Briar House. Being the Story of My Life in Bondage, and My Life in Freedom* (Philadelphia: C.E.P. Brinkloe & Co., 1861), 33–34 (sixth quote); Susan Dabney Smedes, in Jones, ed., *Plantation South*, 275–76.

11 Turner, *Cotton Planters' Manual*, 26 (first quote); *The Westminster Review, American Edition*, no. 152 (July 1862): 265 (second quote).

implicitly reassured potential purchasers that new hands would be immediately productive in the fields and would not slow down operations with clumsy mistakes or time-consuming training.[12]

The difficulties involved in switching slaves from one crop to another also explain why cotton planters often specifically desired *young* migrants from the Upper South because young migrants were less likely to have grown rigidly accustomed to the staple crops in their regions of origin. As Watson Jennison has recently argued, cotton cultivation "required skills that could not easily be acquired if attempted too late in life." In antebellum South Carolina and Georgia, common wisdom even held that any slave older than the age of twenty-five "could never become a '*crack picker*.'" Indeed, one Mississippi planter claimed that "it is much more difficult to acclimate old negroes [i.e. adults] than young ones; and after their removal from their old homes to new ones, they seldom, if ever, become reconciled to the change." Children and young adults who were transplanted to the cotton kingdom, on the other hand, were optimistically viewed by their purchasers as virtual blank slates – and with good reason, for young slaves indeed appear to have learned all aspects of cotton cultivation more easily than older migrants. John Randolph's cotton plantation in Louisiana may serve as a case in point. When three young Virginia slaves named Coley (18 years old), Morris (18 years old), and George (16 years old) were introduced on the plantation in March 1842, they had probably never worked cotton in their lives. During the first week of the harvest season in the late summer, they were indeed tellingly ordered to gather corn while the rest picked cotton. When on September 9 they were finally set to picking cotton, the three predictably lagged behind the rest, with Coley picking 77 lb., and George and Morris each picking 75 lb. The best picker that day was (again) Betsy, who bagged 165 lb. Only days later, however, with the cotton bloom in full swing, the three Virginians were up to 100 lb., and by October 8 – after only a month of picking – Coley and Morris achieved a remarkable 160 lb. each, with George barely trailing at 155 lb. This was an impressive learning curve, although all three still lagged well behind the locals, who averaged 200 lb. on October 8 (Betsy topped 300 lb. that day). Small children also adjusted quickly to cotton because plantation managers tended to allow them more time to grow accustomed. The testimonies of slave migrants who were introduced to cotton before adolescence even tend to underscore the rapidity with which they adapted to working the crop during the seasons rather than the hardships involved. Walter Calloway, who was sold from Virginia to Alabama

[12] Davis, "Bennet H. Barrow," 439; *Louisiana Advertiser*, May 29, 1827 (first quote); *Mississippi Free Trader & Natchez Gazette*, June 9, 1849 (second quote); *Semi-Weekly Mississippian*, Aug. 3, 1860 (third quote). Susan O'Donovan argues that even slaves who were sent westward from the "older" cotton districts to the newer territories had a difficult time adjusting. Although they were set to the same work that they had performed back home, they found the work tempo more brutal and master–slave relations more strained in the western cotton districts. See O'Donovan, *Becoming Free in the Cotton South*, 24.

as a young boy in the early 1850s, proudly related to interviewers that he was first introduced to field labor only after he arrived in the Deep South, and that by the "time I was ten years ole I was makin' a reg'lar han'" in the cotton fields.[13]

Not only did the intricacies of cotton cultivation differ markedly from farm work on a wheat or tobacco plantation, but the tempo and conditions of gang labor on a cotton plantation were also often considered more brutal than what many slaves from the Upper South were used to. In the post-Revolutionary Chesapeake, the shift to mixed farming resulted in a situation in which many bondspeople became jacks of all trades, performing a variety of tasks throughout the working day – from milking cows to farm work and plantation labor. Work was hard, to be sure, and indeed as slaveholding size dwindled, many slaves actually found their workloads increasing, as fewer slaves became responsible for the work of the farm or plantation. But many tasks were accomplished individually, and even gang labor was usually performed at a steady pace and in small groups of three or four. Men, women, and children worked together or in close proximity to one other, often without an overseer. During the harvest season, work could and did continue into the night – shucking corn, threshing wheat, or rolling and packing tobacco – but for most of the year, the working day ended by sundown. Half-Saturdays and free Sundays were common throughout the region. Interstate migrants in the cotton South, however, found themselves assigned to sex-segregated gangs, with white overseers and black drivers rushing them to the end of their rows and the demanding pace of field labor difficult to keep up with. The working day seemed longer as well. Overseer's horns were blown to wake the slaves well before dawn, work commenced at first daybreak, and it continued all day with only a brief pause at midday for lunch. During peak periods, the working

[13] Watson W. Jennison, *Cultivating Race: The Expansion of Slavery in Georgia, 1750–1860* (Lexington: University Press of Kentucky, 2012), 264 (first quotes); Ball, *Fifty Years in Chains*, 149; John Knight to Wm. Beall, May 22, 1845, John Knight Papers, RASP, Series F, Part 1 (microfilm), JFK Institute, Freie Universität, Berlin (second quote); John H. Randolph Papers, Cotton Record Book, vol. 2, Aug. 29–Oct. 8, 1842, RASP, Series I, Part 1 (microfilm), JFK Institute, Berlin; Ibid., Statement by Notary Public William Christt, Mar. 3, 1842, General Financial and Legal, 1841–1857; Ibid., Sale of Slaves, Mar. 3, 1842, General Financial and Legal, 1841–1857; Walter Calloway, in Slave Narratives of the Federal Writers' Project, 1936–1938 (typescript), vol. I, 51 (third quote); Sarah Byrd, in Slave Narratives, vol. IV, 168; Hughes, *Thirty Years a Slave*, 37. Charles Ball overheard one planter complain to an interstate trader in South Carolina that young migrants were in high demand but adults less so because they "could not so readily become expert cotton-pickers." See Ball, *Fifty Years in Chains*, 46. Susan Dabney Smedes, whose slaveholding father moved the family from Virginia to a cotton plantation in Hinds County, Mississippi, in 1835, claimed that the slaves readily adapted to cotton cultivation but that the best cotton pickers – those who picked the most pounds and free of trash – were those who had been "trained in childhood," in other words, those who were born in Mississippi or who were very small when they removed to Mississippi. See Susan Dabney Smedes, in Jones, ed., *Plantation South*, 276.

day was also more regularly extended to include night work and Sunday work than many migrants were accustomed to before arrival in the Deep South. As Ira Berlin has argued, slaves transported to the cotton kingdom entered a world in which "the watch word was 'system,' as slaveowners searched for ways to rationalize and order the plantation," ratcheting up production and squeezing every possible ounce of labor out of their bondspeople.[14]

Whether or not migrants actually worked *harder* than they had back in the Upper South – a subjective claim that is virtually impossible to quantify – they certainly claimed to have felt that the haste and regimentation on cotton plantations were far more grueling than what they were used to. Slave migrants experienced the transition, in other words, as a difficult one, and testimonies from both before and after emancipation stress the long hours and exhausting drudgery of working all day in the cotton fields. Sara Colquitt, who was sold from Virginia to Alabama, claimed to interviewers of the Federal Writers' Project that in the cotton country, "us had to work hard and late. I worked in the fields every day from 'fore daylight to almost plumb dark." At night she was set to spinning, too: "had to do six cuts to de reel." Another slave woman who was sold from the Upper South to Texas related in an interview after emancipation: "Dey work you hard in Texas, [al]most till midnight." William Anderson, sold from Virginia to the "strange land" of Mississippi as a youth, claimed in 1857 that even though slaves in Virginia were forced to perform "hard work," it was nothing compared with the "exceedingly hard" labor that he experienced in the Deep South. In Mississippi, it was "nothing but whipping and driving both night and day – sometimes nearly all Sunday," he contended. Another Virginia migrant sent to Mississippi complained that the pace of work on his new plantation was so high and the heat so stifling that it "made me sick and weakened me down," but under threat of the lash, he "had to keep on." Indeed, such was the intensity of field labor in the cotton South that droves of interstate slave migrants responded by almost immediately running away. One Mississippi planter wrote to a family member in May 1845 that his newly purchased Maryland slaves were "now put to the full test of their skill, strength and willingness and ability to bear fatigue & labor, which they have never before probably experienced; and the consequence will be, I expect... that several will fly the track & run off again," as two already had. Countless runaway slave ads also bear witness newcomers' attempts to flee. Dick Griffin, "just imported from Virginia" to a plantation in the Red River

[14] See Berlin, *Generations of Captivity*, 178, 204 (quote), 212; Susan Eva O'Donovan, *Becoming Free in the Cotton South* (Cambridge, Mass.: Harvard University Press, 2007), 21–22, 27–29; Stevenson, *Life in Black and White*, 187–92; Lorena Walsh, "Plantation Management in the Chesapeake, 1820–1860," *Journal of Economic History* 49, no. 2 (June 1989): 405; Henry Bibb, *Narrative of the Life and Adventures of Henry Bibb, an American Slave* (New York: Henry Bibb, 1849), 110–11; Barrow, *Plantation Life*, 40–41, 45.

region of Louisiana, barely lasted a month in the harvest season of 1844 before absconding.[15]

Newly arrived migrants in the cotton South were also more susceptible to work-related punishments than their local counterparts, as they struggled to adjust to the situation in which they found themselves. Although one Alabama planter claimed that the best way to extract the highest productivity from newly imported Virginia slaves was by "simply assuring them that [the master] intend[s] their good," it may be safe to conclude that many plantation managers had difficulty keeping their tempers under control. Patience in dealing with new slaves from the Upper South may have seemed becoming of a paternalist master, but in reality, southern planters found that the importance of profit maximization made severity and coercion more effective than benevolence, so the planters often fell back on their rights as absolute rulers of the bodies under their control. If newcomers slowed down operations, as they often did, they were placed under close supervision and often brutally "corrected." One Virginia slave who was sold to a cotton plantation in Georgia was "strictly watched while at his labor, by the slave driver, who was himself a black man." William Leftwich, a white Alabamian and the son of slaveholders, recounted in a letter to his brother in 1838 that one of the family's new slaves named Jerry had experienced so much trouble learning to pick cotton that he became the "object of [the master's] special hate," who "would frequently wear out his stick upon his head." Eventually, Jerry could take no more. "As he was not expert in picking cotton," he took to "sometimes run[ning] away in the fall, to escape abuse" but was finally apprehended and sold "farther south." John Warren, a slave from Wilson County, Tennessee, who was sold to a cotton plantation in Mississippi, confided to interviewer Benjamin Drew after escaping to Canada that his body was full of scars "made soon after I went [to Mississippi]." He claimed that during his first season in the cotton fields, he was severely whipped for hoeing out too much cotton and not enough grass. Unaccustomed to the work at which they were put in the cotton South, many

[15] Sara Colquitt, in Slave Narratives, vol. I, 87 (first quote); Blassingame, ed., *Slave Testimony*, 534, 536 (second quote); William J. Anderson, *Life and Narrative of William J. Anderson, Twenty-Four Years a Slave* (Chicago: Daily Tribune Book and Printing Office, 1857), 16 (third quote), 19 (fourth quote); Blassingame, ed., *Slave Testimony*, 382 (fifth quote); John Knight to Wm. Beall, May 7, 1845, John Knight Papers, RASP, Series F, Part 1 (microfilm), JFK Institute Freie Universität, Berlin (sixth quote); *The Times Picayune*, Jan. 5, 1845 (eighth quote). See also Henry Clay Bruce, *The New Man: Twenty-Nine Years a Slave, Twenty-Nine Years a Free Man* (York, Pa.: P. Anstadt & Sons, 1895), 61–62; Campbell, *Bond and Free*, 33; Bibb, *Narrative*, 110–15. William Hall, a Tennessee slave who was moved with his family to Mississippi, where "they drove the hands severely," testified to Benjamin Drew that when his "mother and brothers and sisters ... changed their country, [they] changed their position from good to bad." See Drew, ed., *North-Side View*, 314.

interstate migrants became thorns in their masters' (or overseers') sides and suffered severe consequences for their lack of experience.[16]

II.

Slaves who were snatched up by sugar planters had an even rougher time adapting to new work patterns than bondsmen who were transplanted to the cotton districts. As one British traveler commented in 1842, migrants who were sent to the cotton fields found themselves "in the same dark, degraded, and hopeless state as the African race generally throughout the Southern States," but their condition was at least "better than that of the slaves employed in the cultivation of... sugar." On the sugar plantations, he claimed, "they are more severely worked than anywhere else." Indeed, the excessive labor required of enslaved people in southern Louisiana was hard even by southern standards. Visitors were often appalled by what they found to be the most inhumane work patterns forced on slaves in the entire plantation South. British traveler Thomas Hamilton wrote that the slaves living on Louisiana sugar plantations were all "compelled to undergo incessant labour... [they] are taxed beyond their strength, and are goaded to labour until nature absolutely sinks under the effort." James Stirling, another visitor to the sugar country, opined that "the severe nature of the labour on a sugar plantation... is objectionable both in an economical and social point of view." And George Featherstonhaugh was horrified by rumors that "the duration of life for a sugar-mill slave does not exceed seven years!"[17]

The forced nature of sugar cultivation in southern Louisiana, where the growing season was seriously limited by weather constraints, was the most important factor in determining the work tempo of slaves. "Every planter in the cane world faced a race against time," as historian Richard Follett aptly put it. More than any other southern crop, cane was successfully cultivated only

[16] James O. Breeden, ed., *Advice Among Masters: The Ideal Slave Management in the Old South* (Westport, Conn.: Greendwood Press, 1980), 324 (first quote); Genovese and Fox-Genovese, *Fatal Self-Deception*, 1–2; Blassingame, ed., *Slave Testimony*, 278–79 (second quote); William Leftwich to brother, Dec. 26, 1838, in Thomas Weld, *American Slavery As It Is: Testimony of a Thousand Witnesses* (New York: American Anti-Slavery Society, 1839), 48–49 (third quotes); John Warren, in Blassingame, ẹd., *Slave Testimony*, 184 (fourth quote); See also Anderson, *Life and Narrative*, 18–19; Campbell, Bond and Free, 34–38; Brown, *Slave Life in Georgia*, 28–29; Henry Gowens, in Drew, ed., *North-Side View*, 140–41.

[17] James Silk Buckingham, *The Slave States of America* (London: Fisher & Son, 1842), 1:199 (first quote), 1:376 (second quote); Thomas Hamilton, *Men and Manners in America* (Edinburgh: W. Blackwood, 1834), 2:229 (third quote); James Stirling, *Letters from the Slave States* (1857; reprint New York: Negro Universities Press, 1969), 126 (fourth quote); William Howard Russell, *My Diary North and South* (London: Bradbury & Evans, 1863), 1:404; Pam Drake, *Pictures of the "Peculiar Institution" as It Exists in Louisiana and Mississippi, by an Eye-Witness* (Boston: J.P. Yerrington & Sons, 1850), 8; George W. Featherstonhaugh, *Excursion through the Slave States* (London: John Murray, 1844), 120 (fifth quote).

by working with a furious haste that easily surpassed the tempo necessary to cultivate other southern staples. On sugar plantations, there never seemed to be enough hours in the day. Moreover, slack periods were for all intents and purposes nonexistent throughout the year, as the Louisiana sugar cycle lasted a full twelve months, during all phases of which time was of the essence. After one sugar season had finished, usually around Near Year's, slaves were often given less than a week's rest before commencing work on the next year's crop. Valcour Aime, a sugar planter on the Mississippi River, gave his slaves only three days off between the 1849 and 1850 sugar season; that same winter, his neighbor Octave Colomb allowed his slaves only four days. In early January, slaves were already out in the fields, ditching, plowing, and clearing ground. By the end of February, the seed cane was in the ground, and after the cane sprouted, the rows were repeatedly hoed and plowed throughout the spring and the stifling heat of summer. The secondary chores on the sugar plantations during this period were also endless, from cleaning ditches and repairing levees, to cultivating corn, to chopping thousands of cords of wood for the steam engines and boilers in the sugar house. The "grinding season" in the fall, during which the cane was cut, ground, boiled, and industrially processed into granulated sugar and molasses – an assembly line process that lasted twenty-four hours a day, seven days a week – ushered in a solid two- to three-month block of arduous round-the-clock shifts for the slaves. In most cases, bondsmen were forced to work two nine-hour shifts a day in the sugar house – carrying cane; placing it onto the mechanized conveyer belts; and operating the mill, kettles, vacuum pumps, and other machinery – leaving just six hours a day for sleep. Sunday work was standard.[18]

If labor in the cotton fields was characterized as arduous and overly regulated, it was as nothing compared with work on an antebellum Louisiana sugar plantation. Visitors to the region consistently likened the sex-segregated gangs in the sugar fields to well-disciplined military units that operated with a lock-step cadence. With full Saturdays and Sunday work common, moreover, plantation work appeared to never cease. For slave migrants from other states,

[18] Richard Follett, *The Sugar Masters: Planters and Slaves in Louisiana's Cane World, 1820–1860* (Baton Rouge: Louisiana State University Press, 2005), 93–97, 102–103, 93 (first quote); Berlin, *Generations of Captivity*, 180; Valcour Aime, *Plantation Diary of the Late Mr. Valcour Aime, Formerly the Proprietor of the Plantation Known as the St. James Sugar Refinery, Situated in the Parish of St. James, and Now Owned by Mr. John Burnside* (New Orleans, Clark & Hofeline, 1878), 135; Octave Colomb Plantation Journal, Dec. 23, 1850, in RASP, Series H; T.B. Thorpe, "Sugar and the Sugar Region of Louisiana," *Harper's New Monthly Magazine* 42 (Nov. 1853): 755–67; John C. Rodrigue, *Reconstruction in the Cane Fields: From Slavery to Free Labor in Louisiana's Sugar Parishes* (Baton Rouge: Louisiana State University Press, 2001), 15–17; Olmsted, *Seaboard Slave States*, 650–51, 670–73; Walter Pritchard, "Routine on a Louisiana Sugar Plantation Under the Slavery Regime," *The Mississippi Valley Historical Review* 14 (Sept. 1927): 168–78; Solomon Northup, *Twelve Years a Slave: Narrative of Solomon Northup, a Citizen of New York, Kidnapped in Washington City in 1841, and Rescued in 1853* (Auburn, NY: Derby and Miller, 1853), 208–13.

the difficulty of simply keeping pace and not succumbing to exhaustion often proved a formidable challenge. One literate bondsman from Maryland who was sold to the cane region wrote in a letter back home in 1850: "ha[r]d times here.... I have not Had one [h]our to go out side of the place sence I have bin on it... i put my trust in the lord to halp me." Charlotte Brooks, sold from Virginia to Louisiana, exclaimed to interviewer Octavia Rogers in 1889 that "nobody knows the trouble we poor colored folks had to go through with here in Louisiana." Work was hard, free time was scarce, and during the grinding season, "we all was... busy working night and day." Sunday work was new to her. "In Virginia every body rested and would go to church on Sunday," Brooks recalled, so it "was strange to see every body working on Sunday here." Ceceil George, who was sold with her family from the South Carolina lowcountry to the Louisiana sugar bowl in the 1840s, likewise had few good words to say about the new work patterns with which she and her family were confronted in the Deep South. Similar to Brooks, the transition caused her to become overly nostalgic about work on her old plantation, where she had grown up raising cotton, rice, and corn. Back in South Carolina, the bondswoman claimed, "we'd sing and go at our work in de fields real happy." But in Louisiana, her family experienced "hard times." Everybody worked, "young and old," and the work never stopped. "Sunday, Monday, it all de same. And if you say, 'Lawd a-mercy,' de overseer whip you." The backbreaking labor and lack of free time were particularly trying for her family. "You has to put your candle out early and shut yourself up, den get up while it's still dark and start to work.... Wicked part of de country, wicked, wicked, wicked!" Odel Jackson, whose mother and older siblings had been transported from Virginia and sold off to a sugar planter in Lafourche Parish, similarly claimed that for years after arrival, her "ma had a hard time working" at their new plantation in the Deep South. She was frequently tied and beaten "[al]most to death" for failing to perform.[19]

Indeed, like their counterparts in the cotton belt, slave migrants sent to the sugar fields were often more susceptible to work-related punishments than the

[19] Follett, *Sugar Masters*, 46–47; Charles L. Wingfield, "The Sugar Plantations of William J. Minor, 1830–1860" (MA thesis, Louisiana State University, Baton Rouge, 1950), 72–73; Victor Tixier, *Tixier's Travels on the Osage Prairies*, edited by John Francis McDermott (1844; Norman Okla.: University of Oklahoma Press, 1940), 47; Amos A. Parker, *A Trip to the West and Texas* (Boston, 1836), 227; Walter Pritchard, "A Tourist's Description of Louisiana in 1860," *The Louisiana Historical Quarterly* 21 (Oct. 1938): 12; Solon Robinson, *Solon Robinson, Pioneer and Agriculturalist: Selected Writings*, edited by Herbert Anthony Kellar. 2 vols. Indianapolis: Indiana Historical Bureau, 1936), 167; Northup, *Twelve Years a Slave*, 221; Thomas Duckett to [?] Bigelow, Feb. 18, 1850, in Blassingame, ed., *Slave Testimony*, 89 (first quote); Octavia V. Rogers Albert, *The House of Bondage, or Charlotte Brooks and Other Slaves* (New York: Hunt & Eaton, 1890), 4 (second quote), 10 (third quote), 5 (fourth quote); Ceceil George, in Ronnie W. Clayton, ed., *Mother Wit: The Ex-Slave Narratives of the Louisiana Writers' Project* (New York 1990), 83–84 (fifth quotes); Odel Jackson, in Ibid., 126 (sixth quote).

local slaves, as their superiors sought to keep them moving by using the lash. One visitor to Louisiana was appalled to discover that "if a slave is brought down from Kentucky or Virginia [and] shows the least reluctance at being driven beyond what is consistent and human, he is, as the drivers say, 'getting too smart,' and must have a small touch of the 'Mississippi break down,'" a term used in the Deep South to denote a severe whipping. "And in many cases it is deemed necessary to repeat this 'breakdown' operation a number of times before the 'smartness' will pass out of him." Although most migrants struggled to work as quickly as possible in order to avoid a flogging, some became so frustrated with the furious pace at which they were forced to labor that they resisted. Antebellum newspapers abound with runaway advertisements for slaves new to the sugar country, for example, as innumerable bondspeople responded to the backbreaking work of sugar cultivation by fleeing. Hubbard, a twenty-year-old slave "lately introduced from the state of Virginia," fled his new plantation in southern Louisiana immediately after the planting season of 1845, as did William, "an American Negro" age twenty-four. Even migrants from cotton states often found cane cultivation too much. Mathy and Litty, a couple from Alabama, boarded a flatboat and absconded from their new sugar plantation in St. John the Baptist Parish during the murderously hot month of July. Tom, from Madison County, Mississippi, lasted less than three months in the cane country before fleeing in August 1845. Other migrants entered into a virtual standoff with their masters and overseers, refusing to work as fast as their masters demanded. Francis Doby, a former slave who remembered "coming over [to Louisiana] on a boat" with her mother and being sold to a planter in Opelousas, told interviewers that her mother "was sassy and hardheaded," and that she "used to get plenty [of] beatings" for not submitting to the unreasonable labor demands that she was given in the cane fields. "De master," Doby explained, "he used to stand right near and cry, 'Twenty lashes to Tinette!'"[20]

Mortality rates in southern Louisiana were also appallingly high, due in part, as Michael Tadman has argued, to the unhealthy and diseased environment (with its regular outbreaks of malaria) combined with the excessive labor demands of sugar cultivation. Newly arrived field hands from other states who were not sufficiently acclimated frequently succumbed to the diseases and stifling heat in which they were forced to work. In 1842, for example, one eighteen-year-old man named Jim, a "stoutly formed" and "well looking field hand" from Fauquier County, Virginia, was sold to a sugar planter in East Feliciana Parish, Louisiana, but died five months later while toiling in his new

[20] Philo Tower, *Slavery Unmasked: Being a Truthful Narrative of a Three Years' Residence and Journeying in Eleven Southern States* (1856; New York: Negro Universities Press, 1969), 313–14 (first quote); *The Times Picayune*, Apr. 8,1845 (second quote), Apr. 25, 1845 (third quote), July 19, 1845, Aug. 28, 1845; Francis Doby, in Clayton, ed., *Mother Wit*, 51 (fourth quote); Berlin, *Generations of Captivity*, 180–81.

master's fields. According to one physician, the newcomer died because he was unaccustomed to working in the merciless climate of southern Louisiana. Some sugar planters even explicitly preferred slaves from other unhealthy climates such as the lowcountry, reasoning that if newly imported bondspeople could withstand the heat and malaria of that region, then their chances of surviving in the sugar country were probably better than those of slaves from the more temperate Upper South. And the climate posed only one of many dangers to slave migrants sent to the cane region. During the grinding season, the perils of working in the sugar country were compounded by the ever present possibility of industrial accidents in the sugar house. A slip-up on or near the gears, conveyor belts, and steam engines that operated at full speed night and day in the autumn months could and did result in the maiming or death of locals and newcomers alike.[21]

Although working conditions were appalling to interstate migrants sent to the cane region, crop-specific work incentives did provide migrants with at least limited opportunities to improve their material conditions. The amount of work that had to be done on a sugar plantation was such that planters positively welcomed extra work in return for small payments in cash. Such practices existed throughout the South, but in the sugar country, they were standard. Indeed, Sunday work in Louisiana – so frequently commented on by visitors and newcomers alike – was usually paid work. Victor Tixier, during his travels through the region, found that "Sunday belongs to [the slave]; then he works only for money." Eliza Ripley, the daughter of a sugar planter, recalled after the Civil War that "from Saturday noon till Monday was holiday, when the enterprising men chopped wood, for which they were paid." Chopping wood for the boilers in the sugar house was the most common way for (male) slaves to earn a little bit of money, as some three or four cords of wood were needed to produce a single hogshead of sugar. Planters' account books positively abound with accounts of slaves gathering or chopping wood on Sundays for cash. On Benjamin Tureaud's plantation in 1854, for example, one man named Frank earned $8.80 for driftwood collected by at the Mississippi River. Ben Runt earned $5.00. Smaller payments were more common, however. Isaac Faulk – a fairly typical case – earned $0.40 one week and $0.60 another week for procuring wood on Sundays. On the surface, such incentives appeared to

[21] Michael Tadman, "The Demographic Cost of Sugar: Debates on Slave Societies and Natural Increase in the Americas," *The American Historical Review* 105 (Dec. 2000): 1534–75; Judith Kelleher Schafer, *Slavery, the Civil Law, and the Supreme Court of Louisiana* (Baton Rouge: LSU Press, 1994), 163–64 (quote). One sugar planter advertised in a Charleston newspaper in 1859 for "50 to 150 good plantation negroes, accustomed to either the culture of [sea-island] cotton or rice" to work on his sugar plantation in Louisiana. That he advertised specifically for lowcountry slaves, when Upper South slaves were more cheaply and easily obtained through the domestic slave trade, suggests that he desired slaves who were already accustomed to hard labor in an unhealthy and swampy environment. *Charleston Courier*, Sept. 17, 1859. Follett, *Sugar Masters*, 107–108.

be generous rewards for dutiful labor, and slaveholders – casting themselves in the role of benevolent masters – prided themselves on the "indulgences" they allowed their bondspeople. Yet in reality, paid overtime in the cane country served first and foremost the master's interest because it enticed slaves to perform important extra work for a pittance. As Richard Follett has argued, compensation systems in Louisiana "proved sadly profitable for the sugar masters, who rewrote the mutual obligations of paternalism to exploit their slaves still further." Whatever the underlying motives, however, migrants to the sugar country availed themselves of the opportunity to earn cash for material goods during their limited free time.[22]

III.

Bondspeople who migrated into the southern interior with their masters were confronted with far more primitive conditions than those who arrived on established plantations. Indeed, pioneer slaves throughout the South, especially in the early antebellum period, often arrived on undeveloped patches of land upon which an enormous amount of labor needed to be performed before a new cash crop could even be planted. For them, the drudgery of carving a plantation out of a hostile wilderness – "callousing their hands first with the ax and shovel," in the words of historian Donald McNeilly – had to be undertaken before learning to cultivate a new cash crop. Shelter and sustenance were the first priorities. One white Georgia emigrant to Mississippi declared that upon arrival in 1818, the first order of business was to build houses. As soon as their shelter was taken care of, "the hands went to work, cutting down and clearing the maiden forest to make fields to plant corn in." Virginia slave Francis Fedric recalled in 1863 that when his master moved him and the rest of the slaves out to a new farm in Mason County, Kentucky, the "first thing the negroes did [upon arrival] was to clear the land of bush, and then to sow blue grass seed for the cattle to feed upon." After that, they put up fences for a woodland pasture, tapped the maples in the woods to make maple sugar, and "built a great many log-huts." Unacquainted with such work, both the slaves and their master were guided by the advice of the neighboring

[22] Follett, *Sugar Masters*, 123–216, 153 (last quote); Berlin, *Generations of Captivity*, 184; Olmsted, *Seaboard Slave States*, 651 footnote; Tixer, *Tixier's Travels*, 47 (first quote); Eliza Ripley, *Socials Life in Old New Orleans, Being Recollections of My Childhood* (New York, 1912), 195 (second quote); Roderick A. McDonald, "Independent Economic Production by Slaves on Antebellum Louisiana Sugar Plantations," in Ira Berlin and Philip D. Morgan, eds., *Cultivation and Culture: Labor and the Shaping of Slave Life in the Americas* (Charlottesville: University of Virginia Press, 1993), 284–85; Benjamin Tureaud Plantation Journal, 1858 (microfilm), Tureaud Family Papers, Hill Memorial Library, Louisiana State University; "Account with Negroes for Wood and Work, 1850," Octave Colomb Plantation Journal, 1849–1866 (microfilm), Hill Memorial Library, Louisiana State University; Cashbook and Daybook, Bruce, Seddon and Wilkins' Plantation Records (microfilm), Hill Memorial Library, Louisiana State University.

planters, who regularly "came and showed my master how to manage his new estate."[23]

The frontier character of new plantations could last for several years, as new fields were cleared and new buildings were erected or added on to little by little over time. The daughter of one Virginia slaveholder who removed to a frontier cotton plantation in Mississippi related that her father's "plan in the management of this large estate [was] to bring under cultivation a certain portion of new land every year. His rule was to clear one hundred acres each season." At Araby plantation in Mississippi, new and hired hands spent the winter of 1842 to 1843 chopping "all the logs on about 300 or more acres of land [and] rolling and burning [the] same," a task that was repeated in the following years as well. For slave migrants, the first two or three years of chopping trees, building houses and fences, and clearing fields for planting were arguably the most arduous and certainly the most irregular. Indeed, unlike on established plantations, there was very little "regimentation" on new frontier estates because operations were anything but predictable or systematic. Inexperienced masters frequently gave one set of orders one day and then changed them the next. Slaves were often split up and set to a variety of ad hoc tasks – while some worked on the construction of buildings, others put in provision crops, cleared patches of forest, tended livestock, or were sent to town to acquire supplies. In most cases, work was directed by the masters themselves, who "farmed" alongside their bondsmen, as circumstances on the frontier were more conducive to cooperation than the maintenance of strict boundaries of social and racial hierarchy. Many – perhaps most – masters who emigrated to the southern interior also maintained an element of flexibility in their labor arrangements, regularly hiring out slaves to neighbors and urban employers until they became settled. One Maryland slaveholder who emigrated to Mississippi to become a cotton planter pursued a common course of action when upon arrival he hired out some of his slaves to start generating an immediate cash income. He jotted down in a business memorandum in 1812 that his slaves "Jack and Maria are hired to Mr. John Newman at $19.50 per month . . . and have received of him [a] note for $64.00 (including interest) paid in advance for the hire of Jack and Maria, who are to remain with him till Xmas."[24]

[23] Morris, *Becoming Southern*, 12–41; Berlin, *Generations of Captivity*, 174–76; Malcolm J. Rohrbough, *Trans-Appalachian Frontier: People, Societies, and Institutions, 1775–1850* (Bloomington: Indiana University Press, 2008), 199–200; Donald P. McNeilly, *The Old South Frontier: Cotton Plantations and the Formation of Arkansas Society, 1819–1861* (Fayetteville: University of Arkansas Press, 2000), 133 (first quote); Gideon Lincecum, in Phillips, ed., *Plantation and Frontier*, 195 (second quote); Francis Fedric, *Slave Life in Virginia and Kentucky; or, Fifty Years of Slavery in the Southern States of America* (London: Wertheim, MacIntosh, and Hunt, 1863), 17 (third quotes).

[24] Diane Mutti Burke, *On Slavery's Borders: Missouri's Small-Slaveholding Households, 1815–1865* (Athens: University of Georgia Press, 2010), 93–94, 107–18; Carey, *Sold Down the River*, 104–105; Berlin, *Generations of Captivity*, 174–76; Jonathan Martin, *Divided Mastery: Slave

For those who remained with their masters, however, the transition from subsistence agriculture and homesteading to commercial plantation agriculture was made relatively quickly. As soon as the first patches of forest had been cleared and sufficient accommodations were in place for both the white family and the slaves, newcomers spent most of their working hours cultivating money crops. In the Deep South, these were usually cotton or, in southern Louisiana, cane. Both were difficult transitions, as field hands were set to unfamiliar cultivation techniques, their work tempo was ratcheted up, and resistance to the implementation of gang labor was thwarted by brute force. But in the Appalachian valleys and interior of the Upper South – especially Kentucky, Missouri, and eastern Tennessee – slaves frequently found themselves cultivating the same crops that they had back in the Chesapeake, a situation that set them apart from the mass of interstate slave migrants in the antebellum period. Indeed, as stated in Chapter 1, these regions were largely settled by eastern tobacco and wheat farmers who had exhausted the soil in their native states and who looked to the West as a promising new territory for production. Their slaves remained laboring at familiar crops according to familiar work patterns. Rather than the harsh regimentation of gang labor that migrants in the Deep South were forced into, slaves in the tobacco and wheat frontier performed steady field labor and farm work from sunup to sundown, with half-Saturdays and free Sundays the norm. The scenery in their new destinations was different, but commercial agriculture was not. One visitor to Kentucky in the 1850s observed that in that state, which had been settled by the "hardiest sons of Virginia," slavery appeared virtually the same "as in Virginia and Maryland," with milder work patterns "than farther down in the South, on the cotton, rice and sugar plantations." Another traveler noted in the early 1820s that in newly settled parts of eastern Tennessee, "the heart is less frequently sickened at the sight of large gangs ... broiling under a vertical sun, and goaded to preternatural labour by the brutal lash" than in the "more southern states." There the farm work seemed more reasonable and the pace steadier, and emigrant masters usually worked alongside their slaves in the fields.[25]

Hiring in the Antebellum South (Cambridge, Mass.: Harvard University Press, 2004), 34–43; Susan Dabney Smedes, in Katherine M. Jones, ed., *The Plantation South* (Indianapolis: Bobbs-Merrill Co., 1957), 274–75 (first quote); Journal of Araby Plantation, Jan. 15, 1843, RASP Series F, Part 1 (microfilm), JFK Institute, Freie Universität, Berlin (second quote); Morris, *Becoming Southern*, 65–67; McNeilly, *Old South Frontier*, 123–26; Gen. A. Covington, Business Memorandum 1812, in Phillips, ed., *Plantation and Frontier*, 217 (third quote); Andrew Crane, Bill of Hire, Jan. 7, 1854, Andrew E. Crane Family Papers, Hill Memorial Library, Louisiana State University, Baton Rouge; William Greenleaf Eliot, *The Story of Archer Alexander. From Slavery to Freedom* (Boston: Cupples, Upham and Company, 1885), 35. Henry Clay Bruce claimed that his master lack of experience in frontier farming led to extremely irregular work patterns. "He would give an order one day, and change it the next, causing the loss of many days of labor." Bruce, *The New Man*, 82–83.

25 One Virginia slaveholding family that removed to Alabama in 1845 did not even wait until enough slave cabins had been built to accommodate all of the migrants, who were immediately

V.

Like pioneer slaves from the Chesapeake who were sent to Kentucky or Missouri, other groups of newcomers were also often spared at least the stress of having to learn new cultivation techniques at their new places of residence. Indeed, most local migrants in the antebellum period found themselves performing virtually identical agricultural labor to that on the plantations and farms they had left behind. Although agricultural economies in different regions sometimes varied by degrees within southern states, only in states with two main cash crops – such as South Carolina and Georgia (cotton and rice) or Louisiana (cotton and sugar) – did local migrants run the risk of being transferred to a plantation where they were introduced to completely new crops and cultivation techniques. Such newcomers experienced new work in the same way that interstate migrants did, falling behind the other hands and incurring more than their fair share of work-related punishments. In 1838, a fugitive slave from the cotton-producing South Carolina upcountry, who had been sold to a lowcountry plantation where "great crops of rice" were made, told interviewers in the North that the adjustment to rice cultivation often made him "faint from hard work." He was shown no mercy, however. The rule was that "if a slave goes into the field he must do his task. If he does not, the driver whips him." Because the bondsman often failed to complete his tasks within the allotted time, he was frequently targeted for brutal punishments. "I used to get my full share of whipping," he claimed. "All the scars on my back were made in that way."[26]

Yet in most other states local migrants were usually put to work that they at least knew how to perform. The relative ease with which they were

sent to the cotton fields. Only in 1847, after the first couple of crops had been made, did they build more cabins so that each family had one. See Richard S. Dunn, "Winney Grimshaw, a Virginia Slave, and Her Family," *Early American Studies: An Interdisciplinary Journal* 9 (Fall 2011): 513. McNeilly, *Old South Frontier*, 124–25; Rothman, *Slave Country*, 51–54; Sean M. Kelley, *Los Brazos de Dios: A Plantation Society in the Texas Borderlands, 1821–1865* (Baton Rouge: Louisiana State University Press, 2010), 97–98; Edward E. Baptist, *Creating an Old South: Middle Florida's Plantation Frontier Before the Civil War* (Chapel Hill: University of North Carolina Press, 2001), 71, 191–218; Steven F. Miller, "Plantation Labor Organization and Slave Life on the Cotton Frontier: The Alabama-Mississippi Black Belt, 1815–1840," in Ira Berlin and Philip D. Morgan, eds., *Cultivation and Culture: Labor and the Shaping of Slave Life in the Americas* (Charlottesville: University of Virginia Press, 1993), 155–79; Burke, *On Slavery's Border*, 99; Pulszky, *White, Red, Black*, 14 (first quote); Hodgson, *Remarks during a Journey*, 210–11 (second quote).

[26] Johnson, *Soul by Soul*, 6–7; Deyle, *Carry Me Back*, 157–60. The South Carolina slave's interviewer added in a footnote that "some of the scars are the size of a man's thumb, and appear as if pieces of flesh had been gouged out." See "Recollections of Slavery by a Runaway Slave," *The Emancipator*, Sept. 13, 1838 (quote). Solomon Northup claimed that cotton slaves from the Red River region of Louisiana were often hired out to sugar plantations during the grinding season, a claim backed up by research by Richard Follett. See Northup, *Twelve Years a Slave*, 145, 208; Follett, *Sugar Masters*, 81–84.

integrated into existing field gangs often served to abate their nervousness about moving to new residences; they frequently even pleased their masters and took pride in their work. One Maryland slave related after emancipation that when he was sold to a local planter to work as "a farm hand," the change "did not seem hard" because he had already had plenty of training in all kinds of farm work. Indeed, he proudly claimed that by the second year, the farm "was under my charge," his previous experience allowing him to achieve a managerial position relatively quickly. Similarly, a Mississippi bondsman claimed that he had been a "farm-superintendent" on his home plantation and that when he was subsequently hired out to work on another local cotton plantation, his new master "appointed me to the same position" – a position that was "not easy" but nevertheless left him "contented." Even Bennett Barrow, whose bad experiences with migrant field hands from Virginia turned him off to purchasing interstate migrants altogether, was delighted with the work performed by his local slave migrants. "Never saw hands Work as Well," he noted in his diary in 1840. "Have never said a word to them – feeling an interest, they look a head and see What is to be done." Experts at the crops that they were forced to cultivate at their new homes, few local migrants were exposed to the stress of adapting to completely new cultivation techniques.[27]

Although a majority of local migrants were set to agricultural work that they were already familiar with, however, their experiences nevertheless often entailed *some* measure of adjustment. Every master and overseer had his own way of doing things, and work conditions and tempos could vary by degrees on plantations within the same region or state. Edward Strutt Abdy, a British legal scholar who visited the South in the 1830s, spoke to a slave in northern Virginia who claimed that in the "lower part of the State," where the slave originally was from, "the slaves are most barbarously used." Work conditions also differed by master. Abdy spoke with a Virginia farmer who hired local slaves by the year to work in his fields, for example, who openly admitted that whites who hired slaves worked bondsmen much harder than their owners did. Thinking that "they were naturally a lazy set," the farmer boasted that he himself regularly threatened "to tie them up, and give them a good flogging" if they did not work industriously. These hirelings thus found themselves working with more regimentation than they were used to despite cultivating the same crops and performing many of the same tasks that they had back on their home plantations. Such experiences appear not to have been uncommon for rural hirelings. One Kentucky hireling ran away from his employer, "an Irishman,"

[27] Isaac Mason, *Life of Isaac Mason as a Slave* (Worcester, Mass.: n.p., 1893), 21 (first quote); Charles Thompson, *Biography of a Slave; Being the Experiences of Rev. Charles Thompson, a Preacher of the United Brethren Church, While a Slave in the South* (Dayton, Ohio: United Brethren Publishing House, 1875), 62–64 (second quotes); Bennet Barrow, Diary, Apr. 16, 1840, quoted in Davis, "Bennet H. Barrow," 436 (third quote).

because the white man worked him exceedingly hard to earn back "the value of his money" that he had paid for him.[28]

Slave testimonies also testify to the difficulties of changed work conditions for local migrants. Henry Banks, a local Virginia slave migrant, recalled that on his new farm, the slaves "were worked very late at night and were at it again before day." If his master was "in the least angry," even Sunday work was performed. "It was work, work, and nothing else," Banks related, a situation he had not been used to at his previous residence. Even certain cultivation techniques differed somewhat from those he was used to on his old farm. On one occasion during the wheat harvest, Banks' cradling skills were found wanting, and despite assurances that he was doing "the best I knew how," he was taken into the barn and whipped. Andrew Jackson, a Kentucky slave who changed masters upon the death of his original owner, also found the organization of work on his new tobacco plantation trying, not necessarily because the tempo was more grueling but because his new master forced him to pair up with another slave and work as a team, whereas he had previously been accustomed to working alone. Jackson was assigned to a "girl named Clarida," whom he claimed slowed him down, especially when they were both dragging the plow through the furrows "like cattle." The situation apparently also affected Jackson's masculinity, as he claimed: "I could have borne it, myself, but it was *hard work* to pull the plow with a poor female yoke-fellow." Friday, a North Carolina bondsman, experienced the exact opposite change: "always used to working with a large force of hands," he was "afraid to plough the corn-field by myself" when he was hired out to a local farmer one year. Such cases illustrate that even in situations when migrants did not have to acquire any knew skills, they were forced to adapt to new demands, expectations, and work tempos.[29]

VI.

For most slave migrants in the American South, field work dominated the working day. Although not always employed in the same crops or according

[28] E.S. Abdy, *Journal of a Residence and Tour in the United States of North America, from April 1833 to October 1834* (1835; New York: Negro Universities Press, 1969), 212 (first quote), 176 (second quote); Berlin, Fields, et al., *Freedom*, 540 (third quote). Historian Jonathan Martin has found that as hiring prices rose in the late antebellum period, hirers became especially "adamant that the slaves they rented be considered fully *theirs* for the length of their contracts," claiming full mastery in order to drive their slaves hard enough to earn their investments back. See Martin, *Divided Mastery*. Chapter 4, especially p. 118.

[29] Henry Banks, in Drew, ed., *North-Side View*, 198–99, 73–75, 74 (first quote); Andrew Jackson, *Narrative and Writings of Andrew Jackson, of Kentucky* (Syracuse: Daily and Weekly Star Office, 1847), 8 (second quote); Friday Jones, *Days of Bondage. Autobiography of Friday Jones. Being a Brief Narrative of His Trials and Tribulations in Slavery* (Washington: Commercial Publishing Co., 1883), 1. See also Isaac Johnson, *Slavery Days in Old Kentucky* (n.p., 1901), 11–18; William Grimes, *Life of William Grimes, the Runaway Slave* (New York: n.p., 1825), 14.

to the same work patterns that they were accustomed to back home, few migrants escaped the arduous labor of plantation agriculture. Some, however, were allocated to nonagricultural work, either using skills that they had learned before moving or performing new tasks in which they were trained after arrival at their new destinations. Circumstances relating to such positions were often similar for various groups of migrants. Whether they were transported across state lines, locally, or to towns and cities, for example, slave migrants who were made to perform nonagricultural labor found their experiences profoundly influenced by gender and age. In virtually all settings of antebellum slavery, men (both adults and adolescents) dominated artisanal trades, construction, industrial work, and certain privileged occupations such as driving coaches and serving as butlers, while women and small children overwhelmingly worked in the domestic sphere, cooking, waiting, washing, sewing, and taking care of children.[30]

The chances that migrants (both male and female) would find themselves performing skilled work at their new destinations varied across space, however. Slaves who were sent to towns and cities naturally understood that their fate was *exclusively* to perform nonagricultural labor. Such knowledge indeed underlay many bondspeople's excitement about moving to the city in the first place, as city work was often considered a welcome way of avoiding the physical drudgery of field labor. Peter Randolph, a Virginia slave, claimed that "the slaves in the cities . . . do not fare so hard as on the plantations, where they have farming work to do." Indeed, some slaves arrived in cities and industrial sites already skilled in the work that they were purchased or hired to perform, having learned to perform various useful tasks on the plantation. This is reflected in the sometimes truly exorbitant prices paid in urban and industrial areas for rural slaves with skills that were especially in demand. At the Columbia Mine in Georgia, expenditures for skilled slaves in 1853 were exceptionally high. Frank and Lawson, both engineers, were purchased for $1,800; Simon, a blacksmith, was bought for $2,000. Even Lazy Joe, a miller, was purchased for $1,500.[31]

In rural districts, however, where nonagricultural laborers always constituted a small minority of plantation slaves, opportunities for migrants to perform skilled work often depended on the cash crops. The cotton and sugar regions may serve as cases in point. Some historians, such as Ira Berlin and

[30] I agree with Daina Ramey Berry that the definition of "skilled labor" should include the skills of field laborers. "If skill means that a person has the ability to something well, then some cotton pickers and rice cultivators were certainly skilled," Berry writes. For this analysis, however, I refer to skilled labor as nonagricultural labor, as performed by both men and women. See Berry, *Swing the Sickle*, 16–17. Brenda E. Stevenson, *Life in Black and White: Family and Community in the Slave South* (New York: Oxford University Press, 1996), 196–97.

[31] Peter Randolph, *From Slave Cabin to the Pulpit. The Autobiography of Rev. Peter Randolph: The Southern Question Illustrated and Sketches of Slave Life* (Boston: James H. Earle, 1893), 191 (first quote); "Schedule of property belonging to Columbia Mining Company, Columbia County, Georgia, 1853," Joseph Belknap Smith Papers, Records of Ante-Bellum Southern Industries (hereafter RASI), Series A (microfilm), JFK Institute.

Watson Jennison, have argued, for example, that most male skilled or semiskilled slaves who were transported to the cotton plantations of the Deep South found themselves stripped of their skilled status and put to work in the fields alongside the unskilled laborers. Cotton cultivation, argues Berlin, "demanded little artisanal labor," a situation that "reduced opportunities for slaves to rise within the plantation hierarchy." Jennison likewise found that cotton cultivation deskilled and emasculated male transplants because most were put to the same monotonous work as women: hoeing and picking cotton. Indeed, according to Jennison, cotton was "the great equalizer in terms of gender and work." And although many female slaves took pride in being able to perform the same work and pick the same quotas as their male counterparts, male migrants often found it a humiliating transition.[32]

Cotton indeed required less skilled positions than, for example, rice or sugar, and cotton plantations may have therefore offered migrants fewer opportunities to perform nonagricultural labor than elsewhere, yet the high prices at which imported skilled slaves (usually male) and domestic servants (usually female) sold at markets in the cotton kingdom suggests that at least *some* migrants were purchased specifically to perform their skills at their new places of residence. One Mississippi planter beseeched a relative in Maryland to purchase and send him a number of skilled slaves in 1844: "A good blacksmith, carpenter, midwife and seamstress, I must have if possible," he declared. Interstate migrants who had been trained in various skilled vocations were indeed usually advertised as such in newspapers throughout the cotton South. Slave trader John Harris boasted in an 1834 advertisement in the *Natchez Courier and Journal* that he had 180 "VIRGINIA NEGROES, of both sexes," among whom were "two good carpenters, three blacksmiths, and several house and waiting servants." An 1859 Columbus, Georgia, newspaper announced the arrival of a "large and well selected stock" of slaves from Virginia and North Carolina, including "Field Hands, House Servants, Mechanics, &c." In Jefferson County, Florida, a group of 118 "likely family negroes, originally from Virginia," were advertised for sale in 1858, among them "carpenters, a good plantation blacksmith, a good family cook, and house servants." Although they clearly constituted a tiny minority, such interstate migrants were at least spared the necessity of learning new agricultural work when they arrived in the cotton kingdom. Skilled *local*

[32] For gender and work in the lowcountry, see, for example, Berry, *Swing the Sickle*, 13–51; and in the Upper South, see Stevenson, *Life in Black and White*, 187–205. Berlin, *Generations of Captivity*, 178 (first quote); Jennison, *Cultivating Race*, 246–47 (second quote). Susan O'Donovan, on the other hand, argues that although cotton "planters seldom hesitated to call on slave men to do the jobs slave women performed," they "almost never" called upon women "to work at jobs they understood to be men's." This gave men more access to a wide range of jobs, from skilled work to running errands, but even when it came to plowing tasks, female plow gangs were given simpler equipment to work with then male gangs. See O'Donovan, *Becoming Free*, 36–38.

migrants within the cotton South, moreover, usually remained performing their skills after removal as well.[33]

Sugar plantations showed similar trends. On most sugar plantations, an estimated 85 percent of the slave population occupied unskilled roles, but cane cultivation and sugar manufacturing also required a number of skilled mechanics, artisans, and cutters, among others. Imported blacksmiths and carpenters sold at the New Orleans slave markets for positively exorbitant prices – in the 1830s, they often fetched more than $1,000, and by the eve of the Civil War, some were even being auctioned off for around $2,000. As in the cotton South, skilled labor in the sugar country remained highly gendered. Men dominated nondomestic skilled positions, and southern records confirm that opportunities for male migrants from other states to remain working at their trades upon arrival in the sugar country – or otherwise acquire skilled, semiskilled, or managerial positions on cane plantations – were far greater than those for female migrants, who, with the exception of domestic servants, were almost exclusively sent to the fields. On the plantation of Francois Labarre near New Orleans, twenty-seven full hands (not including minor children) were advertised for sale in the *New Orleans Bee* in January 1850. Of these, seventeen – three young women and fourteen men – were specifically described as "American," meaning that they had been imported from another state. All three American women were labeled "field hands," but among the American men were a cooper, a blacksmith, and a gardener. If "skilled" *agricultural* positions are taken into account, four more male migrants may be ranked above the regular field hands: three plowmen and a driver. In other words, on this particular plantation, 100 percent of the female interstate migrants were put to field labor, working primarily with the hoe, while 50 percent of the male migrants held some kind of skilled, semiskilled, or managerial position. Even domestic servitude was not attainable for many female migrants in the cane country because it was largely limited to "mulattoes and quadroons," a tradition frequently commented on by visitors to the region.[34]

33 A slave trader confided to Ethan Allen Andrews in 1835 that a "good mechanic" from Virginia was worth $1,200 in the cotton kingdom. See Andrews, *Slavery and the Domestic Slave Trade*, 148. *Natchez Courier and Journal*, Dec. 19, 1834 (first quote); John Knight to Wm. Beall, Feb. 7, 1844, John Knight Papers, RASP, Series F, Part 1 (microfilm), JFK Institute, Freie Universität, Berlin (second quote); *Columbus Enquirer*, Sept. 28, 1859, reprinted in Anthony Gene Carey, *Sold Down the River: Slavery in the Lower Chattahoochee Valley of Alabama and Georgia* (Tuscaloosa: University of Alabama Press, 2011), 59 (third quote); *The Charleston Mercury*, Dec. 20, 1858 (fourth quote). See also the testimony of Ambrose Headen, a North Carolina slave who was trained as a carpenter and sold to Alabama, where he continued to work as a carpenter until emancipation. Blassingame, ed., *Slave Testimony*, 743–45.

34 Craig A. Bauer, *A Leader Among Peers: The Life and Times of Duncan Farrar Kenner* (Lafayette: Center for Louisiana Studies, University of Southwestern Louisiana, 1993), 50; Stephenson, *Isaac Franklin*, 85; Follett, *Sugar Masters*, 127–29; Berlin, *Generations of Captivity*, 185; *New Orleans Bee*, Jan. 31, 1850. On a plantation in Plaquemines Parish in 1856, one new male migrant from Virginia was set to work as a domestic servant, gardener, and

Nonagricultural positions on farms and plantations throughout the South were not always fixed, moreover. Especially young migrants who were considered too small to be immediately serviceable in the fields often found themselves being put to nonagricultural work but later transferred to the fields when they were strong enough. One South Carolina cotton mill, for example, employed several "children too small to work in the fields," regularly exchanging them for new ones whenever a child became large enough to perform plantation labor. Phil, a seventeen-year-old Louisiana slave advertised for sale in 1850, was described as "a likely house boy and field hand," having begun his working life in a domestic setting before being promoted to agricultural labor. His twin sister Martha was similarly hawked as a "field hand and good weaver." John Thompson, a Maryland slave, boasted that when he was a young boy, he was given to a new master who made him a "body servant" and that he therefore had "nothing more to do with plantation affairs." Indeed, he admitted that he "thought myself very much superior to those children who swept the yard." But as he grew older, he was sold and hired out several times to local masters who put him back in the field, where his strength was more needed. The shift from nonagricultural back to agricultural work was not always an easy or welcome one; slaves often strongly preferred the former to the latter, not least because it boosted their self-esteem. Indeed, some slaves resented being shifted from skilled work to field labor to the extent that they resisted, fleeing their new masters or going truant for a period of time.[35]

The process of learning and working at new nonagricultural occupations varied widely in practice – as nonagricultural work itself varied widely in nature – but most migrants, both rural and urban alike, initially welcomed the opportunity to work at something other than field labor, dedicating themselves to quickly learning their new tasks. Urban employers often made special note of how rapidly and well newly acquired bondspeople learned new work.

hostler rather than being sent to the cane fields because he was deemed especially "trusty and industrious." Tryphena Blanche Holder Fox to mother, Jan. 4, 1857 (quote) and Aug. 31, 1856, in Wilma King, ed., *A Northern Woman in the Plantation South: Letters of Tryphena Blanche Holder Fox* (Columbia: University of South Carolina Press, 1993), 47, 62. Solomon Northup, a northern black man who was kidnapped and sold to Louisiana in 1841, related that he quickly became an expert cane cutter, "an employment that suited me," and that for three successive years during the harvest season he "held the lead row... leading a gang from fifty to an hundred hands." Northup, *Twelve Years a Slave*, 208 (second quote); Tixier, *Tixier's Travels*, 47–48 (third quote).

35 Elizabeth Fox-Genovese, *Within the Plantation Household: Black and White Women of the Old South* (Chapel Hill: University of North Carolina Press, 1988), 167; E.M. Lander, Jr., "Slave Labor in South Carolina Cotton Mills," *Journal of Negro History* 38 (Apr. 1953): 166 (first quote); *New Orleans Bee*, Jan. 31, 1850 (second quote); John Thompson, *The Life of John Thompson, a Fugitive Slave; Containing His History of 25 Years in Bondage, and His Providential Escape* (Worcester, Mass.: J. Thompson, 1856), 25 (third quote), 44–48, 52–60; William H. Heard, *From Slavery to the Bishopric in the A.M.E. Church. An Autobiography* (Philadelphia: A.M.E. Book Concern, 1928), 25, 28; Johnson, *Soul by Soul*, 194.

One cotton mill owner boasted that his overseer could "learn our [young] negroes ... processes quicker than he can learn any white children." The superintendant of another mill professed that he had "never seen an equal number of entirely new hands become efficient operatives in less time" than at his factory. A Natchez merchant similarly boasted in a letter to a relative in 1835 that his recent slave purchases had been excellent investments: "Henson has proved a most invaluable boy to me, both in my store and home. I could get $1000 or more for him, at a word," the slaveholder wrote. He continued: "Jane will likewise make an excellent servant. And we have a capital cook – and also, a smart, intelligent little errand boy." In narratives and interviews, enslaved people who were put to nonagricultural work also often admitted exerting themselves to excel at their new tasks and please their new masters. Former slave Henry Brown, for example, who was sent from a Virginia farm to work in a Richmond tobacco factory, claimed that upon arrival, he "tried extremely hard to perform my duty." And although he referred to his work as "daily toil" from which he returned every evening "weary and dejected" – logging fourteen to sixteen hours most days – he still concluded that his lot was "comparatively easy" compared with most Virginia slaves. James Lindsay Smith, from Virginia's Northern Neck, was delighted to be bound out to learn the shoemaking trade. "I took hold of shoe-making very readily," he asserted after emancipation. "I had not been there a great while when I could make a shoe, or a boot." William Hayden, a Kentucky slave who was hired out to a ropemaker in Georgetown, claimed that "being very attentive, and quick of apprehension, I became a favorite with my employer."[36]

Such cases are not to suggest, however, that new occupations were always as attractive as slaves thought they would be. Similar to their counterparts in the fields, migrants who were made to perform new nonagricultural labor in various settings often made clumsy mistakes, found to their dismay that certain tasks amounted to mere drudgery, or were otherwise faced with stressful

[36] Lander, "Slave Labor in South Carolina Cotton Mills," 167 (first quote), 168 (second quote); John Knight to Wm. M. Beall, Esq., Feb. 16, 1835, John Knight Papers, RASP, Series F, Part 1, JFK Institute, Freie Universität, Berlin (third quote); Henry Brown, *Narrative of Henry Box Brown, Who Escaped from Slavery Enclosed in a Box 3 Feet Long and 2 Wide. Written from a Statement of Facts Made by Himself* (Boston: Brown & Stearns, 1849), 37 (fourth quote), 41; James Lindsay Smith, *Autobiography of James L. Smith, Including, Also, Reminiscences of Slave Life, Recollections of the War, Education of Freedmen, Causes of the Exodus, etc.* (Norwich: Press of the Bulletin Co., 1881), 13 (fifth quote); William Hayden, *Narrative of William Hayden, Containing a Faithful Account of His Travels for a Number of Years, Whilst a Slave, in the South* (Cincinnati: n.p., 1846), 24 (sixth quote). See also the testimonies of, for example, Noah Davis, a Virginia slave who also learned the shoemaker's trade quickly and expertly, and Charles Ball, who claimed that within a few days of being hired out at the Navy Yard in Washington "the duties of my station became quite familiar to me; and in the enjoyment of a profusion of excellent provisions, I felt very happy." Noah Davis, *A Narrative of the Life of Rev. Noah Davis, a Colored Man* (Baltimore: John F. Weishampel, 1859), 13–16; Ball, *Fifty Years in Chains*, 18.

situations in their new workplaces. For some, nonagricultural work proved to be simply too demanding, even relatively "privileged" migrants such as artisans or hotel butlers. Consider one bondsman hired out as a brickmaker in Missouri, who claimed that his new job "was fun for a while, but soon became very hard," adding that he was often punished because he "could not stand it. Having to carry a double mold all day long in the hot sun[,] I broke down." Lewis Charlton, a Maryland slave who was sold at the age of nine to a local tanner, likewise encountered numerous obstacles while learning to master the skills of his new trade, as he found himself physically incapable of carrying out the orders of his master. His new owner "imposed many laborious duties" on him, for example, "such as no child could possibly do." He would make the young migrant "spread heavy hides, so heavy that men could hardly handle them, and a great many times I have been pulled into the vats, waste deep in water and ice." Every time he made a mistake he was subjected to corporal punishment. Some nonagricultural jobs entailed less physical exertion but longer hours and a more stressful work environment, a situation that drove innumerable migrants to bitterness and even rage. Frederick Law Olmsted encountered numerous hirelings working at hotels throughout the South who were thoroughly dissatisfied with their positions. Most resented the irregular hours and demanding guests. One older hired servant in a Washington inn seethed to Olmsted that he had been "up all night" and that his employer and guests "nebber let de old nigger have no ress – hundred gemmen tink I kin mak dair fires all de same minute; all get mad at an ole nigger . . . ." In Columbus, Georgia, Olmsted found the waiters in his hotel so unenthusiastic that they struck him as "stupid, inattentive, and annoying." And in Savannah, the head waiter of another hotel admitted to him: "I don' like dis place, no how. . . . Dey keeps me up most all night; I haan been used to sich treatem." As one scholar has argued, hirelings at hotels sometimes even feigned incompetence to prevent them from ever being hired out as waiters again. Others openly fought back against guests who became too demanding or abusive. One British sojourner in the South witnessed how a hired hotel chambermaid in New Orleans, who was originally from Virginia, resisted the abuse she received from one particularly demanding guest. When a Creole man "struck her . . . with the fist in the face" for not brining him water quickly enough, the hireling "put herself on the defence," grabbing "the Frenchman by the throat," after which he "ran to his room."[37]

[37] One slave from Mississippi who was sold to a cotton press in New Orleans claimed to a British interviewer in 1858 that he "didn't understand tying the cotton; it was new to me, and I was awkward, so I was flogged." See Tom Wilson, in Blassingame, ed., *Slave* Testimony, 339. Bruce, *The New Man*, 20–21 (first quote); Lewis Charlton, *Sketch of the Life of Mr. Lewis Charlton, and Reminiscences of Slavery*, edited by Edward Everett Brown (Portland, Maine: Daily Press Print, n.d.), 3 (second quotes); Olmsted, *Seaboard Slave States*, 4 (third quote), 548 (fourth quote), 558 (fifth quote); Seth Rockman, *Scraping By: Wage Labor, Slavery, and Survival in*

Working conditions at industrial jobs were even worse. Migrants who were sent to toil in factories, for example, often performed their work in stuffy, loud, and chaotic settings, resenting the repetition and monotony of their tasks. Visiting a cotton factory in Augusta, Georgia, that regularly hired slaves from the surrounding countryside, Swedish traveler Fredrika Bremer claimed that the workers looked miserable and that she "could not believe that the blacks would voluntarily choose this occupation, with its noise, difficulty, and dusty, unwholesome atmosphere – they who had been accustomed to the labor of the open fields." Henry, an eighteen-year-old slave who was hired out to the turpentine manufacturing firm of Wortham and Jackson in South Carolina in 1856, found his new situation dire enough that he fled his new employers, presumed to be making his way back home. Slaves hired out to tobacco factories and flour mills in Chesapeake cities also absconded back to their owners with some regularity, complaining about the long hours and unhealthy working conditions and pleading to be hired out somewhere else. Bondspeople who found themselves hired out or purchased to work on the railroads, dig canals, or mine coal were subjected to working conditions that were arguably even less attractive – and often more dangerous – than factory work. One northern journalist observed that the slaves who were employed laying tracks near Montgomery, Alabama – all of them purchased in Virginia – were "hard worked from sun to sun, and from Christmas to Christmas." Hirelings on the Blue Ridge Railroad in South Carolina averaged twenty-six full workdays in August 1858, foregoing the traditional half Saturday that was common among farmhands in the upcountry region. In Richmond, Virginia, hired immigrant workers who were employed by the James River and Kanawha Company to excavate the James River canal in 1837 found the work so "strenuous and unrelenting," laboring long hours in all weather conditions, that they walked off the job, their places filled by hired slaves who were considered "more manageable and stable." Frances Claiborne, a Virginia slaveholder, filed suit against the hirer of her slave John in 1819, when the hirer fraudulently and in violation of his contract attempted to "send him to the Coal-Pits at which place [Claiborne] has already lost one slave."[38]

Early Baltimore (Baltimore: Johns Hopkins University Press, 2009), 66; James Stuart, *Three Years in North America* (Edinburgh, 1833), 2:241 (sixth quote).

38 Former slave Henry Clay Bruce, who was once hired to a tobacco factory in Missouri, tying lugs of tobacco all day without being permitted to speak to anyone, claimed that this sedentary and monotonous occupation was "prison-like." See Bruce, *The New Man*, 21–22. Fredrika Bremer, in Jones, ed., *Plantation South*, 184 (first quote); *The Weekly Raleigh Register*, Sept. 3, 1856; Midori Takagi, "*Rearing Wolves to Our Own Destruction:" Slavery in Richmond, Virginia, 1782–1865* (Charlottesville: University of Virginia Press, 1999), 50–51; Franklin and Schweninger, *Runaway Slaves*, 33–37; James Redpath, *The Roving Editor; Or, Talks with the Slaves in the Southern States* (1859; New York: Negro Universities Press, 1968), 172 (second quote); Bisset & Hawkins Ledger, 1858, Hawkins Family Papers, SASI, Series B (microfilm), JFK Institute; Takagi, "*Rearing Wolves,*", 32–33 (third quotes); Olmsted, *Seaboard Slave States*, 47–48; Martin, *Divided Mastery*, 138–60; "Frances Claiborne to the County

Domestic servants on plantations and in urban residences, most of them women or children, more frequently disliked their work and failed to please their new masters than perhaps any other type of nonagricultural laborer. On call virtually twenty-four hours a day, seven days a week; forced to perform a variety of unattractive tasks; and often working under the watchful eyes of their owners or employers, domestic servants labored under conditions that all but invited conflicts and friction with their new owners or employers. Many rural newcomers who were set to household labor in urban settings, moreover, had been trained in field work rather than cooking, cleaning, and sewing, forcing them to adjust to new skills in which they may not have been expert. Jane, a Tennessee slave girl age fourteen, was purchased by a Davidson County couple as a house servant but proved "wholy unfit" for the position, having only ever performed farm work. Petitioning the court for permission to sell Jane, the couple claimed to have "taken great pains to train her and qualify her for the duties of a house servant [but] have been wholy unable to accomplish the task. Nature made her a negro and they have been unable to make any thing else of her." Wherever they worked and however much experience they had, the pressure to perform household tasks without evoking the wrath of their masters was great indeed. Louisiana plantation mistress Tryphena Fox constantly had trouble with hired domestic servants, exclaiming in a letter to her mother once that "it requires more watching & telling & running after them to get the work done, than to do it oneself." Frank, a "Creole negro boy" whom she hired in 1856, "annoyed me so much" that she was "glad to get rid of him." Fox claimed that she "tried in vain to make a good dining servant of him, but he was too slow & stupid." Mary, another hireling who was often late with breakfast and "never thought of stirring until called," was also deemed too slow. Eventually, she "got so, that she was never through the washing or the ironing & it seemed impossible to get the kitchen cleaned & everything was getting behindhand." Susan took so long to do the washing one morning that Fox nearly exploded, writing to her mother: "my *temper* is *quite bad* – these darkies 'do plague me to death' sometimes."[39]

Court, Henrico County, Virginia, 1819," in Loren Schweninger, ed., *The Southern Debate over Slavery: Volume 2, Petitions to the Southern County Courts, 1775–1867* (Urbana: University of Illinois Press, 2008), 104–105 (fourth quote). For more on work in Chesapeake tobacco factories and railroads, see Calvin Schermerhorn, *Money over Mastery, Family over Freedom: Slavery in the Antebellum Upper South* (Baltimore: Johns Hopkins University Press, 2011), 147–50, 181–89.

39 Berry, *Swing the Sickle*, 35–51; Takagi, *"Rearing Wolves,"* 44–45. Keith Barton has argued that changing ideas about white women's work among the non-elite in antebellum Bourbon County, Kentucky, resulted in the use of hired slaves "to perform the drudgery that both women and men no longer considered a fit job for housewives." See Keith C. Barton, "'Good Cooks and Washers': Slave Hiring, Domestic Labor, and the Market in Bourbon County, Kentucky," *Journal of American History* 84 (Sept. 1997): 448–57. In Little Rock, a city ordinance prohibited slaves from working on Sundays but exempted "household" work performed by domestic servants. See Paul D. Lack, "An Urban Slave Community: Little Rock, 1831–1862,"

Such friction between domestic migrants and masters was common in southern households, rendering domestics particularly vulnerable to frequent punishments. One Alabama "house wench" who was bought from a slave trader and recommended "as highly as ever a jockey did a horse," was "found wanting in the requisite qualifications" upon arrival at her new residence, falling victim "to the disappointed rage" of the master and frequently tied up and whipped for her shortcomings. Indeed, subjected to such stressful work conditions, many migrants who were put to domestic servitude fled their new owners. Sally, a Louisiana bondswoman from Pointe Coupee who was brought to New Orleans in 1850 to work in the household of one F. Krabbe in 1850, absconded within two months of arrival, presumed to be lurking about the city despite being a "stranger" who "don't know any body in this place."[40]

Whatever the pleasures or disadvantages associated with their work, bondspeople understood that skilled labor came with certain privileges and opportunities, both in rural and urban settings, that were denied common field workers. Urban migrants, especially, could hope to earn extra money in a variety of ways, depending on their occupation, affording them opportunities to not only improve their own material conditions but often even to purchase small luxuries for loved ones back home. Many went to great lengths to take advantage of such incentives. Those employed in hotels, for example, frequently went out of their way to please guests – playing the role of the happy and loyal servant – because they knew they would be tipped for it. Ned, the porter at Norval House in Lynchburg, Virginia, was "an example of politeness when you reward him," one guest noted in 1859. Not only would he take guests' bags and lead them to their rooms – bowing at the foot of the stairs – but he would even "[brush] off the gentlemen" and "caress squalling infants" for a tip. One hireling who worked in a hotel in Washington, DC, likewise admitted to E.S. Abdy in 1833 that the slaves were allowed to keep "presents from the guests," an incentive that induced many to shower visitors with charm and politeness. Thomas Likers, a fugitive slave from Maryland who fled to Canada, claimed during a government interview in 1863 that back home he "had the privilege of hiring my own time;" serving as a waiter in various Baltimore inns, he "earned plenty of money . . . more than I can in Canada." Young female hotel workers charmed male visitors by flirtatiously smiling and accommodating them in a

The Arkansas Historical Quarterly 41 (Autumn 1982): 261–62; Rockman, *Scraping By*, 123; "John and Amanda Wright to the Chancery Court, Davidson County, Tennessee, 1852," in Schweninger, ed., *Southern Debates over Slavery*, 284–85 (first quotes); King, ed., *Letters of Tryphena Blanche Holder Fox*, 65 (second quote), 47 (third quote), 56 (fourth quote), 75 (fifth quote); See also Isaac Mason, *Life of Isaac Mason as a Slave* (Worcester, Mass.: n.p., 1893), 13–14, 19–20; Hughes, *Thirty Years a Slave*, 17–19.62–80; Fedric, *Slave Life in Virginia and Kentucky*, 18–23. For more on female slaves' work as household slaves, see Fox-Genovese, *Within the Plantation Household*, ch. 3.

40 William Leftwich to brother, Dec. 26, 1838, in Weld, *American Slavery as It Is*, 48 (first quote); *The Daily Picayune*, Mar. 13, 1850 (second quote).

polite and courteous manner. Northern reporter James Redpath encountered a chambermaid at a hotel in Augustus, Georgia, who claimed that "gentlemen here sometimes gives me a dollar," although her mistress took "every red" cent of her formal hiring fee. Some hirelings at southern hotels worked for cash after their shifts were over. British geologist Charles Lyell found a footman in Tuscaloosa who worked "on his own account as a bootmaker at spare hours, and another getting perquisites by blacking the students' shoes."[41]

Self-hire arrangements allowed urban migrants to sell their services for more than their masters demanded, pocketing the profit. One Virginia slave claimed that in the cities, where slaves "are employed in factories and work at trades," hirelings could often "do very well, for if they are industrious, they can earn considerably more than is exacted of them by their owners." Many, he claimed, "dress well" and "lay up money." Such practices were common, a testament to hirelings' ability and willingness to bend forced migration into a vehicle for material improvement. James Silk Buckingham was baffled to learn that in New Orleans, slaves who hired themselves "on condition of bringing home a certain portion of wages to their masters" were often able "to accumulate property, though of course very slowly." Joseph Holt Ingraham found during a residence in Mississippi in the 1830s that in Natchez, such hirelings rarely "fail in making up the sum" demanded by their owners, and "generally they earn more, if industrious." Adam Hodgson likewise found in 1819 that some hirelings in Baltimore were "allowed, on paying their masters a certain sum, generally about two dollars a week, to find work for themselves and retain the surplus." Sometimes the surplus hirelings earned amounted to substantial sums. One "country-looking slave" who hired his own time as a carpenter in Montgomery, Alabama, claimed to northern journalist James Redpath that he skimmed almost $100 off the top of his formal hiring fee in 1858. Alonzo, a South Carolina slave who was "a Livery stable keeper by occupation," was permitted the luxury of "working only for whom I chose," paying his master $140 per year to hire out his own time but earning $25 a month. After eighteen years of this arrangement, he had saved enough to buy his own house in Georgetown.[42]

[41] For more on the material conditions of domestic servants in both rural and urban settings, see, for example, Randolph, *From Slave Cabin to the Pulpit*, 160–61; Buckingham, *Slave States of America*, 200; Takagi, *"Rearing Wolves,"* 41; Berry, *Swing the Sickle*, 43–44. J. Alexander Pattern, "Scenes from Lynchburg," in Eugene L. Schwaab, ed., *Travels in the Old South, Selected from Periodicals of the Times* (Lexington: University Press of Kentucky, 1973), 2:542 (first quote); Abdy, *Journal of a Residence*, 89 (second quote); Thomas Likers, in Blassingame, ed., *Slave Testimony*, 395–96 (third quotes); James Redpath, *The Roving Editor: Or, Talks with Slaves in the Southern States* (1859; New York: Negro Universities Press, 1968), 163 (fourth quote); Charles Lyell, *A Second Visit to the United States of North America* (New York: Harper & Bros, 1850), 72 (fifth quote).

[42] For more on the advantages and disadvantages of self-hire, see Martin, *Divided Mastery*, 161–87. Randolph, *From Slave Cabin to the Pulpit*, 191 (first quote); Buckingham, *Slave States of America*, 356 (second quote); Ingraham, *The South-West*, 2:250–51 (third quotes); Hodgson,

Overwork afforded many nonagricultural laborers the opportunity to improve their material conditions. Artisans, both urban and rural, for example, were easily able to hire their services for cash. Peter, a carpenter on Houmas plantation in Louisiana, earned $5 in February 1853 for framing the windows and door of the overseer's house. On the sugar plantations of William Minor, artisans regularly earned extra cash for extra work; indeed, sales to third parties were so widespread that Minor had to specifically instruct his overseer not to "allow the Mechanics to make or sell any of their work without special permission." Urban migrants who were sold or hired out to industrial employers were often paid cash bonuses for working extra hours as well. In Richmond, tobacco factories regularly paid slaves between 50 cents a week to $5.00 a month for overwork. The gold mines of Rowan County, North Carolina, provided hirelings with the opportunity to earn cash credits for extra work in 1859, which were often spent on shoes, tobacco, coffee, sugar, and other minor luxuries. Early Chesapeake ironworks also used the overwork system, "merging [the slaves'] physical and economic interests with those of the ironmaster," as historian Ronald Lewis has argued. Unskilled hands could earn extra meat, bushels of meal, or cash for chopping and hauling wood in their free time. Skilled craftsmen were royally paid for overwork, some of them accumulating more than one hundred dollars in the ironmasters' ledger books.[43]

Nonagricultural work also provided some migrants – especially men – with a degree of latitude and mobility in the work place that they lacked in the fields. Indeed, many found that some or all of their tasks went largely unsupervised, and a few were even permitted limited physical mobility to move about the neighborhood unchecked. In urban settings, especially, migrants frequently took to what historian Midori Takagi has called "losing time," walking off the job or taking extended "breaks" while nobody was watching. Slaves sent on errands, for example, often took longer than necessary, blending in at corner shops, crowded marketplaces, or busy intersections. One Virginia slave who was sold to Savannah as a body servant complained that his master "would never allow me to leave the yard, unless it was for the purpose of taking out his horses to exercise them." When he did take the horses out,

Remarks During a Journey, 28–29 (fourth quotes); Redpath, *Roving Editor*, 173–74 (fifth quote); Testimony of Alonzo Jackson before the Southern Claims Commission, Mar. 17, 1873, in Berlin, Fields, et al., eds., *Freedom*, 813 (sixth). See also Brown, *Narrative of Henry Box Brown*, 49–50.

43 H.M. Seale Diary, Feb. 28, 1850, Hill Memorial Library, Louisiana State University; Charles L. Wingfield, "The Sugar Plantations of William J. Minor, 1830–1860" (MA thesis, Louisiana State University, Baton Rouge, 1950), 47 (first quote); Takagi, "*Rearing Wolves,*" 49–50; Day Book, 1859–1860, Gold Hill Mining Company Records, SASI, Series B (microfilm), JFK Institute; Ronald L. Lewis, "Slave Families at Early Chesapeake Ironworks," *The Virginia Magazine of History and Biography* 86 (Apr. 1978): 169–79, 170 (second quote); Redwell Furnace Account Book, 1791–1813, SASI, Series C, part 1 (microfilm), JFK Institute; Martin, *Divided Mastery*, 161–87.

however, he admitted that he "would often go to the fortune-teller," indulging himself in this small luxury and making no haste to return home. Michael, a slave hired to the Roman Catholic College in Washington, DC, was regularly "sent on errands to Catholic churches" throughout the region on a gray horse, "the property of the College." In the summer of 1822, he took advantage of one such errand to lose time permanently, riding north and absconding from bondage altogether. Stephen, "a carpenter by trade" who was working in Charleston in 1830, likewise slipped off unnoticed one day, presumed to be visiting relatives in one of the surrounding parishes where he was from. And George and Jane, two slaves hired out in Richmond, Virginia, developed a "habit of frequently running away" from their employers while unsupervised; on one particular occasion, they snuck out and hired themselves out as free blacks aboard a schooner bound for New York, attempting to flee the South. Even slaves who worked at supervised industrial work usually found themselves away from the eyes of authority after their shifts were over, a reality that urban southerners constantly complained about. Olmsted learned from a concerned Virginia slaveholder that many of his best hands, who were hired out to work in a furnace, had gotten into the "habit of roaming about" during their off time, because "when they were not at work in the furnace, nobody looked out for them."[44]

Some nonagricultural occupations even afforded slave men the opportunity to travel beyond the plantation or city limits. Carriage drivers made regular trips to town from the rural countryside or even from town to town, exposing them to new sights, sounds, and communities. Such experiences were often welcomed by migrants not only because they broke the monotony of slave life but also because they made them feel superior to their more stationary counterparts, who were confined to their plantations and whose movement was strictly regulated according to the pass system, the cornerstone of what Stephanie Camp has called the "geography of containment." Other laborers traveled even greater distances than carriage drivers, some of them across state lines. Steamboat workers and boatmen, for example, found their horizons significantly broadened as they plied up and down the South's waterways, making contact with riverside communities and spending leisure time unsupervised in cities' grog shops and boardinghouses, a situation that both resembled freedom and often sparked a strong desire for freedom among bondsmen. Largely unsupervised, moreover, they also often combined their travels with "losing time." One frustrated Virginia ironmaster, whose watermen were entrusted

44 Takagi, *"Rearing Wolves,"* 46–47; Grimes, *Life of William Grimes*, 23 (first quote); *Daily National Intelligencer*, June 13, 1822 (second quote); *Charleston Courier*, Jan. 4, 1830 (third quote); "Thomas Cowles to the County Court, Henrico County, Virginia, 1833," in Schweninger, ed., *Southern Debate over Slavery*, 163 (fourth quote); Olmsted, *Seaboard Slave States*, 58 (fifth quote). John Hope Franklin and Loren Schweninger have argued that "accident of location" led many unsupervised slaves living in urban areas to attempt to flee slavery. See Franklin and Schweninger, *Runaway Slaves*, 25–30.

with shipping products and supplies to Richmond, complained in a letter to his manager: "the watermen are the most unfaithful people attached to the estate.... The last trip coming down they were double mann'd and brought half a load – they were about 20 days on their passage, when double handed it might have been done in five days... those rascals only made seven miles a day – let them know I am perfectly acquainted with their rascally behavior."[45]

Slaves enjoyed the lack of supervision and change of scenery. William Wells Brown served on several steamboats during his life in slavery. During one stint as a waiter on a commission merchant's steamboat on the upper Mississippi River, he admitted that he "found a great difference between the work in a steamboat cabin and that in a corn-field." Brown enjoyed "passing from place to place, and seeing new faces every day," but at the same time, he lamented that the white passengers "could go where they pleased" while he was officially trapped in bondage. At times he even felt strongly tempted to leave "the boat at some landing place" and simply disappear from slavery. Indeed, the taste of freedom enjoyed by enslaved riverboat workers induced many to effect their escape from bondage altogether. Blending into urban black communities at ports of call, daring hirelings let their steamboats depart without them. Emanuel, the slave of William Powell of Tennessee but hired "on board of the Steamer Constellation," remained in Natchez during one such flight attempt, eventually discovered and "committed to the Jail of Adams County as a runaway." Jerry, a Kentucky slave hired out to the steamboat *Bunker Hill No 3*, successfully fled slavery while docked in Illinois in 1851.[46]

As they struggled to adjust to new homes in various settings, the hurdle of adapting to new work patterns proved formidable for innumerable antebellum migrants. Arguably the most difficult transition was experienced by interstate migrants who were transported from the Upper South to the cotton and sugar

45 William Robinson, for example, a former slave from North Carolina who was made carriage driver by his new master, was delighted with his new position. Claiming that he "had a great deal of freedom," for he did "nothing but drive Massa Joseph back and forth, to and from town" everyday, he especially liked informing his fellow bondspeople of the latest news he had heard in the city, which elevated his status significantly. See William H. Robinson, *From Log Cabin to the Pulpit, or, Fifteen Years in Slavery* (Eau Claire, Wisc.: James H. Tifft, 1913), 76. For more on the geography of containment, see Stephanie M.H. Camp, *Closer to Freedom: Enslaved Women and Everyday Resistance in the Plantation South* (Chapel Hill: University of North Carolina Press, 2004), 6, 12–34. Schermerhorn, *Money over Mastery*, 70–73; David Ross to William Dunn, Jan. (n.d.) 1813, David Ross Letterbook, SASI, Series C, Part 1 (microfilm), JFK Institute (quote).

46 William Wells Brown, *Narrative of William W. Brown, a Fugitive Slave* (Boston: The Anti-Slavery Office, 1847), 31–35, 35 (first quote), 31 (second quote); Thomas C. Buchanan, "Rascals on the Antebellum Mississippi: African American Steamboat Workers and the St. Louis Hanging of 1841," *Journal of Social History* 34 (Summer 2001): 797–816; *Natchez Daily Courier*, July 1, 1840 (third quote); "A.J. Ballard to the Chancery Court, Louisville, Kentucky, 1851," in Schweninger, ed., *Southern Debates over Slavery*, 270–71; Franklin and Schweninger, *Runaway Slaves*, 25–30.

lands of the southern interior, but even slaves who remained cultivating the same crops they had in their places of origin – such as local migrants and many pioneer slaves – were frequently confronted with the necessity of adapting to new work tempos, techniques, or methods of organizing labor. Falling victim to work-related punishments only compounded the trauma of removal for many migrants. Skilled migrants – male and female, in both rural and urban settings – experienced new work conditions in ways that were both similar and different from their counterparts in the fields. Although most looked forward to the opportunity to escape field labor, they too often experienced difficulties transitioning to new demands and unattractive tasks, evoking the wrath of their masters and employers. Their experiences were to some extent alleviated, however, by the material and physical privileges that nonagricultural labor often brought with it. Seizing opportunities to earn extra money or reclaim a few minutes of valuable time, migrants who were put to nonagricultural work often attempted to reassert their humanity and make the most of their new positions.

5

Managing Newcomers

I suppose I had the misfortune to get a run of bad masters.

Former slave migrant John Brown, 1855[1]

Andrew Crane, a starting sugar planter in southern Louisiana in the 1840s and 1850s, had a reputation for being a tough master. Part of the problem lay in his frugality. During his first few years as a cane producer Crane had difficulties enough simply keeping his business afloat, a predicament that encouraged him to drive his slaves as hard as possible and skimp on their material conditions to save on costs. Indeed, he embarked on his new career in 1849 with only nine slaves, the bare minimum for a crop that was extremely intensive in both labor and capital, and thus usually produced on a far more vast scale. To augment his labor force, Crane secured the necessary credit to gradually purchase more slaves over time, and he also regularly hired local slaves from his neighbors, but his management style remained unchanged and made him deeply unpopular with the bondspeople who toiled under his watch. Whether they were owned or hired by him, records reveal that the slaves who worked for Crane despised him. Runaways were frequent. In 1851 alone, two newly purchased slaves fled, burdening him not only with the loss of their labor but also the costs for newspaper advertisements and jail fees for their recovery. Crane's reputation as a harsh master even irritated some of his peers, especially those who were in the habit of hiring out their slaves to him. E. Herbert, who regularly hired out his slaves to Crane during the fall and winter months, wrote to his fellow slaveholder in 1858: "[My girl Emma] complains mightily about your feeding, if it is so my girl shall not pass the grinding season at your house. As for the

[1] John Brown, *Slave Life in Georgia: A Narrative of the Life, Sufferings, and Escape of John Brown, a Fugitive Slave, Now in England*, edited by L.A. Chamerovzow (London: L.A. Chamerovzow, 1855), 131.

rest of my boys, I have already hired them at Mrs. Heidi Nichols. I was to hire them to you, but they told me they would go anywhere before they would to you.... I hired them according to their wishes."[2]

Crane's unpopularity with the slaves under his command and their attempts to escape or avoid his control reveal important tensions faced by slave migrants who were forced to adapt to new masters. As in other slave societies of the Atlantic world, slavery in the antebellum South rested on the principle of total subordination of one race to another, legally relegating blacks to the subhuman status of "chattels." Yet the development of paternalist ideology in the nineteenth century emphasized reciprocal (if unequal) obligations between masters and slaves that implicitly recognized slaves' humanity. Public discussions regarding the proper "management of negroes" pervaded southern culture, and commentators theoretically agreed that in return for subordination and hard work, antebellum slaveholders should provide their bondspeople with sufficient food, adequate housing, reasonable rules and privileges, and protection from extreme abuse. As Eugene Genovese argued, antebellum slaveholders crafted the ideology of paternalism – positing themselves as benevolent patriarchs of the "childlike" subjects under their command – partly in an attempt to overcome the inherent contradiction that their slaves were both property and people. In the words of Genovese, "paternalism defined the involuntary labor of the slaves as a legitimate return to their masters for protection and direction." More recently, Genovese and Fox-Genovese argued in their book *Fatal Self-Deception* (2011) that slaveholders were sincere in their equation of paternalism with benevolence – though they admit that their behavior was often anything but – and that despite its deceptive and "gaping contradictions," and the countervailing pressures of profit maximization that often compelled masters towards severity rather than kindness, paternalist ideology "bared essential characteristics of a worldview." According to the two historians, slaveholders saw themselves "as the best, the sincerest, indeed the only friends that American blacks had," and they truly believed that their social system was superior to free labor because it "created a floor beneath which the living standards [of their slaves] could not sink."[3]

2 U.S. Bureau of the Census, Nonpopulation Census Schedules, 1850 Agriculture: St. James Parish; U.S. Bureau of the Census, Seventh Population Census, 1850: St. James Parish, Slave Schedules; Andrew Crane, Bills of Sale and Receipts, Mar. 4, 1849, Sept. 21, 1849, Oct. 4, 1849, Jan. 11, 1850, Jan. 21, 1850, Mar. 15, 1850, May 1, 1850, May 25, 1850, Jan. 3, 1851, Jun. 16, 1859, Andrew E. Crane Family Papers, Hill Memorial Library, Louisiana State University, Baton Rouge; *La Messager* (Bringier, La.), Apr. 30, 1852; U.S. Bureau of the Census, Eighth Population Census, 1860: St. James Parish, Slave Schedules; E. Herbert to A.E. Crane, Oct. 6, 1858, Andrew E. Crane Family Papers (quote).

3 Eugene D. Genovese, *The World the Slaveholders Made: Two Essays in Interpretation* (New York: Vintage, 1971), 195–234; Eugene D. Genovese, *Roll, Jordan, Roll: The World the Slaves Made* (New York: Pantheon, 1974), 3–7, 5 (first quote); James Oakes, *Slavery and Freedom: An Interpretation of the Old South* (New York: Knopf, 1990), 137–94; Craig A. Bauer, *A Leader Among Peers: The Life and Times of Duncan Farrar Kenner* (Lafayette, La., 1993),

Yet although slaveholders often boasted that they cared well for their slaves and that their bondspeople were happy under their control, in practice both their commitment to "benevolent rule" and their ideas about what constituted their paternalist obligations were inconsistent, contradictory, and varied widely according to temper, circumstance, and especially economic self-interest. Indeed, as many historians have argued, paternalism was less a reflection of sincere benevolence on the part of the slaveholders than it was "a way of imagining, describing, and justifying slavery." Its tenets were an outgrowth of a system of exploitation for the financial advantage of the masters. Although some slaveholders found it economically expedient to treat the slaves under their command with care and consideration, others, such as Crane, calculated that meager provisions and frequent punishment were more conducive to profit. The paternalist obligations of the master could always be discarded, and they often were; in the end, there was always recognition of the master's absolute authority over the bodies he owned. David Brion Davis noted that even "'welfare capitalist' plantations... were essentially ruled by terror." As a result, forced migrants who changed masters were often confronted with completely different styles of governance – not just by their masters but also by mistresses, overseers, and other whites. Inevitably, they formulated strong opinions about the extent to which their treatment at new destinations was "better" than what they had previously been accustomed to.[4]

How did various types of slave migrants experience and adjust to new masters, overseers, and white populations? To what extent were conditions, punishments, and rules in general different from what they had known in their home societies? This chapter examines the ways in which long-distance, local, and urban slave migrants experienced and adapted to new racial relations at their destinations, delving specifically into themes such as material conditions and punishment and abuse.

I.

Antebellum discussions regarding proper slave management were dominated by discourses about bondspeople's material conditions. Nineteenth-century advice among planters dictated that slaves should be well housed and clothed and adequately fed, not only for their own comfort (a passing nod to paternalist

57–58; Eugene D. Genovese and Elizabeth Fox-Genovese, *Fatal Self-Deception: Slaveholding Paternalism in the Old South* (New York: Cambridge University Press, 2011), 2–3 (second quotes).

4 Peter Kolchin, *American Slavery, 1619–1877* (New York: Hill & Wang, 1993), 111–32; Richard Follett, *The Sugar Masters: Planters and Slaves in Louisiana's Cane World, 1820–1860* (Baton Rouge: Louisiana State University Press, 2005), 151–94; Walter Johnson, *Soul by Soul: Life Inside the Antebellum Slave Market* (Cambridge, Mass: Harvard University Press, 1999), 111 (first quote); David Brion Davis, *Inhuman Bondage: The Rise and Fall of Slavery in the New World* (New York: Oxford University Press, 2006), 196 (second quote).

obligations) but especially to protect slaveholders' valuable chattel investments from physical ailments and death. Thomas Affleck, who authored the widely used *Cotton Plantation Record and Account Book*, expressed the standard view in 1852. "The health of the negroes," wrote Affleck, "is an important matter." Illness and untimely death, he maintained, were often the result of careless mismanagement, such as "unnecessary exposure to rain, insufficient clothing, [and] improper or badly cooked food." Such losses in both labor and life were easily avoided, according to Affleck. He admonished slaveholders and their overseers:

> By exerting yourself to have their clothing ready in good season...; to see that an abundant supply of wholesome, *well-cooked* food, including plenty of vegetables, to be supplied to them *at regular hours*...; in short, by using such means for their comfort as every judicious, humane man will readily think of, you will find the amount of sickness greatly lessened.

Robert Collins, in his classic *Essay on the Treatment and Management of the Slaves* (1852), similarly argued that inadequate material conditions rendered slaves "unprofitable, unmanageable; a vexation and a curse." He advised slaveholders to provide their bondspeople with proper houses, "sufficiently large" and "well ventilated with doors and windows"; rations consisting of "five pounds of good clean bacon, and one quart of molasses, with as much good bread as they require; and in the fall or sickly seasons of the year, or on sickly places, the addition of one pint of strong coffee, sweetened with sugar"; and clothing allowances of "two suits of cotton for spring and summer, and two suits of woolen for winter; four pairs of shoes, and three hats, with such articles of dress as the negro merits."[5]

To the outside world, many antebellum slaveholders claimed to agree with such advice; Genovese and Fox-Genovese even argued that masters' commitment to their slaves' "contentment" and "comfort" was genuine enough that they truly expected their slaves to love them in return, one of the beliefs that proved "deceptive" when the Civil War broke out. In reality, however, few white southerners found it necessary to follow the advice of plantation manuals to the letter, and in practice, material conditions tended to be crude and far from uniform on southern slaveholdings. Indeed, in slave testimonies, one of the most common complaints voiced by migrants who changed masters was that the material conditions in their new places of residence were inferior to what they had been used to at their previous homes – that their clothing was shabby, that their living quarters were cramped and uncomfortable, and especially that

[5] Thomas Affleck, *The Cotton Plantation Record and Account Book, No. 2. Suitable for a Force of 80 Hands, or Under* (Louisville: Morton & Griswold, 1852), n.p. (first quotes); Robert Collins, *Essay on the Treatment and Management of Slaves. Written for the Seventh Annual Fair of the Southern Central Agricultural Society* (Macon, Ga: Benjamin F. Griffin, 1852), n.p. (second quotes). See also James O. Breeden, ed., *Advice Among Masters: The Ideal Slave Management in the Old South* (Westport, Conn.: Greenwood Press, 1980).

their provisions were insufficient. Slaves who were accustomed to certain housing, articles of clothing, or rations at their home plantations expected more or less the same when they changed residences; they felt deprived if their new material conditions appeared lacking or inadequate. As one Louisianan told a visitor to the South, "whatever indulgences, in regard to dress or other things, custom has established, as the right of the slave, he is very particular to require; and if anything is withheld, he remembers it as his due."[6]

Interestingly, interstate migrants often perceived *regional* differences in the material conditions of (rural) slave populations, frequently claiming that housing and allowances at their new destinations differed markedly from those in their regions of origin. In rare cases, the change appeared for the better. One Virginia slave who was forcibly moved to Kentucky claimed in 1863 that "slaves in Kentucky are better fed and clothed, far better, than in Virginia." Complaints of degradation in material conditions were far more common, however, especially in testimonies of interstate migrants from the Upper South who were removed to plantation districts in the Lower South. Long-distance migrants indeed helped craft an image of slaveholders in the Lower South as masters who routinely failed to meet their paternalist obligations. Eli Johnson, who was "born and raised in old Virginia," claimed that his conditions in Virginia were "only middling" but lamented that after he was sold to a Mississippi cotton plantation, he suffered for want of sufficient food because he was only "allowed a peck of corn a week and three pounds meat" by his new master. Interstate migrant William Anderson likewise insisted that in his home state of Virginia, he "fared tolerably well," but in Mississippi, he was forced to work exceedingly hard on nothing but a peck of corn and "two or three pounds of pork or beef" a week. When Henry Bibb was sold along with his family from his native Kentucky – "with Maryland and Virginia said to be the mildest slave States in the Union, noted for their humanity" – to a cotton planter in Louisiana, he was shocked to find the slaves on his new plantation looking ragged and "half-starved." His new master, whom he described as a "devil," only provided his bondspeople with the bare minimum of food, their weekly rations consisting of "one peck of corn for each grown person, one pound of pork, and sometimes a molasses." And when Virginia slave Jourden Banks was deported in a coffle to Alabama, he found that the farther south he got, "the harder the aspect of things looked for coloured people." Indeed, he was "perfectly confounded" at the material conditions on his new plantation. Banks was assigned a log cabin "with the cracks wide open," a dirt floor, and a "mockery for a roof," which he had to share with five others; a bedstead made of "boards put like shelves" without any mattress or blankets (only corn

[6] Ethan Allen Andrews, *Slavery & the Domestic Slave Trade in the United States. In a Series of Letters Addressed to the Executive Committee of the American Union for the Relief and Improvement of the Colored Race* (Boston: Light & Stearns, 1836), 174 (quote). See also Joseph Holt Ingraham, *The South-West. By a Yankee* (New York: Harper Bros., 1835), 2:203.

shucks to lie on); and provisions that consisted of bread "made of Indian corn not really ground" and two and a half pounds of pork per week. To newcomers from the Upper South, slave life in the Deep South appeared hard and inhumane.[7]

Such charges are echoed by the testimonies of white visitors to the South, who likewise frequently observed regional differences in slaves' material conditions and often concluded that bondspeople were better provided for in the Upper South than in the Lower South. Francis and Theresa Pulszky, for example, claimed that bondspeople in Kentucky, "as in Virginia and Maryland, are generally better treated and fed than farther down in the South, on the cotton, rice, and sugar plantations." Frederick Law Olmsted opined at the beginning of his journey through the seaboard slave states that he believed slaves "were much better off... and more kindly treated in Virginia than further South." He was assured by a Virginia slaveholder that bondspeople in that state were allowed at minimum "a peck and a half of meal, and three pounds of bacon a week," and were moreover permitted to raise their own vegetables and fowl to supplement their rations. Even *within* the Lower South, visitors often observed regional differences in the conditions of the slaves. James Buckingham wrote during his journey through the southern states in 1842 that slaves in the cotton districts were afforded "a more liberal allowance of food" than their counterparts in the sugar and rice districts.[8]

In short, most slaves and visitors to the South believed that material conditions in the Upper South were relatively humane but that they gradually worsened the farther one traveled into the cotton, rice, and sugar districts (in that order). Because slavery in the Lower South already had a dreadful reputation among both slaves and whites from other regions, however, it is unclear whether such testimonies were based on objective observations or whether they simply reaffirmed preexisting stereotypes. Most interstate migrants were indignant about having to leave their homes in the first place and were moreover convinced that they were being transported to a region where slavery was infinitely worse than what they had previously experienced. Their negative impressions of the material conditions at their destinations, as well as their

[7] Francis Fedric, *Slave Life in Virginia and Kentucky; or, Fifty Years of Slavery in the Southern States of America* (London: Werheim, MacIntosh, and Hunt, 1863), 91 (first quote); Eli Johnson, ibid., 381–82 (second quote); William J. Anderson, *Life and Narrative of William J. Anderson Twenty-Four Years a Slave* (Chicago: Daily Tribune and Job Printing Office, 1857), 7 (third quote), 17–18 (fourth quote); Henry Bibb, *Narrative of the Life and Adventures of Henry Bibb, an American Slave, Written by Himself* (New York: n.p., 1849), 110 (fifth quote), 117 (sixth quote); J.H. Banks, in James W.C. Pennington, *A Narrative of Events of the Life of J.H. Banks, an Escaped Slave, from the Cotton State, Alabama, in America* (Liverpool: M. Rourke, 1861), 49–52 (seventh quotes).

[8] Francis and Theresa Pulszky, *White, Red, Black* (1853; New York: Johnson Reprint Co., 1970), 14 (first quote); Frederick Law Olmsted, *Journey in the Seaboard Slave States, with Remarks on their Economy* (New York: Dix & Edwards, 1856), 108 (second quote); James Silk Buckingham, *The Slave States of America* (London: Fisher & Son, 1842), 2:199 (third quote).

overly positive memories of conditions in their regions of origin, may have been more rooted in their anger about being deported than about the exact measurements of their provisions (which tended to be meager throughout the South). White travelers' relatively positive impressions of slaves' material conditions in the Upper South, on the other hand, were strongly influenced by the widespread belief that *slaveholding size* was the crucial factor in determining bondspeople's material conditions and not necessarily regional management styles. Betraying an implicit commitment to the master race narrative, many visitors to the South – even those who were opposed to slavery – subscribed to the view that smaller slaveholdings automatically resulted in more intimate and amiable contact between masters and slaves and thus better care and treatment. British sojourner James Stirling, who believed that the salvation of the black population lay in its "constant association with a superior race," claimed during his travels through the South in 1857 that of all slaves, "the farm servants of small proprietors" were "probably, the best off." He argued that these slaves "live much in the farmer's family, work with himself and his children, take an interest in his affairs, and, in return, become objects of his regard." Because slaveholdings in the Upper South and in the upland districts of southern Appalachia were generally smaller than in the cotton and sugar South (where bondspeople were regarded as mere "plantation cattle," according to Stirling), the material conditions of slaves living in those districts were widely assumed to be relatively decent.[9]

Indeed, many slaveholders claimed to agree with such charges because the slaveholding size argument neatly dovetailed with the illusion of paternalist interest in the personal welfare of their slaves that they wished to convey. Grandees and absentee planters regularly complained that the sheer number of slaves they owned or their absence from the plantation for long periods of time made them unable to personally care for their bondspeople as well as they would like. Most felt strong pressure to defend themselves – as Genovese and Fox-Genovese have shown, even southern agricultural reformers and proslavery ideologues lambasted absentee planters for not personally caring for their slaves' material conditions. Attempting to convince critics of their

[9] James Stirling, *Letters from the Slave States* (1857; New York: Negro Universities Press, 1969), 296 (first quote), 291 (second quotes); Charles Lyell, *A Second Visit to the United States of North America* (New York: Harper & Bros, 1850), 2:70–71. E.S. Abdy also claimed that slaves in the mountain districts of southern Appalachia, where masters and slaves lived and worked alongside each other, were better treated than in the plantation districts of the South. See E.S. Abdy, *Journal of a Residence and Tour in the United States of North America, from April 1833 to October 1834* (1835; New York: Negro Universities Press, 1969), 2:291. Olmsted likewise found slavery in North Carolina relatively humane because "the slave more frequently appears as a family servant." See Olmsted, *Seaboard Slave States*, 367. Some scholars have also subscribed to the argument that material conditions were better on smaller slaveholdings than larger ones. See, for example, Diane Mutti Burke, *On Slavery's Border: Missouri's Small-Slaveholding Households, 1815–1865* (Athens: University of Georgia Press, 2010), 149–50.

paternalist *intentions* at least, absentee owners cast themselves in the role of victims, loudly lamenting the heavy burden of being responsible for such large "flocks" while their business (or, in the lowcountry, the perilous climate) called them elsewhere. Unwilling to imperil their honor and admit their shortcomings as kind and generous masters, they defended themselves by blaming others, especially nonslaveholders. Inadequacies in their slaves' material comforts were usually blamed on mismanagement by their overseers. During a visit to a large Louisiana cotton plantation in the 1850s, the Pulzskys were told by the absentee owner that his slaves' material conditions were "better than some, and worse than others," the reason for the latter being that he did not "live amongst them." They were "managed by overseers," the planter explained, "and therefore cannot be treated as well as I would do, if I heard all their complaints and always saw after their wants." Clearly flattering himself in the company of his European guests that his slaves would be happiest and most comfortable if he himself lived on the plantation and had full charge of their daily affairs, the planter underscored his benevolence by claiming to make small investments in their comfort and regularly inspecting his overseers' management of the slaves. More he could not do; his hands were tied. Many grandees and absentee planters indeed dictated to their overseers in writing exactly how to go about providing for their bondspeople to make sure they were adequately cared for. In doing so, they were able to fuse their outward image as generous masters with their financial self-interest but also shift the responsibility for meeting their paternalist obligations away from themselves and onto plantation managers. William Minor, a Louisiana slaveholder obsessed with slave management, drew up a list of "Rules and Regulations" for his overseer, including the order that he "treat all the negroes with Kindness and humanity in both sickness and in health" and that he "must see the various rations given out & that the food (particularly the bread & vegetables) be well cooked & delivered at proper hours to the houses." One wealthy Mississippi slaveholder wrote his overseer an entire essay in 1850 in which he admonished him to "guard as much as possible against sickness" by attending to the slaves' "Diet and cleanliness" and "preventing exposure at night." Among other things, the Mississippian ordered his overseer to see to it that his bondspeople

> have comfortable beds.... Their cabins, clothing & beding [sic] should be kept clean. Prevent as far as possible eating of green fruit, fish or other things – and also from starving themselves by not dividing their allowances into equal dayly [sic] portions.....[10]

[10] Genovese and Fox-Genovese, *Fatal Self-Deception*, 36–37; Pulzsky, *White, Red, Black*, 103 (first quote), 105; William Minor, "Rules and Regulations," reprinted in Charles L. Wingfield, "The Sugar Plantations of William J. Minor, 1830–1860" (MA Thesis, Louisiana State University, Baton Rouge, 1950), 45, 47 (second quotes); *Journal of Araby Plantation*, Mar. 20, 1850, RASP, Series F, Part 1 (microfilm), JFK Institute, Freie Universität, Berlin (third quote). For plantation rules and regulations on Bennet Barrow's Highland plantation in Louisiana, see Bennet H. Barrow, *Plantation Life in the Florida Parishes of Louisiana, 1836–1846, as*

Did interstate newcomers from the relatively small farms of the Upper South thus experience a vast deterioration in their rations, allowances, and housing when they moved to the larger and more anonymous plantations of the Lower South? To be sure, many did. Yet despite claims to the contrary by slave migrants, travelers, and even slaveholders, the extent to which the material conditions of slaves differed structurally by region is in fact far from clear. A stronger argument could be made that they differed by *master* rather than by *region*. Slaves' accommodations may serve as a case in point. Although architectural styles varied across space and time, slave cabins in the antebellum period were generally modest and basic affairs, both in the Upper South and in the Lower South, on large plantations and on small farms. Most were boarded structures or built entirely of logs, consisting of one chamber, crudely furnished, and usually with some kind of fireplace at one end. Cabins with minor luxuries, such as brick fireplaces or glass windows, appear not to have been concentrated in the "humane" Upper South but rather reflected the taste, wealth, or judgment of individual masters throughout the slaveholding states. Olmsted's observations of slave housing in various parts of the South in 1853 are illuminating. On one plantation in Maryland (considered one of the most humane slaveholding states), Olmsted found the slaves housed in "small and rude log-cabins, scattered in different parts of the farm." On the slaveholdings of Virginia (also considered relatively humane), he remarked, most slaves were accommodated in "log-cabins, of various degrees of comfort and commodiousness." The chimneys were "sometimes of brick, but more commonly of lath or split sticks, laid up like log work and plastered with mud." Only occasionally did he see "larger houses, boarded and made ornamental." In South Carolina, Olmsted remarked that the slave cabins on one cotton plantation were "the smallest I had seen," with no windows or even openings for windows, but farther south along the "rice coast" – one of the wealthiest regions in the South – he visited a plantation with small whitewashed "cottages, boarded on the outside, with shingle roofs and brick chimneys." Another slave village in the region, across the river in Georgia, had houses with brick chimneys and "varying quantities of rude furniture." In Louisiana, Olmsted lodged on a plantation with slave cabins that were "exactly like those I described on the Georgia Rice Plantation, except that they were provided with broad galleries in front." Clearly, although slave houses varied by degrees from plantation to plantation, most bondspeople lived in very basic cabins with little luxury and few comforts. Although many interstate migrants may have experienced worsened living conditions upon removal to the Deep South – common complaints included poorly boarded or chinked houses, a lack of furniture and linens, and

Reflected in the Diary of Bennet H. Barrow, edited by Edwin Adams Davis (New York: AMS Press, 1967); Edwin Adams Davis, "Bennet H. Barrow: Ante-Bellum Planter of the Felicianas," *Journal of Southern History* 5 (Nov. 1939): 431–46.

especially overcrowding – others may have actually been assigned quarters that were built slightly better than those on their home plantations.[11]

As for provisions, it is indeed likely that the strict and systematic distribution of meager rations was probably more common on large plantations than on small farms; nevertheless, evidence suggests that provisions in the Upper South often hovered near subsistence level as well. This was especially the case as slaveholders in the region found themselves struggling with gradually diminishing financial means to maintain their slaves because of the economic downturn in the antebellum period. Ethan Allen Andrews, visiting the South in 1836, noted that "the increasing poverty of the planters in Virginia" appeared to result in "their consequent inability to furnish a comfortable support for their slaves." Another traveler in northern Virginia found slaves in the region far from well fed; rations on many farms consisted of only a peck of cornmeal plus a daily herring, and he was told by a worried local that the slave population was "half-starved; to use his own words, they had hardly food enough to keep body and soul together." A young tutor from Vermont who was employed on a Virginia plantation in the early nineteenth century likewise wrote to his family that the slaves "have very little to eat" and that "they will steal whatever they can get a hold of." Indeed, he opined, "who can blame the poor degraded objects?" Surely slaveholders here did not truly believe that their region constituted the epicenter of humane conditions despite its small slaveholdings and intimate contact between white and black.[12]

Tellingly, countless local migrants in the Upper South also decried the material conditions to which they were subjected at their new places of residence despite remaining within the same region. Henry, a Virginia slave who as a young man was sold to a farmer some six or seven miles away from his home in Stafford County, complained to an interviewer in the 1850s that his new

[11] For more on slave cabins, see John Michael Vlach, *Back of the Big House: The Architecture of Plantation Slavery* (Chapel Hill: University of North Carolina Press, 1993); Clifton Ellis and Rebecca Ginsburg, *Cabin, Quarter, Plantation: Architecture and Landscapes of North American Slavery* (New Haven: Yale University Press, 2010); Richard Follett, *The Sugar Masters: Planters and Slaves in Louisiana's Cane World, 1820–1860* (Baton Rouge: Louisiana State University Press, 2005), 179–85; Elizabeth Fox-Genovese, *Within the Plantation Household: Black and White Women of the Old South* (Chapel Hill: University of North Carolina Press, 1988), 149–52; Burke, *On Slavery's Border*, 154–55; Rev. Horace Moulton, in Thomas Weld, *American Slavery as It Is: Testimony of a Thousand Witnesses* (New York: American Anti-Slavery Society, 1839), 19. Olmsted, *Seaboard Slave States*, 11 (first quote), 111 (second quote), 386 (third quote), 416 (fourth quote); 422 (fifth quote), 659 (sixth quote); James Smith, in Blassingame, ed., *Slave Testimony*, 278.

[12] Andrews, *Slavery and the Domestic Slave Trade*, 119 (first quote); E.S. Abdy, *Journal of a Residence and Tour of the United States of North America, from April 1833 to October 1834* (1835; New York, 1969), 1:96, 1:181 (second quote); Elijah Fletcher to Jesse Fletcher Sr., Aug. 29, 1810, Dec. 7, 1810, Feb. 11, 1810, in Martha von Briesen, ed., *Letters of Elijah Fletcher* (Charlottesville: University of Virginia Press, 1965), 14, 23, 26 (third quotes); Genovese and Fox-Genovese, *Fatal Self-Deception*, 86–88.

master "did not clothe nor feed his hands well." One Maryland slave who was sold locally several times likewise had few good words to say about one of his masters, whom he described as "an unfeeling tyrant." The bondsman claimed that he "often... had hardly anything to eat, and many times when I had anything to eat I had no chance to eat it." John Thompson, another Maryland slave, claimed that his original master gave the slaves "a peck of corn, two dozens of herrings, and about four pounds of meat" per week, but when he was hired to an unpopular farmer in the neighborhood, he received only "a quart of meal and two herrings per day." Israel, a Kentucky slave and local migrant, ran away from his new master because, having been accustomed to "having enough to eat" on his old farm, he found the sparse rations at his new residence "more than I was willing to bear." And not just in the Upper South, but local migrants elsewhere in the South made similar complaints. Such testimonies suggest that inadequate material conditions – especially food rations, which slaves most complained about – were not necessarily structural problems unique to the Lower South but rather the consequence of different management styles by individual slaveholders.[13]

Many large, wealthy plantations in the Lower South in fact had elaborate systems of material rewards for hard work – from extra meat to plugs of tobacco – and provided newcomers with extensive opportunities to engage in internal production to augment their weekly provisions. Indeed, as numerous scholars have noted, precisely the regions with the largest plantations and the harshest reputations – the lowcountry and the cane country – had the most developed slave economies in the South. Formal rations may have been meager, but bondspeople supplemented their provisions by taking advantage of numerous incentives offered to them by their masters to acquire extra food. In the Louisiana cane country, local custom dictated that slaves be afforded both garden plots and so-called "negro grounds" – plots along the edges of the plantation where they could grow corn and pumpkins for sale to the master. They also regularly performed overwork for cash on Sundays, which they used to make small purchases at plantation stores. On lowcountry plantations, slave garden plots and the privilege of keeping pigs and chickens were near universal, and the task system – by which slaves performed a set amount of work each day and determined their own work tempo – often afforded bondspeople sufficient free time in the afternoons to amply provide for their own tables. The development of slave economies in both of these regions – and in other parts of the South where slaves had access to garden plots – outwardly appeared to reflect

[13] Henry Banks, in Drew, ed., *North-Side View*, 73 (first quote); Lewis Charlton, *Sketch of the Life of Mr. Lewis Charlton, and Reminiscences of Slavery* (Portland, Maine: Daily Press Print, n.d.), 3 (second quote); John Thompson, *The Life of John Thompson, a Fugitive Slave; Containing His History of 25 Years in Bondage, and His Providential Escape. Written by Himself* (Worcester, Mass: n.p., 1856), 17 (third quote), 52 (fourth quote); Israel Campbell, *Bond and Free: or, Yearnings for Freedom, from My Green Brier House. Being the Story of My Life in Bondage, and My Life in Freedom* (Philadelphia: C.E.P. Brinckloe & Co., 1861), 27 (fifth quote).

benign master–slave relations, but paradoxically, they were designed to financially benefit the slaveholders, who not only encouraged internal production but indeed often purchased slaves' goods themselves at below-market prices. Priding themselves on the "indulgences" they afforded their bondspeople, such masters contented themselves with distributing minimal provisions but also safeguarded their slave communities from idleness and flight and maintained close supervision of their slaves' acquisition of material goods (although in practice, slaves regularly sold their products to third parties without permission).[14]

Whatever the ulterior motives, such privileges allowed enslaved newcomers – interstate and local alike – to at least partially provide for themselves, supplement their weekly rations, and acquire small luxuries. At Ashland plantation in southern Louisiana, which contained several local and interstate newcomers, rations consisted only of cornmeal, pork, and molasses, but slaves supplemented their provisions with vegetables and chickens raised in their garden plots. On Benjamin Tureaud's sugar estate, local slaves and newcomers spent the money they earned through overwork and selling corn to purchase small luxuries at the plantation commissary, including meat, flour, tobacco, clothes, and shoes. Slave testimonies also underscore how widespread economic activities were in these regions. When Maryland slave Charles Ball was sold to one of the wealthiest planters in South Carolina, he was shocked to find that provisions consisted mainly of cornmeal and little else. "Whatever was given us beyond the corn [was considered] over and beyond what we were entitled to, or had a right to receive," he wrote in his autobiography. Yet Ball was quick to point out that his readers "must not suppose, that, on this plantation, we had nothing to eat beyond the corn and salt. This was far from the case." Weekly rations were supplemented by "the gardens, or patches, cultivated by the people," as well as by occasional paid overwork on Sundays. Some of the hands

[14] Roderick A. McDonald, "Independent Economic Production by Slaves on Antebellum Louisiana Sugar Plantations," in Ira Berlin and Philip D. Morgan, eds., *Cultivation and Culture: Labor and the Shaping of Slave Life in the Americas* (Charlottesville: University of Virginia Press, 1993), 280–85; Roderick A. McDonald, *The Economy and Material Culture of Slaves: Goods and Chattels on the Sugar Plantations of Jamaica and Louisiana* (Baton Rouge: Louisiana State University Press, 1993); Richard Follett, *Sugar Masters*, 151–233; Joseph Holt Ingraham, *The South-West. By a Yankee* (New York, 1835), 1:236; Pulzsky, *White, Red, Black*, 2:104; Olmsted, *Seaboard Slave States*, 682; Accounts with the Slaves, 1858, Ledger, Benjamin Tureaud Family Papers, Hill Memorial Library, Louisiana State University, Baton Rouge; Cashbook and Daybook, Bruce, Seddon, and Wilkins Plantation Records, ibid.; Octabe Colomb, Plantation Journal, 1849–1866 (microfilm), ibid.; Larry E. Hudson, Jr., *To Have and to Hold: Slave Work and Family Life in Antebellum South Carolina* (Athens: University of Georgia Press, 1997), 10–12, 25, 32–33; Leslie A. Schwalm, *A Hard Fight for We: Women's Transition from Slavery to Freedom in South Carolina* (Urbana: University of Illinois Press, 1997), 31–33, 59–61; Charles Joyner, *Down by the Riverside: A South Carolina Slave Community* (Urbana: University of Illinois Press, 1984), 26–28; Betty Wood, *Women's Work, Men's Work: The Informal Slave Economies of Lowcountry Georgia* (Athens: University of Georgia Press, 1995); Philip D. Morgan, "The Ownership of Property by Slaves in the Mid-Nineteenth-Century Lowcountry," *Journal of Southern History* 49 (Aug. 1983): 404.

on the plantation made baskets, brooms, and horse collars in their free time, which they sold to local planters for cash, and trapped animals for meat. By such means, most slaves could "gather up a great deal to eat," procuring vegetables from their gardens and exchanging their cash for coffee, molasses, and sugar. Many even secretly left the plantation in the evenings and visited stores in nearby towns. Ball explained that in South Carolina, "the store-keepers are always ready to accommodate the slaves [because they] always pay cash" and because "the shopkeeper knows he can demand whatever price he pleases for his goods." The bondsman admitted that after residing in the region for a few months, he became expert at acquiring extra food and supplies, and his testimony concurs with other accounts of slaves' internal economic activities in South Carolina. One British reporter who visited the lowcountry in 1861 claimed that despite the region's harsh reputation, "the Negroes on the river plantations are very well off."[15]

Outside the lowcountry and cane region, slaves also developed internal economies, especially those who lived in the vicinity of towns. From Baltimore to Little Rock, southern cities teemed with country slaves selling vegetables from their gardens and fowl of their own raising, and both interstate and local migrants participated in such activities where they were available. It is important to note, however, that not *all* slaves were afforded such opportunities. In most parts of the South, the nature and extent of slaves' economies varied widely according to the dictates of the master, whose account books were more important than the living standards his "people" enjoyed. Although many masters – especially those on large plantations – provided their slaves with numerous opportunities to supplement their rations, for example, garden plots were far from universal in the Upper South or cotton regions. Olmsted found that "many planters will not allow their slaves to cultivate patches, because it tempts them to reserve for an to expend in the night-work the strength they

[15] Craig A. Bauer, *A Leader Among Peers: The Life and Times of Duncan Farrar Kenner* (Lafayette, La., 1993), 52–53; Alexander Kenner, in Blassingame, ed., *Slave Testimony*, 392–93; Accounts with the Slaves, 1858, Ledger, Tureaud Family Papers; Charles Ball, *Fifty Years in Chains, or, the Life of an American Slave* (New York: H. Dayton, 1859), 77, 126–30 (first quotes), 195–96; William Howard Russell, *My Diary North and South* (London, 1863), 1:196 (second quote). For more accounts of slaves' economic activities in the lowcountry, see also Plowden C. Weston, "Rules and Management of the Plantation," reprinted in Elizabeth Collins, *Memories of the Southern States* (Taunton: Barnicott, 1865), 114; G.S.S., "Sketches of the South Santee," in Eugene L. Schwaab, ed., *Travels in the Old South, Selected from the Periodicals of the Times* (Lexington, Ken., 1973), 1:8; Adam Hodgson, *Remarks During a Journey through North America in the Years 1819, 1820, and 1821, in a Series of Letters* (1823; Westport, Conn., 1970), 117; Basil Hall, "A Naval Officer Sees All Sections, 1827–1828," in Allan Nevins, ed., *American Social History as Recorded by British Travellers* (New York: Henry Holt & Co., 1923), 154; William Wyndham Malet, *An Errand to the South in the Summer of 1862* (London, 1863), 82; Olmsted, *Seaboard Slave States*, 422, 439; David Doar, *Rice and Rice Planting in the South Carolina Low Country* (Charleston: Charleston Museum, 1936), 32.

want employed in their service during the day, and also because the produce thus obtained is made to cover much plundering of their master's crops, and of his live stock." In the Upper South, gardens were sometimes only given to slaves as rewards for hard work and faithful service, a custom that appeared to legitimate paternalist mutuality by rewarding slaves who met their end of the bargain but that below the surface was designed to spur the other bondspeople to work harder by dangling prizes before their noses. One visitor claimed during his travels in Virginia that only "some" slaves "with indulgent masters" were allowed "a plot of ground to cultivate on their own account; the proceeds arising from the sale of what is grown upon it being their own." Austin Steward, enslaved in Virginia at the turn of the nineteenth century, recalled in his autobiography that "some slaves were permitted to cultivate small gardens, and were thereby enabled to provide themselves with many trifling conveniences. But these gardens were only given to some of the more industrious." Slaves living outside of the lowcountry and cane region – migrants and nonmigrants alike – could therefore not count on gardening privileges, and the testimonies of many migrants are indeed silent about gardens and fowl. One scholar has estimated that only 60 percent of ex-slaves interviewed by the Federal Writers' Project mentioned having access to garden plots.[16]

Throughout the South, and especially on farms and plantations where slaves were not afforded garden plots, local and interstate migrants acknowledged that theft was the most common – and sometimes the only – way of augmenting insufficient rations. Isaac Williams, a Virginia slave who was sold and hired out a number of times, told interviewers that one of his masters only provided his hands with "herrings and a peck of meal a week – never enough," and that if slaves wanted more, they "had to steal it." Interstate migrant John Brown insisted that provisions were insufficient in his home state of Virginia *and* in Georgia – the state to which he was deported – and that both he and other slaves regularly stole corn, meat, and fruit "because [we] were so poorly fed." Allen Parker, sold and hired locally throughout his native North Carolina, recalled after emancipation that on most of the plantations where he lived, provisions were inadequate and that the slaves – including the migrants – stole

[16] Ingraham, *South by South-West*, 54–55; Olmsted, *Seaboard Slave States*, 689 (first quote); Brenda E. Stevenson, *Life in Black and White: Family and Community in the Slave South* (London: Oxford University Press, 1996), 188; Abdy, *Journal of a Residence*, 269 (second quote); Austin Steward, *Twenty-Two Years a Slave and Forty Years a Freeman* (1857; Syracuse: Syracuse University Press, 2002), 3 (third quote); Robert William Fogel, *Without Consent or Contract: The Rise and Fall of American Slavery* (New York: Norton, 1989), 192. I have examined regional differences in slaves' internal economies elsewhere. See Damian Alan Pargas, "'Various Means of Providing for Their Own Tables': Comparing Slave Family Economies in the Antebellum South," *American Nineteenth Century History* 7 (Sept. 2006): 361–87; Damian Alan Pargas, *The Quarters and the Fields: Slave Families in the Non-Cotton South* (Gainesville: University Press of Florida, 2010), 88–113. For more on slaves' internal economies in the Chesapeake, see Loren Schweninger, "The Underside of Slavery: The Internal Economy, Self-Hire, and Quasi-Freedom in Virginia, 1780–1865," *Slavery & Abolition* 12 (Sept. 1991): 1–22.

food from their masters because they believed it was their right to be well fed. "Not feeling that they were getting all that belonged to them," Parker related in his narrative, bondspeople frequently "stole corn, wheat, peas, pork, mutton, or anything else they could eat, or that had a market value." Indeed, similar to their counterparts in the cane region and lowcountry, slaves in Parker's neighborhood sometimes illegally sold a portion of their plundered goods to poor whites in exchange for cash. "There was always some poor white who would either buy the goods or sell them for the benefit of the slaves," he claimed.[17]

By actively seizing illicit opportunities to supplement meager provisions, rural slave migrants not only refused to accommodate themselves to the new conditions with which they were confronted, but they also corrected what they perceived to be the failure of their masters to meet their paternalistic obligations. And as Kathleen Hilliard has recently argued, although white southerners often attempted to reconcile the existence of theft on their plantations with their paternalist ideology, claiming that their slaves *were* well fed but by nature had "no morals nor principles whatever, and are all the most notorious thieves," in rare cases, the slaves' actions were convincing enough that slaveholders decided to increase their allowances. One Mississippi planter who purchased several slaves from Maryland, Virginia, and Louisiana wrote to a relative in Maryland that "fresh pork is unwholesome in this country in summer, and I give none to my negroes." However, he admitted that because his slaves had resorted to stealing meat, he had finally relented and decided to include beef in their weekly provisions.[18]

II.

Slave migrants – both local and interstate, sold and hired – who were sent to work in southern industries, towns, cities, or in plantation households often experienced far different material conditions than their counterparts in rural

[17] Kathleen M. Hillard, *Masters, Slaves, and Exchange: Power's Purchase in the Old South* (New York: Cambridge University Press, 2014), 94–131; Isaac Williams, in Philo Tower, *Slavery Unmasked: Being a Truthful Narrative of a Three Years' Residence and Journeying in Eleven Southern States* (1856; New York: Negro Universities Press, 1969), 57 (first quote); Brown, *Slave Life in Georgia*, 11–13, 53–54 (second quote), 131; Allen Parker, *Recollections of Slavery Times* (Worcester, Mass: Chas. W. Burbank & Co., 1895), 56–58 (third quotes); H.M. Seale Diary, June 23, 1853, Hill Memorial Library, Louisiana State University.

[18] Hillard, *Masters, Slaves, and Exchange*, 94–131, 95 (first quote); John Knight to Wm. Beall, May 22, 1845, John Knight Papers, RASP, Series F, Part I (microfilm), JFK Institute, Freie Universität, Berlin (second quote). In North Carolina, according to E.S. Abdy, the masters of slaves who were inadequately fed and subsequently stole from other whites were liable to recover or repay the damages. See Abdy, *Journal of a Residence*, 182. Along the Mississippi River, many planters specifically built the slave cabins at some distance from the river to prevent slaves from illicitly trading in stolen goods with river merchants. See, for example, Tixier, *Tixier's Travels*, 46–47.

settings. Although such situations did *not* constitute a benign form of bondage, many of these migrants were provided slightly superior living conditions – especially food and clothing – to those of the masses of field hands. Again, however, conditions tended to vary by master and especially by employment.

Working in the households of slaveholders and paraded as testaments to their master's wealth and "paternalistic indulgences," domestic servants in both rural and urban settings usually enjoyed better appearances than most slaves. Rather than receiving the coarse shirts and pantaloons that were distributed to the field hands twice a year, household slave migrants often received hand-me-downs or even specially tailored suits from their masters, who risked loss of face if their domestics appeared as shabby as their field hands. One twenty-four-year old Virginia slave, sold to a household in the small town of Woodville, Alabama, absconded with "a quantity of clothing," including "a blue Wellington coat." Fanny, another Virginia slave who was sold as a domestic servant in New Orleans and subsequently ran way in 1850, was described as a "yellow girl . . . good looking [and] dresses well." Domestic servants indeed often baffled the white population with their genteel dress, and visitors frequently commented on the differences in appearance between field hands and household slaves. One British visitor to Macon, Georgia, found that although the field slaves in the region appeared to be "maintained with as little cost as possible," domestic slaves were "well clad." He explained that as household servants were "continually passing before the eyes of the master and mistress, as well as their visitors and guests," they had to be decently clothed because "the sight of dirty and miserable-looking attendants would be painful to those by whom they are surrounded." Olmsted, remarking on the throngs of slaves – most of them domestics – that crowded the streets of Richmond on the Sabbath, observed that "the greater part of the colored people, on Sunday, seemed to be dressed in the cast-off fine clothes of the white people, received, I suppose, as presents, or purchased of the Jews." Some were dressed "in laughably foppish extravagance, and a great many in clothing of the most expensive materials, and in the latest style of fashion," with the women copying "the latest Parisian mode." Such clothing allowed Olmsted to clearly distinguish between the slaves who lived in Richmond year round and those who had come to town from the surrounding countryside to attend church meetings, who "wore clothing of coarse gray 'negro-cloth,' that appeared as if made by contract, without regard to the size of the particular individual to whom it had been allotted, like penitentiary uniforms." The superior clothing provided to slave migrants who were put to household work constituted status symbols among the slaves themselves; many domestic servants prided themselves on their neat and fashionable appearance compared with the ragged plantation hands.[19]

[19] *Mobile Gazette & Commercial Advertiser*, Feb. 23, 1820 (first quote); *Daily Picayune*, Apr. 4, 1850 (second quote); James Silk Buckingham, *The Slave States of America* (London: Fisher & Son, 1842), 1:200 (third quote); Olmsted, *Seaboard Slave States*, 27–28 (fourth quotes). Former

The accommodations of domestic servants varied throughout the South. On small farms and many urban residences, household slaves were sometimes given their own rooms in the big house; others were lodged in cellars or outbuildings such as kitchens and carriage houses. William, a Virginia slave sold as a domestic servant to a Savannah family, was given "a room up over the carriage house to sleep in" at his new home, furnished with "a bed-stead, or bunk made of boards." Another Georgia woman who was sold to a man in New Orleans to be his household servant, was given her own bedroom with a bed and a wardrobe. Yet many of the larger and wealthier plantations provided their domestic slaves with separate cabins located close to the main residence. Clearly visible to visitors, these cabins were often well built and furnished, and, as with domestics' clothing, the idea was to keep up appearances rather than indulge black "family members." The domestic servants of one Georgia plantation reportedly lived in "brick cabins, adjoining the house and stables," that were "neatly and comfortably furnished," a situation fairly typical for large plantations. Sometimes migrant domestic servants started out living in outbuildings but were later moved to better quarters. One Louisiana slaveholder originally housed his newly purchased domestic slave in a utility room of the house, but when she had a baby, he "indulged" her by building her a proper cabin with a brick fireplace. His wife related in a letter to a relative in 1858 that "expenses will be heavy this year" because they had had "to build Susan a cabin with a *fireplace* on account of her having young children. She has been living in the ironing room next to the kitchen & using my kitchen fireplace, but I find it is not a good plan to allow her to do that; besides, the ironing room was neither large or close enough for health." Indeed, even in urban neighborhoods wealthy slaveholders sometimes built separate living quarters for their domestic servants – compact, brick houses in the yards behind to the main residence, "compounds" that constituted "the urban equivalent of the plantation," according to one scholar.[20]

slave migrants who were put to work as domestic servants admitted in interviews and narratives to being far better clad than their counterparts in the fields, a source of pride. Louis Hughes, a Virginia migrant to Mississippi who was put to household work, claimed after emancipation that the field hands received clothing "of the cheapest" linens, but he "wore pants made of Bosses' old ones," adding that "all his old coats were utilized for me" as well. His shoes were also "made of lighter leather" than the brogans worn by the rest, and eventually his master even provided him with a completely new uniform with a "white bosom shirt" that mimicked the dress of "New York waiters." See Louis Hughes, *Thirty Years a Slave. From Bondage to Freedom. The Institution of Slavery as Seen on the Plantation and in the Home of the Planter* (Milwaukee: South Side Printing Co., 1896), 41–42, 63–64.

20 Paul D. Lack, "An Urban Slave Community: Little Rock, 1831–1862," *The Arkansas Historical Quarterly* 41 (Autumn 1982): 265; William Grimes, *Life of William Grimes, the Runaway Slave. Written by Himself* (New York: n.p., 1825), 30 (first quote); Louisa Picquet and Hiram Mattison, *Louisa Picquet, the Octoroon: or, Inside Views of Southern Domestic Life* (New York: n.p., 1861), 19; Olmsted, *Seaboard Slave States*, 421 (second quote); Tryphena Blanche Fox to mother, Sept. 5, 1858, in Wilma King, ed., *A Northern Woman in the Plantation South:*

Most domestic slaves also enjoyed better food than their counterparts in the fields because they were often given leftovers from the white family's meal rather than standardized rations. Slaves and former slaves openly admitted to such privileges in interviews and narratives. When a Kentucky slave woman who was moved to Missouri and Kansas in the 1850s was asked by a northern reporter about her material conditions, she admitted that she was "well fed; they couldn't have starved me if they had wanted to; for I was their body servant and housekeeper, and had everything else to look after. They allowed me everything." Another North Carolina bondsman claimed in 1861 that when he was sold to an urban slaveholder as a body servant, his "condition was much bettered," as he did not suffer, "as many do, the want of food." Visitors to the South also frequently commented on the better diets of domestic slaves compared with those of the field hands and even the working classes in general. An English visitor to the South claimed that in Georgia "the domestic slaves about the houses of respectable families" were "as well fed... as the free domestic servants of many countries of Europe." In New Orleans, he observed, they were not only "well fed" but indeed appeared "better off" than most free blacks in the cities of the North. Some slaveholders, especially in urban areas, even provided their household servants with luxury foods, doubtless in part because it reflected well on both their paternalistic indulgences and their wealth. Visiting Alabama in 1849, Charles Lyell commented that "the colored domestic servants are treated with great indulgence at Tuscaloosa. One day some of them gave a supper to a large party of their friends in the house of a family which we visited, and they feasted their guests on roast turkeys, ice-creams, jellies, and cakes."[21]

Yet to depict the living standards of all domestic servants as luxurious and enviable compared with the lot of most slaves risks oversimplification. As was the case with rural migrants, the treatment of slaves employed in urban and plantation households differed by master, and certainly not all migrants felt that they were provided superior material conditions when they changed residences. Many domestic newcomers, for example, complained about their living spaces. In urban areas, slave quarters were often overcrowded, poorly ventilated, and crudely furnished. In rural areas, even on large plantations, many young domestic slaves lamented that they were given no private quarters at all, which to many must have seemed worse than even the leaky cabins they

Letters of Tryphena Blanche Holder Fox (Columbia: University of Missouri Press, 1993), 88 (third quote); Richard C. Wade, *Slavery in the Cities: The South, 1820–1860* (New York: Oxford University Press, 1964), 57–61, 61 (fourth quote).

[21] James Redpath, *The Roving Editor: or, Talks with Slaves in the Southern States* (1859; New York: Negro Universities Press, 1968), 319 (first quote); John S. Jacobs, "A True Tale of Slavery," *The Leisure Hour: A Family Journal of Instruction and Recreation* 477 (Feb. 14, 1861): 109 (second quote); Buckingham, *Slave States of America*, 1:200 (third quote), 1:356 (fourth quote); Charles Lyell, *A Second Visit to the United States of North America* (New York: Harper & Bros., 1850), 2:72 (fifth quote).

had been used to back home. One Kentucky bondswoman who was sold to a Missouri family complained that "they made me sleep in their bedroom, on a mattress on the floor, but paid no regard to my feelings, any more than if I was a cat." A North Carolina bondsman who was sold as a house slave to a Georgian woman as a boy claimed that he "did not like my new mistress;" although he "had all I wanted to eat," he "did not have any bed to sleep on, [but] simply slept on the dirt floor by the fireplace in the house like a little dog." Also similar to their rural counterparts, moreover, migrants who were put to work as domestic servants sometimes complained that they were not fed well enough because many masters refused to let their slaves eat the same food that the white family did. As a result, household servants often resorted to theft to secure better provisions or to trade stolen goods for other material products that they could otherwise not acquire. One Louisiana mistress who swore that her domestic servants were "properly clothed and fed" admitted to a relative that she had a constant problem with them stealing food. One of her hired servants was sent back before his contract was up because "he had been badly managed & would steal everything he could lay his hands on. He seemed so remarkably fond of *pilfered* eggs." Another local hireling who was in charge of milking the cow every morning was accused of "steal[ing] the cream, & butter."[22]

Differences in slaves' material conditions can be noted not only between slaves of different masters but also between slaves who were bought (or bequeathed) and those who were hired. Unlike bills of purchase, hiring contracts in the antebellum South usually specified the obligations of the employer to provide for slaves' food, clothing, and allowance. Masters tended to take an interest in the material welfare of their hirelings, though often more out of financial self-interest (seeking guarantees against damage of their valuable property) than paternalist sincerity. In reality, these written agreements did not necessarily prove advantageous for slaves' material conditions per se; indeed, as far as provisions and allowances were concerned, many urban hirelings to southern industries fared much the same as – or even worse than – rural slaves. In Savannah, for example, one company seeking to recruit able-bodied hands to help excavate the Brunswick and Altamaha Canal agreed to provide hirelings "three and a half pounds of pork, or bacon, and ten quarts of gourd-seed corn per week," provisions that were virtually identical to those distributed to slaves in the surrounding countryside. Some poorly managed

[22] Wade, *Slavery in the Cities*, 57–58; Fox-Genovese, *Within the Plantation Household*, 152; Redpath, *Roving Editor*, 322 (first quote); William Henry Singleton, *Recollections of My Slavery Days* (n.p., 1922), 2–3 (second quote); James Currey, in Blassingame, ed., *Slave Testimony*, 132; Catherine Cornelius, in Clayton, ed., *Mother Wit*, 45; King, ed., *Northern Woman in the Plantation South*, 61 (third quote), 47 (fourth quote), 65 (fifth quote). On domestic servants who were forced to simply sleep on the floor in the big house rather than in separate accommodations, see also Hughes, *Thirty Years a Slave*, 14 (second quote); William H. Robinson, *From Log Cabin to the Pulpit, or, Fifteen Years in Slavery* (Eau Claire, Wisc.: James H. Tifft, 1913), 76.

industries had something of a reputation for neglecting to adequately provide for their hirelings. One disgusted Virginia ironmaster became fed up with his managers' "modes of provisions for the estate, and in particular grain," because they "seldom purchased grain until they wanted bread or horse feed – then the speer of the occasion compelled them to give extravagant prices and send for it." As a result, his slaves went with "half of my original allowance, which has always been considered by the servants as their legal right." But other employers, hoping to attract the best slaves and keep their hirelings content on the job, specifically offered better food than plantation owners. A railroad company in Montgomery, Alabama, provided its hands with "five pounds of pork, a pint of molasses, and one peck of meal each per week." A northern visitor to the company commented that the slaves appeared "well fed," at least "for negro slaves." E.S. Abdy spoke with a contractor for a canal in Washington who hired sixty to seventy slaves a year and who insisted that he "fed them well; allowing them meat of the same quality with what he had at his own table," a practice his peers found "mad and impracticable." By feeding them quality food, however, the contractor swore that his hands were "industrious and obedient" and that they often stayed on to work for him the following year as well. Most employers fed their hirelings relatively decently simply because they were specifically obligated to by their contracts, however.[23]

With annual hiring periods spanning the summer and the winter, contracts tended to be quite specific regarding slaves' clothing, and a perusal of antebellum hiring bonds suggests that many hirelings were probably issued better clothing than average farm hands or at least at more regular intervals. One typical bond from Virginia obligated the employer "to cloath the said negro as follows (viz) one German oznaburgs shirt & pantaloons for the spring, one Negro cotton Jackett [sic] and pantaloons, one German oznaburgs shirt, one pair double soal [sic] shoes, one pair plaid or yarn hoes, and one dutch blanket for the winter." Another contract for a slave girl in Kentucky required her employer to "give her 3 shirts 2 linen 2 linsey dresses 1 underdress 2 pr. stockings + shoes and a good blanket." A Virginia factory owner who found his hands "suffering for cloaths" spent more than $440 on clothing for the slaves in 1813, instructing his managers to clothe the bondspeople as follows: "To all the females, a jacket of cotton with long sleeves to shelter their arms from cold & frost. The waggoners are to have coats, vests, and pantaloons of cotton. All the colliers and miners the same. The blue cloth is of good quality

[23] Jonathan D. Martin, *Divided Mastery: Slave Hiring in the American South* (Cambridge, Mass.: Harvard University Press, 2004), 97–99; Robert S. Starobin, *Industrial Slavery in the Old South* (New York: Oxford University Press, 1970), 50–62; Buckingham, *Slave States of America*, 1:137 (first quote); David Ross to George Bailey, Jan. 27, 1827, and David Ross to Thomas Hopkins, Aug. 23, 1813, David Ross Letterbooks, Slavery in Ante-Bellum Southern Industries (hereafter SASI), Series C, Part 1 (microfilm), JFK Institute, Freie Universität, Berlin (second quotes); Redpath, *Roving Editor*, 172 (third quote); Abdy, *Journal of a Residence*, 181 (fourth quote).

and I allot it to the furnace people first & potters, smiths next & forgemen next, a coat of blue cloth & waistcoat of scarlet flannel with sleeves.... As to the distribution of the blankets, the first object is to supply women with young children and next such cases as you may think proper according to the best of your judgment." Even if agreements between slaveholders and employers did not promise any real improvements in slaves' food or clothing, however, hirelings at least profited from the knowledge that their employers were *legally bound* to provide them with the basic provisions stipulated in their contracts. Because slaveholders were anxious to see their valuable slaves returned in good health, most saw to it that contractual obligations were met – voided contracts or even lawsuits often followed if they were not. Slaves knew this, and many wasted no time taking matters into their own hands and informing their owners of inadequate conditions, such as E. Herbert's slaves did when they were hired out to Andrew Crane, as related at the beginning of this chapter.[24]

Hirelings in urban areas were moreover often able to profit from overwork, as discussed in Chapter 4, and some who found themselves largely unsupervised were in a favorable position to steal goods or food from their masters and employers for sale in the black market. One owner of a Richmond iron factory lamented that the hirelings under his command stole pork offal from the kitchen to sell illicitly, complaining that "the slaves feel nearly as great temptation to steal the offall of hoggs as if it was so many dollars scattered on the ground when they are kill'd." However they procured their money, they often spent their earnings on minor luxuries to augment their material conditions. A British visitor to New Orleans commented that employers in that city "leave much more to [the slaves'] management than is ever confided to the free servants of England" and that bondspeople were frequently able to earn some money to "make purchases." Fashionable clothes were especially desired by urban hirelings from rural areas, as migrants attempted to erase any trace of their humble rural origins. Former slaves openly admitted feelings of pride when they spent extra earnings on dressing well, bragging about their "fine" attire and the compliments they received from their companions for their appearance. James Smith, a Virginia slave hired out as a shoemaker in a provincial town, made enough money one year to buy a new suit and a watch, claiming that he "was very proud and loved to dress well, and all the young people used to make a great time over me." Indeed, some hirelings even attempted to pass for

[24] Martin, *Divided Mastery*, 97–99; Starobin, *Industrial Slavery*, 50–62; Bond for hire of slave between Robert & John Smallman and Robert Harress or William Bailey (guardian of William and Betsey Hundley), Jan. 2, 1809, William Bailey Papers, RASP, Series E, Part I (microfilm), JFK Institute, Freie Unviersität, Berlin (first quote); Keith C. Barton, "'Good Cooks and Washers': Slave Hiring, Domestic Labor, and the Market in Bourbon County, Kentucky," *Journal of American History* 84 (Sept. 1997): 443–44 (second quote); David Ross to Robert Richardson, Jan. (n.d.) 1813, and David Ross to William Dunn, Jan. (n.d.) 1813, David Ross Letterbooks, SASI, Series C, Part 1 (microfilm), JFK Institute (third quotes); E. Herbert to A.E. Crane, Oct. 6, 1858, Andrew E. Crane Family Papers.

wealthy from the clothing they purchased with extra earnings. One rural slave who was hired out in Livingston, Alabama, fled his employer wearing "a black cashmere over-coat... and a silver huntsman's watch."[25]

Although often permitted to make minor purchases at shops, however, hirelings could also use their earnings – including earnings from selling stolen goods – to illicitly purchase goods or engage in activities that were forbidden them by their masters or employers, a constant source of anxiety among both slave owners and whites in urban areas. Saloons attracted urban hirelings throughout the South, for example. A northern visitor to Natchez in the 1830s observed that many hirelings earned a bit of money, which they "expended in little luxuries, or laid by in an old rag among the rafters of their houses," but he also saw how some male slaves used their earnings to frequent "the whiskey shops, spending their little all for the means of intoxication." One Virginia slaveholder who regularly hired his hands in Richmond worried that they were "acquiring bad habits" because "they earned money, by overwork, and spent it for whiskey." In 1839, a Kentucky slaveholder sued the steamboat *Mediator* to which her slave Ben was hired for the year, because the officers allowed him to purchase "large quantities of intoxicating liquors [and] wilfully permitted him & the other hands upon said Boat to get drunk," resulting in an accident that claimed Ben's life. Whether to fit in with the free population or to drown their sorrows, the allure of saloons, grog shops, and liquor parties to newcomers from the countryside lay precisely in the fact that they were forbidden by their masters. Spending money like free consumers in the urban marketplace, many migrants to southern towns and cities engaged in behavior that they felt elevated them above their slave status.[26]

The accommodations of slaves hired out or sold to urban employers other than private residences ran the full gamut of available lodging. Most were

[25] David Ross to William J. Dunn, Jan. 9, 1813, David Ross Letterbooks, SASI, Series C, Part 1 (microfilm), JFK Institute (first quote). The presumption that urban slaves sold exclusively stolen goods underlay legislation in several cities that prohibited economic transactions by slaves. In Little Rock, for example, the city council ordered in 1836 that "no person shall buy or received of or from any slave any commodity whatever in this city, unless the said slave shall produce a written permit from his or her master, mistress or overseer." See *Arkansas Gazette*, Jan. 12, 1836. Such laws were rarely enforced and overwhelmingly ignored by slaves. Buckingham, *Slave States of America*, 1:356 (second quote); James Lindsay Smith, *Autobiography of James L. Smith* (Norwich: Press of the Bulletin Company, 1881), 28 (third quote); *Mississippi & State Gazette*, Sept. 5, 1851 (fourth quote). See also Henry Clay Bruce, *The New Man. Twenty-Nine Years a Slave. Twenty-Nine Years a Free Man* (York, Pa.: P. Anstadt & Sons, 1895), 71–72; Ball, *Fifty Years in Chains*, 18.

[26] Ingraham, *South-West*, 251 (first quote), 56 (second quote); Olmsted, *Seaboard Slave States*, 58 (third quote); "Hanna Dubberly to the Chancery Court, Louisville, Kentucky, 1839," in Loren Schweninger, ed., *The Southern Debate over Slavery: Volume 2, Petitions to Southern County Courts, 1775–1867* (Urbana: University of Illinois Press, 2008), 193–94 (fourth quote); Starobin, *Industrial Slavery in the Old South*, 78–80. In rare cases, some southern industries actually rewarded hard working hirelings with liquor. See, for example, Takagi, *"Rearing Wolves to Our Own Destruction,"* 49.

housed as close to their work as possible. One Virginian who hired out one of his slaves to a grain mill in Richmond agreed with the hireling's new employer "that he ought to have comfortable lodgings near the mill and be at hand." How comfortable these accommodations were in practice was often open to interpretation, however; the truth is that most urban slaves' lodgings were often far from enviable. Although some industrial employers provided dank tenements for their hired bondspeople and other small shopkeepers accommodated apprentices in their own households, dismal ad hoc arrangements were the lot of most. With little more than blankets for bedding, hirelings were frequently "housed" right on the floors of the hotels, factories, shops, cellars, or outbuildings at their places of employment. In one Charleston hotel, hirelings were found "laid down for the night in the passages with their clothes on." William, a Virginia slave who was sold to New Orleans and subsequently hired out to a gambling saloon, claimed that he was given no proper living space but rather "slept on a table" in the bar. Noah Davis, a rural slave hired out as a shoemaker's apprentice in Fredericksburg, Virginia, slept in his employer's shop. Steamboat hands often slept in the damp hull of the ship or in the engine rooms, and both railroad and canal companies frequently erected makeshift "camps" for hirelings, with crude "shanties" containing no floors, doors, or fireplaces and often completely exposed to the elements. As one scholar noted, housing conditions for urban hirelings were contingent on the type of industry, locale, and personality of the master, but most large industrial employers did not provide hired slaves with comfortable lodgings by any stretch of the imagination.[27]

A far more preferred – if less common – situation for hirelings in towns and cities was "living out." Living out entailed the freedom of finding one's own accommodations during the duration of one's employment, a practice that hirelings bargained hard for. Usually limited to bondspeople whose masters allowed them to hire their own time, living out provided slaves with the opportunity to live almost like free men and women, often among spouses, family members, or friends in the black community. Indeed, as one historian has noted, the appeal of living out derived not from securing superior lodgings – the rooms and shanties they rented were often physically inferior to slave cabins in rural areas – but rather from the opportunity to live like quasi-freemen and unite scattered family members. It also saved employers from having to quarter hired bondspeople themselves. Although commentators on slave management widely condemned such arrangements and several southern

[27] Martin, *Divided Mastery*, 99; David Ross to John Werth, Jan. 5, 1812, David Ross Letterbooks, SASI, Series C, Part 1 (microfilm), JFK Institute (first quote); Wade, *Slavery in the Cities*, 62–75, 67 (second quote); Thomas W. Henry, *Autobiography of Rev. Thomas W. Henry, of the A.M.E. Church* (Baltimore: n.p., 1872), 9; William Grose, in Drew, ed., *North-Side View*, 84 (third quote); Noah Davis, *A Narrative of the Life of Rev. Noah Davis, A Colored Man. Written by Himself, at the Age of Fifty-Four* (Baltimore: John F. Weishampel, Jr., 1859), 19; Lack, "An Urban Slave Community," 265; Starobin, *Industrial Slavery*, 57–62.

cities legislated against the practice, living out actually increased in the late antebellum period because of a lack of enforcement. In Richmond, tobacco factories and ironworks gave hirelings a dollar per week to rent their own rooms in town. Olmsted visited a Virginia coal-mining town in 1853 where the miners – the majority of whom were hired slaves – were also given a certain amount of money to find their own boarding arrangements. The financial self-interest of some employers, as well as the masters who hired their slaves to such employers, could thus prove advantageous to slave hirelings because their superiors casually discarded their cloaks of benevolent protection and supervision and let them shift for themselves. Paternalist theories of blacks' incapacity to live without white "guidance" and "direction," which according to Genovese and Fox-Genovese were sincere, were conveniently forgotten in such arrangements.[28]

The testimonies of slave migrants reveal that living out often seemed like an infinitely better housing arrangement than that afforded to most bondspeople. Isaac Throgmorton, a Louisville barber who was allowed to hire his own time by one of his masters, arranged to live with free blacks, boasting that "it was just as though I was free." Another Kentucky bondsman claimed in an 1846 testimony that when he hired himself out as a barber in Georgetown, his master allowed him to not only find his own lodgings but also to hire his wife with his surplus earnings so that the two could live together. Henry Brown, who was sent to Richmond to be employed in a tobacco factory, similarly related after his escape from slavery that he was permitted to hire his wife for fifty dollars per year and rent a house in town for seventy-two dollars per year. This arrangement boosted Brown's self-esteem as well as his sense of masculine responsibility, and he often "reflected upon the difference between [country slaves'] lot and mine." The former, he implied, were emasculated by their inability to provide for their own families.[29]

III.

Avoiding punishment was the avowed goal of most slaves, including slave migrants. Yet newcomers were often more susceptible to the lash than local

[28] Martin, *Divided Mastery*, 164–68; Wade, *Slavery in the Cities*, 62–75; Midori Takagi, *"Rearing Wolves to Our Own Destruction": Slavery in Richmond, Virginia, 1782–1865* (Charlottesville: University of Virginia Press, 1999), 37–40; Calvin Schermerhorn, *Money over Mastery, Family over Freedom: Slavery in the Antebellum Upper South* (Baltimore: Johns Hopkins University Press, 2011), 135–40; Genovese, *Roll, Jordan, Roll*, 392; Olmsted, *Seaboard Slave States*, 47; Genovese and Fox-Genovese, *Fatal Self-Deception*, 92–95.

[29] Isaac Throgmorton, in Blassingame, ed., *Slave Testimony*, 432–33 (first quote); Cox, in Blassingame, ed., *Slave Testimony*, 389–90; William Hayden, *Narrative of William Hayden, Containing a Faithful Account of His Travels for a Number of Years, Whilst a Slave, in the South. Written by Himself* (Cincinnati: n.p., 1846), 45–46; Henry Box Brown, *Narrative of Henry Box Brown, Who Escaped from Slavery Enclosed in a Box 3 Feet Long and 2 Wide. Written from a Statement of Facts Made by Himself*, by Charles Stearns (Boston: Brown & Stearns, 1849), 50 (second quotes); Lack, "An Urban Slave Community," 265.

slaves, partly because they were unused to new work patterns, as discussed in Chapter 4, but also because they were unused to new rules, which tended to vary by master. Newcomers were punished for infractions as varied as failing to show their masters and overseers enough respect, arguing with overseers or fellow bondsmen, and not returning from weekend visiting on time. Whatever their crime, corporal punishments were frequently inflicted on recalcitrant migrants who, knowingly or unknowingly, overstepped the boundaries.

The nature of punishment and physical "correction" featured prominently in antebellum discussions on slave management. Depicting slaves essentially as children who needed the firm yet just disciplining of a benevolent white patriarch, contributors to southern periodicals and authors of slave management guides were nearly unanimous in their calls for a more "humane" treatment of enslaved people, especially compared with the colonial period when slaves were perceived more as brutes and savages than children. As with material conditions, however, economic principles, rather than philanthropy, usually underlay such calls, although they were often cloaked in hegemonic claims that slaves' accommodation to the paternalist bargain – rather than terror – was the key to maintaining labor discipline. Most commentators agreed that slaves who were disciplined in a consistent yet humane and reasonable manner were more efficient and contented workers and less prone to flight or aggression than those who were wantonly abused. N.D. Guerry, an Alabama contributor to the *Southern Cultivator*, was convinced that the gradual reduction in barbaric punishments of slaves was the single most important factor in the explosive productivity on southern cotton plantations. "Although negroes cost hundreds more than in the olden time, when men fed little and whipped more," he contended, "you find the yield of cotton increasing by the million bales... for their negroes, treated more leniently, will live longer and perform more efficient service. [...] I have been increasing my force, by purchase, for years from all sorts of masters, from Virginia to Alabama, and have found very little trouble in bringing them all under my system." Robert Collins was even more direct, claiming that "the owner has nothing to gain by oppression or over driving, but something to lose; for he cannot, by such means, extort more work." Collins argued that when disciplining slaves, it was "of great consequence to have perfect system and regularity and a strict adherence to the rules." Indeed, he insisted that regular and predictable punishments for minor infractions would actually promote slaves' "happiness and well-being," because bondspeople supposedly had "no respect or affection for a master who indulges them over-much." Thomas Affleck provided overseers with precise instructions for disciplining slaves in a humane and profitable manner:

> Be *firm*, and at the same time *gentle* in your control. Never display yourself before them in a passion; and even if inflicting the severest punishment, do so in a mild, cool manner, and it will produce a tenfold effect. When you find it necessary to use the whip – and desirable as it would be to dispense with it entirely, it *is* necessary at times – apply it slowly and deliberately, and to the extent you are determined, in your own mind, to be

needful before you began. The indiscriminate, constant and excessive use of the whip, is altogether unnecessary and inexcusable. When it can be done without a too great loss of time, the stocks offer a means of punishment greatly to be preferred.... Always keep your word with them, in punishments as well as in rewards. If you have named the penalty for any certain offence, inflict it without listening to a word of excuse....[30]

Despite such widespread advice, however, the extent and nature of punishment in the South was frequently far from "gentle" or systematic, and exposure to arbitrary and extreme physical abuse was a common complaint among slave migrants who changed masters or who found themselves working under new employers or overseers. Slave testimonies from both before and after emancipation indicate that interstate migrants again clearly perceived regional differences in the punishments dealt to bondspeople in different parts of the South, with the Lower South standing out for its abysmal disciplinary measures. Solomon Bradley, who was "born in North Carolina, in the Northern part of the State," but removed to South Carolina, told government interviewers in 1863 that modes of punishment were "more cruel [in South Carolina] than anything I ever saw in my life." In his native state, Bradley claimed, the "people are not treated... so hard," and it was the custom that "if a master wants to flog a man and the man can break away... there is no attempt made to renew the punishment," unlike in South Carolina. Moses Roper, who was also born in North Carolina but lived in South Carolina, Georgia, and Florida, reported several modes of punishment that he thought were limited to the Lower South. On one plantation, his master adorned apprehended runaways with "iron horns, with bells, attached to the back of the slave's neck," an instrument he claimed was "generally adopted by the slave-holders in South Carolina, and some other slave states." Maryland slave Charles Ball, after witnessing two slaves ordered to lie down on the ground for a whipping in South Carolina, wrote that he "had never before seen people flogged in the way our overseer flogged his people. This plan of making the person who is to be whipped lie down upon the ground, was new to me."[31]

Some states, such as Alabama, Mississippi, and Louisiana, earned particularly harsh reputations among slaves from other regions; migrants specifically

[30] Walter Johnson, "A Nettlesome Classic Turns Twenty-Five," *Common-Place* 1 (July 2001), http://www.common-place.org/vol-01/no-04/reviews/johnson/shtml; N.D. Guerry, "Management of Negroes, Duties of Masters, &c.," *Southern Cultivator* 18 (1860), 177 (first quote); Collins, *Essay on the Treatment and Management of Slaves*, n.p. (second quote); Affleck, *Cotton Plantation Record and Account Book*, n.p. (third quote); Kolchin, *American Slavery*, 121;. Louisiana planter William Minor similarly gave his overseers the order that "when necessary to punish... inflict it, in a serious, firm & gentlemanly manner & endeavor to impress the culprit that he is punished for his bad conduct only and not for revenge or passion." See Wingfield, "Sugar Plantations of William J. Minor," 47.

[31] Solomon Bradley, in Blassingame, ed., *Slave Testimony*, 371 (first quote); Roper, *Narrative of the Adventures and Escape of Moses Roper*, 22 (second quote), 47; Ball, *Fifty Years in Chains*, 125–26 (third quote).

noted the existence of jails and stocks on large plantations in those states, the prevalence of particularly sadistic modes of punishment, and the extensive use of the lash. William Webb, born in Georgia, claimed in an 1873 narrative that on arrival in Mississippi, he "witnessed things I never expected to see." Among other atrocities, he saw "men and women tied down over a log, with their feet on one side and their arms on the other side, and they would whip them from their head to their feet, and their flesh was cut till they had to rub them with salt and red pepper to keep the flies from blowing them." Traveling through the state with his master, Webb reported that he passed "many large plantations... and the same cruelty was going on in every one of them. The whip and whipping post were used as an every day occurrence." A Virginia migrant to Alabama similarly claimed in an 1861 interview that on his new plantation, "scarcely a day passed without a flogging match," the victims often being strung up by their hands or staked down to the ground so as not to escape the crack of the lash. To bondspeople from the Upper South, who often claimed to come from a relatively mild and humane slaveholding region, the Lower South represented a hell in which slaves were routinely exposed to appalling physical abuse for the most minor infractions.[32]

Indeed, both slaves and visitors to the slave states often claimed that the Upper South's mild reputation formed a liability to interstate migrants from those regions, as masters and overseers in the southern interior frequently felt it necessary to "break in" newcomers who came from parts of the South where slaves were thought to be "spoiled." One northern sojourner was horrified to learn of "break-down whippings" in the Deep South inflicted on newly arrived migrants from the Upper South who assumed "a degree of independence unbecoming of a slave." The northerner opined that "the change from Kentucky or Virginia slavery to a large cotton or sugar plantation in the more southern states, is as great almost as liberty and slavery" and contended that interstate migrants who did not "give up their smartness" risked serious corporal punishments in states such as Louisiana and Mississippi. Samuel Hall, a slave from North Carolina who was sold to western Tennessee, recalled after emancipation that his new master attempted to "break" him soon after arrival because he was supposedly "too big feelin'" for a slave, having come from a

[32] William Webb, *The History of William Webb, Composed by Himself* (Detroit: Egbert Hoekstra, 1873), 4 (first quote), 6–7 (second quote); Pennington, ed., *Life of J.H. Banks*, 51 (third quote); Watson, *Narrative of Henry Watson*, 13–15; Hughes, *Thirty Years a Slave*, 19–24, 45–46, 89–90. White visitors also perceived certain regional differences in punishments, often singling out Louisiana for its cruelty. Traveling through eleven slave states in the 1850s, for example, Philo Tower claimed that the punishment of women in Louisiana "differed somewhat in manner from some plantations in other portions of the slave states." There women were made to lie down on the ground with their frocks above their heads, and had their bare skin paddled. See Tower, *Slavery Unmasked*, 311. James Buckingham likewise reported that in Louisiana, the "floggings of the indolent and refractory are cruel and severe, especially among the French and Creole planters." See Buckingham, *Slave States of America*, 1:375–76.

FIGURE 5.1. "Wilson Chinn, a branded slave from Louisiana – Also exhibiting instruments of torture used to punish slaves." c1863. The slave depicted in this photograph was sold from his home state of Kentucky to a Louisiana sugar planter when he was twenty-one years old (in the photograph, he is around sixty years old). His new master, Volson B. Marmillion, branded the initials "V.B.M." onto his forehead with a hot iron. Having fled to a Union contraband camp during the Civil War, Chinn was photographed "exhibiting instruments of torture used to punish slaves" that were common in the Louisiana sugar country that became his new home. *Source:* Kimball, NYC, c1863. Courtesy of the Library of Congress, Prints and Photographs Division, LOT 11662.

reputedly mild slave state. Israel Campbell, moved from Kentucky to Mississippi, claimed that his hired master and overseer attempted to make him "buy the rabbit" – undergo a whipping – on one occasion when he fell short in his cotton-picking task and then fled to the woods. Wary that his new bondsman was setting a bad example for his other hands, Campbell's master exclaimed that "if he did not break me all the niggers would do likewise." In South Carolina, Charles Ball overheard two overseers complaining about "two Yankee niggers . . . brought from Maryland," who "were running away every day" and who were consequently made to wear iron collars around their necks, chains around their ankles, and subjected to a regimen of severe whippings to bring them in line. Testimonies suggest that Upper South newcomers in the Lower South often felt singled out for excessive punishments simply because of their region of origin. Genovese and Fox-Genovese have argued that southerners "sought to instill a sense of inferiority in their slaves" that was predicated on fear and awe; in return, they supposedly genuinely expected their bondspeople "to embrace their masters as absolute others." Yet in reality, the practice of arbitrarily "breaking in" newcomers did not reveal a successful exercise of ideological hegemony; indeed, it had the opposite effect, and slaveholders knew it: it inspired hatred. Most slaveholders, however, appeared little perturbed as long as they achieved absolute obedience.[33]

Both region and slaveholding size may have indeed played an important role in the extent of physical abuse and the severity of punishments throughout the South. Many slaves, for example, claimed that excessive abuse was less common in regions within close proximity to free states and on small farms where overseers were not employed. That meant that slaves living in the Upper South found themselves at an advantage, and a perusal of testimonies from fugitive slaves and former slaves indeed reveals that many bondspeople from that region admitted never to have been excessively punished. Joseph Smith, a Maryland slave who fled to Canada, where he was interviewed in 1863, related that he was treated well by his master. "I can't say that I had a very tough time in slavery," he stated. "I never see anybody tied up and cut and slashed." Smith explained that Maryland "was so near the Northern States" that slaveholders there were "afraid to whip [the slaves], because they knew, if they did, they would run away from them." A.T. Jones, a Kentucky fugitive likewise interviewed in Canada in 1863, claimed that slaves on his small farm were treated relatively well because "there was never any overseer; we were our own managers." Jones explained to his interviewer "it is only on those plantations where they have a number of slaves and where they have overseers,

33 Tower, *Slavery Unmasked*, 313–15 (first quotes); Samuel Hall and Orville Elder, *Samuel Hall, 47 Years a Slave; A Brief Story of His Life Before and After Freedom Came to Him* (Washington, Iowa: Journal Print, 1912), 30 (second quote); Campbell, *Bond and Free*, 34–35 (third quotes); Ball, *Fifty Years in Chains*, 39–40 (fourth quote); Genovese and Fox-Genovese, *Fatal Self-Deception*, 86 (fifth quote).

that the slaves are so cruelly treated." Visitors to the southern states often made similar claims. One traveler through the South remarked on passing through the western valleys and mountains of Virginia – where slaveholdings were small, overseers were rarely employed, and masters often worked alongside their bondspeople in the fields – that slave owners in that region appeared to "have no need of pistols or dirks, as the slaves are generally well treated, and shew . . . that example is a better stimulus than the whip."[34]

A move from a small farm in the Upper South to a large plantation in the Lower South may have therefore indeed entailed an altered master–slave relationship because large plantations – most of which were located in the cotton, sugar, and rice districts, far from the border between North and South – tended to be more formally managed and indeed more frequently employed overseers than small farms. Usually from poor backgrounds, uneducated, and lacking the "check of self-interest" when dealing with slaves, southern overseers embodied the antithesis of benevolent masters in the southern conscience. As a class, they were notorious for their cruelty and nearly universally charged by both blacks and whites with inhumane and sadistic tendencies. One slaveholder, fed up with the managers of his estate, lamented in 1813: "I found overseers in general the most worthless sett [sic] of men and their wives still worse. I have an utter aversion to them after long experience." Slave testimonies – especially those of interregional migrants – did much to help craft an image of overseers in the Deep South as sadists who appeared to actually enjoy inflicting pain on refractory slaves. Henry Watson, a Virginia slave sold to a large Mississippi cotton plantation, claimed that at his new home, "the overseer, who was a drunken, quarrelsome person," was "impossible to please" and took "great delight in inflicting punishment on the slaves." Slaves on Watson's plantation were often whipped excessively, salt being applied to the wounds, or put in specially constructed stocks "for the torture of the slaves." Isaac, a Kentucky interstate migrant who later fled to Canada, declared in an 1863 interview that "the sufferings of the slaves in Louisiana are awful" because the overseers there went too far in disciplining bondspeople. When one of the slaves on his plantation was accused of killing a hog, for example, four overseers "took him, took off every stitch of clothing, and then whipped him from his neck down. One man had hold of each arm, and one hold of each leg." He claimed that his master even "made us all go to see it done. . . . They rang the bell to assemble the slaves to see the flogging." According to Isaac, such excessive and humiliating punishments were commonplace in Louisiana. He went on to relate how on

[34] Joseph Smith, in Blassingame, ed., *Slave Testimony*, 410–11 (first quotes). Smith's wife, also from Maryland, similarly recalled that she "didn't have a hard time" during slavery and that she "never see none of the cutting and slashing that I have heard of." See Mrs. Joseph Smith, in ibid., 411. A.T. Jones, in ibid., 430 (second quote); Abdy, *Journey of a Residence*, 2:291 (third quote).

Haller Nutt's plantation, located in the same neighborhood, slaves were treated "very cruel indeed" by the overseers, sometimes even resulting in death.[35]

Charges of extreme abuse by overseers in slave testimonies certainly achieved their goal of horrifying both interviewers and the general readership, and it is important to note that studies have shown that overseers were usually discharged for excessively cruel treatment. Yet to dismiss slave testimonies of blatant abuse at the hands of overseers risks going to the opposite extreme. Considered necessary to govern bondspeople, the exercise of violence against recalcitrant slaves remained legitimate in the minds of white southerners despite widespread calls for more humane treatment. As late as 1861, the Alabama Supreme Court even clarified that masters may "employ so much force as may be reasonably necessary to secure ... obedience." Planters' records, testimonies of white visitors and residents of the South, and even court documents readily attest that cases of extreme abuse did occur on southern plantations. Indeed, Isaac's testimony is corroborated by Haller Nutt's own plantation account books, in which several incidences of wanton abuse and even murder by the overseer are recorded. Returning home from a short absence in April 1843, for example, Nutt wrote in his journal that he had "lost one woman since I left – not result of ordinary course of disease but proceding from severe punishment in Nov. last for running away – and I think neglect of her afterwards." Weeks later, five of his slaves ran away rather than submit to a flogging. Later that same year, three more slaves – Ben, August, and Tom – died "from cruelty of overseer – Ben drowned[,] August hung – & Tom beat to death when too sick to work ... a horrid account of negligence and ill treatment." Finally, returning from an absence to the North in November, Nutt lost his patience, recording that he "heard most terrible accounts of the severity, cruelty & bad management of my overseer at this place.... I have to day discharged him." It is astounding that the overseer lasted as long as he did – even grandees of course had a financial stake in the health of their bondspeople, and the death of a slave constituted the loss of a significant investment. Nutt's failure to respond appropriately to the abuse visited on his "black family" clearly constituted a breach in his paternalist duties, but he appeared not to dwell on the matter. Masters who placed their plantations under the sole charge of overseers – usually grandees and absentee planters – often left their managers too much liberty

[35] William E. Wiethoff, *Crafting the Overseer's Image* (Columbia: University of South Carolina Press, 2006); David Ross to William Dunn, August (n.d.) 1813, David Ross Letterbooks, SASI, Series C, Part 1 (microfilm), JFK Institute (first quote); Stirling, *Letters from the Slave States*, 290 (second quote); Olmsted, *Seaboard Slaves States*, 486; Watson, *Narrative of Henry Watson*, 14–15 (third quotes); Isaac Throgmorton, in Blassingame, ed., *Slave Testimony*, 433–34 (fourth quotes). Israel Campbell, a Kentucky slave sent to Mississippi and hired out to several farms and plantations, complained of extreme abuse on one cotton plantation with a sadistic overseer, but when he was later hired to a small cotton farmer who "was his own overseer," he admitted that he was treated much better and became satisfied with his lot. See Campbell, *Bond and Free*, 35, 53.

in determining how much and how frequently to "lay it on" or at least failed to catch them when they exceeded the bounds of reasonable punishment.[36]

The a priori fear of abuse – and thus damage of valuable property – indeed underlay many planters' decision to stipulate strict rules for their overseers regarding punishment in the first place. One contributor to the *Farmer's Register* in 1840, who sincerely believed that the overseer "class of men" would be greatly improved if only they were given proper guidelines, commanded his plantation manager not to use the whip too often: "Much whipping indicates a bad tempered or an inattentive manager. The overseer must never, on any occasion, unless in self defence, kick a negro, or strike him with his hand, or a stick, or the but-end of his whip. No unusual punishment must be resorted to without the employer's consent." But even those who closely supervised their plantation affairs often approved of punishments that, by the standards of slave management guides, would have been considered unnecessarily excessive. On Bennet Barrow's Louisiana cotton plantation slaves were routinely punished in sadistic ways – some were given switches and told to "Fight it out," men were sometimes made to wear women's clothes and "paraded" around the plantation, runaways were often treed and bitten by dogs, and numerous slaves were staked down and brutally whipped or locked up in the plantation jail. Barrow admitted that his overseers were "a perfect nuisance," that they "cause dissatisfaction among the negros," and that they were "more possessed of brutal feelings" than was tolerable, and he even went long periods without an overseer for those very reasons, yet he not only agreed that severe punishments were necessary to properly manage his plantation work force, but he indeed often ordered (and sometimes inflicted) the most heinous punishments himself.[37]

Many southern slaveholders and overseers may have been virtually desensitized to punishments that both slave migrants and white visitors to the Lower South considered excessive. One northerner who resided in the Georgia lowcountry in the 1820s insisted that "what is called a moderate flogging at the south is horribly cruel." Thirty-nine lashes on slaves' bare backs, while their hands were tied and attached to a beam, appeared to be the most common form of punishment, but he also knew overseers to "torture" slaves by tying them

[36] Genovese and Fox-Genovese, *Fatal Self-Deception*, 52, 86; William K. Scarborough, *The Overseer: Plantation Management in the Old South* (Baton Rouge: Louisiana State University Press, 1966); "On the Conduct and Management of Overseers, Driver, and Slave," *Southern Agriculturalist* 9 (May 1836): 225–31; "Plantation Life – Duties and Responsibilities," *DeBow's Review* 29 (Sept. 1860): 357–68; Bauer, *Leader among Peers*, 61–62; Anthony Gene Carey, *Sold Down the River: Slavery in the Lower Chattahoochee Valley of Alabama and Georgia* (Tuscaloosa: University of Alabama Press, 2011), 112; *Journal of Araby Plantation*, Apr. 21, 1843, May 16, 1843, Nov. 1, 1843, "Births & Deaths 1843," Haller Nutt Papers, RASP, Series F, Part I, JFK Institute (quotes).

[37] *The Farmer's Register*, vol. 8 (Jan. 31, 1840): 230–31 (first quote); Bennet H. Barrow, *Plantation Life in the Florida Parishes of Louisiana, 1836–1846, as Reflected in the Diary of Bennet H. Barrow*, edited by Edwin Adams Davis (New York: AMS Press, 1967), 40–41, 49–50 (second quotes).

up in awkward positions and leaving them all night, forcing them to wear iron collars with bells, cropping their ears, and clubbing them. A physician called as a witness to a court case in St. Landry Parish, Louisiana, in which a master was charged with inhumanely and excessively abusing his slave Augustin for running away, admitted that Augustin was "severely flogged [and] his skin was off on the shoulders & about the thighs," but went on to argue that the slave had loose skin anyway, and that "the defendant is not considered a severe master [and] is not considered so by his neighbors." What southerners considered routine punishments could easily become excessive if masters and overseers flew into a passion. Legal records reveal that one overseer pursued a recalcitrant slave, who was attempting to escape a whipping, with his cowhide and shotgun and proceeded to fire "the whole load" of his firearm at the bondsman, which became "lodged in [the slave's] back." Although such extreme cases surely constituted exceptions to the rule, they do indicate that cruelty did occur on southern plantations, and newcomers – who did not know the rules and routinely made clumsy mistakes on the job – appear to have received more than their fair share of corporal punishments.[38]

As with material conditions, however, it would be folly to contend that corporal punishments in the Lower South were *systematically* more cruel and excessive than in the Upper South. In states as far away geographically as Maryland and Texas, the most common mode of punishment was a whipping, and severe abuse was not necessarily limited to large plantation districts. One Maryland-based slave trader even claimed that the greatest barbarities he had ever witnessed were in southern Virginia, where he saw slaves "stripped and suspended by their hands, their feet tied together, a fence rail of ordinary size placed between their ankles, and then most cruelly whipped, until, from head to foot, they were completely lacerated." Court cases from the Upper South confirm that bondspeople were sometimes abused in ways that many contemporaries would have associated with the barbarities of Louisiana or Mississippi. In 1826, one Virginia slaveholder, Richard Turner, was indicted for murdering his slave Emmanuel "with force and arms," assaulting the bondsman "with certain rods, whips, and sticks," and "willfully and maliciously, violently, cruelly, immoderately, and excessively beat[ing], scourg[ing] and whip[ping], against the peace and dignity of the Commonwealth." In 1849, Simeon Souther, a slaveholder from Hanover County, Virginia, was charged with fifteen counts of abuse, torture, and murder of his slave Sam. Souther first tied Sam to a tree and beat him with switches and then proceeded to beat him with a shingle,

[38] Horace Moulton, in Weld, *American Slavery as It Is*, 20–21 (first quote); Hodgson, *Remarks During a Journey*, 171–73; "David K. Markham to the District Court, St. Landry Parish, Louisiana, 1830," in Loren Schweninger, ed., *The Southern Debate over Slavery: Volume 2, Petitions to Southern County Courts, 1775–1867* (Urbana: University of Illinois Press, 2008), 151–52 (second quote); Thomas P. Devereux and William H. Battle, *Reports of Cases at Law, Argued and Determined in the Supreme Court of North Carolina, from December Term 1834, to June Term 1836, Both Inclusive* (Raleigh: Turner & Hedges, 1837), 1:122 (third quote).

after which he "did strike, knock, kick, stamp, and beat him, upon various parts of his head, face, and body." The slaveholder then "applied fire to his body, back, sides, belly, groins, & privy parts," and soaked his body in warm water steeped with red peppers. Sam was subsequently untied from the tree and beaten to the ground, dragged to a shed where he was tied by the neck, and slowly suffocated to death, his master beating him and applying fire to his body all the while.[39]

Indeed, many testimonies from slave migrants also suggest that disciplining was often quite harsh in the Upper South. John, a Virginia slave who was sold locally to a "hard-hearted scoundrel," reported to an interviewer after fleeing slavery that he was severely paddled, whipped while tied to an apple tree, forced to work with chains on, placed in stocks, and disciplined in a variety of other ways that were considered typical for the Lower South and not Virginia. Some interstate migrants recalled similar punishments both in the Upper *and* Lower South. Contradicting the charges of many interregional migrants from Virginia, William Anderson insisted that although "some are more cruelly treated than others," most slaves in his native Virginia were "cowed down by the lash" and that his master "sometimes whipped hard." On arrival in Mississippi, he claimed, he was also whipped hard for work-related mistakes and once put in chains for running away, in an attempt to "cow me down... like the rest of the slaves." John Brown, who dictated to his British editor in 1855 that he had "had the misfortune to get a run of bad masters," similarly claimed to have been severely flogged for minor infractions by various masters in both Virginia and Georgia, his abuse in Georgia not necessarily more barbaric than what he suffered in Virginia. Punishments and abuse also varied from plantation to plantation *within* the Lower South, suggesting that the nature of slave punishment was contingent on individual masters' judgment more than anything else.[40]

IV.

Slave migrants to cities, towns, and industrial areas frequently expected better treatment – and thus less and milder physical punishments – than those who

39 Lemuel Sapington, in Weld, *American Slavery as It Is*, 49 (first quote); The Commonwealth vs. Richard Turner, Nov. 1827, in Peyton Randolph, *Reports of Cases Argued and Determined in the Court of Appeals of Virginia; To Which Are Added, Reports of Cases Decided in the General Court of Virginia, Vol. V* (Richmond: Peter Cottom, 1828), 678 (second quote); Southern vs. The Commonwealth, June 1851, in Peachy R. Grattan, *Reports of Cases Decided in the Supreme Court of Appeals, and in the General Court, of Virginia, Vol. VII, From April 1, 1850, to July 1, 1851* (Richmond: Colin & Nowlan, 1852), 673–75 (third quotes); Carey, *Sold Down the River*, 115–17.

40 Tower, *Slavery Unmasked*, 89–93, 89 (first quote); Anderson, *Life and Narrative of William J. Anderson*, 6–7 (second quote), 18 (third quote); Brown, *Slave Life in Georgia*, 11–13, 21–27, 131 (fourth quote); Ball, *Fifty Years in Chains*, 282.

remained in the countryside. Yet migrants were often disappointed to find that city slaves were not immune to severe floggings, painful reminders that whatever its perceived material advantages, urban slavery was still slavery. William Wells Brown, who was moved from Kentucky to St. Louis and subsequently hired out to various employers, insisted that although "slavery is thought, by some, to be mild in Missouri," no part of the South should be "more noted, for the barbarity of its inhabitants, than St. Louis." Brown related that during his time in the city, "numerous cases of extreme cruelty came under my own observation." One domestic slave who lived in his neighborhood, also a migrant, whose new master accused him of being too uppity, had a "ball and chain fastened to his leg" and was made to drive yoke of oxen and perform various duties until it wore out the flesh around his ankles – "all this to '*tame him*.'" Brown also claimed to have been often subjected to abuse by his employers, and indeed when his master once proposed that he find himself "a good master" for the ensuing year, he complained that good masters in St. Louis did not exist. Travelers in the South also frequently admitted surprise at the abuse inflicted on urban slave populations. A visitor to Mobile, Alabama, was shocked at the "barbarity to the Negro servants" that he witnessed during his stay, which were "beyond even what I had anticipated." He complained that in that city, "you continually hear the lash upon their backs, with language which would shock you, even if applied to brutes." Far from privileged and proud, he found that most slaves in Mobile wore an appearance of "abject timidity or idiotic vacancy," and he often saw men, "after receiving a severe flogging... the moment their tyrant's back was turned, burst into a loud laugh... like a school-boy, who wishes to appear as if he 'did not care.'" The records of urban establishments that hired slaves testify to the severe punishments to which some hirelings were subjected. At one iron factory in Richmond, Virginia, managers were directed to punish three slaves for dropping a load of iron into the river while loading it onto a boat as follows: "carry them with ropes round their necks to the boat landing where the load was lost & there have them with stript naked & 39 stripes inflicted well placed on the bare backs of each of those scoundrels.... Punish them as they deserve."[41]

Physical punishment in southern towns and cities was an activity that many slaveholders indeed outsourced to unscrupulous professionals. Gentlemanly urban masters need not get their hands dirty in order to execute their absolute authority over their bondspeople because several cities had notorious whipping pens and jails where slaves were sent to be disciplined, their masters billed for the services rendered. Northern journalist James Redpath, traveling through the South in the 1850s, heard horror stories about the "Sugar House" in

[41] William Wells Brown, *Narrative of William W. Brown, a Fugitive Slave. Written by Himself* (Boston: Anti-Slavery Office, 1847), 27–30 (first quotes), 64–65 (second quote); Hodgson, *Remarks During a Journey*, 157 (third quotes); David Ross to Robert Richardson, Jan. 14, 1813, David Ross Letterbooks, SASI, Series C, Part 1 (microfilm), JFK Institute (fourth quote).

Columbia, South Carolina, from as far away as Richmond, Virginia. On arrival in Columbia, he interviewed a local slave migrant who had been sent there by his new master – "de meanest ole scamp goin,'" according to the bondsman – for such minor infractions as playing cards and staying out too late. Redpath was horrified to learn that slaves sent to the Sugar House were locked up in dark cells for two or three days, fed only hominy, and systematically paddled. When he subsequently went to inspect the jail himself, he almost "suffocated" from the "poisonous air" and found eight slaves performing forced labor on a treadmill next to the reeking privies. The Savannah jail and the Charleston "workhouse," where slaves were routinely sent to be whipped and manacled in solitary confinement, enjoyed similar reputations throughout the southern states. Slave migrants from the countryside were often surprised and shocked to see or hear of such places, and they quickly developed an acute fear of urban jails. When William, a Virginia slave who was sold to Savannah, was recaptured after attempting to flee one of his masters, he was locked up in a local jail that doubled as a whipping post for refractory slaves, who were brought there by their masters to be "whipped three times in one week, forty stripes, save one, and well put on." The sight of slaves being systematically whipped by a professional, he claimed, "struck me with horror." Louis Hughes, dictating his experiences in bondage at the end of the nineteenth century, provided an identical description of the Richmond slave pen in which he was confined before being deported to Mississippi. The pen doubled as a whipping yard, where urban slaveholders of "refinement" sent their slaves to be corrected rather than doing it themselves. "The yard I was in had a regular whipping post to which they tied the slave, and gave him 'nine-and-thirty,'" Hughes recalled. "I saw many cases of whipping while I was in the yard. Sometimes I was so frightened that I trembled violently, for I had never seen anything like it before."[42]

Newcomers were not only often surprised at the brutal and systematic application of corporal punishments in towns and cities but also at some of the infractions for which urban slaves were struck or beaten. Throughout the South, slaves were punished for work-related mistakes, running away, stealing, and talking back to their masters. But in towns and cities, they also had to be careful not to breach additional codes of behavior that were often unknown to slaves from the countryside. For example, rural migrants especially tended to accidentally break rules that governed spatial mobility and racial segregation in southern cities. Although most urban slaves were not restrained by the same "geography of containment" that kept bondspeople captive on plantations and

[42] Redpath, *Roving Editor*, 57–60, 57 (first quote); William Dusinberre, *Them Dark Days: Slavery in the American Rice Swamps* (1996; Athens: University of Georgia Press, 2000), 128–29; "Work-House," *Digest of the Ordinances of the City Council of Charleston, from the Year 1783 to July 1818* (Charleston: Archibald E. Miller, 1818), 254–61; Grimes, *Life of William Grimes*, 35–36 (second quote); Hughes, *Thirty Years a Slave*, 8–9 (third quote).

farms, their movement throughout urban spaces was still strictly curtailed by curfews, laws that prohibited free assembly with other blacks, and especially segregation laws that determined how blacks should navigate city sidewalks. Breaching any one of these codes could evoke the wrath of city patrols. Indeed, as one historian has argued, one of the most striking contrasts between urban and plantation slavery was the "more extensive intrusion of administrative and judicial machinery into the master-slave relationship in the city." In Richmond, alarm bells sounded every night to announce the curfew for blacks, and both a state-appointed Public Guard and city night watch were responsible for the apprehension of slaves out after curfews or suspected of illegal meetings, a form of surveillance that was mimicked in cities across the South after the Nat Turner rebellion in 1831. Less formal reprimands were even meted out by white bystanders who caught slaves breaching segregation laws. On the first day that Isaac Mason, a Maryland slave, set foot in Baltimore, he was severely beaten by two white men for passing between them on the sidewalk. "They were not standing close together," Mason recalled after emancipation, "[and] I could not very well pass around them." As the bondsman was "completely ignorant of the law, forbidding a negro from passing between two or more white men or women who were walking or standing on the sidewalk," he did not know that urban slaves were supposed to "take the street to give place to their superiors." Henry Crawhion, a Kentucky slave who was sent to Charleston, South Carolina, was similarly surprised to learn that "in the city, a black man must get off the side-walk if he meets a white man, or stop on the curb-stone and raise his hat: if he meets a lady and gentleman he must step clear off the walk and raise his hat." Crawhion himself was apprehended and committed to the "calaboose" shortly after arrival to the city for "smoking in the street," another activity that was allowed for whites but forbidden for blacks. "I told them I was a stranger, and did not know the law," the migrant contended. "That made no odds, however; I was sentenced to nine and thirty lashes." Even visitors to southern cities testified to the frequency with which slaves were struck by whites for breaching segregation laws. J. Alexander Pattern, visiting Lynchburg, Virginia, in 1859, wrote that on the city's narrow sidewalks "the pleasures of a walk are not increased by the crowds of blacks, who intercept your way. They are generally polite, but sometimes run the risk of a kick." Olmsted witnessed a white man push a slave woman off the sidewalk with his cane and "three rowdies" beat another slave off the sidewalk and into the middle of the street during his stay in Richmond. Migrants who had no knowledge of urban segregation laws often found themselves disproportionately subjected to maltreatment in city streets.[43]

[43] Stephanie M.H. Camp, *Closer to Freedom: Enslaved Women and Everyday Resistance in the Plantation South* (Chapel Hill: University of North Carolina Press, 2004), 12–34; Marianne Buroff Sheldon, "Black-White Relations in Richmond, Virginia, 1782–1820," *Journal of Southern History* 45 (Feb. 1979): 30 (first quote). Little Rock passed laws in 1836 that instated

Domestic slave migrants in urban settings and on plantations also often found themselves exposed to regular physical abuse because of their constant close proximity to their masters and especially their mistresses, who frequently vented their rage on their servants. Indeed, although some historians have emphasized the shared culture of domesticity that joined mistresses and female slaves in southern plantation households, the testimonies of slave migrants tend to underscore conflict rather than mutual understanding. A common theme is the contention that new *masters* proved to be relatively mild mannered but that new *mistresses* were impossible to please. As Elizabeth Fox-Genovese has argued, many antebellum mistresses, who were in charge of the domestic sphere, found the supervision of slaves difficult and frustrating, and even the kindest often resorted to the whip to maintain order and discipline within an institution that took male violence for granted. One interstate migrant and domestic slave from Kentucky, who eventually secured her freedom, told a northern reporter that her new mistress in Missouri "seemed to be very jealous of me." Although she admitted that her master treated her well, her mistress "could not bear to hear me praised" and seemed to go out of her way to find an excuse to punish her, often hitting her over the head with brooms and other household objects. The bondswoman claimed that only after physically resisting a beating, an infraction that eventually led to her being sold, did her mistress stop maltreating her. Elizabeth Keckley served in southern households in Dinwiddie Court House, Virginia; Hillsboro, North Carolina; and St. Louis, Missouri. In an 1868 testimony, she insisted that her original mistress in Virginia was "a hard task-master," but her North Carolina mistress, who "seemed to be desirous to wreak a vengeance on me for something," was unusually cruel. Although she was treated well by her "good-hearted" master, Keckley insisted that her mistress constantly scolded her, once even allowing a male guest to flog her, an interesting example of how slaveholding women sometimes "managed" their domestic servants by calling on white men to mete out punishments, as Fox-Genovese has argued. Abuse was not limited by gender boundaries, however, and young male migrants also claimed to have been singled out for excessive punishments by frustrated mistresses. Lewis Garrard Clarke, a Kentucky migrant, recalled that after an estate division, he was bequeathed to a cruel mistress, who used to beat him for every "trivial offence." Usually resorting to the "raw hide" or hickory switches,

9 o'clock curfews for all blacks (including free blacks) and prohibited "meetings of slaves held in this City after dark." See *Arkansas Gazette*, Jan. 12, 1836. Abdy, *Journal of a Residence*, 267; Lyell, *Second Visit to the United States*, 42–43; Lack, "An Urban Slave Community," 271; Hogdson, *Remarks during a Journey*, 175–76; Isaac Mason, *Life of Isaac Mason as a Slave* (Worcester, Mass.: n.p., 1893), 23 (second quote); Henry Crawhion, in Blassingame, ed., *Slave Testimony*, 257–58 (third quote); J. Alexander Pattern, "Scenes from Lynchburg," in Eugene L. Schwaab, ed., *Travels in the Old South, Selected from Periodicals of the Times* (Lexington: University of Kentucky Press, 1973), 2:541 (fourth quote); Olmsted, *Seaboard Slave States*, 29 (fifth quote).

Clarke claimed that his new owner sometimes flew into a rage and inflicted blows on him with whatever was at hand, including "a chair, the broom, tongs, shovel, shears, knife-handle, [or] the heavy heel of her slipper."[44]

Other household servants who failed to perform well were abused by their masters or both their masters *and* mistresses. In 1839, an Alabama woman named Eveline Whetstone sued her own husband for his abuse of her domestic servant, a slave woman from another county who had been given to Eveline by her father when she got married. "Never having been accustomed to cooking and washing," the slave failed to please and was subjected to extremely "cruel treatment" from her master, who often "threatened to whip her for not having milk for him" and beat her with a hickory stick for other trivial offences. On one occasion, Mr. Whetstone "loaded in her presence two guns and told her if she did not go home to [Eveline's father] he would blow her brains out." Although extreme, many domestic servants evoked such rage from their new owners that they were indeed gotten rid of. A "negro woman" from Mobile, Alabama, who was sold to a Creole family in Louisiana, for example, clashed so strongly with her new owners that they sold her to a neighboring plantation. The slave's new mistress exclaimed in a letter to a relative that "she was sold by a Frenchman; who like most foreigners, is very hard on negroes." Forced to do all of the household tasks for a family of ten, a position she was "not used to," the Alabama woman had found herself continually being punished by her Creole masters for not working fast enough, the toxic atmosphere in the house exacerbated by the fact that "she did not understand French so her mistress found it impossible to get along with her."[45]

Under such circumstances, the domestic sphere could constitute a site of oppression that rivaled any theater of slavery. For female slave migrants, moreover, the threat or reality of sexual abuse in the master's household heightened tensions even further. Despite widespread condemnation of interracial sexual

44 Marli F. Weiner, *Mistresses and Slaves: Plantation Women in Antebellum South Carolina, 1830–1860* (Urbana: University of Illinois Press, 1997); Fox-Genovese, *Within the Plantation Household*, 22–25, 205–206; Redpath, *Roving Editor*, 319–21, 319 (first quote), 321 (second quote); Elizabeth Keckley, *Behind the Scenes, or, Thirty Years a Slave, and Four Years in the White House* (New York: G.W. Carleton & Co., 1868), 21 (second quote), 32 (third quote), 32–38; Lewis Garrard Clarke, *Narrative of the Sufferings of Lewis Clarke, During a Captivity of More than Twenty-Five Years, among the Algerines of Kentucky, One of the So-Called Christian States of America* (Boston: David H. Ela, 1845), 15 (fourth quote), 18 (fifth quote). North Carolina slave Harriet Jacobs, who was transferred locally to a household run by a difficult mistress as a young girl, contended in her autobiography that she would "rather drudge out my life on a cotton plantation" than to go back and live with a "jealous mistress." See Harriet Jacobs, *Incidents in the Life of a Slave Girl* (1861; Mineola, NY: Dover Publications, 2001), 28–29.

45 "Eveline M. Whetstone and William Ratcliffe to the Chancery Court, Shelby County, Alabama, 1839," in Schweninger, ed., *Southern Debate over Slavery*, 197 (first quote); Trypena Holder Fox to Mother, Dec. 27, 1857, in King, ed., *Northern Woman in the Plantation South*, 67 (second quote).

relations, slave women lived in a society where their bodies were owned by white men and where the rape of a slave woman was not recognized by any state law. Sexual abuse was common, and many migrants – local, interstate, and urban – testified of unwanted attention from their new owners. In the most famous example from the antebellum South, North Carolina slave Harriet Jacobs desperately pursued various recourses to escape sexual harassment by her new master, Dr. James Norcom, even taking a prominent white lover (whom she hoped would protect her) and eventually hiding out in a crawl space in her grandmother's attic for seven years before fleeing to Philadelphia. Although Jacobs' reaction to Norcom's persistence was unique, her abuse was not, and most slave women reluctantly submitted to their masters' desires. Louisa Picquet, a Georgia slave woman who was sold as a household servant to a New Orleans man when she was a young woman, told interviewer Hiram Mattison in 1861 that she became her new master's de facto concubine, delivering four of his children against her will. "I told him, one day," Picquet related, "I wished he would sell me... because I had no peace at all." But her master "got awful mad," and "said nothin' but death should separate us; and, if I run off, he'd blow my brains out." Picquet remained trapped in this situation until her master died. The sexual prowess of overseers was also considered a widespread problem in the South, and newcomers – torn from husbands and family members who might have helped protect them – frequently fell victim to their advances. Winney Grimshaw, a Virginia slave torn away from her husband and transported to a cotton plantation in what is now Hale County, Alabama, had the ill fortune to be assigned as a domestic servant to the overseer, who pursued her relentlessly despite having an ailing wife and children. Unwilling to discharge him, Winney's master attempted to end the abuse by moving the overseer to another location, but to no avail. The bondswoman bore the overseer a son in 1849, a daughter in 1850, another daughter in 1853, yet another daughter in 1854, and another son in 1857. As Genovese and Fox-Genovese have argued, "an efficient overseer was hard to find, and planters tried not to notice [sexual] violations" that did not enflame the slave community as a whole. Such cases occurred with enough frequency that one Louisiana cotton planter felt it necessary to specifically instruct his overseer to stay away from his slave women. Rule number eleven in his plantation list of rules and regulations read:

> Above all things avoid all intercourse with negro women. It breeds more trouble, more neglect, more idleness, more rascality, more stealing, more lieing [sic] up in quarters, more everything that is wrong on a plantation than all else put together. Instead of studying or thinking about women in bed or out of bed, a man should think about what he has to morrow, or for a week... or for a month or year. How to take advantage of this piece of work, or that little job. In fact such intercourse is out of the question – it must not be tolerated.[46]

[46] Kolchin, *American Slavery*, 123–24; Jacobs, *Incidents in the Life of a Slave Girl*, 111–29; Picquet and Mattison, *Louisa Picquet, the Octoroon*, 19–20 (first quote); Richard S. Dunn,

V.

As Anthony Carey has argued, most slave migrants felt that they had little choice but to submit to floggings and harassment at the hands of new masters, overseers, or employers, "for fear of making awful situations worse." But some did openly resist extreme abuse in a variety of ways that testified to their refusal to be treated as dehumanized brutes. Many attempted to flee or went truant for a period of time, for example. Tom Jackson, a slave purchased by James Henry Hammond in Augusta, Georgia, and brought to his South Carolina plantation in 1844, clashed continuously with his new owner and frequently fled back to Georgia as a result of extreme punishments. One time he even fled "with his iron on." Patsey, a slave woman "about 40 or 45 years old" who was sold from Virginia to work in the household of Henry Byrd of Augusta, Georgia, took flight with "two scars on the right cheek, made by the whip." Adam, a hireling under the charge of one Doctor July, of Livingston, Alabama, likewise absconded with "scars on [his] right hand and arm." Will, a Virginia hireling working in Washington, DC, was presumed to be making his way to Pennsylvania, having escaped his employer in 1820 with "a scar near the external angle of one of his eyes," a "recent" wound "the size of a half dollar on one of his legs," a scar "on the back of his head," another scar between his fingers, yet another scar on his left cheek, and missing "the first jaw tooth in his upper jaw on the left side." Virtually all of these wounds were made during his hiring term.[47]

Physical resistance to abuse was also more common than many white masters and overseers liked to admit, as both slave testimonies and court records attest. Many migrants struck, pushed, or wrestled with their overseers and masters rather than submit to a flogging or sexual abuse. One Virginia slave woman named Sukey reportedly shoved her master into a boiling pot of lye in response to his sexual advances, an attack for which she was sold to interstate traders. Frederick Douglass, fed up with six months of whippings and beatings by his hired master Mr. Covey in rural Maryland, "resolved to fight" his employer on one particular occasion, grabbing Covey by the throat and wrestling him to the

"Winney Grimshaw, a Virginia Slave, and Her Family," *Early American Studies* 9 (Fall 2011): 514–16; Genovese and Fox-Genovese, *Fatal Self-Deception*, 58–59 (second quote); "General Rules to Govern Time of Overseer," *Journal of Araby Plantation*, RASP, Series F, Part I, JFK Institute (third quote). See also Keckley, *Behind the Scenes*, 38–39.

47 Carey, *Sold Down the River*, 115 (first quote); John Hope Franklin and Loren Schweninger, *Runaway Slaves: Rebels on the Plantation* (New York: Oxford University Press, 1999), 9–11, 33–37, 42–48; Plantation Records, Jan. 20, 1844, Jan. 22, 1844, Nov. 5, 1844, Mar. 24, 1845 (second quote), Nov. 23, 1845, James Henry Hammond Papers (microfilm), RASP, Series A, Part I, JFK Institute; *Charleston Courier*, Mar. 7, 1835 (third quote); *Mississippi & State Gazette*, Sept. 5, 1851 (fourth quote); *Daily National Intelligencer*, Jan. 8, 1820 (fourth quote). Slave testimonies also testify to the prevalence of absconding to escape abuse at the hands of new masters or overseers. See, for example, Roper, *Narrative of the Adventures and Escape of Moses Roper*, 14–15; Hall, *47 Years a Slave*, 31–32; Bibb, *Narrative of the Life and Adventures of Henry Bibb*, 121.

ground. Describing the incident as a "turning point" in his life in which he felt redeemed in his manhood, Douglass claimed that for the duration of his hire, Covey never laid a hand on him again. In 1826, one Samuel Cowgil, employed as overseer on Magnolia plantation in West Feliciana Parish, Louisiana, sued his employer for "assaults and wounds inflicted by the negroes" of the plantation, which contained several migrants. The slaves "being notoriously rebellious insubordinate & disorderly," Cowgil argued to the court that he often had to inflict severe punishments but that the slaves sometimes resisted and attacked him. One slave named Pompey resisted the lash by slashing the overseer's hand and arm with an axe, "in consequence of which it [Cowgil's arm] hangs by his side in a most Awkward position." Cato, another slave, "Armed with a long knife & a club," also attacked Cowgil, cutting the fingers of his other hand and "using his club on the head & body" of the overseer.[48]

In rare cases, brawls erupted that even resulted in death. In a trial that gripped and deeply divided antebellum Richmond, Jordan Hatcher, a young hireling at a local tobacco factory, was sentenced to death for fatally striking his overseer, William Jackson, with an iron poker after Jackson attempted to whip him. Hatcher was later granted clemency and sentenced to deportation on humanitarian grounds because he had been provoked and had "no design to kill." The case caused such a stir that Richmond newspaper editors ironically began to discuss the need to protect factory *overseers* from abuse by *slaves*. In a similar case, Will, a slave from Edgecombe County, North Carolina, stabbed his overseer to death and succeeded in having his murder charge mitigated to manslaughter after convincing the court that the overseer had been trying to kill him and that he had acted in self-defense. Wesley, an "obedient and submissive" slave in Mississippi, also killed his overseer, one William Ford – "proven to be cruel and violent in his treatment of slaves" – after receiving a severe reprimand in 1859. Having made a mistake at work, Wesley had been beaten and kicked by Ford, then taken to the smoke-house, strapped to the wall, and left there for several hours. When Ford returned to get a piece of meat, Wesley somehow freed himself and with one blow smashed the overseer's skull in with a timber. In Louisiana in 1857, a slave named Henderson "assaulted, struck, cut and stabbed his master, *John Robins*, with a large pocket knife... with the intent to kill and murder" him. He was sentenced to death. Such cases represent the most extreme forms of resistance, but they illustrate that many slaves physically responded to abuse by new masters and overseers, refusing to

[48] Fannie Berry, in Charles L. Perdue, Jr., et al, *Weevils in the Wheat: Interviews with Virginia Ex-Slaves* (Charlottesville: University of Virginia Press, 1976), 48–49; Frederick Douglass, *Narrative of the Life of Frederick Douglass, an American Slave. Written by Himself* (Boston: Anti-Slavery Office, 1845), 71–72 (first quote); "Samuel Cowgil to the District Court, West Feliciana Parish, Louisiana, 1826," in Loren Schweninger, ed., *The Southern Debate over Slavery: Volume 2, Petitions to Southern County Courts, 1775–1867* (Urbana: University of Illinois Press, 2008), 132–33 (second quote).

submit to what they considered arbitrary or excessive punishments upon their bodies.[49]

Hirelings had slightly more leverage in their attempts to escape from abusive employers than purchased slaves because they could often successfully play off their owners' fear of property damage and get them to nullify hiring contracts. It was indeed widely believed in the South that hirers were inherently more cruel than slave owners, because – like overseers – they did not have a lifelong stake in the bondspeople in their charge. The extent to which this was true, of course, differed by employer, but nevertheless the distrust that frequently existed between masters and employers often worked to the advantage of the slave. By complaining of excessive physical abuse to their owners, hirelings pitted their two masters against each other, as Jonathan Martin has argued, in an attempt to determine appropriate boundaries of treatment and remove themselves from abusive environments. When Robert, a slave from Halifax County, Virginia, who was hired out to a Richmond employer, was faced with the prospect of what he perceived to be an unjust flogging, he fled back to his master in the hope that he would interfere. His employer wrote his master:

> Dear Sir,
> I have to report to you that on yesterday your boy Robert, having behaved in such a manner that the overseer was compelled to correct him. He struck him four or five Licks of his shirt and the boy broke and ranaway. I suppose he has gone home. I write this in order you may be on the lookout and return him as soon as he gets home. The boy having been spoken to about idling was very insolent and on being told to take off his shirt refused and after have taken a few licks of the shirt ran off and said he was going to you.

Another Texas slaveholder voided a hiring contract when his slaves informed him that "they were badly treated" by their new employer. A Brazoria County court found that the hirelings were indeed "returned badly injured."[50]

[49] James M. Campbell, *Slavery on Trial: Race, Class, and Criminal Justice in Antebellum Richmond, Virginia* (Gainesville: University Press of Florida, 2007), 103–104 (first quote); Starobin, *Industrial Slavery in the Old South*, 86; The State vs. Negro Will, Slave of James S. Battle, Dec. 1834, Devereux and Battle, *Supreme Court of North Carolina*, 1:121–124; Wesley (a Slave) vs. The State, Oct. 1859, in James Z. George, *Reports of Cases Argued and Determined in the High Court of Errors and Appeals for the State of Mississippi, Vol. XXXVII, Vol. VIII, Containing Cases Determined at a Part of the April Term, 1859, and a Part of the October Term, 1859* (Philadelphia: T. & J.W. Johnson & Co., 1860), 328–29 (third quote); The State v. Henderson, a Slave, Nov. & Dec. 1858, in A.N. Ogden, *Reports of Cases Argued and Determined in the Supreme Court of Louisiana. Vol. XIII for the Year 1858* (New Orleans: Office of the Price Current, 1859), 493 (fourth quote).

[50] Jonathan Martin, *Divided Mastery: Slave Hiring in the Antebellum South* (Cambridge, Mass.: Harvard University Press, 2004), 138–60; Takagi, "*Rearing Wolves to Our Own Destruction*,

Yet such behavior did not always result in direct intervention on behalf of the abused hireling, and complaints did often backfire. Many masters cared little for the punishment or treatment of their slaves as long as they received their annual hiring fee and their slaves were returned employable at the end of the year; as a result, abused hirelings were sometimes – perhaps even often – ignored and sent back to their employers. One young hireling in Nicholasville, Kentucky, owned by a local judge, fled to Union soldiers in 1862 to escape abuse by his employer because his master reportedly ignored his complaints of maltreatment. The employer "beat, bruised and maltreated [the hireling] in a shameful manner," a soldier reported to his superior, "until he had rather die than endure it any longer. . . . The boy further stated that he had repeatedly told his master that he could not endure the treatment he was receiving – whose only reply was, 'go back, you dog.'" Virginia Gunnell Scott, a Virginia slaveholder, wrote in her diary in 1857 that her "servant woman Margaret came home this day complaining of being badly used by Mr. Fairfax, manager for Mrs. Daingerfield," to whom Margaret was hired in Alexandria. Exasperated with her bondswoman, Scott dealt with the situation by simply selling Margaret for $1,000.[51]

Newcomers of all types who changed masters were forced to adapt to new management styles that included changes in their material conditions and in systems of reward and punishments. The experiences of interstate, local, and urban migrants contained some similarities but also appear to have differed in many respects. Interstate migrants who were deported from the small farms of the Upper South to the larger plantations of the Lower South often perceived regional differences their treatment, decrying barbaric living conditions at their new destinations. Although plantation management on large slaveholdings – with the distribution of strict rations and clothing allowances and the widespread employment of overseers – indeed tended to be more systematic and regulated than on small farms, however, charges that slaves were *structurally* worse off in the Lower South than the Upper South appear not to be fully justified. The experiences of local migrants in the Upper South indeed reveal that both material conditions and punishments could be just as inhumane there as they were in the Deep South, and migrants throughout the slave states claimed that treatment often differed markedly on neighboring plantations, suggesting that the (in-)humanity of slave management differed more by individual slaveholder than by region. Slaves who were sent to urban environments, on the other hand, frequently enjoyed somewhat better material conditions than their

49; T.G. Green to Col. Bailey, Aug. 3, n.y., William Bailey Papers, RASP, Series E., Part I (microfilm), JFK Institute (first quote); "Charles K. Reese to the Probate Court, Brazoria County, Texas, 1851," in Schweninger, ed., *Southern Debate over Slavery*, 266–67 (second quote).

[51] Ira Berlin, et al, *Freedom: A Documentary History of Emancipation, 1861–1867, Series I, vol. I* (New York: Cambridge University Press, 1985), 540 (first quote); Virginia Gunnell Scott, Diary (typescript), Apr. 25, 1857 (second quote), May 4, 1857, FCRL.

rural counterparts but quickly found that they were not exempt from physical abuse. Indeed, throughout the slave South, newcomers were more prone to punishments because they made more mistakes at work and often breached rules that they were unfamiliar with.

Adjusting to new masters was equivalent to walking a tightrope for slave migrants, a situation that exacerbated the difficulties of removal. As the next chapter will show, adjusting to new slave communities also posed unexpected obstacles and challenges to interstate, local, and urban newcomers.

6

Slave Crucibles

I began to introduce myself around among [the slaves], but as I came from Mississippi, they looked down on me.

Slave migrant William Webb describing his experiences in Kentucky, 1873[1]

By the time William Grimes escaped bondage aboard a ship bound for New York, he had been owned by ten masters; performed both field work and skilled work; and been an interstate, local, and urban migrant to boot. Grimes' experiences, which he recorded in 1825, ran the full gamut of the trials and obstacles that confronted forced migrants in the antebellum South. Surprisingly, however, his narrative reveals that with each move, he found little support from new slave communities. Indeed, Grimes' frequent conflicts with his fellow bondsmen and constant feelings of alienation pervade his autobiographical account.[2]

When Grimes was first sold away at the age of ten from his native King George County, Virginia, and moved locally to a plantation in Culpeper, for example, he claimed to have felt "heart-broken" at the thought of leaving his home and family. Depressed and unsociable at his new destination, he not only failed to forge any meaningful relationships with the other slaves – describing himself as "a poor friendless boy, without any connexions" – but indeed managed to make enemies almost immediately. Grimes insisted that his hard work in the plantation household "made some of the other servants jealous," especially one Patty, whom he described as a dishonest "brute" with a "malicious temper." Patty seemed to go out of her way to get Grimes in trouble

1 William Webb, *The History of William Webb, Composed by Himself* (Detroit: Egbert Hoekstra, 1873), 19.

2 William Grimes, *Life of William Grimes, the Runaway Slave. Written by Himself* (New York: n.p., 1825). See also Susanna Ashton, "Slavery Imprinted: The Life and Narrative of William Grimes," in Lara Langer Cohen and Jordan Alexander Stein, eds., *Early African American Print Culture* (Philadelphia: University of Pennsylvania Press, 2012), 127–39.

for mistakes he did not commit, to such an extent that the newcomer requested to be transferred to the fields simply to get away from her. There he again made a poor impression on the other hands, regularly evoking the wrath of Voluntine, the black driver, who "punished me repeatedly to make me perform more labour than the rest of the boys." Grimes' only companion during his time in Culpeper was Jourdine, a girl who had originally been owned by his old master and with whom he had grown up back in King George County, and who had coincidentally been sold to a neighboring plantation. Although his master "did not like me to go" see her, Grimes illicitly slipped off to visit his friend whenever he could, grateful for the opportunity to communicate with somebody who had been through the same ordeal that he had.[3]

So it went throughout Grimes' life in slavery: trying to forge new friendships but often getting into conflicts with local slaves and finding himself alone. When he was sold to Savannah, Georgia, for example, he complained that he was forced to work as a house servant with a superstitious lowcountry slave named Frankee, whom he "always believed to be a witch." When Grimes was eventually sold to another Savannah slaveholder, he similarly "got a fighting" with one of his master's other slaves named Cato; on one occasion, Grimes even "bit off his nose, just as my master was going to sell him, which injured the sale of Cato, very much." On a nearby plantation with yet another master, Grimes again felt like "a stranger," claiming that "not one negro on the plantation was friendly to me." There he was also regularly flogged by the black driver, against whom he once retaliated "old Virginia stile (which generally consists in gouging, biting and butting)." During every move, during every conflict, Grimes continually expressed the desire to return to King George County, to familiar ground, to see his parents again.[4]

The experiences of William Grimes underscore the difficulties involved in the social assimilation of antebellum slave migrants. Cast into new slave communities, newcomers often felt – and were treated – like outsiders by their fellow bondspeople and were forced to use various strategies to effect their integration. How did migrants experience the transition to new slave communities? How did they forge new relationships, and what were the bases of these relationships? What institutions and strategies aided in their integration process? And to what extent do their experiences reveal a broad "slave identity" in the antebellum period? This chapter explores these questions for interstate, local, and urban newcomers, respectively.

I.

Interstate newcomers severed all ties with family and community when they left their states of origin. Far from finding comfort in new slave communities,

[3] Grimes, *Life of William Grimes*, 8–9 (first quotes), 10 (second quote), 13 (third quote).

[4] Ibid., 23 (first quote), 28 (second quote), 30, 37–38 (third quotes).

however, their forced confrontations with complete strangers at their destinations often served to compound the trauma of removal and deportation, a fact that contradicts common assumptions regarding an intrinsic social cohesion or identity among slaves in the antebellum South. Such generalizations have a long history. Revisionist scholars in the 1970s and 1980s especially tended to celebrate an antebellum slave culture that was largely homogenous and that stood in stark contrast to the culture of white slaveholders. John Blassingame, for example, portrayed a singular "slave community," with a unified culture consisting of "an emotional religion, folk songs and tales, dances, and superstitions." Sterling Stuckey argued that the memory of "African 'tribalism'" enabled slaves to experience a "sense of community in the traditional African setting and... include all Africans in their common experience of oppression in North America." Even current scholarship tends to assume more cohesion among slaves than perhaps was the case. Ira Berlin, for one, recently argued that in the southern interior slaves from various regions "mixed easily" and that regional identities and even "regional chauvinism" had "no lasting effect on African-American life" in receiving societies.[5]

To be sure, time and especially shared oppression helped dilute feelings of otherness and regional distinction among interstate migrants. Yet to underestimate the friction involved in their initial assimilation process risks oversimplifying the migration experience itself. Friendless, kinless, and carriers of regional cultures that sometimes appeared "foreign" to outsiders (both black and white), interstate migrants were burdened with the awkward task of carving out a new place for themselves within existing slave communities where they did not yet feel at home and where informal social hierarchies relegated them to the bottom of the ladder. Samuel Hall, sold from North Carolina to Tennessee as a young man, related a common story when he claimed that it was "three years before I ever attempted to get out among the young people" at his new destination, not feeling accepted or at home there until long after his arrival. The prospect of adapting to a strange new group was often experienced as daunting by interstate migrants.[6]

[5] John W. Blassingame, *The Slave Community: Plantation Life in the Antebellum South* (New York: Oxford University Press, 1979), 105 (first quote); Sterling Stuckey, *Slave Culture: Nationalist Theory and the Foundations of Black America* (New York: Oxford University Press, 1987), 3 (second quote). Berlin goes on to argue that "one of the consequences of the Second Middle Passage was to attenuate the regional distinctions that had characterized slave life during the seventeenth and eighteenth centuries." Ira Berlin, *Generations of Captivity: A History of African-American Slaves* (Cambridge, Mass.: Harvard University Press, 2003), 170–71 (third quote).

[6] Samuel Hall and Orville Elder, *Samuel Hall, 47 Years a Slave; A Brief Story of His Life Before and After Freedom Came to Him* (Washington, Iowa: Journal Print, 1912), 30 (second quote). Different age cohorts also appear to have experienced different degrees of difficulty in adapting to new communities. Predictably, migrants who were small children readily made playmates among local slaves. Henry Bruce, a Virginia slave who was moved to Missouri as a small boy, claimed after emancipation that he remembered playing with seven or eight boys who lived on a

Indeed, for many migrants, social assimilation was hardly a priority at all upon arrival in new slave communities. Perhaps most telling is the overwhelming evidence of interregional newcomers fleeing new slave communities in desperate attempts to return to their old ones. Continuing to identify themselves with family, kin, and community in their places of origin, migrants often rejected new slave communities outright and bolted in the days, weeks, and even months subsequent to their arrival. Runaway slave advertisements often underscored the presumption that they were returning "home." William, who fled his new plantation near Lexington, South Carolina, in 1830, was presumed to be "mak[ing] his way for North Carolina, as he was purchased . . . and brought from there." A Virginia slave woman named Patsey absconded from her Georgia plantation and was suspected to have "endeavored to get back to Virginia." Interstate migrant Nicholas left his South Carolina plantation in an attempt "to make his way to Maryland," where he was originally from. And Sally, a slave from the estate of George Mason in northern Virginia and purchased by an Alabama slaveholder, ran away "a few days" after arriving in the Deep South, suspected of making her way back home. Southern newspapers from receiving societies are replete with similar ads.[7]

Some runaway slave ads even highlighted cultural differences that must have reinforced feelings of otherness and awkwardness among newcomers. In Louisiana, where local slaves were dubbed "Creoles" and French was widely spoken alongside English, ads frequently labeled interstate fugitives as "Americans" and commented on their accents or (lack of) language skills. In February 1845, one twenty-two-year-old slave woman named Susan absconded from her new plantation in Louisiana, her master describing her as "diffident when spoken to, and in speaking exhibits the broken English dialect of the African raised in Charleston, S.C . . . from whence she was brought but a few months since." In July of that same year, "the young negro BOSTON" took flight, who "answers briskly when spoken to . . . speaks English only [and] was brought three months ago from Mr. J. Hagan, negro dealer." When Elick, age twenty-three, ran away from his new plantation in Plaquemines Parish, his master described him as an "American Negro boy [who] has great difficulty in speaking."[8]

If newcomers' accents, dialects, and even languages appeared that striking and rude to their new masters, who presumably had only limited contact with them, one can imagine how local Creole slave communities perceived them.

neighboring plantation after arrival at his new home, and that they were "the happiest days of my boyhood." See Henry Clay Bruce, *The New Man. Twenty-Nine Years a Slave. Twenty-Nine Years a Free Man* (York, Pa.: P. Anstadt & Sons, 1895), 24.

7 *Charleston Courier*, Nov. 2, 1830 (first quote); *Charleston Courier*, Mar. 7, 1835 (second quote); *Charleston Courier*, Oct. 29, 1830 (third quote); *Huntsvile Democrat*, June 16, 1838 (fourth quote).

8 *The Times Picayune*, Feb. 25, 1845 (first quote); Ibid., July 2, 1845 (second quote); Ibid., June 10, 1845 (third quote).

Some testimonies indeed suggest that Creole slaves looked down on American newcomers and vice versa. Melinda, a Louisiana ex-slave interviewed by the Federal Writers' Project, told interviewers that her Creole grandmother spoke only French and refused to associate with "Americans," slave or otherwise. "She hated the English language; said it was good only to speak to mules, and not to be heard in the mouth of folks, colored or white," the former bondswoman recalled. Over time, most American migrants did learn at least some French, and many fully mastered the language. James Lamar, a Mississippi slave sold to Iberville Parish, Louisiana, absconded in 1845 and was advertised as an American slave who "speaks English and French," for example. Another Virginia migrant claimed that after spending some time in Bayou Sara, he "made considerable progress in learning to speak the French language." Upon arrival, however, language differences surely made migrants feel that they had arrived in a foreign country.[9]

Indeed, Louisiana was undoubtedly the most "foreign" destination possible for migrants from the eastern seaboard, not just because of the language but for other reasons as well. Even white visitors perceived intrinsic cultural differences between Creole slaves and imported newcomers that went beyond communication. Betraying an implicit and almost stereotypical admiration for the Protestant work ethic, for example, one European sojourner in Louisiana concluded that the slaves "who speak English and are Protestants, all work harder, and are less idle than the Frenchified negroes." But for newcomers, perceived differences in religious practices were perhaps most important. Consider the experiences of Charlotte Brooks, a Virginia slave who was sold to Louisiana as a young woman. Relating her experiences to interviewer Octavia Albert in 1890, Charlotte claimed that the first thing she noticed upon arrival in Louisiana, besides the language, was that "every body was Catholic ... and I had never seen that sort of religion that has people praying on beads." For years she refused to worship with the other plantation slaves because she did not recognize the validity of their religion. Instead, she stayed home on Sundays and "thought of my mother's Virginia religion," often replaying in her mind "the old Virginia hymns" that her mother used to sing. Charlotte's isolation from any formal slave church continued for four years, until she learned that another slave woman "from my old State" named Jane Lee had been sold to a neighboring plantation. Perceiving the new arrival as "one of my folks," Charlotte sought out Jane and immediately developed a lasting friendship with her. Having shared the same fate and the same cultural background, the two Virginia migrants commenced to worship together on Sundays, singing

[9] Melinda, in Ronnie W. Clayton, ed., *Mother Wit: The Ex-Slave Narratives of the Louisiana Writers' Project* (New York, 1990), 166 (first quote); *Daily Picayune*, Nov. 2, 1845 (second quote); William Hayden, *Narrative of William Hayden, Containing a Faithful Account of His Travels for a Number of Years, Whilst a Slave, in the South* (Cincinnati: n.p., 1846), 57 (third quote); Berlin, *Generations of Captivity*, 170–71.

and praying in the Virginia style, and eventually even inviting other American migrants to join them. For Charlotte, Jane represented a sense of home, family, and community that she had lost in transit to Louisiana. "Aunt Jane was no kin to me" Charlotte related to Alberts. "But I felt that she was because she came from my old home." Jane was the key to Charlotte's acceptance of her fate, her "mak[ing] my peace with the Lord," and the slow reconstruction of a life she had left behind in Virginia.[10]

But even in other receiving societies of the antebellum South where local slaves were Protestant and spoke English, interstate newcomers often felt that they had entered a strange and inferior country. Consideration must be taken for changes over time because in the early nineteenth century, most newcomers on the frontier entered slave societies in which a majority of "local" slaves were in fact other migrants who had established themselves over a number of years. Yet as the antebellum period progressed and generations of bondspeople native to the Lower South were born, friction between "locals" and out-of-state newcomers become more and more evident. In interviews and conversations with travelers, migrants frequently manifested a sincere and even chauvinistic pride in their regions of origin, which they usually associated with better, more attractive, or more intelligent slaves than the "inferior" slaves born and raised in the Lower South. Indeed, interstate migrants – especially from the Upper South and eastern seaboard – often nostalgically insisted that slaves in their home regions were happier, had higher morals, were more assertive, acted more "free," and were less "cowed down" by the institution of slavery than those in their new destinations. Olmsted's travelogue from his journey through the South in the 1850s reveals several illuminating examples. One North Carolina slave whose master had sent him to South Carolina, for example, responded to the question how he liked being so far from home thusly: "Well, I likes my country better dan dis; must say dat, master, likes my country better dan dis. I'se [like] a free nigger in my country, master." He confessed to Olmsted his opinion that "the niggers did not look so well here as in North Carolina and Virginia" and even that "de niggers ain't so happy heah" and "don't appear so bright as they do there." Slave testimonies also underscore such chauvinism. William Webb, a Mississippi migrant to Kentucky (traveling against the stream), admitted that he found it difficult to make friends in the Upper South: "as I came from Mississippi," he related after emancipation, "they looked down on me." Another Virginia migrant who had been sold to Alabama but later escaped to England recalled to an interviewer his surprise that the local hands in Alabama "were so completely cowed, that they did not need to be tied at all when flogged," contrary to the resistance he had been used to in Virginia. Former slave William Anderson, who was sold from Virginia

[10] Francis and Theresa Pulszky, *White, Red, Black* (1853; New York: Johnson Reprint Co., 1970), 103 (first quote); Octavia V. Rogers Albert, *The House of Bondage, or Charlotte Brooks and Other Slaves* (1890; New York: Oxford University Press, 1988), 4–13 (second quotes).

to Mississippi, similarly insisted in his narrative that slaves in the Deep South were unusually docile toward whites, often seemed to be "great enemies of each other," and were almost completely ignorant of the Bible, something that never ceased to baffle him. In his native Virginia, Anderson claimed, "the Sabbath was observed," but when he got to his new plantation in Mississippi "where they work, curse, swear and dance on Sunday," he felt "awfully" because there was "no preaching." Indeed, shortly after arrival, the local slaves asked him to sing a hymn, "an old Virginia song," but Anderson refused, feeling that he had entered a "strange land" that lacked all morals and spirituality. These very localized cultural differences were often merely *perceived* as regional characteristics – most Mississippi slaves *did* have prayer meetings, after all – but however exaggerated, such perceptions widened the gap between locals and interstate migrants and complicated social assimilation.[11]

II.

Despite such chauvinism and friction, however, no migrant could afford to be an island for long. Although distance and a certain degree of tension sometimes existed between interstate newcomers and local slaves, it would be inaccurate to exaggerate their divisions and describe various groups of bondspeople as diametrically opposed to each other. True, when it came to defining "home" and measuring the merits and shortcomings of certain regions and cultural expressions, local slaves' and newcomers' opinions were often rooted in regional identities. But when it came to defying slavery as an institution, they more often than not shifted their identities along status and racial lines, aiding and assisting each other in their shared experience of slavery. Minor acts of resistance, for example, were often rooted in cooperation between locals and newcomers alike – or newcomers from different regions – revealing how thin the line was between local identities and a broader "slave identity." This is an interesting example of what postmodern cultural studies scholars and social scientists have termed "fluid identities." Current identity theory underscores that identities are not fixed but rather change according to circumstance. Slaves did not necessarily identify themselves broadly as "American slaves" all day every day; they did so when they were overtly confronted with their slave status in such a way that caused them to identify with each other. Virginia migrant Louis Hughes, for example, perceived many differences between slave communities

[11] Frederick Law Olmsted, *Journey in the Seaboard Slave States, with Remarks on their Economy* (New York: Dix & Edwards, 1856), 390–91 (first quote); Webb, *History of William Webb*, 19 (second quote); James W.C. Pennington, *A Narrative of Events of the Life of J.H. Banks, an Escaped Slave, from the Cotton State, Alabama, in America* (Liverpool: M. Rourke, 1861), 58–59 (third quote); William J. Anderson, *Life and Narrative of William J. Anderson, Twenty-Four Years a Slave* (Chicago: Daily Tribune Book and Job Printing Office, 1857), 18 (fourth quote), 8 (fifth quote), 16 (sixth quote), 29. See also Henry Watson, *Narrative of Henry Watson, a Fugitive Slave* (Boston: Bela Marsh, 1848), 17.

in his native state and those in Mississippi, to where he was transported as an adolescent. Indeed, in Mississippi, he identified most strongly with other interstate migrants – his best friend was Tom, "a Virginian, as I was," and like Hughes had been "sold from his parents when a mere lad." Yet witnessing a local bondsman receive a whipping one day made him feel solidarity for his fellow slaves in a more general sense, becoming so indignant about the institution of slavery as a whole that he "wish[ed] I were dead." Other migrants actively aided their fellow slaves who were threatened with punishments, regardless of their regions of origin.[12]

Collective resistance took more indirect forms as well. Interestingly, many interstate migrants who fled their new communities shortly after arrival did so by building *local* networks that allowed them to escape – consorting with and relying on complete strangers with whom they broadly identified as fellow slaves. As Calvin Schermerhorn has argued, forging social relationships with local slaves allowed migrants to gain geographic knowledge that was crucial to their flight plans, but even while on the run, fugitives were forced to depend on strangers to provide them with food, shelter, and advice. And although slave testimonies contain several examples of slaves betraying other slaves, most fugitives could count on the support of the wider slave community, much to the consternation of slaveholders throughout the South. A Massachusetts minister who resided in Georgia for five years observed that his slaveholding neighbors often had great difficulty tracking down newly imported runaways because "the slaves assist one another usually when they can, and not be found out on it." For slaves, assisting fugitives revealed a broader sympathy for a shared plight. Many slaves indeed took major risks by helping strangers. Kitty, a former Alabama slave, told an interviewer after emancipation that she risked a severe whipping one time for "feedin' a runaway nigger!" She added that "dey'd ha' killed me ef they'd ha' found me out den." Andrew Jackson, a Kentucky bondsman, related to interviewers in 1847 that whatever the risks, "it is a very rare thing that one slave ever becomes informer against his brother who intends to take the long walk."[13]

[12] Hazel Rose Markus and Maryann G. Hamedani, "Sociocultural Psychology: The Dynamic Interdependence among Self Systems and Social Systems," *Handbook of Cultural Psychology*, edited by Shinobu Kitayama and Dov Cohen (New York: Guilford Press, 2007), 7; Neil Campbell and Alasdair Kean, *American Cultural Studies: An Introduction to American Culture* (London: Routledge, 2006), 22–23; Tom Postmes & Nyla Branscombe, eds., *Rediscovering Social Identity* (New York: Psychology Press, 2010), chs. 1 and 2; Louis Hughes, *Thirty Years a Slave: From Bondage to Freedom. The Institution of Slavery as Seen on the Plantation and in the Home of the Planter* (Milwaukee: South Side Printing Co., 1896), 101 (first quote), 23 (second quote); William Webb, *The History of William Webb, Composed by Himself* (Detroit: Egbert Hoekstra, 1873), 4; Moses Roper, *A Narrative of the Adventures and Escape of Moses Roper, from American Slavery* (Philadelphia: Merrihew & Gunn, 1838), 26–27.

[13] Calvin Schermerhorn, *Money over Mastery, Family over Freedom: Slavery in the Antebellum Upper South* (Baltimore: Johns Hopkins University Press, 2011), 46–47; Testimony of Rev.

Sometimes migrants even absconded in the company of local slaves who also sought to flee. In Louisiana in 1836, a reward of 75 dollars was offered for the apprehension of three runaway slaves: Jack Hodges, an American slave age twenty-seven; Joseph, "a creole negro [who] speaks but little English;" and Corbon, "an American negro, aged about 30 years." All three had fled together. A Florida slaveholder also advertised for five runaway slaves from his plantation in 1847: four men and one woman. All were local slaves except one Tom, who was suspected of "intend[ing] to make his way to Augusta, Ga., as in that section I purchased him of Mr. Henry B. Ware." In a similar case, two slaves named July and Rhoda absconded together in a skiff from their plantation at Bayou Sara in Louisiana in 1850, July being described as "a small South Carolina negro and lame in one of his hips or leg," and Rhoda was a local woman, "about 45, [and] speaks French." In Orangeburg District, South Carolina, two "Negro Women, both named NANCY," fled a plantation together, one of them purchased in Richmond, Virginia, "where perhaps she may bend her course," and the other aiming "at getting back to the city" of Charleston, where she was originally from. On many occasions, interstate migrants cooperated with fellow interstate migrants – not always from the same state – to flee back to their places of origin. In 1845 one thirty-five-year-old man named Phil, originally from Florence, Alabama, absconded from a Louisiana plantation with another interstate migrant named Jim, twenty-six years old and purchased from a slaveholder living on the South Carolina–Georgia border. Both were presumed to be traveling together and attempting to return to their respective home regions.[14]

Indeed, interstate migrants tended to bond with other interstate migrants in much more intimate ways, outside of the realm of resistance. Sharing a common experience – the trauma of being uprooted and deported – helped to forge bonds of love and affection among victims of the domestic slave trade, even to the extent of establishing new family ties to make up for those lost in removal. This was already evident during removal, as discussed in Chapter 3, but after arrival, it developed even further. A perusal of marriage certificates of emancipated slaves in Louisiana (where records are most detailed and complete) issued by officers of the Freedmen's Bureau during and shortly after the Civil War, for example, reveals how prevalent marriages were between interstate newcomers. Sandy Alexander, a thirty-year-old freedman from North Carolina, formalized his marriage to Malvina Phillip, from Virginia, before a Union chaplain in

Horace Moulton, in: Thomas Weld, *American Slavery as It Is: Testimony of a Thousand Witnesses* (New York: American Anti-Slavery Society, 1839), 21 (first quote); Kitty, in Blassingame, ed., *Slave Testimony*, 536 (third quote); Andrew Jackson, *Narrative and Writings of Andrew Jackson, of Kentucky* (Syracuse: Daily and Weekly Star Office, 1847), 9 (fourth quote).

14 *New Orleans Commercial Bulletin*, Jan. 5, 1836 (first quote); *Tri-Weekly & Advertiser* (Montgomery, Ala.), Mar. 23, 1847 (first quote); *Daily Picayune*, June 30, 1850 (second quote); *Charleston Courier*, May 27, 1840 (third quote); *Daily Picayune*, Oct. 26, 1845; William Henry Singleton, *Recollections of My Slavery Days* (n.p., 1922), 3.

Concordia Parish, Louisiana, on January 12, 1865. Both had been married before in their home states – Sandy for ten years and Malvina for four – and both had been separated from their original spouses "by slave despotism" (in other words, the slave trade). Peter Bumper, of Tennessee, similarly formalized his marriage to Kentucky-born Lucinda Nelson in Louisiana in 1864. Peter had been married before in Tennessee but had been separated from his first wife when "a white man tuk her." Maryland-born Basil Chapman formalized his marriage to thirty-year-old Hariette McKell, of "Eastern Shore, Md.," the mother of seven of his children, when he entered the Union army in 1864. Basil, age forty-four, had been married in Maryland but was separated from his first wife and two children by "being Sold away." The marriage records are replete with similar examples, especially from interstate migrants from the Upper South, who tended to marry each other with striking prevalence. But there are also examples of marriages between migrants from states as far apart as Maryland and Mississippi: Billy Moore of Mississippi married Maria Louisa Bond of Virginia; Edmund Key of Missouri married Patsey Rose of Virginia. In all of these cases, interstate migrants established new families with other interstate migrants in Louisiana, seeking comfort in others who had experienced the same loss and fear and filling the void of the families and spouses they had left behind. Local slaves, on the other hand, tended to marry other local slaves. Slave testimonies reveal a similar picture in other receiving societies of the South.[15]

Marriages between local slaves and interstate migrants also occurred, of course, an indication that some migrants were better able to find acceptance within new slave communities than others. It is important to remember that much depended on the attitude and hospitality of the slaves in the receiving society. Although migrants often reported feeling rejected by local slaves, many

[15] Marriage Certificate of Sandy Alexander to Malvina Phillip, Jan. 12, 1865, Marriage Records of the Office of the Commissioner, Washington Headquarters of the Bureau of Refugees, Freedmen, and Abandoned Lands, 1861–1869 (hereafter "Marriage Records BRFAL"), microfilm 1875, roll 1, National Archives and Records Administration (hereafter NARA), Washington, DC (first quote); Marriage Certificate of Peter Bumper to Lucinda Nelson, Nov. 6, 1864, ibid. (second quote); Marriage Certificate of Basil Chapman to Harriette McKell, Dec. 22, 1864, ibid. (third quote); Marriage Certificate of Billy Moore to Maria Louisa Bond, Jan. 8, 1865, ibid.; Marriage Certificate of Edmund Key to Patsey Rose, Jan. 12, 1865, ibid. Virginia slave Louis Hughes ended up marrying a Kentucky woman in Mississippi, for example, with whom he shared the common experience of deportation. He even recalled that his wife, Matilda, was "a sad picture to look at" when she arrived in Mississippi, as she "was almost heart-broken" about leaving her friends and family behind. Hughes was able to comfort her in a way that local slaves could not because he had experienced the same forced separation from loved ones as Matilda. Hughes, *Thirty Years a Slave*, 91. James Nichols, a Missouri slave who was sold down the river to Mississippi, married a woman who was on the same boat that transported him to Natchez and who was sold to the same plantation. James Nichols, in Blassingame, ed., *Slave Testimony*, 504–505. Slave testimonies are replete with similar stories of interstate migrants marrying each other.

locals in fact sympathized with the plight of newcomers or simply welcomed the arrival of new faces on the plantation or in the neighborhood. Interestingly, various sources suggest that marriages between *male* interstate migrants and *female* local slaves were common, perhaps because local women made more of an effort to comfort newcomers on arrival. One Mississippi slaveholder related to a family member in 1845 that his slave Adam, whom he had recently purchased from Maryland, was "getting on very well," having married one of his other slave women on Christmas Day. A Louisiana plantation mistress wrote to a relative in 1856 that her newly purchased Virginia slave had "tak[en] a wife from the next plantation." The Louisiana marriage certificates issued by the Freedmen's Bureau also contain some illuminating examples. William Lewis, of Georgia, formalized his marriage to Melissa Collins, of Louisiana, in January 1865. Lewis had been married before when he lived in Georgia, but he had been separated from his first wife by the slave trade. Daniel Mines, from Fauquier County, Virginia, similarly married a Louisiana woman named Martha Breskin in 1865. The marriage certificates from other states reveal similar trends (albeit with less prevalence than marriage certificates among interstate migrants). The records for Mississippi, for example, contain several marriage certificates such as that of South Carolina bondsman William Alexander, who legalized his marriage to Mississippi slave Elmira Robinson in September 1865.[16]

Yet however assimilated or settled migrants felt when they established new families at their new destinations, they often continued to identify strongly with their regions of origin. Indeed, similar to migrants of all times and places, antebellum slave migrants often exhibited a "dual orientation" that manifested itself in a wide variety of subtle ways. Naming patterns provide one interesting example. The children of interstate migrant parents were not only often named after family members left behind upon removal, but many were indeed named after the very states, cities, counties, regions, or plantations their parents had come from. When perusing slave inventories from the Lower South, it is striking how many children were named Virginia, Caroline or Carolina, Kentuck, Richmond, Washington, Charlotte, and other references to the sending societies of the domestic slave trade. On one Mississippi plantation that contained several interstate migrants from all over the South, for example, children's names in 1857 included Missouri Ann, Virginia, Breckenridge (a county in Kentucky), Huston (a town in Kentucky), and Caroline. The children on a Georgia

16 John Knight to William Beall, Feb. 1, 1845, John Knight Papers, RASP, Series F, Part 1 (microfilm), JFK Institüt für Nordamerikaatudien, Freie Universität, Berlin (first quote); Tryphena Blanche Holder Fox to mother, Aug. 31, 1856, in Wilma King, ed., *A Northern Woman in the Plantation South: Letters of Tryphena Blanche Holder Fox* (Columbia: University of South Carolina Press, 1993), 61 (second quote); Marriage Certificate of Wm. Lewis and Melissa Collins, Jan. 14, 1865, Marriage Records BRFAL, microfilm 1875, roll 1, NARA; Marriage Certificate of Daniel Mines and Martha Breskin, Jan. 4, 1865, ibid.; Marriage Certificate of William Alexander and Elmira Robinson, Sept. 28, 1865, Marriage Records BRFAL, microfilm 1875, roll 2, NARA.

plantation in 1859 included two Virginias, one Richmond, and a Caroline. Although it is virtually impossible to confirm the reasons such names were given, surely such patterns cannot all be coincidence.[17]

The testimonies of the children of interstate migrants provide another indication that migrants continued to identify with their regions of origin long after they had assimilated and established new family ties. Migrants passed on stories about their roots, origins, and migration experiences to their children. In countless ex-slave interviews from the Federal Writers' Project, for example, former bondspeople related to interviewers that one or both of their parents had come from another state and talked openly about how their parents had been forced against their will to move – information that was passed down to them by their migrant parents. Indeed, this was often the first piece of information that ex-slaves provided during interviews. One Alabama woman told interviewers: "My name is Amy Chapman. My mother was Clary Chapman an' my pappy was Bob Chapman. Dey both come from Virginny; my mammy from Petersburg an' my pappy f'um Richmond. Dey was driv' down to Alabamy lak cattle." Arkansas slave Laura Abromsom similarly began her interview by stating: "My mama was named Eloise Rogers. She was born in Missouri. She was sold and brought to three or four miles from Brownsville, Tennessee. Alex Rogers bought her and my papa.... Rogers got my papa in Richmond, Virginia. He was took outer a gang." The details of such stories and their prominent place at the very beginning of African Americans' life stories, suggest that they were spoken of often in slave households and thus became engrained in the minds of migrants' children. Indeed, one interviewed woman, an Arkansas ex-slave named Betty Curlett, whose mother came from Virginia and paternal grandmother from North Carolina, told interviewers that she could talk "all about my kin folks" because her "Grandma used to set and tell us" all about how the family had ended up in Arkansas.[18]

Finally, interstate migrants continued to manifest a dual orientation between their two "homes" by actively attempting to restore contact – often across truly vast distances – with friends and family that they had lost. Slaves who were moved by their masters or bequeathed to distant family members were in the best position to do this. Many dictated or wrote letters back to their home communities, for example, which were usually sent via their owners. Virginia slave George Pleasant, separated from his wife Agnes and their children when his master migrated to Tennessee, wrote his "biloved wife" a letter in 1833, which he sent by his mistress, "who ar now about starting to virginia" to visit

[17] Slave Inventory 1857, Joseph Jaynes Plantation Journals, Rankin County, Mississippi, RASP, Series F, Part 1 (microfilm), JFK Institüt; Duncan Clinch Slave List, 1859, Camden County, Georgia, RASP, Series C, Part 2 (microfilm), JFK Institüt.

[18] Amy Chapman, Slave Narratives of the Federal Writers' Project, 1936–1938 (typescript), Library of Congress, Washington, DC, vol. I, 58 (first quote); Laura Abromsom, Slave Narratives, vol. II, pt. 1, 160 (second quote); Betty Curlett, Slave Narratives, vol. II, pt. 2, 72 (third quote).

family members. In it he beseeched his wife to rekindle their contact and send him a letter back, and he expressed his hope that "with gods helpe that I may be able to rejoys with you on the earth[.]" He added that if contact in this life was not possible that they would be reunited in the afterlife: "I am determind to nuver stope praying, not in this earth and I hope to praise god. In glory there weel meet to part no more forever." Indeed, some interstate migrants continued to negotiate to be physically reunited with spouses long after they had been deported. Appealing to the moral conscience of his new owner in 1841, one Virginia slave named Reuben, who had been sold to his master's brother in Alabama, convinced his new master to attempt to purchase his wife several months after he had arrived at his new destination. His new master wrote to his brother: "Reuben is very anxious to hear from you respecting the purchase of his wife, the poor fellow is really distressed." Sometimes such negotiations were successful. Charles, a Maryland slave who was given to his master's son-in-law and moved to Mississippi, successfully negotiated with his new master in 1837 to have his wife sent along about a year after arrival in the Deep South. His wife arrived in Mississippi "under very great obligations" to both slaveholders for allowing her to be reunited with her husband, whom she feared she had lost forever when he left Maryland. As this case illustrates, attempts to restore contact came not only from the migrants themselves but from their home communities as well. Some slaves in home communities resorted to drastic measures to be reunited with loved ones. George Ramsey, a Kentucky-born refugee in Canada whose wife and children were carried away from him when his wife's master emigrated to Arkansas Territory, told government interviewers that he "went after her once, and got her, but they took her away from me," adding that it was only after he had "lost her completely [that] I thought I would go to Canada."[19]

Marriage and family formation, whether with local slaves or other newcomers, often facilitated the integration of interstate migrants into new slave communities and helped them establish roots. Religious worship played a similar role. Although the importance of religious *differences* among slaves from various parts of the South have already been discussed, it is crucial to note that religion more often than not served as a vehicle for social cohesion and assimilation among locals and newcomers alike. Sometimes it took several years for newcomers to seek out religious experiences with other slaves, but most eventually did. Emperor Williams, originally from Tennessee, was sold to Louisiana in 1839 but eventually "joined the Church in 1845," for example. Curiosity

[19] George Pleasant to Agnes Hobbs, Sept. 6, 1833, in Elizabeth Keckley, *Behind the Scenes, or, Thirty Years a Slave, and Four Years in the White House* (New York: G.W. Carleton & Co., 1868), 26–27 (first quote); Henry A. Tayloe to Benjamin Ogle Tayloe, May 25, 1841, Tayloe Family Papers (microfilm), RASP, Series E, Part 1, JFK Institüt (second quote); John Knight to Wm. M. Beall, Dec. 28, 1837, in John Knight Papers, RASP, Series F, Part 1, JFK Institüt (third quote); George Ramsey, in Blassingame, ed., *Slave Testimony*, 440 (fourth quote).

led many migrants to church meetings with local slaves. Francis Fedric, a Virginia slave who was moved to Kentucky by his master, related in 1863 that upon arrival, he went "to see several persons baptized," adding that the "social affections" among the slaves during religious ceremonies were so strong that "no hard usage can weaken them." Another Virginia migrant recalled after emancipation that on his new plantation in Mississippi, he regularly attended the Sunday prayer meetings, during which all of the slaves (regardless of their origin) gathered to sing and pray, relate the story of Moses, and urge each other to endure bondage "as good soldiers." Indeed, interstate migrants often initiated collective religious worship themselves. Eli Johnson, a Virginia slave sold to Mississippi, claimed that at his new destination, he "used to hold prayer-meetings Saturday night." Coming together as spiritual brothers and sisters who shared the yoke of oppression, antebellum slaves turned religious worship into the cornerstone of community building. And migrants, who had lost their families and communities in transit, appeared to need religion in their lives to help them cope with their loss.[20]

Collective living conditions and work also served as vehicles to integration over time, as newcomers and locals interacted in their daily lives. Maryland slave Charles Ball related that on arrival in South Carolina, he was assigned to live in the cabin of a young family, whom he described as "companions" who "gave me a part of their boiled greens, and we all sat down together to my first meal in my new habitation." The father of the family made earnest attempts to make the newcomer feel comfortable, making conversation with him and even encouraging him to open up and talk about the wife and children he had left behind in Maryland. Despite insisting that he had arrived in a "land of strangers," Ball referred to his host as "my new friend." Many slave migrants undoubtedly had similar experiences, becoming fictive kin within the slave households in which they were forced to reside. Others forged bonds of friendship in the workplace. John Brown, who was sold from Virginia to Georgia, related in his narrative that on arrival in Georgia, he "used to feel very bad, and wish to die" but that he was comforted by another slave named John Glasgow, who worked in the same field gang and whom he described as one of his only friends. Glasgow took Brown under his wing and "used to tell me not to cry after my father and mother, and relatives.... He encouraged me to try and forget them, for my own sake, and to do what I was bidden." Gradually, his network was expanded as he encountered difficulties in the workplace. When Brown was beaten for work-related mistakes, for instance, another local slave

[20] Emperor Williams, in Blassingame, ed., *Slave Testimony*, 621 (first quote); Francis Fedric, *Slave Life in Virginia and Kentucky; or, Fifty Years of Slavery in the Southern States of America* (London: Wertheim, MacIntosh, and Hunt, 1863), 25 (second quote); Hughes, *Thirty Years a Slave*, 52–54 (third quote); Webb, *History of William Webb*, 19–29, 19; Eli Johnson, in Drew, ed., *North-Side View*, 383 (fourth quote); Albert J. Raboteau, *Slave Religion: The 'Invisible Institution' in the Antebellum South* (New York: Oxford University Press, 1980).

named Uncle Billy "came running up" and beseeched his master: "don't kill the poor boy." Other local bondspeople – whom Brown tellingly referred to as his "fellow-slaves" – even helped wash the blood from his face after the incident. Such situations helped forge bonds of friendship and unity between local slaves and interstate newcomers and encouraged the development of broader slave identities.[21]

III.

Local migrants in the antebellum South manifested a similar dual orientation as their interstate counterparts, but the nature of their dual orientation often differed in a number of important ways. First, local migrants grappled less strongly with regional identities because they usually remained within the same general region and were thus not often confronted with major cultural differences. Although rural slave cultures did vary within southern states, seldom were contrasts perceived as so different that local migrants felt they had arrived at a foreign destination. Regional chauvinism features rarely in the testimonies of local migrants and is usually limited to the testimonies of slaves from communities near urban areas or major thoroughfares (which were often perceived as more cosmopolitan), who were sent to "backwards" slave communities in isolated rural areas. Alexander Kenner, a Louisiana slave interviewed by the American Freedmen's Inquiry Commission in 1863, for example, insisted to government officials that "the negroes on the [Mississippi] river," where he was originally from, "are intelligent, and certainly take care of themselves. Those in the interior, away from the river, are stupid; they see nothing, know nothing, and are very like cattle." Sometimes variations in slave culture within certain states were more pronounced, however, and in such cases, local newcomers did sometimes stand out. Slaves from the lowcountry of South Carolina and Georgia, for example, were perceived as "different" from both black and white residents of the upcountry. Their strange dialects were frequently remarked on. Hercules, a runaway slave from his plantation in the cotton upcountry of Georgia, was advertised in a local newspaper as having "the peculiar brogue of the low country negroes," to give one example.[22]

Second, the dual orientation of local migrants was often more than just a nostalgic mind-set; rather, it was a daily reality because local migrants were better able than their interstate counterparts to actually retain contact with their home communities. As Anthony Kaye has argued, local migration and

21 Charles Ball, *Fifty Years in Chains; or, The Life of an American Slave* (New York: H. Dayton, 1859), 113–15 (first quotes); John Brown, *Slave Life in Georgia: A Narrative of the Life, Sufferings, and Escape of John Brown, a Fugitive Slave, Now in England*, edited by Louis Alexis Chamerovzow (London: L.A. Chamerovzow, 1855), 23–24 (second quote), 26 (third quote), 29, 62–68.

22 Alexander Kenner, in Blassingame, ed., *Slave Testimony*, 393 (first quote); *Greenville Mountaineer*, Aug. 17, 1849 (second quote).

slaves' scattered kinship ties strongly influenced the ways that enslaved people interacted with and gave meaning to the physical landscape. Indeed, the social geography of slave communities was of necessity dynamic, constantly shifting to adapt to the consequences of sales, estate divisions, and long-term hiring. When friends and loved ones were removed locally, slaves focused on "keep[ing] up all the ties . . . that bound neighborhoods together," transcending physical boundaries to maintain relationships that spanned entire regions. As a result, Kaye argues, "slave neighborhoods were in a constant state of making, remaking, and becoming." For local migrants, this meant that adapting to new communities took place within the context of continued contact with their old communities. A strong argument could even be made that local migrants were the key players in the "joining of places" in the antebellum South. The creation of social networks that transcended the geography of containment – or even just the hope of creating such networks – made forced migration fundamentally different for local migrants than for interstate migrants. Whereas interstate migrants often quickly despaired of ever seeing their loved ones again, local migrants more frequently retained the hope of being able to visit with friends and family. Isaac Johnson, a Kentucky bondsman, claimed that after being removed to another plantation as a young boy, he "would gladly have laid down to die" had it not been for the "hope of again seeing my mother and brothers."[23]

It is important to make a distinction between local migrants who were sold within the immediate vicinity of their homes and those who were removed to other counties or parts of the state. The latter were often forced to sever ties with their home communities in whole or in part, much like interstate migrants. Henry Stevenson, a Missouri slave from Howard County, for example, lost all contact with his wife Amanda and their children when his master moved him to Boone County. "I never saw them afterward," Stevenson told interviewers in 1894. Yet even slaves who were removed long distances within the same state or region were sometimes able to obtain permission to visit family members incidentally, especially during the holiday season but sometimes in other seasons as well. Nelly Shanks, an elderly slave in Fairfax County, Virginia, for example, was separated from her daughter Clarissa and her grandchildren in an estate division, the latter being sent to Farmington, some one hundred miles distant. But in October 1827, Clarissa obtained special permission from her master to travel all the way to Fairfax County with her husband and three youngest children to see her mother. Still, incidental visiting was almost never perceived as an ideal arrangement to local migrants, who naturally wished to see their loved ones more often than only once or twice a year. C.H. Hall, a

[23] Anthony E. Kaye, *Joining Places: Slave Neighborhoods in the Old South* (Chapel Hill: University of North Carolina Press, 2007), 4–5 (first quotes); Isaac Johnson, *Slavery Days in Old Kentucky. A True Story of a Father Who Sold His Wife and Four Children. By One of the Children* (n.p., n.y.), 17 (second quote).

Maryland slave who was interviewed by Union officials in 1863, complained that when he was moved forty miles away from his home community, he was "not allowed to see my mother [but] only once or twice a year," an arrangement he clearly found inadequate. Lewis Clarke, a bondsman from Kentucky, similarly lamented that after he was removed some thirty miles from his mother and siblings, he "was only permitted to see them three times" during "ten years of captivity," although his mother "occasionally found an opportunity to send me some token of remembrance . . . a sugar plum or an apple." At least Hall and Clarke saw their loved ones more often than interstate migrants.[24]

Illicit visiting was also possible, however, for those daring enough to risk brief or prolonged periods of truancy to visit friends and family left behind. Albert Patterson, a Louisiana bondsman whose father was sold seventy-five miles away, claimed to interviewers of the Louisiana Writers' Project that his father often "ran away to come back and see his family," for example. Runaway slave ads also provide numerous examples of illicit visiting. Abraham, Benjamin, and Isaac, three brothers who were sold away from their homes in Eastern Shore, Maryland, and brought to the District of Columbia in 1822, absconded in the summer of that year and were suspected of heading back to the place "where they were raised" to visit family members, who were presumed to be harboring the fugitives. Cilla, an eighteen- to twenty-year-old woman belonging to a plantation near the South Carolina–Georgia border, absconded in the summer of 1835 and was suspected to be hiding out on the plantation of "Mr. Joseph F. Bee, who lives on Ashley River, about which place she is supposed to have relations," and from which she was purchased nearly one year before she went missing. Jackey, Sam, and Angelo, three newly purchased slaves from the Cooper River in South Carolina, similarly went missing from their plantation on the Savannah River in 1850 and were suspected of having made their way back home to visit relatives. Margaret, a slave woman owned by a man near New Orleans, went missing in 1850 and was suspected of having made her way back to Lake Providence, Louisiana, where she was raised. Maria ran away from her new owner near Norfolk, Virginia, "known to be lurking in or about Chuckatuch, in the county of Nansemond, where she has a husband, and formerly belonged." Indeed, not only did some local migrants run back home, but their family members often absconded to seek them out as well. One Virginia man ran off "without any known cause," but his master suspected that he was "aiming to go to his wife, who was carried from the neighbourhood last winter." Such cases suggest that, whether they were allowed to or not, many

[24] Henry Stevenson, in Blassingame, ed., *Slave Testimony*, 530 (first quote); Richard Marshall Scott, Sr., Diary, Oct. 27, 1827 (typescript), Fairfax City Regional Library, Fairfax, Va.; C.H. Hall, in Blassingame, ed., *Slave Testimony*, 417 (second quote); Lewis Garrard Clarke, *Narrative of the Sufferings of Lewis Clarke, During a Captivity of More Than Twenty-Five Years, Among the Algerines of Kentucky, One of the So Called Christian States of America. Dictated by Himself* (Boston: David. H. Ela, 1845), 22 (third quote).

local slave migrants who were sent to other parts of the state continued to visit their home communities long after they were removed.[25]

For those who were removed within a ten- to twenty-mile radius of their old homes, formal or illicit weekend visiting with friends and family may have truly provided local migrants with a sense of having two homes instead of one. Slaves' mobility was still circumscribed, however, because weekend visiting was officially contingent on the written permission of their new masters. But although passes were usually forthcoming on such occasions, testimonies suggest that when they were not, slaves went anyway. As Anthony Kaye has argued, "no force of man or nature could prevent neighborhood visiting" by slaves. A fugitive slave from North Carolina claimed to an interviewer that about three weeks after he was sold locally, he "wanted to go back to see my mother," but when his master refused to issue him a pass, the migrant "started and went without the pass, and returned on Sunday evening after dark," a misdemeanor for which he was severely beaten. A slave in Georgia similarly told northern traveler Philo Tower that his wife had been carried some twenty-five miles into the backcountry and "that he had 'run away' several times to see her, although he was always whipped severely on his return." William Green, a Maryland slave and local migrant, was under strict orders by his new master "not to leave the premises," but when he learned that his brother – who lived nearby – was sick, he decided to "not particularly regard [his master's] commands" and visit him anyway despite risks of a severe whipping. Indeed, slaveholders often inflicted gruesome punishments when they caught slaves illicitly visiting with loved ones. Bennet Barrow, the Louisiana cotton planter, forbade any "foreign slaves" from visiting his plantation, whether they were family members of his newly purchased slaves or not. But his diary reveals that many did anyway. On one occasion, Barrow discovered some local slaves visiting with his bondspeople and broke his sword cane "over one of their skulls."[26]

[25] John Hope Franklin and Loren Schweninger, *Runaway Slaves: Rebels on the Plantation* (New York: Oxford University Press, 1999), 49–74); Albert Patterson, in Ronnie W. Clayton, ed., *Mother Wit: The Ex-Slave Narratives of the Louisiana Writers' Project* (New York: 1990), 179 (first quote); *Alexandria Gazette & Advertiser*, July 27, 1822 (second quote); *Charleston Courier*, June 9, 1835 (third quote); *Charleston Courier*, Apr. 11, 1850; *Daily Picayune*, Feb. 21, 1850; *Norfolk Beacon*, Mar. 31, 1838 (fourth quote); *Richmond Compiler*, Sept. 8, 1837 (fifth quote). One scholar noted that slave truancy in the Louisiana sugar country was mainly a result of "a newly acquired bondsman's homesickness and adjustment difficulties with his new surroundings." See Craig A. Bauer, *A Leader Among Peers: The Life and Times of Duncan Farrar Kenner* (Lafayette, La.: 1993), 57.

[26] John Jacobs, "A True Tale of Slavery," *The Leisure Hour: A Family Journal of Instruction and Recreation*, Feb. 14, 1861; Kaye, *Joining Places*, 52 (second quote); John Little, in Philo Tower, *Slavery Unmasked: Being a Truthful Narrative of a Three Years' Residence and Journeying in Eleven Southern States* (1856; New York: Negro Universities Press, 1969), 89 (third quote); Tower, *Slavery Unmasked*, 216 (fourth quote); William Green, *Narrative of Events in the Life of William Green, Formerly a Slave* (Springfield: L.M. Guernsey, 1853), 12 (fifth quote); Bennet

In some cases, weekend visiting was of only limited necessity to retain ties with all family members because local migration did not always completely sever slaves' domestic arrangements in the first place. Slaves were sometimes sold or bequeathed with one or more family members and thus prevented from total separation of all loved ones, and indeed local migration was sometimes even used as a vehicle to *unite* cross-plantation family members, as discussed in Chapter 2. One Maryland slave named John Tydings, for example, successfully arranged for his master to purchase his wife Betsy in 1848. Twelve years later, Cato, a slave on the same plantation, convinced his master to buy his wife Nancy. In both of these cases, neither Betsy nor Nancy were "typical" local migrants because their removal entailed their being united with their husbands rather than torn away from them. Although visiting was necessary for them to retain contact with friends and extended family members, they did not arrive at their new destinations as strangers, as many local migrants did.[27]

Rural hirelings also often negotiated to be hired with family members or at least near to family members. One cross-plantation couple in Alabama arranged for the wife and their four children to be hired to the husband's owner for one hundred dollars in 1861, for example. As stated in Chapter 2, such cases allowed local migrants to turn hiring into a vehicle for being reunited with family members rather than separated from them. Moreover, rural hirelings were afforded the opportunity to see their loved ones during the last week of each year when their contracts expired, and they also made extensive use of the pass system to visit with loved ones on the weekends during the rest of the year. Allen Parker, a hireling in the North Carolina countryside, related after emancipation that when his mother's health began to fail, he "frequently went to see her," obtaining permission from his master to return home regularly. Such contact with home communities was common among rural hirelings. And similar to other local migrants, hirelings often resorted to illicit visiting when necessary, even risking severe punishments if they were caught. Mary, one hired domestic servant on a Louisiana cotton plantation in 1857, was reprimanded when her employer found that she "had been harboring her boy here – feeding him & letting him sleep in her room; he had run away from his master Mr. Salvant." Another new domestic servant on the same plantation was accused of "running out nights" to visit with loved ones. When Jefferson – a hireling in Bourbon County, Kentucky, in 1856 – was confronted by his employer "for his improper visits" to acquaintances on a neighboring plantation, he was beaten so severely that Jefferson's owner eventually filed suit for property damage, his slave being "greatly lessened in value" because of

H. Barrow, *Plantation Life in the Florida Parishes of Louisiana, 1836–1846, as Reflected in the Diary of Bennet H. Barrow*, edited by Edwin Adams Davis (AMS Press: New York, 1967), 49–50 (sixth quote).

27 Jacob Franklin Accounts, "List of slave births, deaths, &c.," Oct. 1848 and May 1860, RASP, Series D (microfilm), JFK Institüt.

"beating & bruising & wounding." Jack, a Tennessee hireling, was eventually sold by his master for "running away from [his] hirer... and lying out for months at times," suspected of being harbored by relatives. Runaway slave ads indeed reveal many examples of hirelings using truancy as a means of visiting loved ones. Bristo, "a very stout Black Man" hired out to a farmer in northern Virginia, went missing in 1828 and was suspected of lurking about his home plantation, where he still had relations.[28]

The ties that bound local migrants to their home communities thus often remained strong even after removal to their new destinations. That is not to suggest, however, that local migrants easily found their places within new slave communities. Even if on arrival they were not perceived as "foreign" by the other slaves, they were still strangers, and adapting to new social orders was a process that many found difficult. Similar to their interstate counterparts, countless local newcomers experienced feelings of difference and isolation at their new destinations or got into conflicts with other slaves. Sometimes even cultural differences lay at the root of such feelings of otherness. Charles, a Mississippi slave and local migrant, lamented after emancipation that when he arrived at his new plantation, he found the slaves of such a different character and so ignorant of religion that he felt out of place. "The men I had to deal with were more to be pitied than blamed," he exclaimed. "They were entirely ignorant of any but the most crude principles of right.... When I talked to them of Jesus they seemed astonished." Another local migrant from Maryland complained that whereas all of the slaves on his new plantation were Catholics, he was a Methodist. Echoing the experiences of interstate migrants in Louisiana, the bondsman claimed that on Sundays he "refused to respond" to the local slaves' calls to prayer and confession. In such instances, social bonds between newcomers and locals were sometimes slow to emerge. The possibility of maintaining contact with their old communities, moreover, diminished the urgency of forging new relationships in the first place and thus possibly extended the amount of time that it took for local migrants to become fully established at their new homes.[29]

[28] Turner Reavis Account Book, Jan. 2, 1861, in RASP, Series C, Part 2 (microfilm), JFK Institüt; Allen Parker, *Recollection of Slavery Times* (Worcester, Mass.: Chas. W. Burbank & Co., 1895), 78 (first quote); Tryphena Blanche Holder Fox to mother, June 8, 1857, in King, ed., *A Northern Woman in the Plantation South*, 56 (second quote); Ibid., Dec. 16, 1860, in King, ed., *A Northern Woman in the Plantation South*, 115 (third quote); Charles Harris to the Circuit Court, Bourbon County, Kentucky, 1856, in *The Southern Debate over Slavery, Volume 2: Petitions to Southern County Courts, 1775–1867*, edited by Loren Schweninger (Urbana: University of Illinois Press, 2008), 310–311 (fourth quote); John W. Franklin to the Circuit Court, Sumner County, Tennessee, 1856, in ibid., 312 (fifth quote); *Phenix Gazette*, Mar. 26, 1828 (sixth quote); Jonathan D. Martin, *Divided Mastery: Slave Hiring in the American South* (Cambridge, Mass.: Harvard University Press, 2004), 57.

[29] Charles Thompson, *Biography of a Slave; Being the Experiences of Rev. Charles Thompson, a Preacher of the United Brethren Church, While a Slave in the South* (Dayton: United Brethren

Yet as was the case with interstate migrants, collective resistance and situations that sharpened the white–black dichotomy served as vehicles for local migrants to bond with other slaves, again revealing an underlying slave identity. Strangers assisted each other in avoiding punishments, stealing food, harboring fugitives, and in numerous other ways. In an 1889 interview, for example, one Georgia slave named Aaron Robinson related that after his master died, he was sold to one J.W. Harris, a large slaveholder in the region. At his new plantation, Robinson was made driver and endowed with the authority to inflict corporal punishments on the other slaves, but the migrant admitted that he "never struck any of them" because he felt it morally wrong to hurt his fellow bondsmen, even if they were strangers. Another local migrant from North Carolina, John, claimed to an interviewer that his first meaningful contact with the slaves on his new plantation revolved around the issue of avoiding punishment. The slaves "told me that Mr. E – was a hard man, and what I had better do to avoid the lash," he related. Henry Gowens, a fugitive slave from Alabama, similarly admitted that his "heart ached to see the suffering and punishment that our people had to undergo" at a plantation to which he was removed as a young man. Lewis, a local migrant from Kentucky, dictated in his life narrative that upon arrival at a new plantation, he cooperated with the other slaves to steal extra food and hide it in "a reserve in the pasture" for communal consumption. Another anonymous fugitive slave likewise told an interviewer that when he was sold locally, he schemed with other slaves to "steal a hog and carry it into the fields and roast it, and share it, and then hide it in the ground and get it as we wanted." Whether avoiding punishments or stealing food together, newcomers and locals often cooperated to overcome shared experiences of oppression and deprivation.[30]

It is important to note that such solidarity was by no means universal, of course, whether for local or interstate migrants. Indeed, the annals of slave testimonies are replete with examples of slaves pitted against each other, even in cases of resistance. John, the North Carolina slave mentioned earlier, for example, found solidarity with fellow bondsmen on his plantation, but when he attempted to flee on one occasion, he was found out and turned in by slaves from another plantation. The migrant complained to his interviewer that "some of [the slaves] will betray another to curry favour with the master, or to get a new coat, or two or three dollars . . . but there are others who would sooner die than betray a friend." Harry Thomas, a Mississippi migrant, was similarly "betrayed by a colored man" in Kentucky when he attempted to flee to Ohio as

Publishing House, 1875), 65 (first quote); Thompson, *Life of John Thompson*, 52 (second quote).

30 Aaron J. Robinson, in Blassingame, ed., *Slave Testimony*, 498 (first quote); John Little, in Drew, ed., *North-Side View*, 199 (second quote); Henry Gowens, in ibid., 140 (fourth quote); Clarke, *Narrative of the Sufferings of Lewis Clarke*, 29–30; "Recollections of Slavery. By a Runaway Slave," *The Emancipator*, Sept. 13, 1838 (fifth quote); Robert S. Starobin, *Industrial Slavery in the Old South* (New York: Oxford University Press, 1970), 75–94.

a young man. When a local migrant from Mississippi went truant to visit his a relative, he became "fearful" that a suspicious slave on his relative's plantation "would betray me." Such fears were legitimate, and they reveal the limits of slave solidarity in the antebellum South. Yet in general, minor acts of slave resistance rested on cooperation between bondspeople who did not necessarily know each other personally.[31]

Similar to their interstate counterparts, local migrants effected their integration into new slave communities by using a variety of different strategies, including joining local slaves in religious worship. One Maryland bondsman claimed that when he was forced to move locally, he was comforted by the religiosity of the slaves on his new plantation, declaring that he "felt thankful that I had once more got among Christians." Although religious differences sometimes isolated newcomers from local slave communities, religion more often than not served as a vehicle of integration. The importance of the slave church for community building can hardly be overstated; it was indeed great enough that some slaveholders perceived it as a threat and attempted to prohibit or severely circumscribe unsupervised slave worship. One South Carolina slaveholder became livid when one of his local migrants asked for a pass to "join the Methodist church" in 1831. Although he granted the pass, he simultaneously resolved "to break up negro preaching & negro churches." William Minor, a Louisiana slaveholder, instructed his overseer that "he must not allow preaching of any sort on the place nor allow the negroes to go off the place to hear any kind of exhortation." To local migrants – and their interstate counterparts – such restrictions frustrated attempts to forge new relationships with other slaves from the community. Henry, a Virginia slave who eventually fled to Canada, told interviewer Benjamin Drew that after being sold to a plantation in a neighboring county, he was unable to attend local religious meetings because his new master refused to issue him a pass on Sunday. "I did not hear a sermon preached during all the time I lived with S – ," the former bondsman related. "I would sometimes hear of there being meetings about there, but I had no chance to go." Another South Carolina slave similarly lamented that he had "lived with a good many masters, but never found any who cared to let their slaves go to meeting." Such cases illustrate the desire with which many newcomers wished to attend services with local strangers, both for the religious content of the meetings and for their social nature, but ultimately their ability to interact with the local community depended on the rules of their new masters and the extent of opportunities for illicit visiting.[32]

31 John Little, in Drew, ed., *North-Side View*, 200 (first quote); Harry Thomas, in ibid., 304 (second quote); Thompson, *Biography of a Slave*, 80 (third quote).

32 John Thompson, *The Life of John Thompson, a Fugitive Slave; Containing his History of 25 Years in Bondage, and His Providential Escape. Written by Himself* (Worcester, Mass.: n.p., 1856), 40–41 (first quote); Silver Bluff Plantation Records, Dec. 16, 1831, James Henry Hammond Papers, RASP, Series A, Part 1 (microfilm), JFK Institüt (second quote); William J. Minor, "Rules and Regulations," in Charles L. Wingfield, "The Sugar Plantations of William

Courting, marriage, and family formation were also ways in which local migrants integrated into new slave communities, just like their interstate counterparts. Sometimes relationships were forged within relatively short amounts of time, suggesting that newcomers attempted to deal with the trauma of removal by immediately rebuilding family and community ties that they had lost. Julia Woodrich, a Louisiana ex-slave, claimed that her "ma had fifteen children and none of us had de same pa. Every time she was sold she would get another man." John Thompson, a Maryland slave, admitted that when he was removed to one particular slaveholder as a young man, he immediately began to court some of the "pretty girls" on a neighboring farm – illicitly – often risking a whipping to forge a romantic relationship. Charles Ball similarly related that "soon after" a local removal within Maryland, he married a girl named Judah, who lived on a neighboring farm. "I was at the house of [Judah's master] every week," Ball claimed. Yet other local migrants integrated far more slowly, however, sometimes taking several years to finally "settle" at their new homes. A perusal of the James Henry Hammond plantation records from Edgefield District, South Carolina, reveals some illuminating examples. Harry, a slave from the Savannah River purchased in 1844, married a local woman named Rachel and became the father of a boy named Emanuel in 1848. Juliana, a slave woman from Hamburg whom Hammond also purchased in 1844, was listed as the mother of a baby from a cross-plantation marriage in 1854. George, likewise purchased from the Savannah River in 1844 and who attempted to run away several times during the following two years, finally settled down and was listed as the husband of a local slave named Binah and the father of a baby named Zedick in 1854. All of these newcomers gradually accepted their fate and adapted to local slave communities during the course of several years.[33]

Finally, the workplace served as a site in which local newcomers could forge bonds with local slaves, as various testimonies reveal. Josiah Henson "obtained great influence" with the local slaves on his new plantation in Maryland, whom he referred to as his "companions," mainly by assisting them with their tasks and performing his work quickly and well. Isaac, a Kentucky slave who was removed far away from his family members as a young boy, was taken under the wing of one local bondsman named Peter, who let the newcomer lodge with him and who trained him in his duties. William, a North Carolina slave who was sold locally as a boy, claimed that he was trained at his new work by another slave named Fannie, who showed great patience in teaching him how to milk the cows and perform other tasks on the farm. Fannie became a

J. Minor, 1830–1860" (M.A. thesis, Louisiana State University, Baton Rouge, La., 1950), 46 (third quote); Henry Banks, in Drew, ed., *North-Side View*, 74 (fourth quote); "Recollections of Slavery. By a Runaway Slave," *The Emancipator*, Sept. 20, 1838 (fifth quote).

33 Julia Woodrich, in Clayton, ed., *Mother Wit*, 217 (first quote); Thompson, *Life of John Thompson*, 67 (second quote); Ball, *Fifty Years in Chains*, 21 (third quote); "Slave Births, 1832–1855," Papers of James Henry Hammond, RASP, Series A, Part 1 (microfilm), JFK Institüt.

surrogate mother to William, and within three months, his bond with her had grown so strong that he even dared "talk to [her] about running away." For local migrants, thus, cooperation in the workplace frequently led to friendships and fictive kinships that transcended mere collegiality, providing them with opportunities to rebuild social relationships that they had lost in removal.[34]

IV.

Urban migrants' experiences with social assimilation reveal important similarities to those of both interstate and local migrants, but they were also unique in a number of respects, mainly because the urban environment itself was so unique. Many slaves who were forcibly removed to towns and cities initially felt like outsiders, continued to manifest a dual orientation between their old and new communities, and used basic strategies to effect their integration. All of these factors, however, were strongly influenced by the very nature of urban slavery.

The dual orientation that urban newcomers manifested subsequent to removal, for example, differed slightly from that of other migrants. As discussed in Chapter 2, most bondspeople who were removed to towns and cities were local migrants (especially hirelings) from the surrounding countryside, and many of them initially looked forward to living in an urban environment because they were convinced that slave life in the city was more exciting and "freer" than it was in the countryside. Their initial impressions of urban communities were therefore often positive. Anticipation of a better life in the city did not, however, translate into a desire to sever ties with their old communities in the countryside. Indeed, similar to other local migrants, urban migrants did everything in their power to retain strong relationships with loved ones back home, requesting passes to visit friends and family on the weekends and sometimes even having visiting privileges included in their hiring contracts. One hireling to Augusta, Georgia, told a northern visitor that he was married to a woman "out in [the] country," where he was originally from but that he had permission to visit her "bout once every two or three months." Urban newcomers also resorted to illicit visiting and long-term truancy to visit loved ones when authorization from their masters or employers was denied them. Jerry, a slave hired out in Alexandria, Virginia, went missing from his employer in the fall of 1851, suspected of hiding out in the neighborhood "of Dr. E. H. Henry, of Fauquier [County]," his original owner. Daniel Solomon ran away from his employer in the District of Columbia, area residents being warned that "has an extensive acquaintance & relations in Fairfax County" and that

[34] Josiah Henson, *The Life of Josiah Henson, Formerly a Slave, Now an Inhabitant of Canada, as Narrated by Himself* (Boston: Arthur D. Phelps, 1849), 8 (first quote); Johnson, *Slavery Days in Old Kentucky*, 13; William H. Robinson, *From Log Cabin to the Pulpit, or, Fifteen Years in Slavery* (Eau Claire, Wisc.: James H. Tifft, 1913), 53–58, 58 (second quote).

he was likely lurking about Cedar Grove plantation, "where he has relations." Sally, a Louisiana migrant to New Orleans, absconded and was suspected of having returned to her native Pointe Coupee parish, her owner adding that she was unlikely still in the city as she was "a stranger, and don't know any body" there. Stephen, another migrant to Charleston, was presumed to have fled in the direction of St. James, Goose Creek, "having formerly belonged to the estate of David Deas." Such cases demonstrate the efforts that urban migrants undertook to reconnect with their home communities in the countryside, especially when relations with their employers or new masters in the city began to sour or when formal visiting was prohibited. Indeed, some industrial employers preferred single men because married ones often absconded to be with their wives. One North Carolina agent for a railroad company informed his boss that he did not find many suitable hirelings at an auction in 1845 because the "negroes had wives in this neighborhood and would lose at least two months [out] of the year."[35]

Urban newcomers – especially male hirelings – were also able to retain and even enhance certain roles within their families and households despite being separated from them in the domestic sense. Many, for example, were able to earn extra money in the city, which they could use to purchase minor luxuries for their loved ones back on the farm or plantation. The ability of male hirelings to contribute to the improvement of the material conditions of their wives, children, and other family members "greatly enhanced their self-esteem in the family and in the quarters," according to one historian, because it allowed slaves to "act out the role of family provider." Account books from early ironwork furnaces throughout the Chesapeake, for example, reveal that hirelings often performed overwork in order to purchase food and clothing for their families back home, maintaining a tangible connection to their original communities. Male hirelings employed at North Carolina gold mines similarly spent money earned through overwork to purchase items such as "chil[dren]'s shoes" and "women's shoes," which were clearly meant to be sent back to their families. Slave testimonies underscore the importance of such opportunities as well. Henry Brown, a Virginia slave sent to work in a tobacco manufactory in Richmond as a young man, proudly claimed after escaping slavery that he often obtained "money to buy things with, to send to my mother." Parke Johnston, a Virginia slave permitted to hire himself out in Petersburg and Farmville, told an interviewer that with the extra money he earned by "jobbing," he was able to buy "many little comforts for himself and his family." Such behavior reveals

[35] Ronald L. Lewis, "Slave Families at Early Chesapeake Ironworks," *The Virginia Magazine of History and Biography* 86 (Apr. 1978): 173–76; Redpath, *The Roving Editor*, 162 (first quote); *Alexandria Gazette and Virginia Advertiser*, Oct. 17, 1851 (second quote); *Alexandria Gazette*, May 9, 1822 (third quote); *Daily Picayune*, Mar. 13, 1850 (fourth quote); *Charleston Courier*, Jan. 4, 1830 (fifth quote); Franklin and Schweninger, *Runaway Slaves*, 49–74; W.H. Jozned to John D. Hawkins, Franklinton, Dec. 31, 1845, Hawkins Family Papers, SASI, Series B, Subseries 1.1 (microfilm), JFK Institüt (sixth quote).

that despite when rural slaves were moved to towns and cities, their focus and their "homes" remained on the plantation.[36]

When urban migrants came from longer distances – such as other states or regions – attempts to reconnect and retain contact with home communities were, of course, either impossible or at least far more difficult. That did not prevent migrants from trying to reestablish networks they had lost in transit, however. Some desperately sought out information about loved ones by consulting other newcomers and travelers from their home regions. William Hayden, a Virginia migrant to Frankfort, Kentucky, never "lost the hope of again seeing my parents," and even years after his removal, he "inquired of every traveller with whom I met, if they were not from the vicinity of Falmouth, Virginia." Flight attempts to these migrants' home regions were far less frequent, but when they did occur, they took on a more permanent nature. Such fugitives were not intending to "visit" loved ones but rather escape their new destinations for good, like other runaway interstate migrants. When newcomer Isaac ran away from Vicksburg in 1845, for example, his new owner did *not* suspect that he had gone truant. Isaac was rather believed to be "making his way back" to his native Livingston Parish, Louisiana, where he had relations by whom he would presumably be harbored indefinitely. Winter, a slave "raised near Georgetown, S.C.," absconded from Montgomery, Alabama, in 1835, and was also suspected of "endeavour[ing] to make [his] way" back home to his native lowcountry district. Jerry, a new migrant who absconded from Charleston, South Carolina, was presumed to be headed back to "the back part of Georgia," where he was from.[37]

Desperate attempts to become reunited with loved ones who had been sent to distant cities were undertaken by both migrants themselves and by family members from home communities, who also often absconded in search of loved ones sold away. Such acts were rare, and their chances of success were minute, but they do demonstrate how strong the desire was for slave communities to retain bonds that were severed by forced migration. Sometimes truly vast distances were traversed in these attempts. Dick, a thirty-seven-year-old slave from Kentucky, ran all the way to New Orleans to be with his wife, who was "living in that city" after being sold out of state. The urban environment,

[36] Lewis, "Slave Families at Early Chesapeake Ironworks," 171 (first quote), 171–73; Gold Hill Day Book, 1859–1860, Gold Hill Mining Company Records, Records of Ante-Bellum Southern Industries (hereafter SASI), Series B (microfilm), JFK Institüt; Henry Box Brown and Charles Stearns, *Narrative of Henry Box Brown, Who Escaped from Slavery Enclosed in a Box 3 Feet Long and 2 Wide. Written from a Statement of Facts Made by Himself. With Remarks Upon the Remedy for Slavery"* (Boston: Brown & Stearns, 1849), 37 (second quote); Parke Johnston, in Blassingame, ed., *Slave Testimony*, 490–91 (third quote).

[37] William Hayden, *Narrative of William Hayden, Containing a Faithful Account of His Travels for a Number of Years, Whilst a Slave, in the South* (Cincinnati: n.p., 1846), 36 (first quote); *Daily Picayune*, Aug. 1, 1845 (second quote); *Charleston Courier*, Sept. 14, 1835 (third quote); *Charleston Courier*, Sept. 19, 1835 (fourth quote).

moreover, lent itself well to illicit contact because fugitives could often blend in with urban slave populations, find work, and be harbored by blacks in the community. Consider the case of William, a Virginia slave who was sold to New Orleans. William related in an interview to Benjamin Drew that the slave trade had separated him from his wife, a free woman. His wife knew that he had been transported to New Orleans, and within one year, she showed up in the city and found work as a domestic servant. In the end, their contact was eventually discovered; William claimed that "when my master found out that I had a free-woman for a wife... he was angry about it." Indeed, his master threatened to turn her in to the authorities because she was an illegal migrant. As a free black from Virginia, William's wife had to obtain special permission to remain in Louisiana, but the costs involved were prohibitive, and in the end she was forced to leave. William resolved to escape bondage altogether, eventually reaching Canada.[38]

Similar to other migrants, urban migrants often felt awkward about living and working with strangers on arrival at their new destinations. It often took time for them to forge meaningful contacts with other slaves and feel like they were at home in their new communities. At a Washington hotel, for example, one hireling informed a guest that he was "let out, as many others are, to the landlord: – there are many here who do not know each other, even by name." Another newcomer to Columbia, South Carolina, told a northern reporter: "I's a stranger in the city: I's not bin here quite two years yet." Even though he admitted that after two years he had finally made friends with other slaves in the city, he still did not feel at home at his new destination. A young Virginia slave sent to Richmond to work in a tobacco factory similarly admitted in his narrative that at his new destination, "no one appeared to sympathize with me" and that he indeed "felt alone in the world." Newcomers even frequently came into conflict with locals, both at the workplace and in public. One rural hireling to Vicksburg, Mississippi, "got into a dispute with another slave" one Sunday afternoon, which came to blows and which ended when the newcomer "stabbed him." Another migrant who ended up working as a store clerk in Carrolton, Alabama, claimed that the other "negroes [were] envious of me in the position of assistant clerk" and that he therefore made few friends when he started his new employment. Sometimes violent confrontations emerged between hirelings and local *white* co-workers as well. At Columbia Mine in Georgia, a white engineer named Morris got drunk one night in 1857 "and went into the blacksmith shop [in the] morning, and beat Simon [a hired slave] over the head... with a pick handel and used him very rough all for nothing." The manager on duty discharged Morris on sight.[39]

[38] *Lexington Intelligencer*, July 7, 1838 (first quote); William Grose, in Drew, ed., *North-Side View*, 84–85 (second quote).

[39] E.S. Abdy, *Journal of a Residence and Tour in the United States of North America, from April 1833 to October 1834* (1835; New York: Negro Universities Press, 1969), 2:59 (first quote);

Class divisions also arose between rural slaves (comprising the bulk of newcomers) and more "sophisticated" urban blacks. One northern visitor to Natchez in the 1830s insisted that city slaves "look down upon [rural newcomers] as infinitely beneath themselves." On one occasion, he overheard two city slaves comment on the appearance of a newcomer, one of them remarking smugly that the migrant appeared to be a "field nigger" and that he "nebber has no 'quaintance wid dat class." On another occasion, the northerner saw an assembly of urban slaves try to impress a group of newcomers "ob de field nigger class" by "imitating the manners, bearing, and language of their masters... convers[ing] with grave faces and in pompous language....." By such means the city slaves attempted to demonstrate their superiority to their rural counterparts. Appearances were also an important marker of difference. Urban slaves often referred to rural newcomers as dirty and poorly dressed. One slave in Savannah, whose master hired him to a local hotel, complained to Frederick Law Olmsted that he had to work and live with other hirelings from the countryside. The bondsman remarked that he often went to sleep at his wife's house because he refused to "sleep heah wid dese nasty niggers." Indeed, the fact that rural newcomers often tried to acquire the means to dress "fashionably" upon arrival in towns and cities, as discussed in Chapter 4, indicates that they felt ashamed of their country appearance and wished to fit in with local urban blacks.[40]

Even skin color divided urban black communities in some cases. In New Orleans, mulattoes and quadroons formed a class apart from local slave and free black communities. Composed of the illegitimate offspring of white men and "colored" women, many quadroons were educated, pampered, and considered the elite of the black community. Indeed, they navigated more within white circles than black ones. When one quadroon woman named Mary Jane – a "good faithful and trusty house servant" – was sent to New York aboard a southern schooner with her master, she was even allowed to "eat at table with white people, and in other respects [was] treated by the captain of said ship... as an equal of white people." Such treatment often amazed visitors to the city. As Olmsted put it, quadroons in New Orleans were "too much superior to the negroes, in general, to associate with them," mainly because of their "habits of early life, the advantages of education, and the use of wealth." Some of them, he added, and comported themselves with the "graceful and elegant carriage" of "the women of Paris." Another northern sojourner in New

Redpath, *Roving Editor*, 57 (second quote); Brown and Stearns, *Narrative of Henry Box Brown*, 37 (third quote); Henry Watson, *Narrative of Henry Watson, a Fugitive Slave* (Boston: Bela Marsh, 1848), 28 (fourth quote); Sella Martin, in Blassingame, ed., *Slave Testimony*, 724–25 (fifth quote); B. Broomhead to Joseph Belknap, Columbia Mine, June 22, 1857, Joseph Belknap Smith Papers, SASI, Series A (microfilm), JFK Institüt (sixth quote).

40 Joseph Holt Ingraham, *The South-West. By a Yankee* (New York: Harper & Bros., 1835), 2:256 (first quote), 2:30 (second quote), 2:56 (third quote); Olmsted, *Seaboard Slave States*, 558–59 (fourth quote).

Orleans remarked that many quadroons were "whiter, more talented, better looking, and more accomplished than many of the southern white population." Although the law permitted them to marry "colored freemen," many chose not to because "such an alliance would not raise them above their class." White companionships – although legally not recognized – were preferred to both enslaved and free blacks.[41]

Despite such divisions, however, the urban environment provided enslaved newcomers with ample unique opportunities to socialize with other slaves on friendly terms. Migrants found it advantageous to "network" with other slaves through a series of ties and exchanges, actions that constituted a "strategy for survival," as Calvin Schermerhorn has argued. Urban and industrial slaves were often under less direct supervision from their masters, enjoyed more spatial mobility than their rural counterparts, and indeed frequently had leisure time at the end of the workday to spend in relative freedom. Under such conditions, they often had occasions to meet up with other slaves, both during and outside of working hours. In Lynchburg, Virginia, one visitor noted in 1859 that throngs of enslaved hirelings to the local tobacco factories assembled out of doors in the evenings, socializing with one another in public spaces throughout the city. "They hang about the corners, they perch on the fences and walls; and... keep up a continual whistling. All along the streets, come the notes of this boy-beloved music... from groups, where they have made wagers as to harmony and wind.... It is the tunes of the plantations where they were born [and] of the factories, where the song lightens their labor." Indeed, the traveler added that slaves in Lynchburg "whistle away the evening hours," often walking along in gangs or simply "with their backs to the palings and walls, their hands in their pockets" until the curfew went into effect, when "the streets are deserted by the negroes for their blankets in outbuildings and garrets, from which the earliest dawn will call them." In other cities, such scenes were also common. White citizens in Richmond complained about the "tumultuous assemblies of negroes in the streets of our City on Sundays." In Little Rock, slaves "took advantage of their leisure to seek the company of other blacks, often meeting in small groups." In Washington, slaves threw makeshift "balls and parties" in their free time, which made the city "much enjoyed" by rural newcomers. When Charles Ball was hired out to Washington, he "was permitted to spend the afternoon in my own way," and he often took long walks through the city, making "many new acquaintances with the slaves." Assembling with other slaves in an informal setting, even in public spaces, allowed newcomers to mingle with locals and develop social networks outside of their direct places of employment and residence.[42]

41 "James Thompson to the District Court, Orleans Parish, Louisiana, 1839," in Schweninger, ed., *Southern Debate over Slavery*, 2:195–96 (first quote); Olmsted, *Seaboard Slave States*, 594 (second quote); Tower, *Slavery Unmasked*, 326 (third quote).

42 Calvin Schermerhorn, *Money over Mastery, Family over Freedom: Slavery in the Antebellum Upper South* (Baltimore: Johns Hopkins University Press, 2011), 24 (first quote); J. Alexander

Indeed, white urban residents (both slaveholders and nonslaveholders alike) frequently lamented that the spatial mobility and lack of supervision that characterized slavery in southern cities exposed rural newcomers to "vices" that encouraged petty crime, ruined their character and monetary value, and endangered the community at large. One commentator opined that in Natchez, slaves who were "hired, and, free from restraint in a great degree, compared with their situations under their masters, or in the country... soon become corrupted by the vices of the city [by] associating indiscriminately with each other...." Alcohol, gambling, and "frolicking" topped the list of vices to which rural migrants were exposed. One rural hireling to a shoemaker's shop in Fredericksburg, Virginia, recalled that "in order to get along pleasantly" with the other slaves in the shop, he learned to sneak out and "bring liquor among the men with such secrecy as to prevent the boss, who had forbidden it to come on the premises, from knowing it." In this way, he made friends at his new place of employment. A slave migrant to Columbia, South Carolina, similarly related to a northern visitor that he often turned the attic of his master's house into a small gambling room for his newfound friends in the city. On one occasion, his master "came up... and caught us – a few boys and myself – playin' [cards]," a crime for which he was sent to the local workhouse and severely whipped. On another occasion, the same bondsman was punished when his master found out that he had gone "to the races," where he "met some friends." Olmsted noted that in Richmond, a great number of "drinking shops are frequented chiefly by the negroes" and that "dancing and other amusements are carried on in these at night." In New Orleans, citizens complained that "hundreds [of hirelings] spend their nights drinking, carousing, gambling, and contracting the worst of habits, which not only make them *useless to their owners*, but dangerous pests to society."[43]

Pattern, "Scenes from Lynchburg," in Eugene L. Schwaab, ed., *Travels in the Old South, Selected from Periodicals of the Times* (Lexington: University of Kentucky Press, 1973), 2:541 (second quote); Marianne Buroff Sheldon, "Black-White Relations in Richmond, Virginia, 1782–1820," *Journal of Southern History* 45 (Feb. 1979): 38 (third quote); Paul D. Lack, "An Urban Slave Community: Little Rock, 1831–1862," *The Arkansas Historical Quarterly* 41 (Autumn, 1982): 271 (fourth quote); John S. Jacobs, "A True Tale of Slavery," *The Leisure Hour: A Family Journal of Instruction and Recreation*, Feb. 21, 1861 (fifth quote); Charles Ball, *Fifty Years in Chains, or, the Life of an American Slave* (New York: H. Dayton, 1859), 18–19 (sixth quote).

43 Ingraham, *The South-West*, 2:253 (first quote); Noah Davis, *A Narrative of the Life of Rev. Noah Davis, a Colored Man. Written by Himself, at the Age of Fifty-Four* (Baltimore: John. F. Weishampel, 1859), 15 (second quote); Redpath, *Roving Editor*, 58–59 (third quote); Olmsted, *Seaboard Slaves States*, 52 (fourth quote); *New Orleans Crescent*, reprinted in Olmsted, *Seaboard Slave States*, 592–93 (fifth quote); Lack, "An Urban Slave Community," 271; Richard C. Wade, *Slavery in the Cities: The South, 1820–1860* (New York: Oxford University Press, 1964), 151–60; James M. Campbell, *Slavery on Trial: Race, Class, and Criminal Justice in Antebellum Richmond, Virginia* (Gainesville: University Press of Florida, 2007), 10–40. See also Henry Watson, *Narrative of Henry Watson, a Fugitive Slave* (Boston: Bela Marsh, 1848), 26–27.

Similar to their local and interstate counterparts, urban newcomers were also drawn to religious gatherings to help initiate them into local slave communities and provide them with a source of comfort and inspiration after enduring removal and forced separations. Slave religion in southern cities was more formally organized than it was on the plantations, however, with real meeting houses, formal membership, and frequently even manumitted preachers. Visiting Louisville, Kentucky, in the 1850s, northerner evangelist Philo Tower remarked on the "colored people's church," which he described as a dilapidated "building that looked as though it might once have been a chapel where the whites worshipped, but [was] now for the exclusive use of the poor slaves to worship in." Yet despite the "superannuated" appearance of the church itself, slaves in the city were grateful for a private place to "sen[d] up a living flame to the throne of God." The preacher at this particular church had even been emancipated when the congregation pitched in to purchase his freedom. So it was in towns and cities across the South. In Little Rock, blacks withdrew from white-dominated churches during the course of the antebellum period and gravitated toward several independent black congregations. One newcomer to Richmond, Virginia, attended meetings and eventually joined the black Baptist church there, among other reasons because the popular minister "thought it was wicked to hold slaves." Another migrant to Richmond admitted that on arrival, he began "thinking more or less about seeking religion," partly because he "long[ed] to join" the other slaves in their worship. In the "large tobacco factories" in the city, the migrant claimed, he "daily heard of many converts" among the rural newcomers, and he often accompanied his new friends who set out to "seek religion" in one of the city's many churches or in clandestine meetings. In St. Louis, another hireling recalled, "the M.E. Church, South, allowed the colored people to meet in the basement . . . and their minister preached to them every Sunday."[44]

Such gathering places provided sites of socialization and integration for rural newcomers, who came into contact with urban slave communities and built support networks. Tower interviewed one Virginia slave who had been hired out in the city who claimed that he did not formally belong to the church but admitted that he "goes thar to meetin" to mingle with the other slaves. Noah Davis, a young hireling in Fredericksburg, Virginia, related that during his time in the city, he "commenced to visit the girls, which induced me to go still more frequently to church." He had "no particular preference for any one [of the] denominations [but] went wherever my favorites went," eventually meeting his future wife at the Baptist church, which he subsequently joined. Olmsted also

44 Tower, *Slavery Unmasked*, 251 (first quote); Lack, "An Urban Slave Community," 269–70; Brown and Stearns, *Narrative of Henry Box Brown*, 40 (second quote); Thomas Lewis Johnson, *Africa for Christ. Twenty-Eight Years a Slave* (London: Alexander and Shepherd, 1892), 19 (third quote); Henry Clay Bruce, *The New Man. Twenty-Nine Years a Slave. Twenty-Nine Years a Free Man* (York, Pa.: P. Anstadt & Sons, 1895), 71 (fourth quote).

viewed places of religious worship as sites of contact between rural and urban slaves. Observing a slave funeral procession in Richmond, Virginia, he noted that "most of the company" consisted of what appeared to be rural migrants, "of a very poor appearance, rude and unintelligent" but that several others were obviously urban blacks, "neatly-dressed and very good-looking." Black churches in southern cities served to bring together rural and urban slaves as members of the same community.[45]

The urban environment provided newcomers with other "organized" institutions that served as sites of integration as well. Some of them were clandestine and rooted in resistance to slavery, at least in theory, but they nevertheless attracted swarms of migrants and locals alike. For example, in several antebellum cities, slaves secretly learned to read, attending underground meetings conducted by literate slaves and free blacks. One British traveler through the South remarked that white citizens in both Richmond and Columbia had informed him that some "negroes regularly teach reading in the evenings to their fellow-slaves, receiving a fee of a dollar a month." He even remarked that in the Lower South, "intelligent" slave migrants from the "mild" Upper South were most often suspected of teaching local bondspeople to read. Charles Lyell also reported that schools existed in cities in Kentucky and Tennessee "for teaching negroes to read." Some of these "schools" worked in close conjunction with local black churches. In Baltimore, for example, both slaves and free blacks could take reading classes offered by the local black Bible Association. The presence of literate slaves in urban environments facilitated flight and unsupervised mobility for rural newcomers, as a black market in forged passes emerged to accommodate bondspeople who wished to visit loved ones or flee slavery altogether.[46]

As in rural areas, collective resistance to slavery helped to forge bonds of solidarity between newcomers and local slaves in urban areas. Runaways from the countryside were often hidden and assisted by local and migrant slaves in the cities, for example, and newcomers often interfered or at least expressed anger when they witnessed the physical abuse of their fellow slaves, regardless of their origins. Henry, a rural newcomer to a Richmond factory, became especially

[45] Tower, *Slavery Unmasked*, 256 (first quote); Davis, *Life of Rev. Noah Davis*, 18 (second quote), 26; Olmsted, *Seaboard Slave States*, 24–25 (third quote); Wade, *Slavery in the Cities*, 160–72. See also James Lindsay Smith, *Autobiography of James L. Smith* (Norwich: Press of the Bulletin Company, 1881), 26–27.

[46] James Stirling, *Letters from the Slave States* (1857; New York: Negro Universities Press, 1969), 295–96 (first quote); Charles Lyell, *A Second Visit to the United States of North America* (New York: Harper & Bros., 1850), 2:215 (second quote); Adam Hodgson, *Remarks During a Journey through North America in the Years 1819, 1820, and 1821, in a Series of Letters* (1823; Westport, Conn.: Negro Universities Press, 1970), 55; Lack, "An Urban Slave Community," 270; *New Orleans Crescent*, reprinted in Olmsted, *Seaboard Slave States*, 592–93; Gregg D. Kimball, *American City, Southern Place: A Cultural History of Antebellum Richmond* (Athens: University of Georgia Press, 124–32; Wade, *Slavery in the Cities*, 173–77.

indignant at the sight of a colleague being whipped by the foreman one day but lamented that he could do nothing to help his fellow bondsman "for I was a slave, and any interference on my part would only have brought the same punishment upon me." Another hireling to a railroad company in Charleston similarly complained after fleeing slavery that "nobody can tell how badly the slaves [were] punished" by his industrial employers. "They [were] treated worse than dumb beasts." Solomon, a hireling to the Charleston and Savannah railroad, was "made almost wild one day" when he witnessed the excessive whipping of a female slave. And when William Wells Brown was hired to a hotel in St. Louis, he felt awful at having to witness the whipping of a fellow colleague named Aaron. "The poor fellow's back was literally cut to pieces," he recalled. In all of these cases, migrants' sympathy for the physical abuse of other slaves revealed a broader identification with the plight of all slaves.[47]

Yet slave solidarity in urban environments also manifested itself in unique ways, partly because of the relatively large presence of free black populations. Indeed, an argument could be made that urban environments were conducive not only to the development of a broader *slave* identity but of a *black* identity that transcended slave status. In southern towns and cities, the boundaries between slavery and freedom were vague and fluid. Slaves hoped to become free, free blacks had usually once been slaves, many families consisted of both free blacks and slaves, and many hirelings who were permitted to hire their own time had one foot in slavery and the other in freedom. The shared experience of racial oppression and discrimination in urban areas often brought all of these groups together. Escape attempts from slavery usually rested on the cooperation of other urban blacks, for example, often via local churches but also in the workplace. Some professions were indeed seen as crucial links in the road to freedom. One scholar has noted that on the antebellum Mississippi River, free black "boat workers helped fugitive slaves" reach free territory, often concealing runaways in steamships and forwarding them on to friends in St. Louis and from there to freedom. Indeed, contact with free urban blacks fanned the desires of many migrants to be free themselves. Isaac, a hireling in Louisville, told interviewers in 1863 that he was "put at a trade with a free man, and I lived with free people, and it was just as though I was free, only when [my master] would send for me to come round, and let me know that I was not altogether free." When he was turned over to another owner, "who kept me close round," he became dissatisfied because he "was not a freeman [and] all the privileges were taken from me, that I had when I was working with freemen." He eventually escaped the South and fled to Canada. In 1833, a

[47] Lack, "An Urban Slave Community," 279–80; Brown and Stearns, *Narrative of Henry Box Brown*, 44 (first quote); "Recollections of a Runaway Slave," *The Emancipator*, Oct. 21, 1838 (second quote); Solomon Bradley, in Blassingame, ed., *Slave Testimony*, 372 (third quote); William Wells Brown, *Narrative of William W. Brown, a Fugitive Slave* (Boston: The Anti-Slavery Office, 1847), 24–25 (fourth quote).

Virginia slave named George became so dissatisfied with slavery after being hired out among free blacks in Richmond that he began to pass "himself off as a freeman & hired himself as a cook on bord of [a] schooner," eventually gaining the assistance of other blacks to attempt to escape to New York aboard cargo ship.[48]

Even intermarriage between enslaved newcomers and free blacks was not uncommon. Although such relationships were forged on the basis of love and affection, they also carried certain practical advantages for bondspeople. A slave woman who married a free man could rest assured that her husband would not be forcibly torn away from her; indeed, a free husband enjoyed (relative) spatial mobility and could even follow his wife if she were ever to be sold. When Lizzie Hobbs, a Virginia slave woman who developed a relationship with a free black man in Virginia, was removed by her master to St. Louis, her partner was able to follow her and marry her at her new urban destination, thereby preventing definitive separation. Slave women married to free black men could also hope to one day be purchased or at least hired by their husbands. William Williams, a free black man in Washington, DC, was able to purchase his enslaved wife and child in 1831 and successfully bring suit against their former owner, who attempted to sell them to interstate traders. A slave man who married a free woman, on the other hand, knew that his children would be free. James Redpath, a northern journalist, interviewed a hireling in Raleigh who married a local free woman and whose sons were therefore free. "I've five children," the migrant related, "but my wife is a free woman, and they are free, although I am a slave." He claimed that he was "giving them as good an education as we dare give them; so that, if the time does come when I'm going to be sold, they may buy me."[49]

Relationships and marriage between rural newcomers and city slaves were far more common, however, an indication that newcomers were gradually integrated within urban slave communities over time. Such relationships were

[48] In Richmond, Virginia, the African Baptist Church assisted slaves escape to freedom and it aided church members in finding and maintaining contact with loved ones who fled slavery. See Kimball, American City, *Southern Place*, 124–58. Seth Rockman, *Scraping By: Wage Labor, Slavery, and Survival in Early Baltimore* (Baltimore: Johns Hopkins University Press, 2009), 52–53; Campbell, *Slavery on Trial*, 146–85; Thomas C. Buchanan, "Rascals on the Antebellum Mississippi: African American Steamboat Workers and the St. Louis Hanging of 1841," *Journal of Social History* 34 (Summer 2001): 797–817 (first quote); Isaac Throgmorton, in Blassingame, ed., *Slave Testimony*, 432–34 (second quote); "Thomas Cowles to the County Court, Henrico County, Virginia, 1833," in Schweninger, ed., *Southern Debate over Slavery*, 2:163 (third quote).

[49] Kimball, *American City, Southern Place*, 139; Elizabeth Keckley, *Behind the Scenes, or, Thirty Years a Slave, and Four Years in the White House* (New York: G.W. Carleton & Co., 1868), 46; William Williams vs Thomas Duvall, Mar. 9, 1831, Petition 20483101, Digital Library on American Slavery, http://library.uncg.edu/slavery/details.aspx?pid=4283; James Redpath, *The Roving Editor: or, Talks with Slaves in the Southern States* (1859; New York: Negro Universities Press, 1968), 39–40 (first quote).

not only forged at churches or in public spaces but also in the workplace, where newcomers most frequently came into contact with their urban counterparts and other migrants. Indeed, even newcomers who worked in domestic settings, where contact with other slaves was limited, managed to develop strong bonds of love and affection for local urban slaves. Louisa, a hireling in Mobile, Alabama, met a suitor while working as a domestic servant in town. A carriage driver for a local urban family, her suitor came by her house regularly, and after becoming acquainted with her, he commenced "to come and see me Sundays" as well. The development of such relationships was important to migrants' assimilation, and indeed when Louisa was later sold to New Orleans, she complained that her new master "never let me go out anywhere," which isolated her from the black community. Male industrial slaves often found themselves at a disadvantage in this regard because they were more often sent to work in more isolated areas with few female slaves. One hireling to the Hamburg and Charleston Rail Road in South Carolina claimed that he worked with "a great many hands" at his new destination but only "some of them [were] women," which prevented the development of many romantic relationships among the hirelings. Redpath spoke with a group of migrant slaves who were sent to work on the railroad from West Point, Georgia, to Montgomery, Alabama, and not one of them was married because the entire gang was male. Some of them had been married back home, but their relationships had been broken in the removal, and others claimed that they sometimes "cohabited with plantation slaves" along the route but were unable to maintain relationships because they were constantly moving as their work continued down the line. As a result, Redpath noted, these slaves appeared "condemned for life to Alabama celibacy and adultery."[50]

Interstate, local, and urban migrants experienced difficulties adjusting to new slave communities, and their experiences revealed both striking similarities and important differences. All three groups manifested a dual orientation, for example, as they settled into their new communities but simultaneously remained "attached" to their old homes. Interstate migrants were the least successful in their attempts to maintain contacts with their old communities, but they compensated by forging strong relationships with other interstate migrants, frequently from the same regions that they were from. Local and urban migrants, on the other hand, were more often better able to navigate between their two "homes," visiting friends and family members on the weekends or when hiring contracts expired at the end of the calendar year.

Migrants from all three groups also all manifested local and regional identities and therefore often found it challenging to find their places among strangers

50 Louisa Picquet and Hiram Mattison, *Louisa Picquet, the Octoroon: or Inside Views of Southern Domestic Life* (New York: Hiram Mattison, 1861), 8 (first quote), 19 (second quote); "Recollections of Slavery, by a Runaway Slave," *The Emancipator*, Oct. 11, 1838 (third quote); Redpath, *The Roving Editor*, 172–73 (fourth quote).

within new slave communities – with interstate migrants again experiencing the most difficult transition. Moreover, they all revealed a broader slave or even black identity when confronted with the shared experience of oppression at the hands of masters, employers, overseers, and the white community in general. Such manifestations underscore the fluidity of slave identity in the antebellum period.

Finally, long-distance, local, and urban migrants all effected their assimilation and integration into new slave communities by using institutions such as marriage, religious worship, social gatherings, and collegiality in the workplace. Their experiences again differed in some respects but remained fundamentally the same. Integration was a more pressing need for long-distance migrants than it was for local migrants because migrants who were removed great distances were completely severed from ties with their home communities and thus more in need of forging new social networks to make up for the ones they had lost in transit.

Conclusion

> *I know it may be said that the slave in this country is not stolen: that it is a purchase, a fair business transaction. But who is the owner of this man thus sold and purchased? None other, most certainly, than himself... It is the stealing of a man from himself.*
>
> Henry Peterson, Junior Anti-Slavery Society of Philadelphia, 1838[1]

William Grose, a twenty-five-year-old fugitive slave, stole his body back from his southern master and arrived nearly destitute in Ontario in 1851. During a perilous journey that commenced in New Orleans, Grose risked his life and suffered a tremendous ordeal in order to live in freedom, especially psychologically, as he struggled along the way with "many doubts" about his chances of successfully escaping the institution of bondage. Smuggled on board canal boats and traversing vast distances on foot, Grose was plagued by the nightmare of being caught and sent back. Indeed, the entire time he "felt a dread – a heavy load on me all the way." He preferred even death to reenslavement. Relating his story to interviewer Benjamin Drew five years later in St. Catherines, he recalled: "I said to myself – I recollect it well, – I can't die but once; if they catch me, they can but kill me." When he finally arrived in the North, his initial intention was to remain in the United States, but he "saw so many mean-looking men," that he "did not dare to stay." He eventually found a friend "who helped me on the way to Canada," where he placed his valuable body out of reach of the Fugitive Slave Law and recapture.[2]

1 Henry Peterson, *An Address on American Slavery, Delivered Before the Semi-Annual Meeting, of the Junior Anti-Slavery Society, of Philadelphia, July 4th, 1838* (Philadelphia: Merrihew and Gunn, 1838), 5.

2 William Grose, in Benjamin Drew, ed., *A North-Side View of Slavery. The Refugee: Or the Narratives of Fugitive Slaves in Canada. As Related by Themselves, with an Account of the History and Condition of the Coloured Population of Upper Canada* (Boston: John P. Jewett &

Born near the confluence of the Shenandoah and Potomac Rivers in northern Virginia, Grose grew up in the danger zone – a mountainous region in which slavery had never really become firmly entrenched in the first place, whose waterways provided the main arteries for the interstate slave trade to the Deep South, and whose superfluous slave population was constantly at risk of being deported and forcibly separated from loved ones. Similar to many slaves of the Upper South, Grose long feared and was ultimately unable to avoid this dreaded fate. He had even heard rumors of his impending sale, but he refused to believe them until he – along with two of his brothers – was deceivingly delivered into the hands of traders one day and deported. The move turned Grose's world upside down. Separated from his grief-stricken wife (a free woman), chained in a coffle, marched to town and locked up in a local slave pen, and then dispatched to Baltimore to be shipped to the South, he experienced the worst of forced migration in the antebellum period.[3]

Arrival in Louisiana hardly improved his situation. The newcomer was sold as a house servant to a moody widower in New Orleans, who deemed him "unacclimated" and sent him to a "watering hole" in Alabama for three months until he got used to the southern climate. When he returned, he found himself forcibly hired out to various difficult employers in the city, including a gambling saloon owner (who fed him only two meals a day and made him sleep on a table) and a steamboat captain who was "impossible to please." Even worse, Grose's new master forced him to take another slave as his wife, a woman named Cynthia who worked in their master's household. "I was scared half to death," Grose recalled, "for I had one wife whom I liked, and didn't want another." Homesick, unaccustomed to his new work, unable to avoid conflicts with his new master and employers, and forcibly coupled to a local stranger, Grose longed for home, family, and familiar ground. The haunting realization that he may never be reunited with his loved ones again sank in a year later when his free wife traveled all the way to New Orleans to live near her husband, only to be denied residency in the state of Louisiana and ordered to leave. After her departure, Grose "felt very uneasy." Rather than accept his fate and assimilate to his new home in the largest urban center of the South, he decided that he

Co., 1856), 85–86 (quotes). For some recent studies on the Fugitive Slave Law, see, for example, Stanley W. Campbell, *The Slave Catchers: Enforcement of the Fugitive Slave Law, 1850–1860* (Chapel Hill: University of North Carolina Press, 2011); Earl M. Maltz, *Fugitive Slave on Trial: Anthony Burns and Abolitionist Outrage* (Lawrence: University Press of Kansas, 2010); R.J.M. Blackett, "Dispossessing Massa: Fugitive Slaves and the Politics of Slavery after 1850," *American Nineteenth-Century History* 10 (June 2009): 119–36.

[3] Grose, in Drew, ed., *North-Side View*, 82–84. For more on slavery in northern Virginia and the Virginia Appalachians, see, for example, Brenda E. Stevenson, *Life in Black & White: Family and Community in the Slave South* (New York: Oxford University Press, 1996); Wilma A. Dunaway, *Slavery in the American Mountain South* (New York: Cambridge University Press, 2003); Wilma A. Dunaway, *The African-American Family in Slavery and Emancipation* (New York: Cambridge University Press, 2003).

had endured enough and fled slavery altogether. In Canada, he was also a newcomer surrounded by strangers, but at least he felt "like a man," whereas before he felt "more as though I were but a brute," valuable only as a beast of burden and not as a human being.[4]

The market mechanisms that reduced the body of young William Grose to an anonymous and mobile cog in the vast machine of southern slavery also wrought havoc on the lives of millions of his fellow bondsmen. Indeed, because slavery was based on the twin principles of labor mobility and legal ownership of enslaved people's bodies, most antebellum slaves found themselves removed at one point or another during their lives. Some were sold, others moved with their masters, yet others were hired out, and still others were bequeathed to distant family members of their late masters. Some slaves were indeed confronted with several or even *all* of these methods of removal. Yet not all migrants experienced individual relocations in quite the same way. When analyzed through a comparative lens, it becomes clear that in the antebellum South, enslaved people's experiences of forced migration often varied – sometimes subtly, sometimes widely – according to several factors but most important according to migration type. A strong argument could be made that those who were forcibly relocated to other states and other parts of the South – and especially those who, like William, were removed via the domestic slave trade – endured the most extreme trials during their migration and assimilation experiences. These migrants were subjected to relatively arduous and uncomfortable journeys, had little chance of ever seeing or hearing from loved ones again, were often forced to learn new work patterns, and felt the most out of place in new slave communities. Local and urban migrants were often spared wearisome journeys, stressful adjustments to unattractive new work, and permanent separation from loved ones. Urban migrants indeed often looked forward to their new lives in cities and towns. Yet similarities in the experiences of all of these groups can be found as well. Forced migration could be a traumatic experience for local and urban migrants, for example, depending on the nature of work at their new destinations, the temper and personality of their new masters or employers, and especially the possibility of frequent contact with their home communities.[5]

The importance of family in slaves' experiences with forced migration can indeed hardly be emphasized enough. Whether confronted with interstate, local, or urban removal, the prospects for contact with loved ones largely determined how slaves perceived and responded to the threat or reality of

[4] Grose, in Drew, ed., *North-Side View*, 82–85, 84 (first quote), 85 (second quote), 86 (third quote).

[5] Walter Johnson, *Soul by Soul: Life Inside the Antebellum Slave Market* (Cambridge, Mass.: Harvard University Press, 1999), 19–44; James W.C. Pennington, *The Fugitive Blacksmith; or, Events in the History of James W.C. Pennington, Pastor of a Presbyterian Church, New York, Formerly a Slave in the State of Maryland, United States* (London: Charles Gilpin, 1849), iv–xv.

removal. Interstate migrants were threatened with the most definitive and permanent separations from loved ones, so their fear of deportation and resistance against sale to the Deep South (from negotiation to running away to physical violence) were the most extreme. Local migrants and urban migrants, on the other hand, were often able to maintain contact with loved ones, sometimes returning home to visit family members on weekends (with passes or illicitly) or when their hiring terms were up at the end of the year. When they were confronted with separation across great distances, they too responded in ways that were virtually identical to those of interstate migrants. The fear of forced migration for enslaved people in the antebellum South was synonymous with the fear of forced separation from family, kin, and community. No other aspect of forced migration loomed as large in their minds.[6]

Forced migration did not end on arrival at new destinations. The daunting process of assimilation was a major part of the migration experience and should be integral to any study of domestic slave migration in the antebellum period. As enslaved newcomers reached their new homes, they found that their trials had only just begun. Adjustments to new work could prove stressful – especially for interstate and urban migrants – and migrants' frequent mistakes often made them susceptible to a disproportionate amount of punishment compared with local slaves. Local migrants often found themselves in the least stressful situations regarding work, but even they had to make an effort to justify the pricey acquisition of their bodies or risk severe punishments. New masters and overseers proved difficult to get used to as well, not only for interstate migrants – who dreaded southern masters long before they were deported – but also for local and even urban migrants.

Finally, enslaved newcomers had to assimilate into new slave communities, a thorny process that has largely eluded the attention of historians. For interstate migrants, regional identities often thwarted opportunities for integration with local slaves at their destinations, but the shared experience of forced migration did facilitate their forging bonds with other migrants, both during the journey itself and after arrival in new communities. For local and urban migrants, frequent contact with home communities sometimes eased the pressure to assimilate at new destinations, although urban migrants especially appear to have striven to fit in with urban blacks (both free and enslaved), copying their dress and mannerisms and seeking social contact. All migrants manifested a dual orientation: they continued to identify with their old homes

[6] For the importance of family in migrants' experiences, see, for example, John Hope Franklin and Loren Schweninger, *Runaway Slaves: Rebels on the Plantation* (New York: Oxford University Press, 1999), 49–74; Calvin Schermerhorn, *Money over Mastery, Family over Freedom: Slavery in the Antebellum Upper South* (Baltimore: Johns Hopkins University Press, 2011), 18–21; Stevenson, *Life in Black and White*, 204–207; Heather Andrea Williams, *Help Me to Find My People: The African American Search for Family Lost in Slavery* (Chapel Hill: University of North Carolina Press, 2012), 21–88; Damian Alan Pargas, *The Quarters and the Fields: Slave Families in the Non-Cotton South* (Gainesville: University Press of Florida, 2010), 171–200.

even while creating new lives for themselves in their new ones. Moreover, all newcomers appear to have shifted their identities and used the same strategies for integration in new slave communities, especially attending local religious gatherings, courting and marrying local bondspeople, and providing collective assistance and resistance when necessary. Bondspeople's identities, orientation, and loyalties were thus fluid and not fixed. Under certain circumstances, newcomers distanced themselves from strangers, but under others, they sought contact and forged unifying bonds that transcended cultural distinctions or places of origin.[7]

As a central feature of southern slavery – indeed, *the* central feature – forced migration proved impossible for slaveholders to adequately reconcile with their paternalist ideology, although outwardly they certainly tried to justify their actions through a paternalist framework. As "benevolent masters" participated in the forced transfer of valuable bodies on the slave marketplace, as both buyers and sellers, they struggled to perform the remarkable feat of convincing themselves and outsiders that they were acting humanely and in the slaves' best interest. Yet time and again, the "twisted logic [that] lay at the heart of [the] paternalist apologetic," as Walter Johnson put it, proved unstable and unconvincing, underpinned as it was by contradictions and untruths. Slaveholders claimed that the familial bond between masters and slaves was sacred, but they recognized that their black family members had monetary values and could be liquidated at will to serve the interests of the white family members. They cloaked themselves in self-righteousness as protectors of slave families but casually orchestrated forced separations. They professed to be "saving" unfortunate bondspeople when they purchased them from auction houses, but they cared little for their histories and inspected their bodies like those of beasts of burden before admitting them to their "households." As owners of newcomers, southern masters congratulated themselves on providing unwanted slaves with good homes but skimped on their provisions and inflicted, or tolerated the use of, excessive force on their bodies, both in and out of the workplace. When an illusion of paternalism seamlessly dovetailed with their financial self-interest, the southern slaveholding class showered itself with self-adulation. When friction arose, however, financial self-interest trumped paternalist obligations – not some of the time but nearly all of the time.

[7] John W. Blassingame, *The Slave Community: Plantation Life in the Antebellum South* (New York: Oxford University Press, 1979), 105; Starling Stuckey, *Slave Culture: Nationalist Theory and the Foundations of Black America* (New York: Oxford University Press, 1987), 3; Ira Berlin, *Generations of Captivity: A History of African-American Slaves* (Cambridge, Mass.: Harvard University Press, 2003), 170–71; Hazel Rose Markus and Maryann G. Hamedani, "Sociocultural Psychology: The Dynamic Interdependence among Self Systems and Social Systems," *Handbook of Cultural Psychology* (New York: 2007), 7; Neil Campbell and Alasdair Kean, *American Cultural Studies: An Introduction to American Culture* (London: Routledge, 2006), 22–23; Tom Postmes & Nyla Branscombe, eds., *Rediscovering Social Identity* (New York: Psychology Press, 2010), chs. 1 and 2.

Southern masters surely cannot have failed to see the lies and contradictions in their own rhetoric, which took the form of a dishonest and ludicrous justification for their institution rather than a sincere commitment to a deceptive ideology. Their actions and attitudes reflected not benign master–slave relations but rather the brutal and logical consequences of an institution that defined people as property and black bodies as market commodities. The acts of resistance to forced migration that many slaves undertook, moreover, consisted of such fundamental rejections of the commodification of their bodies that they can hardly be dismissed as mere localized challenges to slaveholders' authority that reflected accommodation to slaveholders' hegemony. Quite the opposite, by challenging the very basis on which forced migration rested – dehumanization and commodification – slaves demonstrated their rejection of both their owners' ideology and the basic tenets of slavery itself. Falling back on the need to use extreme force to execute forced migrations and bring newcomers into their regime, slaveholders implicitly acknowledged that their attempts to impose hegemony over their slaves were unsuccessful.[8]

Only the fiery collapse of slavery during the Civil War ended the fear and reality of forced migration for the four million African Americans who lived to experience emancipation. Yet even as the filthy slave pens and dusty auction houses were abandoned and legal codes were rewritten to transform the valuable bodies of chattels into human beings in the eyes of the law, freedmen continued to migrate in droves – some for economic reasons, others in search of family lost during slavery, and still others to escape violence and harassment at the hands of an enraged white population. After the guns fell silent in 1865, however, waves of African-American migration would never again be forced.[9]

[8] Walter Johnson, *Soul by Soul: Life Inside the Antebellum Slave Market* (Cambridge, Mass.: Harvard University Press, 1999), 29–30 (quote), 107–13; Eugene Genovese and Elizabeth Fox-Genovese, *Fatal Self-Deception: Slaveholding Paternalism in the Old South* (New York: Cambridge University Press, 2011), 1–5, 14, 37–39; Walter Johnson, "A Nettlesome Classic Turns Twenty-Five," *Common-Place* 1 (July 2001), http://www.common-place.org/vol-01/no-04/reviews/johnson.shtml.

[9] See Ira Berlin, *The Making of African America: The Four Great Migrations* (New York: Viking, 2010).

Bibliography

I. Archival Sources

Fairfax City Regional Library, Fairfax, Virginia

Fairfax County Will Books (microfilm)
Diary of Richard Marshall Scott, Sr. (typescript)
Diary of Richard Marshall Scott, Jr. (typescript)
Diary of Virginia Gunnell Scott (typescript)

Hill Memorial Library, Louisiana State University, Baton Rouge, Louisiana

Ashland Plantation Record Book
Boucry Family Record Books
Louis Bringier and Family Papers
Bruce, Seddon & Wilkins Plantation Records
Andrew E. Crane Family Papers
Keller Family Plantation Records
George Mather Account Books
Records of Ante-Bellum Southern Plantations: From the Revolution through the Civil War, edited by Kenneth M. Stampp (microfilm series)
H. M. Seale Diary
Benjamin Tureaud Family Papers
Uncle Sam Plantation Papers
Welham Plantation Record Books
William Webb Wilkins Papers

Howard-Tilton Memorial Library, Tulane University, New Orleans

Octave Colomb Plantation Journal
Jean Baptiste Ferchand Journal
Eugene Forstall Letterbooks

John F. Kennedy Institut für Nordamerikastudien, Freie Universität, Berlin

19th Century U.S. Newspapers Database
Records of Ante-Bellum Southern Plantations: From the Revolution through the Civil War, edited by Kenneth M. Stampp (microfilm series).
Slavery in Ante-Bellum Southern Industries, edited by Charles B. Dew (microfilm series).

Library of Congress, Washington, D.C.

MANUSCRIPT DIVISION
Custis-Lee Family Papers
Stephen D. Doar Papers
Edward Frost Papers
William Lowndes Papers
Bushrod Washington Papers
David Wilson Scott Papers

National Records and Records Administration, Washington, D.C.

Records of the Field Offices for the State of Louisiana, Bureau of Refugees, Freedmen, and Abandoned Lands, 1861–1869 [RG 105]. Marriage Records of the Office of the Commissioner.
U.S. Bureau of the Census, Population and Nonpopulation Census Schedules

South Carolina Historical Society, Charleston, South Carolina

R. F. W. Allston Papers
Cheves-Middleton Papers
Gourdin-Gaillard Family Papers
Pringle Family Papers
Joshua John Ward Plantation Journals

South Caroliniana Library, University of South Carolina, Columbia, South Carolina

Cleland Kinloch Huger Papers
Miles, C. R. "In equity, Charleston District: Emily Frances Weston, executrix of Plowden C.J. Weston, deceased." 1864.
Davison McDowell Papers
Read-Lance Family Papers
James Ritchie Sparkman Papers

St. James Parish Courthouse, Convent, Louisiana

St. James Parish Probate Records, 1800–1860

Union Parish Courthouse, Spearsville, Louisiana

Union Parish Deed Book I

II. Periodicals

Alexandria Gazette and Advertiser
Arkansas Gazette
Charleston Courier
Charleston Mercury
Cleveland Herald
Columbus Enquirer
The Cultivator
Daily Missouri Republican
Daily National Intelligencer
Daily Picayune
DeBow's Review
The Emancipator
The Farmer's Register
Fayetteville Observer
Floridian & Advocate
Genius of Universal Emancipation (Baltimore, Md.)
Georgia Journal and Messenger
Greenville Mountaineer
Huntsville Democrat
Illustrated London News
Kentucky Statesman
Lexington Intelligencer
Louisiana Advertiser
Louisiana Gazette
Lynchburg Virginian
La Messager (Bringier, La.)
Mississippian and State Gazette
Mobile Gazette & Commercial Advertiser
Natchez Courier and Journal
Natchez Gazette
New Orleans Argus
New Orleans Bee
New Orleans Commercial Bulletin
New York Tribune
Norfolk Beacon
Pensacola Gazette
Phenix Gazette
Richmond Compiler
Richmond Whig
Semi-Weekly Mississippian
Southern Agriculturalist
The Times Picayune
Weekly Flag & Advertiser (Montgomery, Ala.)
The Weekly Raleigh Register
The Westminster Review, American Edition
Winyah Intelligencer

III. Websites

Documenting the American South. http://www.docsouth.unc.edu. Consulted Jan. 5, 2014.

Digital Library on American Slavery. http://library.uncg.edu/slavery/details.aspx?pid=4283. Consulted Sept. 1, 2013.

US GenWeb Archives. http://files.usgwarchives.net/va/shiplists/slavship.txt. Consulted Mar. 6, 2012.

IV. Unpublished Literature

Crawford, Stephen C. "Quantitative Memory: A Study of the WPA and Fisk University Slave Narrative Collections." PhD dissertation, University of Chicago, Chicago, Ill., 1980.

Sweig, Donald M. "Northern Virginia Slavery: A Statistical and Demographic Investigation." Ph.D. dissertation, College of William and Mary, Williamsburg, Va., 1982.

Wingfield, Charles L. "The Sugar Plantations of William J. Minor, 1830–1860." M.A. thesis, Louisiana State University, Baton Rouge, 1950.

V. Published Sources

Abdy, E.S. *Journal of a Residence and Tour in the United States of North America, from April 1833 to October 1834*. First published 1835. Reprint New York: Negro Universities Press, 1969.

Adams, Nehemiah. *A South-Side View; or, Three Months at the South, in 1854*. Boston: T.R. Marvin and B.B. Mussey & Co., 1854.

Affleck, Thomas. *The Cotton Plantation Record and Account Book, No. 2. Suitable for a Force of 80 Hands, or Under*. Louisville: Morton & Griswold, 1852.

Aime, Valcour. *Plantation Diary of the Late Mr. Valcour Aime, Formerly the Proprietor of the Plantation known as the St. James Sugar Refinery, Situated in the Parish of St. James, and Now Owned by Mr. John Burnside*. New Orleans: Clark & Hofeline, 1878.

Albert, Octavia V. Rogers. *Charlotte Brooks and Other Slaves*. First published 1890. Reprint New York: Oxford University Press, 1998.

Allen, William Frances. *Slave Songs of the United States*. New York: Simpson & Co., 1867.

Anderson, William J. *Life and Narrative of William J. Anderson, Twenty-Four Years a Slave*. Chicago: Daily Tribune Book and Job Printing Office, 1857.

Andrews, Ethan Allen. *Slavery and the Domestic Slave Trade in the United States, in a Series of Letters Addressed to the Executive Committee of the American Union for the Relief and Improvement of the Colored Race*. First published 1836. Reprint Freeport, N.Y.: Books for Libraries Press, 1971.

Ashton, Susanna. "Slavery Imprinted: The Life and Narrative of William Grimes." *Early African American Print Culture*. Edited by Lara Langer Cohen and Jordan Alexander Stein. Philadelphia: University of Pennsylvania Press, 2012.

Bailey, David Thomas. "A Divided Prism: Two Sources of Black Testimony on Slavery." *Journal of Southern History* 46 (Aug. 1980): 381–404.

Ball, Charles. *Fifty Years in Chains; Or, the Life of an American Slave*. New York: H. Dayton, 1859.

Bancroft, Frederic. *Slave-Trading in the Old South*. First published 1931. Reprint Columbia: University of South Carolina Press, 1996.

Baptist, Edward E. *Creating an Old South: Middle Florida's Plantation Frontier Before the Civil War*. Chapel Hill: University of North Carolina Press, 2001.

______. "'Cuffy,' 'Fancy Maids', and 'One-Eyed Men': Rape, Commodification, and the Domestic Slave Trade in the United States," *The American Historical Review* 106 (Dec. 2001): 1619–50.

Barton, Keith C. "'Good Cooks and Washers': Slave Hiring, Domestic Labor, and the Market in Bourbon County, Kentucky," *Journal of American History* 84 (Sept. 1997): 436–60.

Bauer, Craig A. *A Leader Among Peers: The Life and Times of Duncan Farrar Kenner*. Lafayette: Center for Louisiana Studies, University of Southwestern Louisiana, 1993.

Berlin, Ira. *The Making of African America: The Four Great Migrations*. New York: Viking, 2010.

______. *Generations of Captivity: A History of African-American Slaves*. Cambridge, Mass.: Harvard University Press, 2003.

______. *Many Thousands Gone: The First Two Centuries of Slavery in North America*. Cambridge, Mass.: Harvard University Press, 1998.

Berlin, Ira, et al, eds. *Freedom: A Documentary History of Emancipation, 1861–1867, Series I, Volume I*. New York: Cambridge University Press, 1985.

Berry, Daina Ramey. *Swing the Sickle for the Harvest is Ripe: Gender and Slavery in Antebellum Georgia*. Urbana: University of Illinois Press, 2007.

______. "'We'm Fus' Rate Bargain': Value, Labor, and Price in a Georgia Slave Community." *The Chattel Principle: Internal Slave Trades in the Americas*. Edited by Walter Johnson. New Haven: Yale University Press, 2004.

Bibb, Henry. *Narrative of the Life and Adventures of Henry Bibb, an American Slave*. New York: The Author, 1849.

R.J.M. Blackett. "Dispossessing Massa: Fugitive Slaves and the Politics of Slavery after 1850." *American Nineteenth-Century History* 10 (June 2009): 119–36.

Blassingame, John W. *The Slave Community: Plantation Life in the Antebellum South*. New York: Oxford University Press, 1979.

______. ed. *Slave Testimony: Two Centuries of Letters, Speeches, Interviews, and Narratives*. Baton Rouge: Louisiana State University Press, 1977.

______. "Using the Testimony of Ex-Slaves: Approaches and Problems." *Journal of Southern History* 41 (Nov. 1975):473–92.

Breeden, James O., ed. *Advice Among Masters: The Ideal Slave Management in the Old South*. Westport, Conn.: Greendwood Press, 1980.

Breene, T.H. *Tobacco Culture: The Mentality of the Great Tidewater Planters on the Eve of Revolution*. Princeton: Princeton University Press, 1985.

Bremer, Fredrika. *The Homes of the New World: Impressions of America*. 2 vols. New York: Harper & Bros., 1853.

Briesen, Martha von, ed., *Letters of Elijah Fletcher*. Charlottesville: University of Virginia Press, 1965.

British and Foreign Anti-Slavery Society. *Slavery and the Internal Slave Trade in the United States of North America*. London: Thomas Ward and Co., 1841.

Brown, Henry. *Narrative of Henry Box Brown*. Boston: Brown & Stearns, 1849.
Brown, John. *Slave Life in Georgia: A Narrative of the Sufferings, and Escape of John Brown, a Fugitive Slave, Now in England*. Edited by Louis A. Chamerovzow. London: L.A. Chamerovzow, 1855.
Brown, William Wells. *Narrative of William Wells Brown, a Fugitive Slave*. Boston: The Anti-Slavery Office, 1847.
Bruce, Henry Clay. *The New Man: Twenty-Nine Years a Slave, Twenty-Nine Years a Free Man*. York, Pa.: P. Anstadt & Sons, 1895.
Buchanan, Thomas C. "Rascals on the Antebellum Mississippi: African American Steamboat Workers and the St. Louis Hanging of 1841." *Journal of Social History* 34 (Summer 2001): 797–816.
Buckingham, J. S. *The Slave States of America*. 2 vols. London: Fisher, Son & Co., 1842.
Burke, Diane Mutti. *On Slavery's Border: Missouri's Small-Slaveholding Households, 1815–1865*. Athens: University of Georgia Press, 2010.
Camp, Stephanie M.H. *Closer to Freedom: Enslaved Women and Everyday Resistance in the Plantation South*. Chapel Hill: University of North Carolina Press, 2004.
Campbell, Israel. *An Autobiography. Bond and Free: Or, Yearnings for Freedom, from My Green Briar House. Being the Story of My Life in Bondage, and My Life in Freedom*. Philadelphia: C.E.P. Brinkloe & Co., 1861.
Campbell, James M. *Slavery on Trial: Race, Class, and Criminal Justice in Antebellum Richmond, Virginia*. Gainesville: University Press of Florida, 2007.
Campbell, Neil, and Alasdair Kean. *American Cultural Studies: An Introduction to American Culture*. London: Routledge, 2006.
Campbell, Stanley W. *The Slave Catchers: Enforcement of the Fugitive Slave Law, 1850–1860*. Chapel Hill: University of North Carolina Press, 2011.
Carey, Anthony Gene. *Sold Down the River: Slavery in the Lower Chattahoochee Valley of Alabama and Georgia*. Tuscaloosa: University of Alabama Press, 2011.
Cashin, Joan. *A Family Venture: Men and Women on the Southern Frontier* Baltimore: Johns Hopkins University Press, 1991.
Chaplin, Joyce E. "Creating a Cotton South in Georgia and South Carolina, 1760–1815," *Journal of Southern History* 57 (May 1991): 171–200.
Charlton, Lewis. *Sketch of the Life of Lewis Charlton, with Reminiscences of Slavery*. Portland, Maine: Daily Press Print Co., n.d.
City of Charleston. *Digest of the Ordinances of the City Council of Charleston, from the Year 1783 to July 1818*. Charleston: Archibald E. Miller, 1818.
Clarke, Lewis Garrard. *Narrative of the Sufferings of Lewis Clarke, During a Captivity of More than Twenty-Five Years, among the Algerines of Kentucky, One of the So-Called Christian States of America*. Boston: David H. Ela, 1845.
Clayton, Ronnie W., ed. *Mother Wit: The Ex-Slave Narratives of the Louisiana Writers' Project*. New York: Peter Lang Publishing, 1990.
Cobb, Thomas R.R. *An Inquiry Into the Law of Negro Slavery in the United States of America*. Philadelphia: T. and J.W. Johnson & Co., 1858.
Collins, Elizabeth. *Memories of the Southern States*. Taunton, England: Barnicott, 1865.
Collins, Robert. *Essay on the Treatment and Management of Slaves. Written for the Seventh Annual Fair of the Southern Central Agricultural Society* Macon, Ga: Benjamin F. Griffin, 1852.

Conway, M. D. *Testimonies Concerning Slavery*. First published 1865. Reprint New York: Arno Press, 1969.

Craven, Avery Odell. *Soil Exhaustion as a Factor in the Agricultural History of Virginia and Maryland, 1606–1860*. Urbana: University of Illinois Press, 1926.

Crenshaw, Kimberlé, et al, eds. *Critical Race Theory: The Key Writings that Formed the Movement*. New York: New Press, 1995.

Davis, David Brion. *Inhuman Bondage: The Rise and Fall of Slavery in the New World*. New York: Oxford University Press, 2006.

Davis, Edwin Adams. "Bennet H. Barrow: Ante-Bellum Planter of the Felicianas." *Journal of Southern History* 5 (Nov. 1939): 431–46.

______. ed. *Plantation Life in the Florida Parishes of Louisiana, 1836–1846, as Reflected in the Diary of Bennet H. Barrow*. New York: AMS Press, 1967.

Davis, Noah. *A Narrative of the Life of Rev. Noah Davis, a Colored Man*. Baltimore: John F. Weishampel, 1859.

Devereux, Thomas P., and William H. Battle. *Reports of Cases at Law, Argued and Determined in the Supreme Court of North Carolina, from December Term 1834, to June Term 1836, Both Inclusive*. Raleigh: Turner & Hedges, 1837.

Deyle, Steven. *Carry Me Back: The Domestic Slave Trade in American Life*. New York: Oxford University Press, 2005.

Dimond, Arthur E. Grey, and Herman Hattaway, eds. *Letters from Forest Place: A Plantation Family's Correspondence, 1846–1881*. Oxford, Miss.: University Press of Mississippi, 1993.

Doar, David. *Rice and Rice Planting in the South Carolina Low Country*. Charleston: Charleston Museum, 1936.

Douglass, Frederick. *Narrative of the Life of Frederick Douglass, an American Slave*. First published 1845. New York: Dover, 1995.

Drago, Edmund, ed. *Broke by the War: Letters of a Slave Trader*. Columbia: University of South Carolina Press, 1991.

Drake, Pam. *Pictures of the "Peculiar Institution" as It Exists in Louisiana and Mississippi, by an Eye-Witness*. Boston: J.P. Yerrington & Sons, 1850.

Drew, Benjamin, ed. *A North-Side View of Slavery. The Refugee, or Narratives of Fugitive Slaves in Canada*. Boston: John P. Jewitt & Co., 1856.

Dunaway, Wilma. *The African-American Family in Slavery and Emancipation*. New York: Cambridge University Press, 2003.

______. *Slavery in the American Mountain South*. New York: Cambridge University Press, 2003.

Duncan, Georgena. "'One negro, Sarah... one horse named Collier, one cow and calf named Pink': Slave Records from the Arkansas River Valley." *The Arkansas Historical Quarterly* 69 (Winter 2010):325–45.

Dunn, Richard S. "Winney Grimshaw, a Virginia Slave, and Her Family." *Early American Studies: An Interdisciplinary Journal* 9 (Fall 2011): 493–521.

Dupre, Daniel S. *Transforming the Cotton Frontier: Madison County, Alabama, 1800–1840*. Baton Rouge: Louisiana State University Press, 1997.

Dusinberre, William. *Them Dark Days: Slavery in the American Rice Swamps*. New York: Oxford University Press, 1996.

Easterby, J.H. ed. *The South Carolina Rice Plantation as Revealed in the Papers of Robert F.W. Allston*. Chicago: University of Chicago Press, 1945.

Eliot, William Greenleaf. *The Story of Archer Alexander: From Slavery to Freedom*. Boston: Cupples, Upham, & Co., 1885.

Ellis, Clifton, and Rebecca Ginsburg, eds. *Cabin, Quarter, Plantation: Architecture and Landscapes of North American Slavery*. New Haven: Yale University Press, 2010.

Epstein, Dena J. *Sinful Tunes and Spirituals: Black Folk Music to the Civil War*. Urbana: University of Illinois Press, 1977.

Evans, Estwick. *A Pedestrious Tour of Four Thousand Miles Through the Western States and Territories during the Winter and Spring of 1818*. Concord, NH: Joseph C. Spear, 1818.

Featherstonhaugh, G.W. *Excursion through the Slave States*. London: John Murray, 1844.

Federal Writers' Project. Slave Narratives: A Folk History of the United States of America from Interviews with Former Slaves. 17 vols. Washington, D.C., 1941.

Fedric, Francis. *Slave Life in Virginia and Kentucky; or, Fifty Years of Slavery in the Southern States of America*. London: Wertheim, MacIntosh, and Hunt, 1863.

Fields, Barbara Jeanne. *Slavery and Freedom on the Middle Ground: Maryland during the Nineteenth Century*. New Haven: Yale University Press, 1985.

Flint, Timothy. *Recollections of the Last Ten Years*. First published 1826. Reprint New York: De Capo Press, 1968.

Fogel, Robert William. *Without Consent or Contract: The Rise and Fall of American Slavery*. New York: Norton, 1989.

Fogel, Robert William, and Stanley L. Engerman. *Time on the Cross: The Economics of American Negro Slavery*. Boston: Little, Brown, 1974.

Follett, Richard. *The Sugar Masters: Planters and Slaves in Louisiana's Cane World, 1820–1860*. Baton Rouge: Louisiana State University Press, 2005.

Foshee, Andrew W. "Slave Hiring in Rural Louisiana," *Louisiana History* 36 (Winter 1985): 63–73.

Fox-Genovese, Elizabeth. *Within the Plantation Household: Black and White Women of the Old South*. Chapel Hill: University of North Carolina Press, 1988.

Franklin, John Hope, and Loren Schweninger. *Runaway Slaves: Rebels on the Plantation*. New York: Oxford University Press, 1999.

Frederickson, George M. *The Black Image in the White Mind: The Debate on Afro-American Character and Destiny, 1817–1914*. Middletown, Conn.: Wesleyan University Press, 1987.

Frobel, Anne S. *The Civil War Diary of Anne S. Frobel of Wilton Hill in Virginia*. Florence, Ala.: M. H. and D. M. Lancaster, 1986.

Gamble, Robert S. *Sully: The Biography of a House*. Chantilly, Va.: Sully Foundation, 1973.

Gardeur, René J. Le, Jr. "The Origins of the Sugar Industry." *Green Fields: Two Hundred Years of Louisiana Sugar*. Compiled by the Center for Louisiana Studies, University of Southwestern Louisiana. Lafayette, La.: The Center for Louisiana Studies, 1980.

Genovese, Eugene. *Roll, Jordan, Roll: The World the Slaves Made*. New York: Vintage, 1976.

———. "Yeoman Farmers in a Slaveholders' Democracy." *Agricultural History* 49 (April 1975): 331–42.

______. *The World the Slaveholders Made: Two Essays in Interpretation.* New York: Vintage, 1971.

Genovese, Eugene D. and Elizabeth Fox-Genovese. *Fatal Self-Deception: Slaveholding Paternalism in the Old South.* New York: Cambridge University Press, 2011.

George, James Z. *Reports of Cases Argued and Determined in the High Court of Errors and Appeals for the State of Mississippi, Vol. XXXVII, Vol. VIII, Containing Cases Determined at a Part of the April Term, 1859, and a Part of the October Term, 1859.* Philadelphia: T. & J.W. Johnson & Co., 1860.

Gill, Harold B., Jr. "Wheat Culture in Colonial Virginia." *Agricultural History* 52 (1978): 380–93.

Grattan, Peachy R. *Reports of Cases Decided in the Supreme Court of Appeals, and in the General Court, of Virginia, Vol. VII, From April 1, 1850, to July 1, 1851.* Richmond: Colin & Nowlan, 1852.

Gray, Lewis Cecil. *History of Agriculture in the Southern States to 1860.* 2 vols. Washington: The Carnegie Institution of Washington, 1933.

Green, William. *Narrative of Events in the Life of William Green.* Springfield, Ill.: L.M. Guernsey, 1853.

Greenblatt, Steven, et al, eds. *Cultural Mobility: A Manifesto.* New York: Cambridge University Press, 2009.

Greene, Jack P., ed. *The Diary of Colonel Landon Carter of Sabine Hall, 1752–1778.* Charlottesville: University of Virginia Press, 1965.

Grimes, William. *Life of William Grimes, the Runaway Slave.* New York: n.p., 1825.

G.S.S., "Sketches of the South Santee." *Travels in the Old South, Selected from the Periodicals of the Times.* 2 vols. Edited by Eugene L. Schwaab. Lexington, Ky.: University of Kentucky Press, 1973.

Gudmestad, Robert H. "Slave Resistance, Coffles, and Debates over Slavery in the Nation's Capital." *The Chattel Principle: Internal Slave Trades in the Americas.* Edited by Walter Johnson. New Haven: Yale University Press, 2004.

______. *A Troublesome Commerce: The Transformation of the Interstate Slave Trade.* Baton Rouge: Louisiana State University Press, 2003.

Gutman, Herbert G. *The Black Family in Slavery and Freedom, 1750–1925.* New York: Vintage, 1976.

______. *Slavery and the Numbers Game: A Critique of Time on the Cross.* Urbana: University of Illinois Press, 1975.

Hall, Capt. Basil. "A Naval Officer Sees All Sections, 1827–1828." *American Social History as Recorded by British Travellers.* Edited by Allan Nevins. New York: Henry Holt & Co., 1923.

______. *Travels in North America, in the Years 1827 and 1828.* Edinburgh: Cadell & Co., 1829.

Hall, Samuel, and Orville Elder. *Samuel Hall, 47 Years a Slave; A Brief Story of His Life Before and After Freedom Came to Him.* Washington, Iowa: Journal Print, 1912.

Hamilton, Thomas. *Men and Manners in America.* 2 vols. Edinburgh: W. Blackwood, 1834.

Hayden, William. *Narrative of William Hayden, Containing a Faithful Account of His Travels for a Number of Years, Whilst a Slave, in the South.* Cincinnati: W. Hayden, 1846.

Heard, William H. *From Slavery to the Bishopric in the A.M.E. Church: An Autobiography*. Philadelphia: A.M.E. Book Concern, 1928.

Henry, Thomas W. *Autobiography of Rev. Thomas W. Henry, of the A.M.E. Church.* Baltimore: n.p., 1872, 9.

Henson, Josiah. *The Life of Josiah Henson, Formerly a Slave, Now an Inhabitant of Canada, as Narrated by Himself.* Boston: Arthur D. Phelps, 1849.

Hilliard, Kathleen M. *Masters, Slaves, and Exchange: Power's Purchase in the Old South.* New York: Cambridge University Press, 2014.

Hodgson, Adam. *Remarks During a Journey through North America in the Years 1819, 1820, and 1821, in a Series of Letters.* First published 1823. Reprint Westport, Conn.: Negro University Press, 1970.

Hudson, Larry E., Jr. *To Have and to Hold: Slave Work and Family Life in Antebellum South Carolina.* Athens: University of Georgia Press, 1997.

Hughes, Louis. *Thirty Years a Slave: From Bondage to Freedom.* Milwaukee: South Side Printing Co., 1896.

Hughes, Sarah S. "Slaves for Hire: The Allocation of Black Labor in Elizabeth City County, Virginia, 1782 to 1810." *William & Mary Quarterly* 35 (April 1978): 260–86.

Ingraham, Joseph Holt. *The South-West. By a Yankee.* 2 vols. New York: Harper & Bros., 1835.

Jackson, Andrew. *Narrative and Writings of Andrew Jackson, of Kentucky.* Syracuse: Daily and Weekly Star Office, 1847.

Jacobs, Harriet. *Incidents in the Life of a Slave Girl.* First published 1861. Reprint Mineola, N.Y.: Dover, 2001.

Jacobs, John S. "A True Tale of Slavery." *The Leisure Hour: A Family Journal of Instruction and Recreation.* Feb. 14, 1861.

Janney, Werner L., and Asa Moore Janney, eds., *John Jay Janney's Virginia: An American Farm Lad's Life in the Early 19th Century.* McLean, Va., EPA Publications, 1978.

Jennison, Watson W. *Cultivating Race: The Expansion of Slavery in Georgia, 1750–1860.* Lexington: University Press of Kentucky, 2012.

Jervey, Edward D., and C. Harold Huber. "The *Creole* Affair." *Journal of Negro History* 65 (summer 1980): 196–211.

Johnson, Isaac. *Slavery Days in Old Kentucky.* n.p., 1901.

Johnson, Thomas L. *Africa for Christ: Twenty-Eight Years a Slave.* London: Alexander & Shepherd, 1892.

Johnson, Walter. *River of Dark Dreams: Slavery and Empire in the Cotton Kingdom.* Cambridge, Mass.: Harvard University Press, 2013.

———. "On Agency," *Journal of Social History* 37 (Autumn 2003): 113–24.

———. "A Nettlesome Classic Turns Twenty-Five: Re-Reading Eugene D. Genovese's *Roll, Jordan, Roll*," *Common Place* 1 (July 2001): http://www.historycooperative.org/journals/cp/vol-01/no-04/reviews/johnson.shtml.

———. *Soul by Soul: Life Inside the Antebellum Slave Market.* Cambridge, Mass.: Harvard University Press, 1999.

Johnson, Walter, ed. *The Chattel Principle: Internal Slave Trades in the Americas.* New Haven: Yale University Press, 2004.

Jones, Friday. *Days of Bondage. Autobiography of Friday Jones. Being a Brief Narrative of His Trials and Tribulations.* Washington: Commercial Publishing Co., 1883.

Jones, Katherine M. *The Plantation South*. Indianapolis: Bobbs-Merrill Co., 1957.

Joyner, Charles. *Down by the Riverside: A South Carolina Slave Community*. Urbana: University of Illinois Press, 1984.

Katz, Bernard, ed. *The Social Implications of Early Negro Music in the United States*. New York: Arno Press, 1969.

Kaye, Anthony E. *Joining Places: Slave Neighborhoods in the Old South*. Chapel Hill: University of North Carolina Press, 2007.

Keckley, Elizabeth. *Behind the Scenes, or, Thirty Years a Slave, and Four Years in the White House*. New York: G.W. Carleton & Co., 1868.

Kelley, Sean M. *Los Brazos de Dios: A Plantation Society in the Texas Borderlands, 1821–1865*. Baton Rouge: Louisiana State University Press, 2010.

Kimball, Gregg D. *American City, Southern Place: A Cultural History of Antebellum Richmond*. Athens: University of Georgia Press, 2000.

King, Wilma, ed. *A Northern Woman in the Plantation South: The Letters of Tryphena Blanche Holder Fox, 1856–1876*. Columbia: University of South Carolina Press, 1997.

Klein, Herbert. *The Atlantic Slave Trade*. New York: Cambridge University Press, 2000.

Klingaman, David. "The Significance of Grain in the Development of the Tobacco Colonies." *Journal of Economic History*, vol. 29, no. 2 (June 1969): 268–78.

Kolchin, Peter Kolchin. *American Slavery, 1619–1877*. New York: Hill & Wang, 1993.

Kulikoff, Allan. *Tobacco and Slaves: The Development of Southern Cultures in the Chesapeake, 1680–1800*. Chapel Hill: University of North Carolina Press, 1986.

______. "Uprooted Peoples: Black Migrants in the Age of the American Revolution, 1790–1820," in Ira Berlin and Ronald Hoffman, *Slavery and Freedom in the Age of the American Revolution* (Charlottesville: University of Virginia Press, 1983, pp. 143–71.

Lack, Paul D. "An Urban Slave Community: Little Rock, 1831–1862." *The Arkansas Historical Quarterly* 41 (autumn 1982): 258–87.

Lander, E.M., Jr. "Slave Labor in South Carolina Cotton Mills." *Journal of Negro History* 38 (Apr. 1953): 161–73.

Leon, J.A. *On Sugar Cultivation; in Louisiana, Cuba, & the British Possessions*. London: J. Ollivier, 1848.

Lewis, Ronald L. "Slave Families at Early Chesapeake Ironworks," *The Virginia Magazine of History and Biography* 86 (April 1978): 169–79.

Lightner, David L. *Slavery and the Commerce Power: How the Struggle Against the Interstate Slave Trade Led to the Civil War*. New Haven: Yale University Press, 2006.

Lyell, Charles. *A Second Visit to the United States of North America*. 2 vols. New York: Harper & Bros., 1850.

Maltz, Earl M. *Fugitive Slave on Trial: Anthony Burns and Abolitionist Outrage*. Lawrence: University Press of Kansas, 2010.

Markus, Hazel Rose, and Maryann G. Hamedani. "Sociocultural Psychology: The Dynamic Interdependence among Self Systems and Social Systems." *Handbook of Cultural* Starling Stuckey, *Slave Culture: Nationalist Theory and the Foundations of Black America*. New York: Oxford University Press, 1987. *Psychology*. Edited by Shinobu Kitayama and Dov Cohen. New York: Guilford Press, 2007.

Martin, Jonathan D. *Divided Mastery: Slave Hiring in the Antebellum South*. Cambridge, Mass.: Harvard University Press, 2004.

Mason, Isaac *Life of Isaac Mason, a Slave*. Worcester, Mass.: n.p., 1893.
McClelland, Peter, and Richard Zeckhauser. *Demographic Dimensions of the New Republic: American Interregional Migration, Vital Statistics, and Manumissions, 1800–1860*. New York: Cambridge University Press, 1982.
McDonald, Roderick A. *The Economy and Material Culture of Slaves: Goods and Chattels on the Sugar Plantations of Jamaica and Louisiana*. Baton Rouge: Louisiana State University Press, 1993.
______. "Independent Economic Production by Slaves on Antebellum Louisiana Sugar Plantations." *Cultivation and Culture: Labor and the Shaping of Slave Life in the Americas*. Edited by Ira Berlin and Philip D. Morgan. Charlottesville: University of Virginia Press, 1993.
McNeilly, Donald P. *The Old South Frontier: Cotton Plantations and the Formation of Arkansas Society, 1819–1861*. Fayetteville: University of Arkansas Press, 2000.
Miller, James David. *South by Southwest: Planter Emigration and Identity in the Slave South*. Charlottesville: University of Virginia Press, 2002.
Miller, Steven F. "Plantation Labor Organization and Slave Life on the Cotton Frontier: The Alabama-Mississippi Black Belt, 1815–1840." *Cultivation and Culture: Labor and the Shaping of Slave Life in the Americas*. Edited by Ira Berlin and Philip D. Morgan. Charlottesville: University of Virginia Press, 1993.
Moody, V. Alton. *Slavery on Louisiana Sugar Plantations*. New Orleans: Cabildo, 1924.
Moore, John Hebron. *The Emergence of the Cotton Kingdom in the Old Southwest: Mississippi, 1770–1860*. Baton Rouge: Louisiana State University Press, 1988.
Morgan, Philip D. *Slave Counterpoint: Black Culture in the Eighteenth-Century Chesapeake & Lowcountry*. Chapel Hill: University of North Carolina Press, 1997.
______. "The Ownership of Property by Slaves in the Mid-Nineteenth-Century Low Country." *Journal of Southern History*, vol. 49, no. 3 (Aug. 1983): 399–420.
Morris, Christopher. *Becoming Southern: The Evolution of a Way of Life, Warren County and Vicksburg, Mississippi, 1770–1860*. New York: Oxford University Press, 1995.
Netherton, Nan, et al. *Fairfax County, Virginia: A History*. Fairfax, Va.: Fairfax County Board of Supervisors, 1978.
Nevins, Allan, ed. *America Through British Eyes*. 2 vols. New York: Oxford University Press, 1948.
Northup, Solomon. *Twelve Years a Slave: Narrative of Solomon Northup, a Citizen of New York, Kidnapped in Washington City in 1841, and Rescued in 1853*. Auburn, N.Y.: Derby & Miller, 1853.
Oakes, James. *Slavery and Freedom: An Interpretation of the Old South*. New York: Knopf, 1990.
O'Donovan, Susan Eva. *Becoming Free in the Cotton South*. Cambridge, Mass.: Harvard University Press, 2007.
Ogden, A.N. *Reports of Cases Argued and Determined in the Supreme Court of Louisiana. Vol. XIII for the Year 1858*. New Orleans: Office of the Price Current, 1859.
Olmsted, Frederick Law. *A Journey in the Seaboard Slave States in the Years 1853–1854, with Remarks on their Economy*. New York: Dix and Edwards, 1856.
Pargas, Damian Alan. "In the Fields of a 'Strange Land': Enslaved Newcomers and the Adjustment to Cotton Cultivation in the Antebellum South." *Slavery & Abolition* 34 no. 2 (Apr. 2013): 1–17.

———. "The Gathering Storm: Slave Responses to the Threat of Interregional Migration in the Early Nineteenth Century." *Journal of Early American History* 2 no. 3 (Fall 2012): 286–315.

———. *The Quarters and the Fields: Slave Families in the Non-Cotton South*. Gainesville: University of Florida Press, 2010.

———. "'Various Means of Providing for Their Own Tables': Comparing Slave Family Economies in the Antebellum South," *American Nineteenth Century History* 7 (Sept. 2006): 361–87.

Parish, Peter J. *Slavery: History and Historians*. New York: Harper Collins, 1989.

Parker, Allen. *Recollections of Slavery Times*. Worcester: Chas. Burbank & Co., 1895.

Parker, Amos A. *Trip to the West and Texas*. Boston: Benjamin B. Mursey, 1836.

Parsons, C.G. *An Inside View of Slavery*. First published 1855. Reprint Savannah: The Beehive Press, 1974.

Pattern, J. Alexander. "Scenes from Lynchburg." *Travels in the Old South, Selected from Periodicals of the Times*. 2 vols. Edited by Eugene L. Schwaab. Lexington: University Press of Kentucky, 1973.

Pennington, James W.C. *A Narrative of the Events of the Life of J.H. Banks, an Escaped Slave, from the Cotton State, Alabama, in America*. Liverpool: M. Rourke, 1861.

———. *The Fugitive Blacksmith; Or, Events in the History of James W.C. Pennington, Pastor of a Presbyterian Church, New York, Formerly a Slave in the State of Maryland, United States*. London: Charles Gilpin, 1849.

Perdue, Charles L., Jr., et al, eds. *Weevils in the Wheat: Interviews with Virginia Ex-Slaves*. Charlottesville: University of Virginia Press, 1976.

Peterson, Henry. *An Address on American Slavery, Delivered Before the Semi-Annual Meeting, of the Junior Anti-Slavery Society, of Philadelphia, July 4th, 1838*. Philadelphia: Merrihew and Gunn, 1838.

Phillips, Ulrich B., ed. *Plantation and Frontier: Documents, 1649–1863, Illustrative of Industrial History of the Colonial and Ante-Bellum South*. 2 vols. Cleveland: The Arthur H. Clark Co., 1909.

Picquet, Louisa. *Louisa Picquet, the Octoroon: Or, Inside Views of Domestic Slave Life*. New York: The Author, 1861.

Postmes, Tom & Nyla Branscombe, eds. *Rediscovering Social Identity*. New York: Psychology Press, 2010.

Price, Richard, and Sidney W. Mintz. *The Birth of African American Culture: An Anthropological Perspective*. Boston: Beacon, 1992.

Pritchard, Walter. "Routine on a Louisiana Sugar Plantation Under the Slavery Regime." *The Mississippi Valley Historical Review* 14 (Sept. 1927): 168–78.

———. "A Tourist's Description of Louisiana in 1860," *The Louisiana Historical Quarterly* 21 (Oct. 1938): 11–15.

Pritchett, Jonathan B. "The Interregional Slave Trade and the Selection of Slaves for the New Orleans Market," *Journal of Interdisciplinary History* 28 (summer 1997): 57–85.

Pulszky, Francis and Theresa. *White, Red, Black*. First published 1853. New York: Johnson Reprint Co., 1970.

Raboteau, Albert J. *Slave Religion: The 'Invisible Institution' in the Antebellum South*. New York: Oxford University Press, 1980.

Randolph, Peter. *From Slave Cabin to the Pulpit. The Autobiography of Rev. Peter Randolph: The Southern Question Illustrated and Sketches of Slave Life.* Boston: James H. Earle, 1893.

Randolph, Peyton. *Reports of Cases Argued and Determined in the Court of Appeals of Virginia; To Which Are Added, Reports of Cases Decided in the General Court of Virginia, Vol. V.* Richmond: Peter Cottom, 1828.

Redpath, James. *The Roving Editor; or, Talks with the Slaves in the Southern States.* First published 1859. Reprint New York: Negro Universities Press, 1969.

Ripley, Eliza. *Socials Life in Old New Orleans, Being Recollections of My Childhood.* New York, 1912.

Robinson, Solon. *Solon Robinson, Pioneer and Agriculturalist: Selected Writings.* Edited by Herbert Anthony Kellar. 2 vols. Indianapolis: Indiana Historical Bureau, 1936.

Robinson, William H. *From Log Cabin to Pulpit, or, Fifteen Years in Slavery.* Eau Claire, Wisc.: James H. Tifft, 1913.

Rockman, Seth. *Scraping By: Wage Labor, Slavery, and Survival in Early Baltimore.* Baltimore: Johns Hopkins University Press, 2009.

Rodrigue, John C. *Reconstruction in the Cane Fields: From Slavery to Free Labor in Louisiana's Sugar Parishes.* Baton Rouge: Louisiana State University Press, 2001.

Rohrbough, Malcolm J. *Trans-Appalachian Frontier: People, Societies, and Institutions, 1775–1850.* Bloomington: Indiana University Press, 2008.

Roper, Moses. *A Narrative of the Adventures and Escape of Moses Roper, from American Slavery.* Philadelphia: Merrihew & Gunn, 1838.

Rothman, Adam. *Slave Country: American Expansion and the Origins of the Deep South.* Cambridge, Mass.: Harvard University Press, 2005.

______. "The Domestification of the Slave Trade in the United States." *The Chattel Principle: Internal Slave Trades in the Americas.* Edited by Walter Johnson. New Haven: Yale University Press, 2004, pp. 32–54.

Russell, William Howard. *My Diary North and South.* 2 vols. London: Bradbury & Evans, 1863.

Scarborough, William K. *The Overseer: Plantation Management in the Old South.* Baton Rouge: Louisiana State University Press, 1966.

Schafer, Judith Kelleher. *Slavery, the Civil Law, and the Supreme Court of Louisiana.* Baton Rouge: LSU Press, 1994.

Schermerhorn, Calvin. *Money over Mastery, Family over Freedom: Slavery in the Antebellum Upper South.* Baltimore: Johns Hopkins University Press, 2010.

Schwalm, Leslie A. *A Hard Fight for We: Women's Transition from Slavery to Freedom in South Carolina.* Urbana: University of Illinois Press, 1997.

Schweninger, Loren, ed. *The Southern Debate over Slavery: Volume 2, Petitions to Southern County Courts, 1775–1867.* Urbana: University of Illinois Press, 2008.

______. "The Underside of Slavery: The Internal Economy, Self-Hire, and Quasi-Freedom in Virginia, 1780–1865." *Slavery & Abolition* 12 (Sept. 1991): 1–22.

Sheldon, Marianne Buroff. "Black-White Relations in Richmond, Virginia, 1782–1820." *Journal of Southern History* 45 (Feb. 1979): 27–44.

Singleton, William Henry. *Recollections of My Slavery Days.* N.p., 1922.

Sitterson, J. Carlyle. *Sugar Country: The Cane Sugar Industry in the South, 1753–1950.* Lexington, Ken.: University of Kentucky Press, 1953.

Smith, James Lindsay. *Autobiography of James L. Smith, Including, Also, Reminiscences of Slave Life, Recollections of the War, Education of Freedmen, Causes of the Exodus, etc.* Norwich: Press of the Bulletin Co., 1881.

Smith, John David, ed. *Florida Plantation Records from the Papers of George Noble Jones*. Gainesville: University Press of Florida, 2006.

Smith, Mark M. *Debating Slavery: Economy and Society in the Antebellum South*. New York: Cambridge University Press, 1998.

Sobel, Mechal. *The World They Made Together: Black and White Values in Eighteenth-Century Virginia*. Princeton: Princeton University Press, 1987.

Starobin, Robert S. *Industrial Slavery in the Old South*. New York: Oxford University Press, 1970.

Stephenson, Wendell Holmes. *Isaac Franklin: Slave Trader and Planter of the Old South*. First published 1938. Reprint Gloucester, Mass.: P. Smith, 1968.

Stevenson, Brenda E. *Life in Black and White: Family and Community in the Slave South*. New York: Oxford University Press, 1996.

Steward, Austin. *Twenty-Two Years a Slave and Forty Years a Freeman*. First published 1857. Reprint Syracuse, N.Y.: Syracuse University Press, 2002.

Still, William. *The Underground Railroad: A Record of Facts, Authentic Letters, &c.* First published 1872. New York: Negro Universities Press, 1968.

Stirling, James. *Letters from the Slave States*. First published 1857. Reprint New York: Negro Universities Press, 1969.

Stroyer, Jacob. *Sketches of My Life in the South*. Salem: Salem Press, 1879.

Stuckey, Starling. *Slave Culture: Nationalist Theory and the Foundations of Black America*. New York: Oxford University Press, 1987.

Sydnor, Charles S. *Slavery in Mississippi*. First published 1933. Reprint Baton Rouge: Louisiana State University Press, 1966.

Tadman, Michael. "The Demographic Cost of Sugar: Debates on Slave Societies and Natural Increase in the Americas." *The American Historical Review*, vol. 105, no. 5 (Dec., 2000): 1534–75.

______. "The Hidden History of Slave Trading in Antebellum South Carolina: John Springs III and other 'Gentlemen Dealing in Slaves.'" *South Carolina Historical Magazine* 97 (Jan. 1996): 6–29.

______. *Speculators and Slaves: Masters, Traders, and Slaves in the Old South*. Madison: University of Wisconsin Press, 1989.

Takagi, Midori. "Rearing Wolves to Our Own Destruction": *Slavery in Richmond, Virginia, 1782–1865*. Charlottesville: University of Virginia Press, 1999.

Taylor, Rosser H. *Antebellum South Carolina: A Social and Cultural History*. New York: De Capo Press, 1970.

Thompson, Charles. *Biography of a Slave; Being the Experiences of the Rev. Charles Thompson, a Preacher of the United Brethren Church, While a Slave in the South, Together with Startling Occurrences Incidental to Slave Life*. Dayton, Ohio: United Brethren Publishing House, 1875.

Thorpe, T.B. "Sugar and the Sugar Region of Louisiana." *Harper's New Monthly Magazine* 42 (Nov. 1853): 747–48.

Tixier, Victor. *Tixier's Travels on the Osage Prairies*, edited by John Francis McDermott. First published 1844. Reprint Norman: University of Oklahoma Press, 1940.

Torrey, Jesse. *American Slave Trade; Or, An Account of the Manner in Which the Slave Traders Take Free People*. London: J.M. Cobbett, 1822.

Tower, Philo. *Slavery Unmasked: Being a Truthful Narrative of a Three Years' Residence and Journeying in Eleven Southern States*. First published 1856. Reprint New York: Negro Universities Pres, 1969.

Troutman, Phillip. "Correspondences in Black and White: Sentiment and the Slave Market Revolution." *New Studies in the History of American Slavery*. Edited by Edward E. Baptist and Stephanie M.H. Camp. Athens: University of Georgia Press, 2006.

______. "Grapevine in the Slave Market: African-American Geopolitical Literacy and the 1841 Creole Revolt." *The Chattel Principle: Internal Slave Trades in the Americas*. Edited by Walter Johnson. New Haven: Yale University Press, 2004.

Turner, J.A. *The Cotton Planter's Manual: Being a Compilation of Facts from the Best Authorities on the Culture of Cotton*. New York: Orange Judd & Co., 1857.

Veney, Bethany. *The Narrative of Bethany Veney, a Slave Woman*. Worcester, Mass.: n.p., 1889.

Vlach, John Michael. *Back of the Big House: The Architecture of Plantation Slavery*. Chapel Hill: University of North Carolina Press, 1993.

Wade, Richard C. *Slavery in the Cities*. New York: Oxford University Press, 1964.

Walsh, Lorena S. "Plantation Management in the Chesapeake, 1620–1820," *Journal of Economic History* 49 (June 1989): 393–406.

Watson, Henry. *Narrative of Henry Watson, a Fugitive Slave*. Boston: Bela Marsh, 1848.

Webb, William. *The History of William Webb, Composed by Himself*. Detroit: Egbert Hoekstra, 1873.

Weiner, Marli F. *Mistresses and Slaves: Plantation Women in Antebellum South Carolina, 1830–1860*. Urbana: University of Illinois Press, 1997.

Weld, Thomas. *American Slavery As It Is: Testimony of a Thousand Witnesses*. New York: American Anti-Slavery Society, 1839.

Whitten, David O. "Slave Buying in 1835 Virginia as Revealed by Letters of a Louisiana Negro Sugar Planter." *Louisiana History* 11 (summer 1970): 231–44.

Whittier, John G., et al, *Voices of the True-Hearted*. Philadelphia: Merrihew & Thompson, 1846.

Wiethoff, William E. *Crafting the Overseer's Image*. Columbia: University of South Carolina Press, 2006.

Williams, Heather Andrea. *Help Me to Find My People: The African American Search for Family Lost in Slavery*. Chapel Hill: University of North Carolina Press, 2012.

Wood, Betty. *Women's Work, Men's Work: The Informal Slave Economies of Lowcountry Georgia*. Athens: University of Georgia Press, 1995.

Index